Dying in Character

MEMOIRS ON THE END OF LIFE

Jeffrey Berman

UNIVERSITY OF MASSACHUSETTS PRESS

Amherst and Boston

Copyright © 2012 by University of Massachusetts Press
All rights reserved
Printed in the United States of America

ISBN 978-1-55849-965-2 (paper); 964-5 (library cloth)

Designed by Sally Nichols
Set in Adobe Garamond Pro
Printed and bound by Thomson-Shore, Inc.

Library of Congress Cataloging-in-Publication Data
Berman, Jeffrey, 1945–
Dying in character : memoirs on the end of life / Jeffrey Berman.
p. cm.
Includes bibliographical references and index.
ISBN 978-1-55849-965-2 (pbk. : alk. paper) — ISBN 978-1-55849-964-5 (library cloth
: alk. paper) 1. Authors, American—Biography—History and criticism. 2. Ameri-
can prose literature—20th century—History and criticism. 3. Critically ill—United
States—Biography—History and criticism. 4. Terminally ill—United States—
Biography—History and criticism. 5. Autobiography. 6. Death in literature.
7. Self in literature. 8. Death—Psychological aspects. I. Title.
PS366.A88B45 2013
810.9´3548—dc23
                                                2012030821

British Library Cataloguing in Publication data are available.

Dying in Character

For my wife, Julie

The British psychoanalyst D. W. Winnicott began an autobiography that he never finished. The first paragraph simply says, "I died." In the fifth paragraph he writes, "Let me see. What was happening when I died? My prayer had been answered. I was alive when I died. That was all I had asked and I had got it." Though he never finished his book, he gave the best reason to write in the world for writing one, and that's why I want to write mine—to make sure I'll be alive when I die.

—*Anatole Broyard*

CONTENTS

ACKNOWLEDGMENTS

Dying in Character is my seventh book published by the University of Massachusetts Press, and I'm grateful to everyone associated with the press: Bruce Wilcox, director; Clark Dougan, senior editor and trusted friend; Carol Betsch, managing editor; and Anne R. Gibbons, copy editor par excellence, my infallible guide to the grammatical and stylistic mysteries of English. I'm also grateful to the two outside readers who offered so many constructive comments on strengthening the manuscript. Thanks also to David E. Balk, the editor in chief of the indispensable *Handbook of Thanatology*. Part of my discussion of Philip Roth's psychoanalysis with Hans J. Kleinschmidt has appeared in *The Talking Cure: Literary Representations of Psychoanalysis* (New York University Press, 1985) and "Revisiting Philip Roth's Psychoanalysts," appearing in *The Cambridge Companion to Philip Roth,* edited by Timothy Parrish (Cambridge University Press, 2007), 94–110. Portions of this book were read at the 27th and 28th International Conference on Literature and Psychology held in Pecs, Hungary, and Roskilde, Denmark, in 2010 and 2011. I thank the students in my fall 2010 course Writing about Love and Loss for allowing me to quote their impressions of my return to class after being struck by a car. I am grateful to Robert J. DeFatta, MD, PhD, for his surgical skills, without which I might still resemble Frankenstein's creature. I am also grateful to my friend and colleague Randy Craig for his many personal and professional acts of kindness. My greatest debt is to my wife, Julie, who nursed me back to health, helped me to write about my accident, offered me her profound insights into love and loss, and brought joy back into my life.

Dying in Character

INTRODUCTION
"It Is When Faced with Death That We Turn Most Bookish"

In his memoir *Nothing to Be Frightened Of,* a witty meditation on how writers confront their own mortality, the contemporary British novelist Julian Barnes quotes an observation by Jules Renard, the late nineteenth-century French novelist, playwright, and philosopher: "It is when faced with death that we turn most bookish." Countless novelists, poets, and memoirists have turned bookish to deal with their death fears. They have turned bookish in a double sense: they read and write books on death. For many creative writers, particularly those who realize they are approaching the end of life, death is the undying muse of art. Asking himself whether his own death awareness is connected with his desire to write, Barnes is uncharacteristically evasive. "Perhaps. But if so, I don't want to know, or investigate" (66).

Ironically, Barnes then spends the remainder of his memoir investigating his fear of death. He imagines a dialogue in which he concedes that his awareness of death is intimately connected to his stories. He also admits that one of the motives behind his writing is the quest for immortality, even if it is only the illusion of immortality. "You make up stories so that your name, and some indefinable percentage of your individuality, will continue after your physical death, and the anticipation of this brings you some kind of consolation" (66). He then raises a startling question: Suppose someone devised a new brain operation that takes away the fear of death but also removes the desire to write. Would Barnes opt for this surgery? He hopes he would decline such an offer or at least negotiate a better deal. "How about eliminating not the fear of death but death itself? That would be seriously tempting. You get rid of death and I'll give up writing. How about *that* for a deal?" (67).

It is not likely, alas, that either the fear of death or death itself will be eliminated in our lifetime. How, then, do writers deal with these twin problems? By continuing to do what they have always done: writing about death.

Penning *Nothing to Be Frightened Of* was like whistling in the dark for Barnes, a way to talk—or write—himself out of the fear of death. Asked by a friend how often he thinks about death, he replies, "At least once each waking day. . . . And then there are the intermittent nocturnal attacks. Mortality often gatecrashes my consciousness when the outside world presents an obvious parallel: as evening falls, as the days shorten, or towards the end of a long day's hiking" (24). Barnes refers to many other thanatophobes who turn to writing or other forms of artistic creativity to hold their demons at bay, including the Soviet composer Shostakovich, who maintained that one way "to make the fear familiar" is to write about it. "I don't think writing and thinking about death is characteristic only of old men. I think that if people began thinking about death sooner, they'd make fewer foolish mistakes" (27). Shostakovich had two overwhelming problems: his fear of death and living in a repressive country in which death was politically incorrect, a taboo subject for art. Nevertheless, he found a way toward the end of his career to write musical compositions that contain, in Barnes's words, "long, slow meditative invocations of mortality" (27).

Barnes's bookishness is evident on every page of *Nothing to Be Frightened Of,* as when he quotes Montaigne's observation that "To be a philosopher is to learn how to die," and then reminds us that "Montaigne is quoting Cicero, who is in turn referring to Socrates" (40). Barnes next jumps to Philippe Ariès's influential *The Hour of Our Death,* which demonstrates that people in the twentieth century became so terrified of death that they stopped talking about it.

As a rule, we can talk about our own dying but not our actual deaths. There are exceptions to this rule, however, as Barnes points out. He refers to the late eighteenth-century Swiss physiologist Albrecht von Haller who, monitoring his own pulse as it weakened, "died in character" with the last words, "My friend, the artery ceases to beat." Voltaire similarly clung to his own pulse "until the moment he slowly shook his head and, a few minutes later, died" (*Nothing to Be Frightened Of* 110). I'm not aware of any examples of authors who are able to write about their actual deaths in real time: One can imagine writing about the loss of one's consciousness but not about its actual extinction.

Barnes mentions briefly a number of writers who die in character. The great eighteenth-century German man of letters Johann Wolfgang von Goethe wrote until the end of his long life. On his death day, in extreme pain and unable to speak, "he continued to trace letters on the rug over his knees (still taking his usual care over punctuation—a wonderful example of dying in character)" (*Nothing to Be Frightened Of* 196). Another example is Stendhal, who wrote, after suffering a stroke, "I find that there's nothing ridiculous about dropping dead in the street, as long as one doesn't do it deliberately." Barnes adds that Stendhal's wish came true "on the pavement of the Rue Neuve-des-Capucines" (218). Barnes can't help wondering whether he, too, will die in character, something we can never know in advance.

Dying in character contains an "extra option," as Barnes points out. "You may die in your personal character, or in your literary character. Some manage to do both" (174). Either form of dying may be more complicated than Barnes implies, for there are often significant shifts in a "real" and "fictional" character's attitude toward death, especially over a long period of time. What may be in character early in one's life may be out of character decades later.

What do we mean when we refer to dying in character? The expression implies a consistency between the way we live and the way we die. It would be "in character" for those who have loving relationships with relatives and friends to die expressing love and gratitude to these people. So, too, would it be in character for those whose lives were filled with anger, bitterness, rejection, or violence to expire while venting these dark emotions.

Last Words

One of the most famous examples of dying in character is Socrates, who, sentenced to death in 399 BCE for corrupting Athenian youths, stoically accepted his fate. His last words—"Crito, we owe a cock to Asclepius. Do pay it. Don't forget"—reveal his preoccupation with ethics and virtue. Socrates had the opportunity to escape or avoid execution, as his friends begged him to do, but he chose death to defend his moral philosophy of life, his commitment to wisdom and truth. As T. Z. Lavine points out in his survey of Western philosophy, many people regard Socrates' martyrdom as the secular counterpart to that of Christ (17). James Miller suggests in *Examined Lives* that Socrates appeared to welcome death. "His serenity in the face of death seemed to confirm the perfection of his goodness: he was a man completely at peace with himself in his final hours" (35).

Our fascination for "last words" arises largely from our curiosity over whether a person dies in character. Some of the deathbed utterances found in *Famous Last Words,* compiled by Ray Robinson, reflect dying in character. As Robinson writes in his introduction, the "beauty of some of these last words is that they may open a window through which we feel we can catch a glimpse, if only for a moment, of the entire life that preceded it" (ix). Many of the people Robinson cites in his book were creative writers. Annoyed by the question whether he finally recognized the divinity of Jesus, Voltaire exclaimed on his deathbed, presumably while his artery was still beating, "In the name of God, please let me die in peace" (147), a statement that leaves open the question of his religious belief. Goethe's dying words were "More light," which, Robinson suggests, may have been literal—to open a window and allow the sun in—or metaphorical (60). (Were these the letters he traced on his rug?) Isaac Babel's last recorded words before being shot to death by the Soviet secret police in 1939, at the age of forty-four, for the trumped-up charges of espionage and terrorism, were in character: "I am only asking for one thing—let me finish my work" (23).

John Keats admits in "Ode to a Nightingale" that he has been "half in love with easeful Death," and, fittingly, he expired with the words, "Lift me up, for I am dying. I shall die easy. Don't be frightened. Thank God it has come" (Robinson 79). In his celebrated poem "Do Not Go Gentle into That Good Night," Dylan Thomas exhorts readers to "Rage, rage against the dying of the light," but he drank himself into oblivion, boasting shortly before his death in 1953, at the age of thirty-nine, "I have just had 18 whiskeys in a row. I do believe that is a record" (123). Gertrude Stein's last words to her companion Alice B. Toklas were both ironic and gnomic: "What is the question? If there is no question, there is no answer" (30). Virginia Woolf penned her final words in a suicide note to her husband immediately before drowning herself at the age of fifty-nine in 1941: "If anybody could have saved me it would have been you. Everything has gone from me but the certainty of your goodness. I can't go on spoiling your life any longer. I don't think two people could have been happier than we have been" (140–41). Given the dark motives behind suicide and the Freudian belief that suicide is symbolic murder of the other, Woolf scholars continue to debate whether her last words should be read sincerely or ironically.

Artists, composers, actors, and impresarios often make deathbed statements that are in character with their lives. Ever the businessman, P. T. Barnum billed his circus as the "greatest Show on earth" and died with the question, "How were the circus receipts in Madison Square Garden?" (Robinson 7). While on his deathbed, Laurence Olivier, one of the twentieth-century's greatest Shakespearean actors, was so annoyed when his nurse spilled water on him as she tried to moisten his parched lips that he cried out, "This isn't Hamlet, you know. It's not meant to go in my bloody ear!" (49). Beethoven's final words were either "I shall hear in heaven" or "Friends, applaud. The comedy is over" (119). The first statement reflects the composer's heroic side, creating revolutionary compositions that he himself could not hear; the second statement betrays his cynical, misanthropic side. Before shooting himself in the chest in 1890 at the age of thirty-seven, Van Gogh wrote his final words that hint at the mysterious relationship between creativity and madness: "I paint as a means to make life bearable. Don't weep. What I have done is best for all of us. No use, I shall never be rid of this depression" (138).

All of these deathbed expressions are in character, allowing us to see a continuity between a person's life and his or her last (or almost last) conscious thoughts. "Death is the great heightener," remarks Edward S. Le Comte in the preface to his *Dictionary of Last Words*. "When the thing that is said would have been under any circumstances wise or fine, it is especially so under *this* circumstance. Death can make even triviality momentous, and delirium oracular. Last words have an aura about them, if not a halo" (vii). Most people, however, do not die uttering quotable words. According to psychiatrist Avery D. Weisman, dying patients are generally too ill to be articulate, witty, profound, or pious (189).

Is it good to die in character? It depends on whether one's character has been good. We value, for the sake of consistency, those men and women who, living good lives, die in character. On the other hand, as Emerson states in his essay "Self-Reliance," a "foolish consistency is the hobgoblin of little minds, adored by little statesmen and philosophers and divines. With consistency a great soul has simply nothing to do" (137). The brutal Roman emperor Nero, convinced that he was a great soul, died in character. Responsible for many executions (including those of his mother and stepbrother) and the destruction of a great city—he "fiddled while Rome burned"—Nero opined, before committing suicide, "What an artist the world is losing in me" (Robinson 109). There are many examples where dying in character reveals consistency, not goodness. "Tell my mother I died for my country," John Wilkes Booth proclaimed shortly before he was fatally shot in the neck in a burning barn after assassinating Abraham Lincoln. "Useless, useless" were his last ambiguous words (Robinson 11). Shortly before he was put to death by electric chair in 1928 for killing a police officer, George Appel called attention to his surname: "Well, folks, you'll soon see a baked Appel" (51). It is hard to disagree with Robert Kastenbaum's blunt conclusion about last words: "Although wise people may have wise things to say as they near the end of their lives, it is possible that foolish, boring, and neurotic people stay in character by saying foolish, boring, and neurotic things" (Kastenbaum 281).

The fear of not dying in character—dying *out* of character—has prevented many people from actions that they would otherwise take. I heard a story at a conference on death education about a world-famous thanatologist who was so devastated by his wife's death that he contemplated suicide. He decided against it mainly because committing suicide would have destroyed his entire life's work—the prevention of suicide. The thanatologist rejected suicide, went into psychotherapy, and died at an advanced age.

Dying in character implies consistency, not goodness, and it should not be regarded as the same as a "good death." In his book *Dying of Cancer,* the sociologist Allan Kellehear lists five features of a good death: (1) being aware of approaching death (2) saying goodbye to relatives and friends (3) making final preparations for death (4) ending formal work responsibilities and (5) waiting for death. One may die in character, that is, die in a way that is consistent with one's life, and yet not experience a good death.

Unless we choose suicide, which almost always creates a lifetime legacy, or illegacy, of anguish, guilt, and anger among relatives and friends, we do not get to choose our own deaths. We cannot always "die at the right time," as Nietzsche quipped. (He died ten years too late, spending the last years of his life in an insane asylum, the result of untreated syphilis). Nor can we know when, how, why, and where we will die.

How many of us die in character? I've never seen any research on this question. In their book *Final Gifts,* Maggie Callanan and Patricia Kelley, both experienced hospice nurses, offer their clinical answer to this question. "To some degree, most people die—and react to someone else's death—in ways reflecting their usual style of handling of crises. Quiet people remain quiet; angry, controlling people continue to be angry and controlling; people known for taking care of others may be trying to do so with their last breaths" (55). The clinicians' generalization sounds plausible, but much hinges on the words "to some degree."

The Dilemmas of Death

One of the difficulties of writing about our own death is that we may not have the time to complete the story. Barnes raises this issue in a particularly clever way: "Dying in the middle of a wo , or three-fifths of the way through a nov . My friend the nov ist Brian Moore used to fear this as well, though for an extra reason: 'Because some bastard will come along and finish it for you.' Here is a novelist's would-you-rather. Would you rather die in the middle of a book, and have some bastard finish it for you, or leave behind a work in progress that not a single bastard in the whole world was remotely interested in finishing?" (109). Joyce Carol Oates voices a similar fear in *Where I've Been, and Where I'm Going.* "Normal men and women—by whom I mean, I suppose, non-novelists—may be surprised to learn that novelists are haunted by a quickened sense of mortality when they are writing novels; the terror of dying before the work is completed, the interior vision made exterior, holds us in its grip" (363). Those who write end-of-life memoirs experience an even greater sense of mortality: the terror of dying casts a shadow from which there is no escape.

Death poses other challenges for writers of fiction and nonfiction. Garrett Stewart's observation about the "dilemma of death" for the novelist is no less true for the memoirist. "To write of death is for the novelist to speak of something that cannot *talk* back, that must be worded from without, from this side of its arrival" (63). Memoirists writing about their own deaths must also contend with their physical suffering, which, as Elaine Scarry notes in *The Body in Pain,* cannot be conveyed in words. "Physical pain is not only resistant to language but also actively destroys language, deconstructing it into the pre-language of cries and groans. To hear those cries is to witness the shattering of language" (172). Another dilemma is, as Todd May indicates, perhaps the central paradox of death: "It grants us the possibility of a meaningful life even as it takes it away. It gives us the promise of each moment, even as it threatens to steal that moment, or at least reminds us that some time our moments will be gone." Still another dilemma is that death is part of the unknowable future. Kierkegaard's insight—we can understand our life only backward, but we must live it forward—reminds us that no matter how much we reflect on or brood over death, we cannot grasp its meanings. Without death, we might not take our lives seriously, but death eventually destroys our lives.

Assumptive World

Many people assume that they will die of the same diseases as their parents or siblings—and die around the same age as their relatives. The age at which we will die becomes part of our "assumptive world," which Colin Murray Parkes defines as a "strongly held set of assumptions about the world and the self which is confidently maintained and used as a means of recognizing, planning, and acting. . . . Assumptions such as these are learned and confirmed by the experience of many years" (132). Hope Edelman reports in *Motherless Daughters* that the "fear of a foreshortened future is a common one among motherless women," especially if the mother dies young (223). Many people who have lost a close family member to cancer believe they are doomed by the same disease. And sometimes they are. Jacques Derrida, the founder of deconstruction, died in 2004 at the age of seventy-four from pancreatic cancer, the age his father was when he died from the same disease. Cancer survivors fear the return of their disease no matter how long they are in remission. A grim riddle: How do we know that we will not die of cancer? Only by dying of something else.

The concept of an assumptive world enables us to understand the meaning of dying in character. According to Ronnie Janoff-Bulman, there are three fundamental beliefs that are at the core of one's assumptive world: the world is benevolent, the world is meaningful, and the self is worthy (6). Trauma shatters these assumptions and requires the adoption of new assumptions. Death—or, more precisely, the news that one is terminally ill—calls into question one's fundamental beliefs about the world.

Dying in Harness

"It is indeed impossible to imagine our own death," Freud writes in "Thoughts for the Times on War and Death," and "whenever we attempt to do so we can perceive that we are in fact still present as spectators." From this, Freud concludes that "at bottom no one believes in his own death, or, to put the same thing in another way, that in the unconscious every one of us is convinced of his own immortality" (289). Nevertheless, even though our unconscious may not be able to confront our own death, Freud urges us to contemplate our mortality, concluding with a statement that is consistent with the title of his essay: "If you want to endure life, prepare yourself for death" (300).

Freud's earliest writings reveal his preparation for and preoccupation with death. "As far back as we know anything of his life he seems to have been possessed by thoughts about death, more so than any other great man I can think of except perhaps Sir Thomas Browne and Montaigne," observes biographer Ernest Jones. "Even in the early years of our acquaintance he had the disconcerting habit of parting with the words 'Goodbye; you may never see me again.' There were the repeated attacks of what he called *Todenangst* (dread of death). He hated growing old, even as early as his forties, and as he did so the thoughts of death became increasingly clamorous. He once said he thought of it every day of his life, which is certainly unusual. On the other hand there was a still more curious longing for death. After his fainting spell in Munich in 1912, his first remark upon regaining consciousness was: 'How sweet it must be to die'" (279). Another biographer, Max Schur, who was also Freud's personal physician, points out Freud's "preoccupation with dates at which he might die, a preoccupation which in contrast to his travel phobia never yielded completely to his self-analysis. It was first focused on the numbers 41 and 42, later even more strongly on the number 51. In 1899, he began to be preoccupied with the numbers 61 and 62, and in 1936 with the number 81½" (159).

Schur injected the dying Freud, in irremediable pain from the ravages of cancer, with a lethal dose of morphine in fulfillment of an agreement they had made years earlier. Schur quotes on the final page of his biography Freud's poignant plea for physician-assisted suicide: "My dear Schur, you certainly remember our first talk. You promised me then not to forsake me when my time comes. Now it's nothing but torture and makes no sense any more" (529). Freud died on September 23, 1939, and Peter Gay quotes on the final page of his own biography a letter Freud had written to his friend Oskar Pfister nearly four decades earlier: "Let us die in harness, as King Macbeth says" (651). Freud fulfilled his vow to die in harness, as Gay's closing sentence suggests: "The old stoic had kept control of his life to the end" (651).

Not all writers are fortunate enough to die in harness, but many of them write to the end of their lives. Some of these authors write about their own impending deaths. What better way is there to endure life and prepare for death than by reading stories of writers' own deaths? It is hard to find a story in which a novelist does *not* imagine the death of one or more fictional characters, but a story about the writer's own death takes on special significance. Writers cannot fully describe their own impending deaths—the moment of death can never be captured on paper—but they can take us to the edge of mortality. One need not be a creative writer to write a memoir about death, but literary writers' final words are especially noteworthy because they have often spent their entire lives imagining death in their stories, poems, and plays. Creative writers' fictional deaths become rehearsals for their own deaths.

One cannot help feeling ambivalent when reading stories about death and dying. It is the same ambivalence that Harold Bloom admits in the introduction to his anthology *Till I End My Song: A Gathering of Last Poems.* "We turn to last poems at whatever age because we both desire and fear finalities. We want to know and not know the extent of our temporal spans, and we hope to learn from the poets not how to die but how to stand against uncertainty" (xxv–xxvi). Bloom's introduction and commentary reveal the same self-elegiac mood of farewell as the "last poems" in his anthology. "Myself seventy-nine years of age," he writes in the second paragraph, "I grieve still for many of these poets who were my friends" (xvii). Bloom reminds us of his advanced age *six* more times in the book, identifying with the poets who, young, middle-aged, or old, confront their own mortality. "If your next birthday will be your eightieth, and you have read the greatest poetry all your life, then you begin to know that in the face of dying and death, the imagination is at once nothing and everything" (xxiv). For the secular Bloom, there is no consolation for death except, perhaps, the beauty of art. "Confronting illness, pain, and dying, we quickly learn that eloquence is not enough. Neither are even the most authentic poems of consolation. Still, the beauty and wisdom of these poems reverberate into the coming silence" (xxviii).

End-of-Life Memoirs

In *Companionship in Grief* I focus on authors who write spousal loss memoirs—C. S. Lewis, John Bayley, Donald Hall, Joan Didion, and Calvin Trillin—but there is no easy way to describe stories that explore the death and dying of the writer or a loved one. I asked a colleague if there is a Latin term for memoirs on death and dying that would flow like the well-known memento mori, which means "remember—you too shall die." The French rendering of death and dying memoirs is *mémoires de la mort,* while the Latin might be *commentarii de morte et moriendo.* Neither expression flows trippingly off the tongue, however. Nor is *autothanatography,* the word Nancy K. Miller uses to describe "narratives of the dying other" ("Facts, Pacts, Acts" 13), much of an improvement. Instead, I'll use the term *end-of-life memoir* to describe a story about death and dying, either one's own story or that of a relative or friend.

Whatever we call it, the memoir is ideally suited to convey the approach of death. "This is the age of the memoir," declares William Zinsser at the beginning of *Inventing the Truth.* "Never have personal narratives gushed so profusely from the American soil as in the closing decade of the twentieth century. Everyone has a story to tell, and everyone is telling it" (3). Zinsser refers to memoirs about drug and alcohol addiction, rape, sexual abuse, incest, eating disorders, codependency, depression, and suicide, all of which are "fashionable talk-show syndromes" (5). Zinsser and other literary theorists, such as Sven Birkerts and Thomas Larson, have rightly complained about the tendency of certain memoirists to fabricate or sensationalize the truth. Freud would have allied himself with those who mistrust memoirs and biographies. "Anyone turning biographer commits himself to lies, to concealment, to hypocrisy, to flattery, and even to hiding his own lack of understanding, for biographical truth is not to be had, and even if it were it couldn't be used" (*Letters* 430). One need not agree entirely with Freud's cynical view to observe that biographers and memoirists are always selective in what they reveal and conceal. "No biography"—or memoir—"can be definitive or wholly truthful," writes Edwin Haviland Miller in his biography of Nathaniel Hawthorne: "It is only fitting that all individuals should have an inalienable right to their mysteries" (xviii). No one need fear that those who write about death and dying demystify the end of life. Death remains a mystery, perhaps the ultimate mystery, and the dying take to the grave their final thoughts on the end of life.

There are far fewer memoirs about writers' or loved ones' death and dying, if only because there is less of an inclination to fabricate death, which comes sooner or later—usually sooner in the memoirs I discuss here. "The reports of my death have been greatly exaggerated," Mark Twain is reported to have said upon hearing about the publication of his obituary in a newspaper. No one can claim that the death and dying of those writers or characters appearing in the following memoirs have been greatly exaggerated.

I have selected authors in *Dying in Character* who have spent their entire professional lives writing about death, and who then write memoirs either about their own impending death or about that of a parent. Some of these writers demonstrate an exceptionally intense awareness of death throughout their long careers; they are *haunted* by death. In some cases, their preoccupation with death spans several decades. All are students of death. There are no experts on the subject, since we cannot live to experience death and then talk (or write) about it. Quoting Flaubert's statement, "Everything must be learned, from reading to dying," Barnes responds, "but we don't get much practice at the latter" (97). True, but reading about death is a form of practice—and learning. Some of the writers seek to demythologize death, but in doing so, they create their own mythology of death. All interpretations of death are subjective, revealing more about the interpreter than about the object of interpretation, death.

As I was working on this book, immersed in writing about others' deaths, I had my own close call. Had I died, my death would have been in character, though certainly not the one I have long imagined. I begin with this experience, which gave me a partial insight into the challenges of writing about one's ending. Then I turn to Elisabeth Kübler-Ross, whose first book, *On Death and Dying,* published in 1969, remains a classic. I discuss in detail her controversial stage theory of dying and then trace the changes in her attitude toward death in her later books, which describe out-of-body and near-death experiences that fascinated the general public but dismayed the scientific community. Her memoir *The Wheel of Life,* published in 1997, seven years before her death, describes her life before and after a series of devastating strokes that left her paralyzed and despondent. Throughout her life she rejected the idea that terminally ill patients should be allowed to end their own lives, but she struggled to heed her own advice at the end. Whether her death was in character remains ambiguous. The thanatophilic Kübler-Ross is the only writer in the study who looked forward to her own death, believing it would lead to a rebirth beyond human experience. She would agree with the Russian writer Turgenev that "the most interesting part of life is death" (cited by Barnes 129).

Philip Roth is one of America's greatest novelists, and his 1991 memoir *Patrimony* remains one of the most poignant studies of a father's death. Roth insists that everything in *Patrimony* is true, but he omits crucial information about his relationship to Herman Roth that appears in the countertexts and countervoices surrounding the writer's life. What Roth excludes from the story of his father's death turns out to be as revealing as what he includes. It is a truism to say that memory is highly selective, even or especially when a memoirist writes about a parent's death, but in *Patrimony* we can show specifically what Roth left out. We cannot know the extent to which writing *Patrimony* was a reparative act until we first know that the story was preceded by an angry act.

Next I turn to Harold Brodkey, an immensely gifted novelist who suffered from long periods of writer's block. Once he was diagnosed with AIDS in the 1990s, however, he turned to the story of his own impending death and produced a remarkable memoir, *This Wild Darkness,* published in 1996, the year of his death. The countertexts and countervoices of *This Wild Darkness* appear not only in Brodkey's earlier stories but also in the two novels written by his wife, Ellen Schwamm. Brodkey writes unflinchingly about his own death, and he is a striking example of dying in character.

Susan Sontag's death was both in and out of character, as we can see in the memoir *Swimming in a Sea of Death*, written by her son, David Rieff. Sontag was one of the leading American intellectuals of the second half of the twentieth century, the author of groundbreaking books on photography and illness. She survived two different forms of cancer that are often fatal, breast cancer and uterine cancer, and when she developed a third form, blood cancer, she believed that what helped her survive in the past, excellent medical treatment and a heroic determination to live, would once again help her prevail. It became apparent to nearly everyone except Sontag that she was dying and did not have much time left. Was her denial helpful or harmful? Rieff is never able to answer this question. Sontag died in 2004, and *Swimming in a Sea of Death*, published four years later, dramatizes the plight of caregivers who find themselves telling the dying what they want to hear. By withholding the truth of her medical condition, Rieff finds himself implicated in denials, evasions, and equivocations that undermine his own health and sanity.

Following Sontag, I turn to two other major public intellectuals, Edward W. Said, professor of English and comparative literature at Columbia University, and Tony Judt, professor of modern European history at New York University. Both the Palestinian-born Said and the British-born Judt were distinguished and prolific writers before being diagnosed with terminal illnesses, leukemia and amyotrophic lateral sclerosis (ALS), respectively, but they were not known for being autobiographical writers. Upon learning they were terminally ill, both felt compelled to write memoirs in which they explored how their sense of being outsiders influenced their life work. Said's memoir *Out of Place* was published in 1999, four years before his death, and Judt's *The Memory Chalet* appeared in 2010, the same year in which he died. Both men died in character, leaving behind fascinating stories of their lives and their abiding commitment to humanistic values.

Unlike Sontag, Said, and Judt, Art Buchwald was able to joke about his dying. The legendary humorist checked himself into a hospice in Washington, D.C., in 2006 after he made the decision to go off dialysis, when his kidneys shut down. Buchwald held court in hospice, becoming a "media star" for death, and then, unexpectedly, his kidneys began working again. Calling himself the "man who would not die," Buchwald shatters one taboo after another, proclaiming that he never realized "dying could be so much fun." He checked out of hospice, began writing *Too Soon to*

Say Goodbye, arranged his own funeral, and then died, thoroughly in character, in 2007.

Next I turn to two books that have become publishing sensations, Mitch Albom's *Tuesdays with Morrie* and Randy Pausch's *The Last Lecture.* Morrie Schwartz and Randy Pausch were both academics committed to teaching. Terminal illness gave them an opportunity to share their insights on death and dying with their students and the reading public. Both believed in using the classroom for death education, which they knew was also life education. Schwartz, a sociology professor at Brandeis University, died of ALS in 1995; Pausch, a computer science professor at Carnegie Mellon University, died of pancreatic cancer in 2007. Schwartz's own account of living and dying with a terminal illness appears in *Letting Go,* published in 1996, one year before *Tuesdays with Morrie.* All three books, *Letting Go, Tuesdays with Morrie,* and *The Last Lecture,* are surprisingly upbeat in their portraits of the end of life. They speak powerfully to a generation of baby boomers who take more than an academic interest in stories of death and dying. Both Schwartz and Pausch would agree with Harold Bloom's statement that the "purpose of teaching is to extend the blessing of more life" (xxvii). Ironically, Schwartz and Pausch became far better known when they were ill than when they were well.

Of all the memoirs in my study, none came into existence in a more unusual way than Jean-Dominique Bauby's *The Diving Bell and the Butterfly.* The victim of a massive stroke in 1995, Bauby was afflicted with "locked-in syndrome," a rare neurological disorder. The only way he could communicate was by blinking his left eye (his right eye was sewed shut to prevent ulceration). Entrapped by his body, Bauby was nevertheless able to create, through blinking, a masterful memoir that affirms the power of the imagination to survive the most horrific illness. Bauby died in 1996, two days after the publication of his memoir, which became the number one bestseller throughout Europe.

I had planned to end my study with *The Diving Bell and the Butterfly,* but the publication of Roland Barthes's *Mourning Diary* in 2010, thirty years after his death, compelled me to explore the ways in which it reveals a profound split between the writer's private and public selves. Nothing could be more *out* of character for Barthes than *Mourning Diary.* The literary theorist who claims, disingenuously, that there are many bad reasons for keeping a diary turns out to have written a profoundly moving and insightful *mourning diary.*

In the conclusion, I discuss the end-of-life memoir as a new death ritual, a secular example of the long tradition of *ars moriendi,* the art of dying. Each day sees the publication of a new end-of-life memoir by a major author. Death may have gone into hiding in the twentieth century, as many thanatologists claim, but the increasing popularity of the end-of-life memoir is slowly bringing death into the open again, where it can be viewed as the natural end of life.

Posterity Self

The memoirists in my study reveal striking differences in the way in which death shattered their assumptive worlds. There are also differences in the way in which they created new assumptive worlds. But they share one striking characteristic: all turned to writing to record the approach of death. They left a paper trail that we can follow as we try to understand their lives and deaths. They created what I call a *posterity self* that lives on after their own deaths. Edwin Shneidman has proposed the term *postself* (28) to describe a deceased person's reputation and influence that will be remembered by relatives and friends. Unlike postself, posterity self refers to a writer's published works that become his or her legacy. The desire to create a posterity self is one of the main motives for writing about death. We write not only for the present but also for the future, a future in which we will no longer be alive. Such writing requires a leap of faith, as Kent L. Koppelman suggests in the following Greek proverb: "A society grows great when old men plant trees whose shade they know they shall never sit in" (xi). Not everyone takes comfort in a posterity self, however, as Woody Allen wryly observed. "I don't want to achieve immortality through my work. I want to achieve it through not dying."

Notwithstanding that wish, dying authors are in a race against time to complete their final work. The French physician David Servan-Schreiber, a clinical professor of psychiatry at the University of Pittsburgh School of Medicine and cofounder of the Center for Complementary Medicine, was diagnosed with brain cancer when he was thirty-one. He underwent surgery, chemotherapy, and radiation therapy, and his cancer went into remission for several years. Servan-Schreiber popularized the importance of a healthy diet and balanced lifestyle for the treatment of cancer, both of which he believed should supplement traditional treatments. He wrote about his story in *Anticancer: A New Way of Life,* which became an international bestseller. When his brain cancer returned, he struggled to complete *Not the Last Goodbye* before dying at age fifty. Emile Servan-Schreiber notes in the epilogue that his brother was cheered by readers' enthusiastic response to his new book. "With his strength dwindling, just days before he died, he held up the French best-seller list to his eyes, to see his book at the top. It gave him the feeling of having defied the cancer in a most meaningful way. He had not allowed it to get in the way of his being useful, of his helping alleviate other people's suffering" (162).

"Do we create art in order to defeat, or at least defy, death? To transcend it, to put it in its place?" Barnes raises these questions and implies the answer to each of them is yes (200). I am reminded of the poet Donald Hall's statement in *Goatfoot Milktongue Twinbird:* "Art is created against death" (16). In *Nothing to Be Frightened Of,* Barnes quotes Montaigne, who believed that "since we cannot defeat death, the best form of counterattack is to have it constantly in mind" (42). All of the writers in my study would be inclined to agree with these statements. And I suspect they would agree with another statement Barnes makes about Montaigne: "To anticipate death in this way is to release yourself from its servitude: further, if you teach someone how to die, then you teach them how to live" (42).

Montaigne is a key figure in the study of death, and his monumental *Essays,* a collection of 107 essays written between 1572 and 1592, are filled with his insights not only on "how to live" but also on "how to die." Few studies of death, my own included, do not have an apt quote by Montaigne. Biographers note that one of the turning points in his life was the death of his beloved friend Étienne de La Boétie in 1563. "The two became soul mates," James Miller states, "joined in a shared love of wisdom, not unlike Seneca and Lucilius—and joined, too, in a shared love of the other, not unlike the Platonic love that Socrates expressed toward Alcibiades" (176). Sarah Bakewell reports that after his friend's death, Montaigne felt compelled to write his *Essays,* largely to work through his devastating grief. In the process, Bakewell notes, Montaigne "discovered the therapeutic benefits of writing. By passing on La Boétie's death narrative and farewell to the world in written form, he helped himself to relive the scene, and thus outlive it. He never fully got over La Boétie, but he learned to exist in the world without him, and, in so doing, to change his own life. Writing about La Boétie eventually led him to write the *Essays:* the best philosophical trick of all" (108).

Reading memoirs about dying in character tells us little about death but much about dying. I don't know whether reading these memoirs will help us die in character—we can't know that in advance. Nevertheless, these memoirs deepen our understanding of the end of life. They are not how-to books, and, with the exceptions of *Letting Go, Tuesdays with Morrie,* and *The Last Lecture,* they do not contain didactic advice that is easily transferable to all readers. Nevertheless, they record lives that readers will find insightful, moving, and inspirational. Bloom quotes in *Till I End My Song* a poem by Theodore Roethke that opens with a startling line: "In a dark time, the eye begins to see" (394). Without exception, the authors in my study attempt to illuminate this darkness.

"Write As If You Were Dying"

"Write as if you were dying," Annie Dillard exclaims in *The Writing Life.* "At the same time, assume you write for an audience consisting solely of terminal patients. That is, after all, the case. What would you begin writing if you knew you would die soon? What could you say to a dying person that would not enrage by its triviality?" (68). The memoirists in my study would identify with Annie Dillard's startling command. Those writing about their own impending deaths feel an urgency because they know they don't have much time left. And those writing about the death of a father or a mother, like Philip Roth, Roland Barthes, and David Rieff, feel a solemn duty to honor the memory of parents who are no longer able to speak for themselves. Regardless of whether they are writing about their own deaths or those of a parent, the memoirists all bear witness to life's final event.

There are many reasons to write about one's mortality, as Max Lerner asserts in *Wrestling with the Angel: A Memoir of My Triumph over Illness:*

> This is one man's journey away from death, toward life. It is at once
> a narrative of a cluster of illnesses and a meditation on them. There
> are many reasons a man gives himself for writing a memoir about

an illness: his friends have egged him on; he wants to reach other sufferers; he thinks his example may do something to change the climate within which life-threatening illnesses are treated. There is a kernel of truth for me in each. Yet my real reason is an experiential one. I passed through a searing experience that tested and changed me in ways I never foresaw. And like the Ancient Mariner I want to tell my story, to whatever listeners it finds. (20)

Lerner's memoir describes his battle with two different forms of cancer followed by a heart attack, all within a five-year period, and though he felt like Job, he never doubts the value of writing. Quoting a statement made by the twelfth-century Christian writer Bernard of Clairvaux—"every word we write is a blow struck at the Devil"—Lerner adds that even if he should fail to overcome the diseases assailing his body, he knows he has written something that will survive his own death (64).

Reading the memoirs of deceased authors is a communion with the dead, and regardless of whether we die in or out of character, we can hope to be alive when we die, to quote the dying writer Anatole Broyard in *Intoxicated by My Illness* (29–30) as he quotes from the dying psychoanalyst D. W. Winnicott's unfinished autobiography. For Winnicott and Broyard, "I was alive when I died" means enjoying life to the end, using their days to the fullest, feeling fulfilled in love and work, and leaving written records of the stories of their lives. They wrote for posterity—for us—and they encourage us, by their example, to write our own stories for those who follow us. Memoirists of death and dying turn bookish when confronting the end of life, and they remain alive for us for as long as we read and ponder their stories.

"I Never Saw or Heard the Car Coming"
My Close Call with Death

I end my book *Death in the Classroom* with a chapter called "Teacher's Self-Eulogy," in which I imagine dying in character— teaching until my eighties, believing, with George Steiner, that there is no more privileged craft than teaching: "To awaken in another human being powers, dreams beyond one's own; to induce in others a love for that which one loves; to make of one's inward present their future: this is a threefold adventure like no other" (Steiner 183–84). My imagined death is, admittedly, a fantasy, but it reflects my passion for teaching and my belief in pedagogical love: "He taught many thousands of students over a career that spanned more than half a century, and although he forgot most of their names, he never stopped feeling affection for them, even love" (*Death in the Classroom* 225).

The idealized death I blissfully imagined was far different from the real death I miraculously escaped on the morning of October 6, 2010, when I was hit by a car while running with my two Belgian sheepdogs, Caleb and Sabrina. It was raining hard as dawn was breaking when we were struck from behind by an elderly woman who did not see us. I never saw or heard the car coming. Because there are no sidewalks in my neighborhood, I was running on the extreme right of the road, with the dogs running a foot or two to my left. All I remember was a horrific impact. I went flying through the air, crashing into the road with my head. I arose immediately, shocked that I was still alive and could walk. Bleeding profusely from my scalp, I used my T-shirt to soak up the gushing blood that soon covered my sweatshirt, pants, and running shoes. I remember seeing Caleb and Sabrina lying motionless and soundless on the road, and hearing the driver repeating plaintively, over and over again, "Oh, my God, I didn't see you." She did not have a cell phone to call an ambulance, but after a few minutes other drivers stopped and offered assistance. Soon a police car and an ambulance arrived, and what is ordinarily a quiet residential street was suddenly transformed into a surreal scene of flashing lights, wailing sirens, and scurrying emergency medical paramedics and police.

Upon impact, my glasses had flown off my head, and, nearly blind without them, I kept pacing back and forth on the road, vainly looking for them. After several minutes a school bus driver, to whom I had waved a few minutes earlier when she passed me in the opposite direction, honked, anxious to continue on her route. I picked up Caleb and Sabrina and gently moved them onto the grass. They were breathing slowly, with their eyes slightly opened, but they remained motionless and mute. I recall imploring those who had stopped in their cars to awaken my companion, Julie, who was home sleeping, less than a block away. By this time it was about 7:00 a.m., and many neighbors had come out of their houses and were standing quietly on their lawns. Traffic began to move slowly, and it was now fully light.

As I remained standing on the grass, an emergency medical technician came and placed my neck in a brace, despite my repeated assertions that it wasn't necessary. I was then put on a backboard near the ambulance. I heard one of the attendants say, "Make sure he's laying comfortably." I started to say, "it should be *lying* comfortably," but I decided to withhold my professorial correction; now was not the time for a grammar lesson. I was then carried into the ambulance, where I *lay* for several minutes. Julie suddenly appeared at my side, calm but with a look of terror. She didn't believe me when I said I was okay—there was too much blood for my assurance to be credible. She said she'd meet me at the ER; I asked her to bring me a backup pair of glasses. As she left the ambulance, I heard her ask to see the dogs. The ambulance then sped me to the city's major hospital, where I was wheeled into a large emergency room.

An ER physician asked me to move my head, arms, fingers, and legs, which I had no difficulty doing. Astonishingly, I did not have a head-ache or any pain except for my throbbing left leg. I was still without my eyeglasses, so the world continued to look disorienting and dreamlike. A nurse removed my blood-stained clothes and gave me a surgical gown.

Julie arrived soon with my glasses, which was a great relief. After clean-ing up the scalp wound—pebbles from the road were now sticking to the skin, glued, as it were, by the dried blood—the ER physician started to staple the scalp wound closed, but he decided that the area, which he said was about the size of a half dollar, was too large. The ER physi-cian removed the staple and consulted with an otolaryngologist, who examined the wound, agreed that it could not be stapled closed, and recommended Dr. D, "one of our best plastic surgeons." Would he have told me, I wondered at the time, if Dr. D. were *not* one of the best plastic surgeons? "Don't be fooled by Dr. D.'s southern drawl," he continued, "he's not a hillbilly. He'll come in and say 'Hi y'all,' but he is the one I would choose for myself or my family." Clearly the otolaryngologist was not from the South.

Closing the Wound

I was told that I would have to wait several hours before Dr. D. would be free, but as it turned out, he soon arrived. A self-confident man in his thirties, he explained that when my head slammed into the pavement, I suffered an *avulsion,* which meant, essentially, that part of my scalp was still on the road. I later learned on the Internet that avulsions are among the "ugliest" injuries and carry a high risk of infection. (Avulsion equals repulsion, I thought to myself.) The surgeon told me he would close my wound by using a relatively simple procedure called a "flap," which entailed making an incision halfway around the crown of my skull, thereby enlarging the wound substantially but providing access to healthy tissue that he would then be able to pull over the wound and staple closed. He used this surgical procedure, he said, when someone had squamous cell skin cancer that had to be removed from the scalp. Given the complicated reconstructive surgery he does every day, often in the ER, there must be few challenges to creating a flap, but that was fine with me. At that point, they gave my glasses to Julie and wheeled me off to surgery.

I was given general anesthesia; the entire procedure, I was later told, took about an hour. Afterward Dr. D. said he was pleased with the outcome. He placed gauze on the stapled wound and told me to return in about ten days so that he could remove the staples. The wound continued to bleed and ooze while I was in recovery, but a nurse assured me that was normal and nothing to be concerned about.

I remained in recovery for several more hours, again, without my glasses. I found myself needing to urinate every few minutes. An attendant assisted me to the bathroom. Ten minutes later, I needed to urinate again. I didn't want to bother the attendant again, and so I hobbled slowly, holding onto the wall for support. I felt unsteady on my feet, probably a result of the anesthesia and the fact that my legs were becoming sore from crashing into the road nearly a dozen hours earlier. Despite the intense urge to void and pressure from my bladder, only a few drops of urine came out each time. That pattern repeated itself while I waited for Julie and my friend and colleague Randy Craig to return from transporting Caleb and Sabrina from the vet's office to an emergency clinic, where they would be monitored throughout the evening. Julie and Randy returned with my eyeglasses, and it was a relief to see again. The drive home from the hospital is only twenty-five minutes, but twice I needed to stop so that I could pee. I felt like an escapee from a mental institution, a sixty-five-year-old man with an oozing bloody dressing, wearing hospital socks and a surgical gown flapping open in the wind, trying desperately to relieve myself on a darkened street while cars streamed by a few feet away and dogs barked.

Catheterization

It was eight o'clock when we arrived home, thirteen hours after the accident. I was exhausted but unable to lie in bed more than ten minutes before I needed to urinate again. Nothing came out. My body was becoming increasingly sore from the accident, and though the bathroom was only a few feet from the bed, it was painful to go back and forth every few minutes. Just as I would find a comfortable position in bed, I had to pee again. We could not sleep. At one point I felt like sleeping on the toilet. Finally, at three o'clock in the morning, Julie called the plastic surgeon's office to explain the situation. Surprised to get Dr. D. on the phone, she was told the discomfort was probably due to a combination of the IV fluids pumped into me during surgery, the anesthesia, and my enlarged prostate. The walnut-size gland that surrounds the urethra, the prostate, when enlarged, blocks the flow of urine and may cause a burning sensation—exactly my situation. If the problem didn't correct itself by the morning, Dr. D. said, I should either return to the ER or see a urologist. The next morning I called my primary physician, who was able to arrange an appointment with a urological nurse practitioner later that day. In the interim, my overall discomfort increased. Elizabeth, the nurse practitioner, began taking my medical history. She struck me as conscientious but not overly friendly. I told her that although I have known for the last decade that I have an enlarged prostate, as most men do my age, I have never taken medication for it; instead, I limit my liquid intake in the late afternoon and evening. While speaking, I needed to go to the bathroom—no surprise there—with the same result, or nonresult.

When I returned, Elizabeth told me that I would need to be catheterized, to which I readily, though unenthusiastically, agreed. Anything would be preferable to hobbling urgently to the toilet every ten minutes only to void a drop. As I lay on her examining table, I told her that I needed to go again; she grinned enigmatically and told me that I could if I wanted to but that it wouldn't make a difference. She used a sonogram to measure my distended bladder, numbed my penis with a gel, and then, hardly waiting long enough for the gel to take effect, inserted a long catheter, attached to a bag, into my penis. Closing my eyes and squeezing my hands on the table, I steeled myself as best as I could. The catheter stung more than I anticipated. I later told my students that I preferred the impact of the car smashing into me than the insertion of the catheter: I didn't anticipate the former, but I dreaded the latter. Sting notwithstanding, I felt instant relief. It turns out I was retaining 1.5 liters of urine.

Following the catheterization, I was ready to leave but Elizabeth ordered me to place my elbows on the table so that she could check my prostate. Unfortunately, this must be done rectally. My father died of a virulent form of prostate cancer when he was seventy-six. The physical discomfort of the procedure pales in contrast to the fear of being told I have prostate cancer. As I positioned myself awkwardly at her table, spread-eagled, Elizabeth examined me, concluding that I had enough prostate for my neighbor and me. It was indeed enlarged, but it did not appear to be cancerous. Afterward I remarked ruefully that if one's companion can witness both a catheterization and a digital rectal exam without wanting to flee, romantic love will survive anywhere. Julie reminds me that she looked out the window for most of the two procedures.

I left Elizabeth's office with a leg bag and prescriptions for two different medications, one to relax the muscles in the bladder and prostate, which relieves the symptoms of benign prostatic hyperplasia; the other to shrink my enlarged prostate. She provided us with instructions on how to apply, change, and clean the leg bag, which I had to wear during the daytime, and the night bag, which rested on a chair near our bed. By the time we left Elizabeth's office, my mind couldn't absorb any more information, but Julie listened carefully to everything that was said. Elizabeth told us that we could either visit her a week later, when she would remove the catheter, or Julie could remove it herself. She gave Julie instructions, which seemed straightforward at the time, and we left her office.

Wearing a leg bag for a week gave me a tiny insight into the world of disability. Mechanically declined, I had trouble tightening the leg straps. Sometimes the bag, which was supposed to be fastened high on my leg, near my briefs, began to slip—an embarrassment when I was outside walking and it fell to my ankle. Once, after emptying the bag at the university, which I did every couple of hours, I felt a warm liquid on my leg and realized, to my chagrin, that I had forgotten to close the valve. (Fortunately, I had the foresight to wear dark pants.) I had difficulty sleeping at night, afraid I'd forget I was attached to a bag that was attached to a chair and that the catheter would pull out—a gruesome thought. For the first few mornings Julie helped me change from the night bag to the day bag. I then went solo, and sometimes I found myself sprayed with urine. An aging man's penis is not a thing of beauty and a joy forever. I tend to be a fast and careless walker, often bumping into objects and losing my balance—I can't run on sidewalks because I'm always tripping over uneven pavement—but for the week I had the catheter and leg bag, I moved slowly, cautiously, fearfully, afraid that if the catheter came off, so would my manhood, another gruesome thought.

I returned to the scene of the accident two days later, looking for my eyeglasses. A neighbor pointed out exactly where the accident had occurred, and within a few minutes I found the two lenses, badly scratched and chipped, about twenty feet apart from each other on the grass. The frames were nowhere in sight. Near one of the lens was Caleb's leather leash, snapped cleanly in two. On the pavement was a sterile gauze wrapper. A police report indicated the name and address of the driver of the car. I immediately recognized Mrs. M.'s name. I'm neither angry nor upset with her; I'm grateful that she decided to stop after hitting me. Not everyone would have done so. Julie and I later said that we would rather be struck by a car than be a driver responsible for a serious accident.

Turning Black and Blue

Apart from my scalp avulsion and minor abrasions on my left hand, left elbow, and left knee, I had no other physical injuries on the day of the crash. Sore and aching, I took ibuprofen several times a day, not the strong prescription pain medication I was given. The ER nurses warned me I would probably feel worse before I felt better, a prophecy that came true with a vengeance. Three days after the accident I was horrified to discover that my right calf was hugely swollen and had turned a ghastly black and blue. I have strong calves as a result of running every day, but my right calf was now double in circumference. Then my right foot and toes began to swell and turn black and blue, as did my right eye, which became swollen shut. The same happened with my left foot. For the first time I looked like I was struck by a car. Julie and I each spoke with physician-friends who confirmed that in the absence of heat, fever, or severe pain, these bruises did not require treatment. I stopped taking the large doses of ibuprofen and my daily 81 mg aspirin, used to lower the risk of a heart attack or stroke. Both ibuprofen and aspirin, it turns out, can increase internal bleeding.

Because of my swollen leg and feet, it became increasingly difficult to walk, bend, or lie down. People began to stare at me when I was outside. The dried blood on my head, which made the white gauze turn black, gave me a hideous appearance. The plastic surgeon told me not to get the wound wet for three days; on the fourth day Julie began to clean the blood off my scalp and remove the gauze. By that time, the gauze was like a hard black shell. Friends and neighbors were startled when they saw me.

The accident occurred on a Wednesday, and that afternoon I had called the English Department from the hospital and asked one of the secretaries to cancel my two classes the next day. I didn't tell her why. I didn't want the department to send out a "sad news" email detailing the accident. I knew that no matter how much I insisted I was not seriously hurt, everyone would reach the opposite conclusion: there are not too many people who are able to walk after being struck by a car. It was the first time in decades that I called off classes because of illness or injury.

I could have spent several weeks at home, not teaching—I have more than a year's worth of sick leave accrued, the maximum—but I was eager to return to work as soon as possible. Teaching is as much a part of my life support system as is breathing; I can't imagine not being in the classroom. I've had six one-semester sabbaticals since I began teaching at the University at Albany in 1973, and in each case I couldn't wait to return to the classroom. I dread the idea of retirement, and I'm grateful there is no mandatory retirement age. I don't love every aspect of teaching: reading student essays, especially poorly written ones, is not something I look forward to, though I take this responsibility seriously. The two highest forms of praise I receive from students are that I have inspired them to do their best *and* helped them to improve their writing. The following Tuesday I limped into my two classes. My Frankenstein's monster leer horrified my students. Had the accident occurred three weeks later, I would have looked properly ghoulish during Halloween. Julie had placed a strip of fresh gauze on the top of my head, covering part of the wound. I could have worn a baseball cap when I was teaching, but it would have been too much out of character, and besides, I didn't want to look goofy. I decided not to look into a mirror to see the extent of the wound until the staples were removed, but Julie said that its size and shape were about half the perimeter of a yarmulke. "God works in mysterious ways," she joked, adding that if I was self-conscious about the scar that would remain in the end, all I needed to do was wear a yarmulke! She put one on my head, which gave me a Talmudic appearance, and we both laughed. Julie hopes that my miraculous survival will make me, if not a believer, then at least open to the possibility of a Higher Power.

I continue to be amazed that I was not killed or seriously maimed by the accident. Nearly all of the doctors and nurses who saw my head were also astonished that only part of my scalp, not my brains, remained on the road. No less incredible is that I did not suffer a concussion or loss of consciousness. Given all of the internal bleeding that later occurred, it was also remarkable that I did not suffer an intracranial hemorrhage.

The day before my accident, one of my Love and Loss students, Marilyn, had read aloud an essay that I couldn't stop thinking about. The paper assignment, "Writing a Wrong," emboldened her to write a letter to her biological father, who had abandoned her mother when she became pregnant. Marilyn's missive, written in the form of a letter to her father, reveals the depth of her rage and hurt over his rejection, not unlike Sylvia Plath's "Daddy" in which the poet portrays her father as a monster. The most striking moment in Marilyn's essay is her depiction of a broken doll. "When I was little, I had a doll that I slept with every night. Being careless, I accidently dropped her, and her head split open. My mom glued the split in her head, and assured me that she was okay. To me, she wasn't okay; I still see the line of glue that held her together. I was afraid of playing with her because I feared the glue would come undone, and her brains would come spilling out. I was always afraid that my mom would come unglued too; that she would come unglued where she had stitched herself back together and her insides would also come spilling out. When you left, you created a hole in my mother that she has been trying to stitch up and fix ever since you left."

In class I had praised this paragraph, in particular, a concrete image of how both Marilyn and her mother felt as a result of parental and spousal rejection. While singling out this paragraph, I had no idea that it foreshadowed my own head almost splitting open one day later. I began to fear after the accident that my brains would spill out if I stumbled and hit the pavement.

I felt self-conscious walking into my first class, the Fiction of Thomas Hardy and D. H. Lawrence. Julie had reminded me that humor could be a lifesaver, and in an effort to explain my absence on the preceding Thursday and my medical condition, I read to my students a few paragraphs of "My Close Call with Death," which I had started to write. The students were unusually quiet and subdued during class. To lighten the classroom atmosphere, I bet a dollar that no one would be able to tell when I was peeing during our discussion. Many laughed, but no one took me up on the bet. After class Marilyn and another student came up to me to say that they knew something was wrong when they heard I had canceled class the previous week. Marilyn said she feared I was terminally ill when she heard me say I was writing a book called *Dying in Character*.

Putting Caleb Down

Throughout the ordeal I kept thinking how fortunate I was to survive. My thirteen-year-old dog, Caleb, was less lucky. He was frail before the accident, running like a puppy with Sabrina and me in the morning but sleeping the remaining twenty-three hours of the day. Many times he was in such a deep sleep that Julie and I both thought he was dead. Caleb was suffering from acute shock and respiratory distress, and a chest tap was performed to remove air from around his lungs. He also had severe heart arrhythmia that required constant treatment, we were told, for an indefinite period of time. Sabrina suffered labored breathing and some abrasions, but her lungs were clear. When Julie and I picked them up the morning after the accident to transport them back to our local vet, Caleb was hardly moving, and we made the painful decision to put him down. The vet seemed at first taken aback by our decision, but after a few seconds she said, "That's the decision I would make if he were my pet. It's the most selfless thing to do." By this time, Julie and I had been awake for over twenty-four hours. We were with him when he was euthanized, and the entire process, though sad, was calm and peaceful. We said our good-byes. We took Sabrina home that day, and though she appeared dazed and lethargic, no doubt a result of the traumatic injury and the absence of her buddy Caleb, she made a steady recovery. Julie's dog has helped keep Sabrina company, and we are glad we have at least two dogs.

Had I not survived the accident, I would have certainly died in character, for nearly every day during the last thirty-five years, I have run in the morning, regardless of rain, snow, sleet, or ice, typical upstate New York weather. I'm a slow, steady runner, and a slow, steady writer, and I try to run, and write, every day. Both activities are central to my identity. Admittedly, there is something obsessional about my daily running and writing, two activities that allow me to keep my demons at bay. I marvel at my "good bad luck" on October 6. There are advantages to dying quickly, but I hope that the guardian angel who may have been looking over my shoulder on that nasty morning will allow me to die many years from now in a warm classroom or, better yet, in my university office, a death that would truly be in character.

I have long assumed that I will die of cancer, like nearly everyone else in my family, many of them in their forties or fifties. Never have I imagined that I will die in a car accident—and certainly not as a runner or pedestrian. I've never had any close calls during any of my runs. Decades earlier I ran on a busy street, but I changed my route to the present one, where there are few cars early in the morning. After the accident, while I was in the ER, Julie recalled the words from Joan Didion's *The Year of Magical Thinking:* "Life changes fast. Life changes in the instant." Indeed, the words appear throughout the memoir like a Wagnerian leitmotif. Life changed for Didion in an instant when her husband, the writer John Gregory Dunne, died of a heart attack in the middle of a sentence while having dinner. The death was shocking to her even though her husband had a family history of heart disease, had undergone major heart surgery, and had written several books, fiction and nonfiction alike, in which he imagined he would die of a heart attack. Didion wrote *The Year of Magical Thinking* "to make sense of the period that followed, weeks and then months that cut loose any fixed idea I had ever had about death, about illness, about probability and luck, about good fortune and bad, about marriage and children and memory, about grief, about the ways in which people do and do not deal with the fact that life ends, about the shallowness of sanity, about life itself" (7).

I was grateful for being alive before the accident, but I was even more grateful afterward. After my accident, Julie nursed me back to health in her funny and bossy way, dressed my wounds, drove me to doctors' offices, iced my swollen legs and feet, removed dried blood from my scalp, washed my hair, cleaned my catheter bags, removed my catheter, cheered me up when I worried about my appearance, and reminded me that life is a gift. She said that the little stubs of hair growing back on top of my head looked so cute. She sees my scar not as disturbing or disfiguring but as a battle wound, a sign of being alive, like the rings of a tree.

After my injury I told Julie that many people in her situation would walk away from such a relationship. She disagrees vehemently and says that the exact opposite is true: crises like this bring people closer if they are meant to be together—when you are faced with the pain of wondering what if—and then the gratitude of not having to wonder anymore.

"I Was Shocked"

How did my students view this ordeal? On Thursday, October 13, seven days after my accident, the students in my Love and Loss course turned in their weekly diaries, and though I didn't ask them to offer their impressions of my injury or the brief narrative I had given them on Tuesday, five of them did so, four using the word *shocked* to describe my appearance. Sherry devoted the first half of her diary to describing her feelings about my return to class:

> I returned from class today, my fingers itching to write my diary entry. I think this past class was one of the most emotionally charged classes we have had since the semester began. I found myself wishing that my computer would turn on faster, impatiently anticipating the moment my hands would hit the keyboard, and then realizing that I did not even know where to start. I guess I will go in order of events.
>
> On Wednesday night, I received a message from an unfamiliar email address, with my class number in the subject. The email was forwarded to the rest of the class, as well, and informed us that our class on Thursday had been cancelled. My roommate was in the room when I opened the mail and heard me mumble the words "uh-oh." When she heard this, she became concerned and asked me why I reacted this way. I replied that I was not sure, but that my class was canceled for Thursday and that I had a bad feeling about the reason for the cancellation.
>
> You walked into the classroom as I was reading *Dying to Teach*. I did not look up. Instead, I tried to finish the paragraph I had been reading. Once you began talking, I realized the class had started and put away my book. I looked up to the sight of half of your scalp in stitches and your face bruised. I was shocked; this is the only word I can think of to describe my reaction. I tried my best to ignore the vision, trying not to be rude by staring, and instead focused on the paper you gave us, which described the ordeal. I was shaken after hearing what had happened to you. The daily ritual you had taken upon yourself to rid yourself of demons was now forever changed by this monumental accident.
>
> Your humor struck me. It makes me happy to know that there are people who can forgo their pain and make light of a scary situation. In this class, we hear many stories of the bad and how people have risen above their demons. The essays are written in a way that

make us believe that beneath the optimism, there is still pain, but the writers continue to find joy in life as well.

My head was spinning as I walked out of the classroom, both because of seeing you and because of the last essay read aloud [about a classmate's rape]. I had a dual desire to comfort those who had spoken in any way I could, and also to run from that room as quickly as my feet would take me. As strong as I try to be, I am horrible with sorrow. I hide my feelings and hate to hear of other people's pain. It is terrifying to imagine that there are people in the world who would treat others as my fellow classmates have been treated. It is even harder to imagine these scenarios after being in a class such as this, in which everyone is sympathetic and supportive. As much as I wish I knew what they were feeling, it frightens me to put myself in everyone else's shoes. My eyes are being truly opened to the evil that lies in this world, and I am both excited and afraid to continue my discoveries in this class.

Another student also remarked on how my humor helped her to deal with her anxiety arising over my appearance. "Everyone in the classroom was talking about the accident they heard through word of mouth, from his other students. When I saw him walk in I was terrified. Not by the staples or black eye but I worried he wouldn't be funny and have a sense of humor like he does in most classes. Luckily the accident just led to more material for him to joke about." Another woman assumed, upon seeing me walk into the classroom, that I was the victim of a violent crime. "Last class was perhaps the most eye-opening and disturbing class for me. First, upon Jeff entering the class with his head injury, I was shocked. The wound looked horrible. I got queasy, not because of the appearance of the wound, but because of the mere thought of what may have possibly happened. Living in Albany instills in me an automatic negative response to situations like this. Immediately, I found myself assuming that Jeff was harmed purposely, or anything that did not suffice as an 'accident.' I was almost relieved to discover that this truly was an unfortunate accident." Another person wrote how glad she was that I returned to teaching so quickly. "It seems weird that I am saying this, because I am just a student and I hardly know you. But I am proud that you didn't let this accident affect your working career. Even though you said you were afraid to come to class looking the way you did, you never gave up on us, and, most importantly, you didn't give up on yourself."

Sherry's dilemma of whether or not to look at me highlights the problem of those who encounter people with disfiguring scars or disabilities. Does one look or not look? Can one see without staring? I found myself in this dilemma for the three or four weeks after the accident when the wound was still nasty looking, except that now I was the object of others' stares. I didn't know whether or not to establish eye contact whenever I was in the presence of other people. Usually I look at people when I walk, especially when I'm on campus, and I always say hello to the many students, faculty members, and staff I know, but there were times when I kept my eyes down, so that I wouldn't have to explain the accident. Ironically, keeping my eyes and face down made the full extent of my head wound more visible. When I looked around while walking, as I usually do, I noticed that some people seemed to stare at me without their facial expression changing. Others stared and grimaced in horror. Strangers came up to me in the supermarket and exclaimed, "What happened to you?!" I felt ambivalent toward these people, annoyed by their indiscreetness but willing to tell my story, albeit briefly. Sometimes, curiously, I found myself irritated when people looked at me without asking about my injury.

Sherry's diary raises another pedagogical question. How much pain can a student experience without feeling overwhelmed? I urge my students to be as empathic as possible, but like everything else, empathy has its limits. Her diary reveals what Dominick LaCapra calls "empathic unsettlement," in which "secondary witnesses" feel partial identification with victims of atrocities. Sherry, however, was a primary witness, and she was profoundly disturbed by seeing her professor's gaping head injury and hearing about her classmate's rape. Notice, though, how eager she is to write her diary, eagerness that approaches excitement; how thoughtful and well written it is; how much compassion she has for her teacher and classmates; how honest she is in exploring her feelings; and how she captures so many of the complexities of love and loss. Faced with the choice of feeling too much empathy or too little, I suspect she would choose the former. I would too.

Twelve days after my accident, Dr. D. removed the staples and said that I was healing well. He pointed out a raised pouch on the top of my forehead that he said would eventually disappear. He laughed when I told him that I was sorry my case didn't pose more of a challenge to him. "Sometimes it's nice to have a chip shot," he replied. I showed him my black-and-blue calf and feet, and he said that they, too, were healing. When I told him about my extreme bladder discomfort and catheterization, he said he had heard that the pain associated with the inability to void after being injected with fluids for surgery is comparable to the pain of kidney stones for men. As we were leaving, I think we may have embarrassed him with all of our "thank-yous" and handshakes. Julie and I walked out of his office beaming. Another milestone.

Dr. D. told me after he removed the staples to rub vitamin E oil on my scalp to lessen the possibility of permanent scarring. When I began to do so, I realized that I was reluctant not only to look at myself in a mirror but also to touch the wound. I am not generally squeamish—I always look at the blood drawn from my arm when I donate plasma and platelets several times a year at the American Red Cross. The wound felt bumpy, crusty, and larger than I had imagined. For the next several days Julie applied the oil, and I found myself wincing even though the wound was not painful. When I told Julie that I didn't want to look at or touch the wound, she said to imagine how a woman with a mastectomy must feel when she looks in the mirror after her surgery.

Gratitude

I began writing about the accident one day after it occurred. Why? Like Didion, I needed to understand everything that had occurred—the details of the accident, the ways in which my body was bruised, the treatments I received, and the reactions of those who saw me. I needed to reflect on injury and illness, good luck and bad luck, love and loss, friendship and trust, life and death. I needed to understand my "story" before I could tell it to others. Writing about the accident helped me to remember details I was already beginning to forget or had not fully grasped at the time. For example, I was too much in shock to remember Dr. D.'s explanation of my avulsion, but when Julie reminded me of it, I went on the Internet to learn more about it. I needed to know about the catheterization and the medications I was prescribed for my enlarged prostate. I needed to know Julie's impressions of the accident and how it affected our relationship.

I was also curious about my students' reactions, especially those in my Love and Loss course. The accident was an all-too-timely example of life changing in an instant.

I'm not sure I would describe the accident as "traumatic": I never saw the car coming and, therefore, could do nothing to avert it. I have not dreamed of the accident, as I have of other traumatic events in my life. Nevertheless, I needed to write every detail down so that I could impose an order to it, thereby achieving a degree of self-awareness, self-control, and self-mastery. I wanted to share my story with relatives, friends, colleagues, and students. As painful as the experience and its aftermath were, I took pleasure in crafting every word, trying to make the story as compelling, both aesthetically and psychologically, as possible. Hours went by in an instant as I tried to reconstruct faithfully everything that happened. I found myself having what the psychologist Mihaly Csikszentmihalyi calls a "flow" experience, in which we lose all sense of time.

I now remember my accident as much from the story I wrote as from the accident itself. As Arthur W. Frank observes in *Letting Stories Breathe*, stories "*enact* realities: they *bring into being* what was not there before" (75). Our stories become our lives as much as our lives become our stories. "Stories by themselves may not determine whether people have fuller or diminished lives," Frank adds, "but by setting the terms in which lives are or are not narratable, stories create conditions for enrichment or diminishment" (75).

What did I learn about my encounter with death? The world looks so good to me even though I may not look so good to the world. One of the most memorable diaries I received about my scars was from a student who had several scars of her own as a result of a nearly fatal automobile accident:

> I was surprised when I learned about Professor Berman's unfortunate accident. When he walked into the class, I immediately noticed the incision scar on his head. I wanted to console him after he called himself a "freakoid." I am a freakoid too. I have a scar that is at least a foot long going straight down my stomach. In addition to that scar, I also have one on my chest, one on my hip, and a few on my side. I know that incision scars are the best scars to have. If the incision is done right, it will heal very well, and I believe that Professor Berman's head will look lovely with time.

That is not to say that I don't find scars beautiful. I wear mine with pride, as evidence that I have survived something difficult. People often get tattoos to externalize a struggle they have overcome; it is my belief that scars do the same thing.

It can be difficult to deal with people staring at you. I work as a waitress, and I usually can't go a week without a drunk person asking to hear my story. When napping on the beach, I open my eyes to people staring at my stomach. Over time, you learn to deal with it.

I was definitely upset after I got my scars. It was painful to look in the mirror and remember how I once looked. Now, I love my scars because they are a sign of my strength. I believe Professor Berman will be able to look at his scar in the same way with time.

I also learned, to my amazement, that there are cultures in which a more violent version of my accident is part of a ritual in which men and women willingly participate—without experiencing any pain:

> In East Africa, men and women undergo an operation—entirely without anaesthetics or pain-relieving drugs—called 'trepanation', in which the scalp and underlying muscles are cut in order to expose a large area of the skull. The skull is then scraped by the doktari as the man or woman sits calmly, without flinching or grimacing, holding a pan under the chin to catch the dripping blood. Films of this procedure are extraordinary to watch because of the discomfort they induce in the observers, which is in striking contrast to the apparent lack of discomfort in the people undergoing the operation. There is no reason to believe that these people are physiologically different in any way. Rather, the operation is accepted by their culture as a procedure that brings relief [from] chronic pain. (Melzack and Wall 17)

In his book *A Hole in the Head*, Charles G. Gross notes that trepanation is the oldest known surgical procedure, "practiced from the late Paleolithic period and in virtually every part of the world" (3). My hole in the head, it turns out, links me to the beginning of Western and non-Western medicine.

I have long believed that life is a tragedy filled with joy. Much of what I learned I relearned: that life is precious, that we should live each day as if it were the last, that we should be grateful for being alive, and that our gratitude extends to the living and the dead. My brief experience with a catheter has sensitized me to the courage of those who find themselves in this life situation for months or years. I have heightened admiration for those who are the objects of others' stares, whether because of disfigurement, disability, or simply difference. I recall Eric J. Cassell's observation in *The Nature of Suffering and the Goals of Medicine:* "All around us in the contemporary world there are persons with long-term chronic illness and disability who are weighed down by their suffering, although they may not have any of the prominent symptoms that alert us to the possibility of suffering" (xii). I am also reminded of George Eliot's statement in *Middlemarch:* "If we had a keen vision and feeling of all ordinary human life, it would be like hearing the grass grow and the squirrel's heart beat, and we should die of that roar which lies on the other side of silence. As it is, the quickest of us walks about well wadded with stupidity" (189). My accident removed some of that wadding.

I've made three changes since the accident. First, after three years of procrastination, I have finally gotten a hearing aid. Until the accident, vanity had trumped hearing. It's nice to hear my students without asking them repeatedly to speak louder. (I haven't started to wear the hearing aid to departmental meetings: no great loss.) Second, Julie and I are now running together in the morning—in the light. (One night, not long after the accident, when I was driving home from work, I saw a man in dark clothes running on the road and thought to myself, "Look at that stupid idiot!") And third, we are now married. As close as we were before the accident, we are now closer. She was right: that's how it is with love.

CHAPTER 2

"Death Itself Is a Wonderful and Positive Experience"
Elisabeth Kübler-Ross and *The Wheel of Life*

lisabeth Kübler-Ross, known famously and infamously as the "death and dying lady," was the most influential thanatologist of the second half of the twentieth century. Nearly every researcher in the field still cites her first book, *On Death and Dying*, published in 1969. The book's many psychiatric insights challenged the entrenched conventional wisdom of the age, including the belief that physicians should withhold the truth from terminally ill patients. Kübler-Ross postulated in *On Death and Dying* the "stage theory" of dying, in which terminally ill patients experience a sequential series of emotions, beginning with denial and ending in acceptance. Following *On Death and Dying*, she wrote more than a dozen books in which she shared her experiences working with terminally ill children and adults. Clinicians have accepted, with qualification, many of her psychiatric recommendations, but in her later work she became increasingly mystical, describing out-of-body experiences, cosmic consciousness, conversations with Jesus, and encounters with the dead that called into question her scientific judgment. In a December 26, 2004, article published in the *New York Times Magazine*, Jonathan Rosen quotes a psychiatrist as saying that Kübler-Ross's belief in life after death is a form of denial that has the effect of destroying the credibility of her earlier work, a judgment that speaks for many physicians and scientists.

Derek Gill captures much of the controversy of Kübler-Ross's life in his biography *Quest*. He acknowledges in the introduction the contradictory feelings she awakened in him when they met for the first time in 1977. "When she talked of her mystical experiences, my mind hovered between outright incredulity and a genuine desire to believe" (xii). He found her admirable yet disconcerting. "In the months ahead I was to discover that she was so rocklike in her convictions—convictions that I could not always support—that we had many clashes. Indeed, there were times when we regretted having set out on the task of writing her story. Then there were times when I believed (and still do) that destiny, the stars in their courses and the moon—what you will—played a part in this project" (xii). *Quest* often reads like an authorized biography, which prevents the biographer from being sufficiently critical of his subject. Gill ends his story in November 1969, when Kübler-Ross resigned from the University of Chicago Medical School and began her new career giving lectures and workshops—a career that, for many readers, seemed less about science than science fiction.

Never one to shrink from medical or theological controversy, Kübler-Ross became a cult figure despite her aversion to New Age spirituality, speaking to as many as fifteen thousand people per week for twenty years. During the middle and late 1990s she suffered a series of strokes that left her partly paralyzed, and she died in 2004 at the age of seventy-eight. The woman who spent a lifetime chronicling her patients' end-of-life-experiences wrote about her own experience in *The Wheel of Life: A Memoir of Living and Dying* (1997), where, in the last two chapters, she impatiently awaits death. The memoir, which is fascinating for many reasons, allows us to see the ways in which her own belief system influenced her vision of death. Writing the memoir enabled her to practice what she had preached for most of her life, namely, that death is a "wonderful and positive experience" (280). Or as she observes wryly in *Death Is of Vital Importance*, "I'm *not* the 'death and dying lady.' I hope in the next fifty years I will be known as the 'life and living lady' "! (137). Waiting for death proved harder than she imagined.

The Stage Theory of Dying

During the early years of her professional work, dying in character meant, for Kübler-Ross, going through the stages of dying that she formulated in

On Death and Dying, one of the groundbreaking books in thanatology. Most of her ideas are intuitive and have withstood the test of time. She begins by making a paradoxical observation that is as true today as it was fifty years ago: "The more we are making advancements in science, the more we seem to fear and deny the reality of death. How is this possible?" (6–7). She never fails to acknowledge that she has learned the most about death and dying not from her medical school professors or psychiatric textbooks but from terminally ill patients, who are her best teachers. By helping dying patients realize they can teach the living, she validates their existence and gives them a reason to live as fully as possible while they prepare for the end.

Kübler-Ross's experience as a young country doctor in Switzerland taught her that dying patients do best when they are in familiar and comfortable environments. It is less frightening and isolating to die in one's home than in a cold, impersonal hospital. She describes in the book the Interdisciplinary Seminar on Death and Dying that she began teaching in 1965 as an assistant professor of psychiatry at the University of Chicago Billings Hospital. After two years the seminar became an accredited course for the medical school and the Chicago Theological Seminary. *On Death and Dying* reveals the intense opposition she encountered from physicians who refused to allow her to interview their terminally ill patients; indeed, the physicians did not even acknowledge their patients were dying.

Denial

Kübler-Ross begins the chapter on denial and isolation with a question she never answers: "Who was it who said, 'We cannot look at the sun all the time, we cannot face death all the time'"? (xx). The answer is La Rochefoucauld: "Neither the sun nor death can be looked at steadily." Not that she would have had much in common with the cynical seventeenth-century French writer who believed that everything is reducible to self-interest.

One of Kübler-Ross's most important insights in *On Death and Dying* is that the terminal patients she interviewed knew they were dying despite protestations to the contrary from their physicians and family. The patients sensed they were dying by the "changed attention, by the new and different approach that people take to them, by the lowering of voices or avoidance of rounds, by the tearful face of a relative or an ominous, smiling member of the family who cannot hide their true feelings" (32). Avery D. Weisman reaches a similar conclusion in *On Dying and Denying.* "To tell or not to tell is seldom an urgent question. Contrary to popular expectations, to be informed about a diagnosis, especially a serious diagnosis, is to be fortified, not undermined. In any case, patients soon are aware that something is amiss, and that their closest relatives and friends are poor actors" (17). The patient's need for denial, Kübler-Ross theorizes, is in direct proportion with the physician's need. But this is only part of the problem, she admits. The other part of the problem is that denial is the first response to, or stage of, the news of terminal illness. "Among the over two hundred dying patients we have interviewed, most reacted to the awareness of a terminal illness at first with the statement, 'No, not me, it cannot be true'" (34). Curiously, Kübler-Ross does not devote a separate stage to "shock," which would seem to precede denial. In her later books she refers to shock and denial as a single stage, though they appear to be different. Shock is a sudden, often violent physical response to a horrifying event, whereas denial is a rejection or a dismissal of the horrifying event.

In her next book, *Questions and Answers on Death and Dying,* Kübler-Ross points out that she doesn't tell patients they are dying until they are ready to hear this. "As soon as the diagnosis is confirmed a patient should be informed that he is seriously ill. He should then be given hope immediately, and by this I mean he should be told of all the treatment possibilities. We usually then wait until the patient asks for more details. If he asks for specifics I would give him an honest, straightforward answer. I do not tell the patient that he is dying or that he is terminally ill" (2). There is an art to sharing this painful news with a patient, she writes in *On Death and Dying.* "The simpler it is done, the easier it is usually for a patient who recollects it at a later date, if he can't 'hear it' at the moment" (32–33). A small minority of patients—1 percent, in Kübler-Ross's view—remain in denial until the end of their lives, and she urges physicians not to be judgmental about these patients. Nor should one be judgmental of patients who decide to forgo medical treatment in order to complete "unfinished business," her term for unresolved personal conflicts or issues.

Many of Kübler-Ross's insights foreshadow those in Ernest Becker's

Pulitzer Prize–winning book *The Denial of Death*. Becker does not refer to Kübler-Ross's work, but she refers to his, describing his book, on the back cover of the paperback edition, as a "brilliant and desperately needed synthesis of the most important disciplines in man's life." Both Kübler-Ross and Becker emphasize the use of denial as a defense mechanism against the realization of human mortality. She would agree with his statement about the basic duality in human nature: "Man is literally split in two: he has an awareness of his own splendid uniqueness in that he sticks out of nature with a towering majesty, and yet he goes back into the ground a few feet in order blindly and dumbly to rot and disappear forever. It is a terrifying dilemma to be in and to have to live with" (*The Denial of Death* 26). She would also agree with his statement that "*consciousness of death* is the primary repression, not sexuality" (96). And both Kübler-Ross and Becker would endorse E. M. Forster's observation in *Howards End:* "Death destroys a man: the idea of Death saves him" (239).

Anger

"When the first stage of denial cannot be maintained any longer," Kübler-Ross writes, "it is replaced by feelings of anger, rage, envy, and resentment" (*On Death and Dying* 44). These dark feelings are often displaced onto everyone—relatives, friends, doctors, and nurses. The challenge for those working with the terminally ill is to accept these emotions without becoming threatened by them. Only those who have confronted their own fears of death and dying will be able to tolerate a patient's anger. Just as the expression of these emotions is therapeutic, the inability to express these emotions is countertherapeutic. Allowing the dying to express their feelings not only helps them to feel better, released from toxic rage, but also enables them to feel less isolated and withdrawn. The dying want and need to be heard, Kübler-Ross insists; sometimes it is enough simply to hear them without offering consolation, false hope, or judgment. Unlike Freud, who rarely spoke about the importance of empathy, and who was distinctly insensitive with some of his patients, such as Dora, Kübler-Ross places empathy at the center of her therapeutic strategy.

A dying patient's anger or resentment can easily awaken the same feelings in those who attend them. To defuse this anger in hospital staff, Kübler-Ross advocated the use of "screaming rooms." As she writes in

Questions and Answers on Death and Dying, "Every helping person needs a screaming room—perhaps a little room beside the nursing station, the hospital chapel, or any other room where you can cry, where you can curse, where you can express your anger, where you can disappear with a friend and tell nasty things about your co-workers who aggravated you or prevented you from staying with a needy patient" (22–23). Her language, here and elsewhere, is simple, commonsensical, clear, and earthy. Her sense of humor is often evident. One could never infer from her highly readable prose that English was not her first language.

Like her other books, *On Dying and Death* abounds in clinical vignettes that transcend the dry discussions of most case studies. The protagonists in her books are her patients; the antagonists are unenlightened doctors, nurses, and administrators. One of her patients is Sister I., who is hospitalized for the eleventh time with what turns out to be advanced Hodgkin's disease. Kübler-Ross devotes a twenty-five page section of the book to a transcript of an interview among the psychiatrist, chaplain, and patient. Sister I. was an angry, demanding patient, and her physicians believed that the rashes on her body were a psychosomatic illness rather than, as Sister I. suspected—she was a nurse by profession—cancer. "I felt like a leper and they thought I had a psychological problem" (51). Sister I.'s simile is the same one C. S. Lewis uses in his memoir *A Grief Observed* to describe the stigmatization surrounding death and dying: "Perhaps the bereaved ought to be isolated in special settlements like lepers" (11). Kübler-Ross never refers to Lewis, but she would be sympathetic to his belief that "passionate grief does not link us with the dead but cuts us off from them" (54).

Throughout the interview, Kübler-Ross listens attentively to Sister I., particularly when she talks about the need for increased pain medication. Sister I. criticizes the rigid hospital policy that restricts the amount and timing of medication even when patients are in excruciating pain. She states sarcastically that physicians should not worry that the dying will become addicted to drugs: "This patient isn't going to live long enough" (*On Death and Dying* 58). The psychiatrist not only listens empathically to her patient but she also summarizes pithily—and bluntly—the meaning of her comments: "If you have to die you would like it to be without agony and pain and loneliness," to which Sister I. responds: "That's very true" (59). As the interview progresses, Sister I. talks about the need to decorate her hospital walls to make them less sterile. She also wants to be with visitors who will provide companionship. "When I am in tears or depressed I know I have to do something to stop thinking about myself and whether I am in pain or not I have to drag myself to somebody else, to concentrate on them" (60). Kübler-Ross immediately picks up on this theme and responds pragmatically, "Well, that's something, you know, where we can help" (60). The patient then begins to cry, saying that no one has helped her in this way. Without offering false praise, Kübler-Ross compliments Sister I. on her articulateness. "You know, you put this so much in words what we have been doing here for this whole year and what we have attempted to do in many ways. I think you really put it in words" (62).

Kübler-Ross encourages Sister I. to reflect on her past to have a better understanding of the present. Throughout the interview she empathizes with her patient's fears, mirrors her words, and shores up her self-esteem. As a result of the interview, Sister I. became less hostile, and the other nurses began to visit her more often. Kübler-Ross relates how, in one of her last visits, Sister I., close to death, asked her to read her a chapter from the Bible. The psychiatrist is unexpectedly troubled by this request, finding it "peculiar and beyond the usual things I was asked to do," but she reminds herself that she has promised to try to fulfill Sister I.'s needs. "I recall the dreaded thought that some of my colleagues might come in and laugh at my new role," she confesses, with admirable honesty, "and I was relieved that nobody entered her room during this 'session'" (*On Death and Dying* 71). A few days later Sister I. visits Kübler-Ross to bid farewell. "She looked cheerful, almost happy. She was no longer the angry nun who alienated everybody, but a woman who had found some peace if not acceptance and who was on her way home, where she died soon thereafter" (71).

Bargaining

Kübler-Ross devotes only three pages in *On Death and Dying* to "bargaining," the third stage. She gives the example of a child who attempts to bargain with a parent to receive a special favor. "If I am very good all week and wash the dishes every evening, then will you let me go?" (72). In Kübler-Ross's view, the dying attempt to bargain with someone for more time. Terminally ill patients use the same strategy as children. Bargaining seems a reasonable response to news of terminal illness, but Kübler-Ross claims that none of her patients have kept their promise. Since most dying people attempt to bargain with God, they may feel guilty or unworthy if their wishes aren't answered, and for this reason she recommends that the patient speak with a chaplain.

Depression

Kübler-Ross divides the fourth stage, depression, into two types, reactive depression, a response to learning that one is dying, and preparatory depression, the grief that one experiences in undertaking the final separation from life. The first type of depression looks backward; the second type, forward. She maintains that while it is helpful for dying patients who experience reactive depression to look at the bright side of life, telling a dying mother, for example, that her children are playing happily while their father works, it is not helpful to cheer up those suffering from preparatory depression. "It would be contraindicated to tell him not to be sad, since all of us are tremendously sad when we lose one beloved person" (*On Death and Dying* 77). Kübler-Ross suggests that while psychotherapy may be helpful for reactive depression, it is not useful for preparatory depression, since patients prefer to remain silent. "In the preparatory grief there is no or little need for words. It is much more a feeling that can be mutually expressed and is often better done with a touch of a hand, a stroking of the hair, or just a silent sitting together" (77).

Acceptance

Kübler-Ross spends the most time in *On Death and Dying* describing the final stage, acceptance, which, she implies, is the most desirable. Acceptance is neither resignation, defeat, surrender, nor happiness. "It is almost void of feelings. It is as if the pain had gone, the struggle is over, and there comes a time for 'the final rest before the long journey' as one patient phrased it" (100). She does not elaborate here on the nature of this long journey, though she does so in her later books. Rather, she contents herself with describing how this stage looks to the attentive physician. "The patient may just make a gesture of the hand to invite us to sit down for a while. He may just hold our hand and ask us to sit in silence. Such moments of silence may be the most meaningful communications for people who are not uncomfortable in the presence of a dying person" (100). Silence becomes eloquent during these moments, suggesting that the dying person and the visitor have accepted the inevitability of death. She invests this silence with peace and dignity, the two words she uses to describe the final stage of death.

Anticipating criticisms of her stage theory, Kübler-Ross makes several key qualifications, often in her later books. She admits in *Questions and Answers on Death and Dying* that "patients do not necessarily follow a classical pattern from the stage of denial to the stage of anger, to bargaining, to depression and acceptance. Most of my patients have exhibited two or three stages simultaneously and these do not always occur in the same order" (25–26). If patients reach genuine acceptance and then regress, it is usually because someone has urged them to cling unnecessarily to life. She insists that it is not the physician's goal to push patients from one stage to another. "If a patient has been angry all his life long or was a revolutionary or a fighter, it is much more likely that he will remain in the stage of anger until the moment he dies" (36–37). Those who have been struggling with depression their entire lives may die depressed. Such patients, she implies, die in character. She concedes that some terminally ill patients do not experience all five stages, and those who do may not proceed chronologically through them.

After describing the various responses to death, Kübler-Ross then discusses the complicated question of hope, observing that all dying patients hope for a miraculous cure even toward the end of their lives. However unrealistic this hope may be, she urges physicians not to contradict it. "This does not mean that doctors have to tell them a lie; it merely means that we share with them the hope that something unforeseen may happen, that they may have a remission, that they will live longer than is expected" (*On Death and Dying* 123).

In the remaining chapters of *On Death and Dying*, Kübler-Ross includes several interviews with terminally ill patients, summarizes the responses to her Seminar on Death and Dying, and offers recommendations for working with dying patients. She argues that patients' families experience the same emotional reactions as the patients themselves. Once again she insists that families who are emotionally honest will do better than those who mask or conceal their feelings. Relatives and friends should not feel rejected if a patient wishes to be left alone. She rejects offering religious consolation to the family. "Once the patient dies, I find it cruel and inappropriate to speak of the love of God" (156). Instead, she encourages relatives and friends to express all of their emotions, especially anger, bitterness, and despair. Such "ventilation"—one of the most significant words in the book—is always valuable. In the chapter devoted to interviews, she allows patients to do most of the talking, limiting her own role to asking questions and then validating the patient's feelings.

Throughout *On Death and Dying* Kübler-Ross maintains that if discussions of death were as commonplace as discussions of birth, everyone would have a far healthier attitude toward life and death. "If this book serves no other purpose but to sensitize family members of terminally ill patients and hospital personnel to the implicit communications of dying patients, then it has fulfilled its task" (126). She is modest here, for her book, more than any other in the past half century, has effected a revolution in the treatment and understanding of terminally ill patients. Named one of the hundred most important books of the twentieth century by the New York Public Library, *On Death and Dying* changed the way we think about end-of-life issues.

On Death and Dying remains Kübler-Ross's most "medical" book. She never reveals her religious beliefs, nor does she suggest that one must make a choice between science or religion, as Freud and Becker do. She implies that one can live a fulfilling life and accept the inevitability of death without maintaining or denying belief in God or in an afterlife. Only in her later books does a strong spiritual and mystical impulse emerge. There is little in *On Death and Dying* that foreshadows her dramatic turn to spirituality.

Kübler-Ross remains cautious about revealing her spiritual beliefs in her second book, *Questions and Answers on Dying and Death*. She tells us in the introduction that she has excluded chapters on "religion and life after death" and "bereavement and grief" not only because of lack of space but also because "there are others who are more qualified to answer these questions" (xii). Nevertheless, she admits midway through the book, in a chapter called "Questions of Humor and Fear, Faith and Hope," that she feels comfortable sharing her views about God with her patients as long as she doesn't impose her own religious and philosophical beliefs onto them (157). She is forthright about her own faith: "I believe that the soul or the spirit continues to live and it is conceivable that this is the reason why it is so difficult for us to conceive of our own death" (155). Near the end of the book she discloses how she has acquired her faith: "Before I started working with dying patients, I did not believe in a life after death. I now do believe in a life after death, beyond a shadow of a doubt" (167).

Criticisms of the Stage Theory

As Michèle Catherine Gantois Chaban points out, most of the criticisms of *On Death and Dying* have focused on Kübler-Ross's stage theory. "Critics have come to dismiss the staging theory at its outset, saying people do not die in stages" (35). Edwin Shneidman observes in *A Commonsense Book of Death*, "My own limited work has not led me to conclusions identical with those of Kübler-Ross. Indeed, while I have seen in dying persons isolation, envy, bargaining, depression, and acceptance, I do not believe that these are necessarily 'stages' of the dying process, and I am not at all convinced that they are lived through in that order, or, for that matter, in any universal order" (12). Robert Buckman contends that the stage theory does not pay sufficient attention to emotions such as fear, guilt, hope, and despair (145). Kenneth J. Doka criticizes Kübler-Ross for her method of collecting clinical data and for her failure to discuss the diverse ways people cope with death. David Wendell Moller asserts that she "has established in *On Death and Dying* an Imperial Journey of Dying that monolithically defines a good death as one grounded in peaceful, tranquil acceptance." He likens her and those who accept her ideal of the "good death" to "travel agents for the dying, offering therapeutic intervention to a singular destination: tranquil, peaceful death" (51).

In *The Truth about Grief,* the journalist Ruth Davis Konigsberg views Kübler-Ross as the key figure in creating what has become a "grief culture" based on flawed scientific assumptions. "Despite her medical training, Kübler-Ross was always more of a spiritualist than a scientist, more a believer than an empiricist" (88). She also suggests that Kübler-Ross failed to acknowledge other clinicians who had earlier developed similar stages of dying, including A. Beatrix Cobb, a Texas Tech University psychologist, and two British psychiatrists, Colin Murray Parkes and John Bowlby.

On Death and Dying is surprisingly psychoanalytic in its theoretical assumptions and clinical recommendations. Kübler-Ross endorses Freud's belief in the talking cure and his conviction that knowledge is power. She lists five Freudian texts in her extensive bibliography, exceeded only by her seven references to Cicely Saunders, the British physician who is credited with the creation of hospice in the United Kingdom. Kübler-Ross's belief that "in our unconscious, death is never possible in regard to ourselves" (2) is certainly Freudian, as is her view that "in our unconscious mind we cannot distinguish between a wish and a deed" (2)—what Freud calls the "omnipotence of thought." She doesn't cite "Mourning and Melancholia," Freud's landmark 1917 essay, but she accepts his belief that the dying engage in "decathexis," withdrawal of interest in the outside world. She also affirms Freud's model of defense mechanisms, including projection and internalization, along with his theory of resistance, transference, and countertransference. She is careful to avoid projecting her spirituality onto her patients; she neither agrees nor disagrees with a patient's remark that he expects "to be at home with the Lord when I die" (100). She never offers religious consolation or false hope to any of the patients in the book.

In the mid-1960s Kübler-Ross was in psychoanalysis at the prestigious Chicago Institute for Psychoanalysis, the second oldest psychoanalytic institute in the country, and while she does not discuss this experience in *On Death and Dying*, she does in *The Wheel of Life*. She speaks tersely about her initial interview there with an authoritarian male analyst who thought she had a speech impediment. " 'I don't know why the institute considered you for a training analysis,' he said. 'You can't even speak.' " Insulted, she stormed out of the office. A second session with the same analyst was no better, and she vowed never to return. She did not give up on psychoanalysis, however, and she found an analyst, Dr. Helmut Baum, with whom she developed a good therapeutic relationship. "I eventually realized there was some value to analysis. I got some new insight into my personality, why I was so headstrong and independent" (*The Wheel of Life* 138). She tells us that she was in psychoanalysis for thirty-nine months, though Gill reports she "tackled her psychoanalysis with such vigor and intensity that she completed in twenty-six months the full analytical course, which normally took four to five years" (300). Regardless of which figure is correct, she never became enamored with classical psychoanalysis, objecting to the time and expense of analysis and the emphasis on publishing scientific papers. Nor was she a fan of mainstream psychiatry, with its growing reliance upon medication.

An Unwanted Child

Kübler-Ross never commented in detail on how her personal psychoanalysis influenced her life or work, but in an important moment of self-analysis, she reveals in *Death Is of Vital Importance* that being born a triplet had a formative influence on her. She describes herself as being an unwanted child who had to struggle harder than her sisters to gain parental approval. "Not that my parents didn't want a child. They wanted a girl very badly, but a pretty, beautiful, ten-pound girl. They did not expect triplets and when I came, I was only two pounds. I was very ugly and had no hair, and I was a terribly, terribly big disappointment to my parents" (1). A stormy relationship with her father reinforced her fear of being underappreciated. In *The Wheel of Life* she relates how her controlling father wanted her to be a secretary, not a physician. Crushed, she snaps, "No, thank you!" (22) and then relates how she defied his wishes, even at the risk of banishment from her family. Years later, when she became a physician, she repaired the relationship with her father, who by this time was proud of her achievements. Her writings convey her intolerance of authoritarian males and her willingness to speak up for herself and her patients. Her angry arguments with her father, who loved her only as long as she obeyed him, taught her the value of unconditional love, which she affirms in all of her books. She viewed unconditional love not as an abstract ideal, to be pursued but never obtained, but as a transcendent reality that was within the reach of everyone.

Kübler-Ross's perception of being an unwanted child sensitized her to patients like Sister I., who also felt underappreciated. Aware of her own anger, Kübler-Ross encouraged her patients to express their feelings, however dark they might be. Regardless of whether patients' anger was rational (an appropriate response to dying) or irrational (a displacement of anger onto an innocent passerby), she urged dying patients to talk about their feelings. Invariably they felt not only better but often, for the first time, understood by another person. She never doubted that a physician's empathy could take the sting out of a patient's death.

Heinz Kohut and the Power of Empathy

Kübler-Ross never mentions Heinz Kohut (1913–81), the world-famous analyst who was professor of psychiatry at the University of Chicago and a training analyst at the Chicago Institute for Psychoanalysis, but she seems to have had an intuitive understanding of his approach to psychological disorders. The creator of a new movement called "self-psychology," Kohut, unlike orthodox Freudian analysts, urged an empathic, nonjudgmental attitude toward patients, especially those suffering from narcissistic disorders, which he believed arose from insufficient love and attention in early childhood. Kohut believed that the treatment for narcissistic patients is not the traditional talking cure, insight therapy, but the analyst's empathy, approval, and validation, which help to strengthen the patient's fragile self. Kohut departs radically from the orthodox view of the analyst as purely objective and detached. He rejects the "blank screen" model of classical analysis and replaces it with empathy, which, he asserts, in *The Search for the Self*, is the "power that counteracts man's tendency toward seeing meaninglessness and feeling despair" (2:713). Since narcissistic injuries are caused by empathic failure, Kohut recommends nothing less than a new paradigm for therapeutic cure, one based not on insight but on unwavering empathic support and validation. He also expands the role of the analyst-as-mirror. Unlike the reflecting pool in Ovid's myth of Echo and Narcissus, which is emotionally unresponsive, in Kohut's writings mirroring assumes an active, joyful quality. He celebrates the "glint in the mother's eye" in mirroring the child's buoyant strivings. Empathic mirroring remains for Kohut a Kantian imperative, and he affirms, with almost religious fervor, the child's search for empathically responsive selfobjects. In *How Does Analysis Cure?* Kohut makes the heretical claim that excellent therapeutic results can be maintained as long as the analyst remains empathic, even if the analyst's interpretation of the patient's conflicts is in error (91).

Psychoanalysts tend to limit the scope of narcissistic disturbances to developmental fixations or arrests, but it is easy to see how death is the fundamental narcissistic blow, as Darcy Harris suggests. "No matter how much one accomplishes in life or how great an individual's contribution to society has been, death is the ultimate insult that returns all beings, no matter what their level of achievement has been, back to the earth through the process of decay. Death is essentially the ultimate narcissistic wound, bringing about not just the annihilation of self, but the annihilation of one's entire existence, resulting in a form of existential shame for human beings, who possess the ability to ponder this dilemma with their high-functioning cognitive abilities" (77–78). Death reminds us of the finite nature of life, and regardless of whether we personify death as the Grim Reaper or a ticking clock, we know that our time on earth is limited.

And here we return to *On Death and Dying,* for without referring to Kohut, Kübler-Ross urges an empathic, nonjudgmental approach to end-of-life issues. Both Kübler-Ross and Kohut regard empathy as an indispensable tool of observation, an antidote to fear and destructiveness, and a psychological nutriment that sustains human life. Related to empathy is the power of love, which becomes increasingly important in Kübler-Ross's writings. She risks sounding utopian, as Kohut often does, in her affirmation of unconditional love, as a passage from her 1983 book *On Children and Death* reveals. "It is my hope that more young parents will begin to comprehend the importance of raising their children by allowing them the expression of natural emotions and showing them unconditional love. If this could be done with one generation of children, we could eliminate places of pornography, most prisons, and many other institutions! We could spend less time consoling families whose children were murdered, fewer hours trying to identify bodies of runaway children in cold morgues, and less time and energy trying to comprehend the ever-increasing number of childhood suicides" (73–74).

Far from being a blank screen to her patients, Kübler-Ross is not afraid to admit that she cries with her patients. "Sometimes I have tears in my eyes when I sense this is my last visit with a patient I have cared for for a long time. I do not feel that it is unprofessional to have tears in your eyes. It is not a question of not having worked through enough of your own feelings; it is rather a question of how much you are willing to share your own humanness" (*Questions and Answers on Death and Dying* 106–7). In writing about working with dying patients, Kübler-Ross anticipated by two decades the movement toward "relational" psychoanalysis, or intersubjectivity, where analyst and analysand share their feelings toward each other. She doesn't use the words "transference" or "countertransference" to describe the patient's or therapist's conscious or unconscious projective tendencies, but this is what she has in mind when she discusses the therapist-patient relationship.

On Death and Dying would not have generated much medical controversy if it were Kübler-Ross's only book. But within a few years she published several other books, each becoming more outspoken in its spiritual and mystical claims. By the end of the 1960s she had become a household name, known to millions of people. Her movement toward spirituality and out-of-body experiences provoked immediate criticism from the medical and scientific communities. Undeterred by these criticisms, she began to write about experiences, both her own and others', that defined a new image of dying in character.

A shift in Kübler-Ross's thinking appears in her third book, *Death: The Final Stage of Growth,* published in 1975. She is listed as the sole author of the book, but it is an edited volume consisting of fifteen essays, one of which, "Death as Part of My Own Personal Life," is by her. She remarks in the introduction that death is the muse of art, citing Thomas Mann's statement that "without death there would scarcely have been poets on earth" (2). She then suggests that "death was the great instructor of those noble characters in history whom we venerate as heroes, saints, or martyrs of science" (2). The "one message" she hopes to convey in the book is that "death does not have to be a catastrophic, destructive thing; indeed, it can be viewed as one of the most constructive, positive, and creative elements of culture and life" (2). The assertion that death can be a positive experience, the final stage of growth, contradicts her statement early in *On Death and Dying* that "death has always been distasteful to man and will probably always be" (2). In "Death as Part of My Own Personal Life" she discloses that her experience working with the terminally ill has "helped me to find my own religious identity, to know that there is life after death and to know that we will be reborn again one day in order to complete the tasks we have not been able or willing to complete in this lifetime" (119). Finding her own religious identity proves to be, from a medical point of view, increasingly out of character for her.

The Out-of-Body Experience

Death not only lost its sting for Kübler-Ross but soon became a consummation devoutly to be wished, as Hamlet exclaims in his "to be or not to be" speech. Unlike Hamlet, she never fears shuffling off this mortal coil. Nor does she experience dread or indecision when contemplating the "undiscovered country from whose bourn / No traveller returns." She describes in *Working It Through* her first out-of-body experience, which occurs while she is giving one of her workshops at her retreat near San Diego called Shanti Nilaya, which means Home of Peace in Sanskrit. While drifting into a deep, trancelike sleep, she sees herself lifted out of her physical body and compares the experience, mechanistically, to bringing an automobile to a repair shop. She awakens two hours later energized, as if she has been sleeping for nine hours, and looks with astonishment at a nurse who informs her with a "knowing smile" that she has had an out-of-body experience.

The most dramatic shift in Kübler-Ross's thinking appears in *On Life after Death,* first published in 1991, a decade after the appearance of *Working It Through.* She bases her new view of death on her study of "twenty thousand cases of people all over the world who had been declared clinically dead and who later returned to life" (2). She once again proposes a stage theory, not the five-stage theory she uses to describe the process of dying, but a three-stage one to depict the transition from life to death. The first stage she compares to a butterfly emerging from a cocoon: the dying person escapes from a body that is no longer needed. The second stage consists of "psychic energy" when the deceased realize they will be made whole again. This stage is so pleasurable that the deceased are reluctant to return to life, reinhabiting a decaying or diseased body. One of the reasons this stage is so peaceful, Kübler-Ross maintains, is that no one dies alone. Now the dead can speak to whomever they wish. The dying have a guardian angel or spirit guide who accompanies them to the "other side," a journey that involves traversing a bridge, tunnel, or mountain pass. The third and final stage involves embracing pure light. "It is extremely bright, and the more you approach this light the more you are embraced by the greatest indescribable, unconditional love you could ever imagine. There are no words for it" (10).

Kübler-Ross is never at a loss for words, however, and immediately after explaining these three stages, she tells us why we need to change our attitude toward death. "If you accept your life as something you were created for, then you will no longer question whose lives should be extended and whose should not. No one would ask if someone should be given an overdose in order to shorten his or her life. But dying must never mean having to suffer. Nowadays, medical science is so fantastic that anyone can be kept pain-free. If your dying ones can be kept without pain, dry, and nursed with care, and you have the courage to take them all to your homes—I mean all, if possible—then none of them will ask you for an overdose" (*On Life after Death* 12–13).

How do we respond to Kübler-Ross's lofty claims? Despite the statement later in *On Life after Death* that she engages in reality testing when she converses with a deceased patient, her stage theory of life after death has not received scientific confirmation. She describes mystical experiences that speak authentically to mystical readers: nonmystical readers remain incredulous. Many scientists believe in God, an afterlife, and reunion with the dead, but few would claim there is irrefutable scientific proof for these truth claims.

Science can neither prove nor disprove Kübler-Ross's truth claims, but physicians challenge her assertion in *On Life after Death* that "nowadays medical science is so fantastic that anyone can be kept pain-free." Significant progress has been made in palliative care, but physicians admit that many patients remain in irremediable pain despite the use of massive amounts of morphine. As the oncologist Alan Astrow concedes, "the line between relief of suffering and end of life is often blurred" (45). Medical ethicist Margaret Battin argues in *The Least Worst Death* that "even a patient receiving the most advanced and sympathetic medical attention may still experience episodes of pain, perhaps alternating with unconsciousness, as his or her condition deteriorates and the physician attempts to adjust schedules and dosages of pain medication. Many dying patients, including half of all terminal cancer patients, have little or no pain, but there are still cases in which pain management is difficult and erratic. Finally, there are cases in which pain control is theoretically possible but for various extraneous reasons does not occur" (105). Though some physicians, such as Ira Byock, *guarantee* that their dying patients will not suffer physical pain—"eighteen years of clinical hospice experience has taught me . . . that physical distress among the dying can *always* be alleviated" (215)—other physicians are more guarded. In their edited volume *Physician-Assisted Dying*, Timothy Quill and Margaret Battin reveal the gap between the promise and reality of palliative medicine:

> Most experts in pain management believe that 95 to 98 percent of pain among those who are terminally ill can be adequately relieved using modern pain management, which is a remarkable track record—unless you are unfortunate enough to be in the 2

to 5 percent for whom it is unsuccessful. However, among hospice patients who were asked about their pain level one week before their death, 5 to 35 percent rated their pain as "severe" or "unbearable." An additional 25 percent reported their shortness of breath to be "unbearable" one week before death. This says nothing of the physical symptoms that are harder to relieve, such as nausea, vomiting, confusion, and open wounds, including pressure sores, which many patients experience. (323)

No one can fail to agree with Kübler-Ross's statement in *On Life after Death* that "from the scientist, humility is demanded!" (5), but one hopes for the same humility from all researchers and practitioners, including Kübler-Ross herself. Her certainty of belief in the books following *On Death and Dying* is exasperating for nonbelievers. She acknowledges in *On Life after Death* that many of her skeptical colleagues dismiss her patients' near-death stories as "projections of wishful thinking" (7), but she insists she has scientific proof. She never doubts the truth claims of her patients' stories, whether they are from a woman with multiple sclerosis who imagines dancing again or from a woman with breast cancer who suddenly feels whole. Nor does she doubt why children die young. "The answer is quite simple. They have learned in a very short period what one has to learn, which could be different things for different people" (11). It is comforting to believe Kübler-Ross's promises in *On Life after Death* that "after seeing the light nobody wants to go back" (11), that "If you live well, you will never have to worry about dying" (18), and that "death does not exist" (34). Comforting promises, however, are not always convincing.

Nevertheless, some physicians find the idea of near-death experiences comforting as they themselves approach death. David Servan-Schreiber states in *Not the Last Goodbye* that several of his patients told him about their own near-death experiences. "They did so spontaneously, without my asking them" (125). He admits that he is filled with joy over the prospect of joining a community of human and animal souls bathed in light, connectedness, and love. "Nothing proves that NDE visions actually reflect any kind of reality. It's quite possible that they are no more than the hallucinated product of a handful of neurons misfiring due to a cocktail of chemicals. But from my vantage point today, I'd rather imagine that my death will resemble the famous tunnel leading me to a white light" (132).

The publication of Raymond A. Moody's *Life after Life* in 1975—the 1981 edition has a foreword by Kübler-Ross—made near-death experiences known to millions of readers who now believed that there was scientific proof supporting this phenomenon. But as Hayden Ebbern and his associates point out, those who report these experiences were never clinically dead, since their brains were still functioning, albeit in a reduced condition. (The brain can continue functioning for several minutes after cardiopulmonary arrest.) Ebbern and others argue that if near-death experiences originate from changes in brain physiology, they are not a glimpse of an afterlife.

How do philosophers and theologians respond to the question of life after death? John Hick, a renowned philosopher of religion, does not discuss Kübler-Ross by name in *Between Faith and Doubt,* but he offers some support for her theories. He cites a 1976 British National Opinion Poll of about two thousand people indicating that 36 percent reported having religious or mystical experiences, a figure that is consistent with polls taken in other countries. Hick quotes from David Hay's 1982 book *Exploring Inner Space* about those who have religious or mystical experiences:

> What we found was that over a third of all adults in Britain would claim to have had experiences of this kind. Generally speaking, women are rather more likely to claim these experiences than men, in the ratio of four to three. As one moves up the social scale, more people will talk about religious experience; also, the more education people have, the more likely they are to talk about their experience. The happier people are, and the older they are, the more likely they are to claim experience. Most interesting of all, those who report religious experience are more likely than others to be in a good state of psychological well-being." (39–40)

An eloquent advocate of religious pluralism, Hick suggests that the "great mystics of all traditions have always developed a holistic spirituality which involves their whole lives, not just temporary 'highs' provided by drugs or any other means" (91). Quoting Erich Fromm's statement that the "tragedy in the life of most of us is that we die before we are fully born," Hick points out that "all the religions teach that this life is only a small part of our total existence" (144). He does not believe in traditional ideas of heaven and hell, but he does believe, in agreement with Kübler-Ross, that "there must be an opportunity for further moral and spiritual growth beyond this life" (151).

Kübler-Ross reveals, toward the end of *On Life after Death,* her own near-death experience. To gain the credibility of her readers, she tells us that in her early years she had no guru or comprehension of a higher consciousness. Nor was she able to meditate. Working with dying patients, however, enabled her to reach a higher level of consciousness. Each time a patient or a life experience made her aware of a "negativity" within her, she tried to externalize it so that she could reach a "harmony" among the four quadrants she believes exists in all people: physical, emotional, spiritual, and intellectual. Soon she began to have more and more mystical experiences, including out-of-body experiences.

One of these out-of-body experiences occurred when she was in a laboratory filled with "several skeptical scientists" in the Blue Ridge Mountains in Virginia. During her first out-of-body experience there she was "slowed down" by the laboratory chief who felt she "went too fast" (*On Life after Death* 66). Much to her dismay, he interfered with her own needs and personality. Determined to have a second out-of-body experience, she induced herself "to go faster than the speed of light and further than any human being has ever gone during an out-of-body experience" (66). The result, she avers, is that she left her body at an incredible speed. Upon returning to life, she had only one memory, hearing the words *Shanti Nilaya,* which had no meaning or significance to her at the time. She asserts that the mysterious out-of-body experience cured her of two serious medical problems she had at the time, a bowel obstruction and a painful slipped disk. Everyone present pressed her for information about her strange experience, but she was unable to explain it even to herself. The next night, while trying to sleep in a lonely guesthouse, she realized that she had "gone too far" and that she had to accept the "consequences" of the eerie event. "I tried to fight sleep during that night, having a vague, inner-knowledge that 'it' would happen, but not knowing what 'it' would mean. And the moment I let go I had probably the most painful, most agonizing experience any human being has ever lived through. I literally experienced the thousand deaths of my thousand patients" (67).

"Rebirth Beyond Human Description"

Kübler-Ross concludes from this experience that she has the strength and courage to endure the unendurable—and that people are never given more suffering than they can bear. Her agony ends when she is able to move from "rebellion" to "submission." This gives rise to a "rebirth beyond human description." The experience begins with a "very fast vibration, or pulsation" in her abdominal area, spreads to her entire body, and then to everything her eyes can see, beginning with the ceiling and wall of the guesthouse and eventually to the "whole planet earth" (*On Life after Death* 69). She then sees something that looks like a lotus flower behind which appears the "light" glimpsed by her patients. Traveling through the open lotus flower, she emerges into the light, which she identifies as unconditional love, and becomes one with it. She falls into a deep trancelike sleep and wakes up about an hour and a half later, having experienced "probably the greatest ecstasy of existence that human beings can ever experience on this physical plane" (70). She finds herself in "total love and awe of all life" around her, literally walking above the ground so that she doesn't step on and hurt anyone or anything. It takes her several days before she is able to return to her normal physical existence and several months before she can share it with anyone. She speaks about the experience for the first time when a "beautiful, non-judgmental, understanding group" located in Berkeley invites her to speak on transpersonal psychology. They give her experience a label, *cosmic consciousness,* and explain the meaning of *Shanti Nilaya.* She ends the chapter by declaring that this experience "has touched and changed my life in ways that are very difficult to put into words" (71).

How do we interpret Kübler-Ross's rebirth experience? The messianic imagery is striking. Like Jesus, she suffers for others, in her case, reliving the agonizing deaths of her patients, but she is also prepared to suffer verbal crucifixion in the form of condemnation by her medical colleagues. She never believes she is Jesus, but she maintains she has a special calling to convince people that dying and death are nothing to be feared. Her later books reveal an evangelical fervor as she tries to persuade her readers that they can be saved by the truths she preaches. Rescue fantasies are common among physicians and mental health professionals, but they are especially strong in her work. She "rescues" her patients and readers, first, by reassuring them they have nothing to fear about dying and death; second, by promising them they will ecstatically merge with God's unconditional love; and finally, by telling them they must resolve their unfinished business lest they be forced to return to life and relive painful experiences.

Kübler-Ross's near-death experience constitutes the aesthetic and psychological climax of *On Life after Death,* though there is an additional chapter, "Death of a Parent," that serves as a coda. Between the publication of *On Life after Death* in 1991 and *The Wheel of Life* in 1997, she wrote five books, including *Death Is of Vital Importance, The Meaning of Suffering, The Cocoon and the Butterfly, Healing in Our Time,* and *Say Yes to It,* but most of these are distillations of her earlier works. Many of the events in *The Wheel of Life* are a retelling of notable chapters in her earlier books. For example, the three-stage theory of dying she first proposed in *On Life after Death* is now expanded to a four-stage theory; the last stage includes "life review," in which the deceased reflect on the totality of their lives. She also discloses in *The Wheel of Life* her belief in a special destiny to be a healer, her rejection of the conventional wisdom surrounding death and dying, and her initiation into the world of spirits and guardian angels. In writing about the deaths of her relatives, friends, and patients, she foreshadows the way in which she writes about her own end-of-life experience. Part valedictory, part eulogy, part obituary, and part credo, *The Wheel of Life* ends with the physician who is now the patient, confined to a wheelchair, longing for death.

Early Deaths in Kübler-Ross's Life

Three of the earliest deaths in *The Wheel of Life* have a formative influence on Kübler-Ross's life. The first occurred when she was five years old, around the time her family moved to a small Swiss village not far from Zurich. She developed a high fever that turned into pneumonia, and she was rushed to the hospital, where she felt scared and alone. The examining room was cold, and no one spoke to her, not even to offer comfort. After the doctor asked her mother to leave the room, "I was weighed, poked, prodded, asked to cough and treated like a thing rather than a little girl as they sought the cause of my problems" (28). This frightening event was the first of many unpleasant experiences, both as a patient and as a physician, with cold, impersonal hospitals. Sharing the room with her was a dying girl two years older who reminded her of an "angel without wings, a little porcelain angel," whom no one visited (28). At first they do not speak to each other, but they communicate through thought transference. When they do begin to speak, the porcelain angel reveals she will be leaving later that night. "I grew concerned. 'It's okay,' she said. 'There are angels waiting for me.'" The porcelain angel adds that her "real family was 'on the other side' and assured me that there was no need to worry." They trade smiles before falling asleep, and Kübler-Ross recalls that she "had no fear of the journey my new friend was embarking on" (29).

Kübler-Ross was in her early seventies when she wrote *The Wheel of Life,* and it is remarkable that she remembers this experience so vividly. One wonders whether she recalls accurately all these details, including the actual dialogue and, more importantly, her religious certainty of life after death, or whether some of these details are reconstructions created decades later, when she became certain of the existence of life after death. Memory is often unreliable, especially when it involves events occurring in early childhood, yet she never doubts the accuracy of these details. We can see from the description of the porcelain angel that the young Elisabeth imagines death as a journey to the "other side." She experiences no fear of death, no uncertainty over why children die, no dread over the possibility of her own death. Nor does she experience anything like survivor guilt, which many in her situation would feel.

The two deaths that occurred when Kübler-Ross was ten could not have been more different from each other. One was a bad death, the other a good death. A young doctor moves into her small Swiss village, and soon his daughter, Suzy, stops going to school, suffering from meningitis: "First paralysis set in, then deafness, and finally she lost her eyesight" (*The Wheel of Life* 38). Fearing they will catch the terrible disease, the villagers shun the doctor and his family. Unlike most of her classmates, young Elisabeth continues to have contact with the dying girl. Suzy's death fills her with sadness because of the way she dies. "I will never forget that when Suzy died her bedroom curtains were shut. I recall being sad that she was closed off from the sunshine, the birds, the trees and all the lovely sounds and sights of nature. It did not seem right to me" (39).

Would Suzy's death be more acceptable had she died in a brighter room? Suppose Suzy's room was airy and bright—would that have made much of a difference to a person who didn't want to die? Can a child's death ever seem right? Are there "simple" answers for a child's death, as Kübler-Ross asserts in *On Life after Death?* Kübler-Ross never raises these questions.

The good death, which does seem right to her, is that of one of her parents' friends, a farmer who had once befriended her and her family when she was ill with pneumonia. The farmer does not die from an illness, like Suzy, but from an injury—he breaks his neck falling from an apple tree. He does not die immediately, however, and after the doctors at the hospital declare that his condition is hopeless, he is taken home, where his family and friends say good-bye to him. Unlike Suzy's room, the farmer's room is bright and cheerful. "His room overflowed with wildflowers, and his bed was positioned so that he could look out the window on his fields and fruit trees, literally the fruits of his labor that would survive the drift of time. The dignity and love and peace I saw made a lasting impression" (*The Wheel of Life* 39). Contrasting the two deaths, she sees Suzy as cut off from the beauty of nature while the farmer is at one with it. "The farmer had died what I now call a good death—at home, surrounded by love and given respect, dignity and affection. His family said all they had to say and grieved without any regrets or unfinished business" (39).

A good death, for Kübler-Ross, is one that occurs not in a cheerless hospital, where a patient is isolated from family and friends, and where children cannot see a parent, but in a familiar home environment, where the sun streams through the windows and loved ones gather to say good-bye. That remained one of Kübler-Ross's fundamental beliefs. Her aversion to hospitals, which can be seen from early childhood, helps to explain her decision to quit her job working in a Chicago hospital and devote the rest of her career to giving workshops and lectures, where she did not have to contend with institutional bureaucracy and her medical colleagues' disapproval.

The Death of Her Father

Ernst Kübler was also suspicious of hospitals, and his daughter sees in his death a confirmation of her belief that it is better to die at home. He developed septicemia as a result of a "botched" operation on his elbow, and his health rapidly declined while in the hospital. "Medicine was not helping him anymore," Kübler-Ross writes in *The Wheel of Life*. "All my father wanted was to go home. Nobody heard him. His doctor refused to discharge him, and so did the hospital" (122–23). Fearful of dying away from home, like his father, who had died in a nursing home, Kübler threatened to commit suicide if he was not allowed to go home—and his wife was "so weary and distraught" that she threatened to join him. The hospital physicians did not want to discharge him, warning that the trip home would probably kill him, but Kübler-Ross intervened. She and her mother kept a constant vigil by his bedside at home, but his health continued to decline. Finally he stopped eating, asking only for different bottles of wine from his wine cellar. On the last night, he was in excruciating pain, and his daughter gave him an injection of morphine.

The next afternoon "the most extraordinary thing happened": he asked his daughter to open his window so that he could hear the church bells ring. "For a few moments we listened to the familiar chimes of the Kreuzkirche. Then my father began conversing with his own father, apologizing for letting him die in that dreadful nursing home" (*The Wheel of Life* 124). She never questions whether her father's conversations with his deceased father are hallucinations. Though she cannot hear her grandfather's words, she never doubts that they are audible to her father. Nor does she doubt that her father's present suffering is due to "unfinished business." Ernst Kübler's death does not force his daughter to change her belief system. The family's grieving does not last long, and "none of us were left with any regrets" (125)—a surprising statement for a daughter to make about a father who was so unsupportive of her medical career. She closes the chapter, aptly entitled, "Living until Death," with a statement she wrote in her journal immediately after the funeral: "My father truly lived until he died" (125).

"I Want You to Terminate My Life"

Eva Kübler's death was far more difficult. One of the turning points in everyone's life is the death of one's mother, and the death of Kübler-Ross's mother proves to be no exception. In 1969 Kübler-Ross flew with her two young children to visit her seventy-seven-year-old mother in Switzerland, and during an otherwise joyous vacation, Eva Kübler said, "Elisabeth, we don't live forever" (*The Wheel of Life* 154). In retrospect, Kübler-Ross believed that her mother had a premonition of her death, which the psychiatrist could have easily inferred from her mother's next statement: "You are the only doctor in the family and if there is an emergency I will count on you" (154). To eliminate any ambiguity over the meaning of her statement, the mother continued, "If I ever become a vegetable, I want you to terminate my life" (154). Finding herself annoyed and angered by her mother's statements, Kübler-Ross tries to change the subject. When that fails, she tells her mother that nothing bad will happen to her—a promise the daughter knows she cannot keep. She then adds that she is irrevocably opposed to assisting anyone to commit suicide, especially her mother. " 'If something happens, I will do the same for you that I do for all my patients,' I said. 'I will help you live until you die' " (155). A few weeks later Eva Kübler suffers a massive stroke, and her daughter returns to Switzerland to visit her in the hospital. "Unable to move or speak, she stared at me with a hundred words in her deep, injured, pained and frightened eyes. They added up to one plea, which I understood. But I knew then—as I'd known before—that I could never fulfill her request. I could never be an instrument of her death" (155).

Filled with questions about what to do while she watches her mother "languish in her cocoon of helplessness and torment" (*The Wheel of Life* 156), Kübler-Ross feels like screaming out loud for divine guidance— which is slow to come. Finally she decides, with her two sisters, to send her mother to a rest home where she will receive nursing care but no artificial efforts to prolong her life. Eva Kübler remains alive for four years, and her daughter cannot stop thinking about her refusal to assist in her mother's death. She doesn't report on any further conversations with her mother, or on what her mother may have said to her other daughters, but she concludes that she made the right decision in keeping her mother alive. "My mother continued to feel love and give love. In her own way, she was growing and learning whatever lessons she needed to learn" (157).

Is this affirmative interpretation the mother's or the daughter's? It is impossible to know from the evidence presented in *The Wheel of Life*. When Eva Kübler died, on September 12, 1974, the day Kübler-Ross completed her third book, *Death: The Final Stage of Growth*, the psychiatrist once again finds herself "asking God why He made this woman, who, for eighty-one years, gave only love, shelter and affection, a vegetable and kept her in that state for so long" (*The Wheel of Life* 195). As she curses God, she has an epiphany that gives her the answer she seeks. "Then, as unbelievable as it sounds, I changed my mind and was actually thanking Him for his generosity. It sounds insane, right? It did to me too—until it dawned on me that my mother's final lesson had been to learn how to receive affection and care, something she had never been good at. From then on, I praised God for teaching her in just four years. I mean, it could have been a lot longer" (195).

Kübler-Ross's interpretation here never sounds insane, but it is highly subjective, as all interpretations are. Who wouldn't like to believe that one's bedridden mother can find meaning and growth in a four-year experience that most people would dread? Who wouldn't like to believe that suffering has a positive meaning? Or that everything happens for a reason, part of a benevolent God's grand design? Or that everything is bearable if there is love? We cannot enter into the mind of the dying Eva Kübler, and, therefore, we cannot validate her daughter's affirmative interpretation. Curiously, Kübler-Ross never describes any of these deaths in terms of her stage theory, not even her mother's death, which is the most protracted of those discussed in *The Wheel of Life*. Did the psychiatrist believe that she needed to cite no additional empirical proof to support her stage theory? Or did she have no evidence to cite?

Linda's Story

Of the several patients mentioned in *The Wheel of Life*, Linda holds a prominent position. When Kübler-Ross was asked by her supervisor at the University of Colorado Medical School, Sydney Margolin, to lecture on psychiatry while he was traveling in Europe, she became understandably anxious. He was a charismatic speaker, and she feared she would not be able to hold his students' attention. Unsure what to lecture on, she chose the subject of death, "probably the greatest mystery in medicine. The biggest taboo too" (130). She thought of Linda, a sixteen-year-old girl suffering from leukemia. "Her doctor's impersonal treatment drained whatever hope she had, but she also freely and eloquently expressed her anger toward her family, who weren't coping well with her dying" (131). Linda's bravery fascinates Kübler-Ross, and she urges the girl to speak to the medical students about what it is like to die. During the first hour of the talk, Kübler-Ross's presentation bores her students, who chatter disrespectfully among themselves, but they quickly become quiet and apprehensive when Linda is wheeled into the center of the auditorium's stage. Kübler-Ross asks the students to raise questions for the young patient to answer, but they can think only of technical ones about her illness. Linda becomes incensed by their failure to confront her dying, and she proceeds to pose and answer the questions she wanted her physicians to ask: "What was it like to be sixteen and given only a few weeks to live? What was it like not to be able to dream about the high school prom? Or go on a date? Or not worry about growing up and choosing a profession? Or a husband? What helps you make it through each day? Why won't people tell you the truth?" (132).

The biographer Derek Gill reports that it was Kübler-Ross herself, not the patient, who poses these questions to Linda (255). The difference is significant because in Gill's version of the story, the psychiatrist raises questions that may strike readers as inappropriate and intrusive, whereas in Kübler-Ross's version the patient raises these questions. There are other subtle differences between the two accounts. Gill describes Linda during the beginning of the question period as quiet and shy, while Kübler-Ross characterizes her as angry and impatient. Kübler-Ross's account is the more dramatic of the two, and she portrays Linda as *dying* to speak about her illness, an image that is less apparent in Gill's account. Regardless of whose version is correct, we can understand why Kübler-Ross's students were apprehensive. These questions are daunting to anyone, including experienced physicians, mental health professionals, philosophers, and theologians. Kübler-Ross tells us that after speaking for nearly thirty minutes, Linda tired and returned to her bed, leaving the students "in a stunned, emotional, and almost reverential silence" (*The Wheel of Life* 133). The lecture time was over, but no one left the room, and during the following discussion most admitted that Linda's story had moved them to tears.

I don't doubt that hearing Linda's story reminded the students of their own fears of dying and death, as Kübler-Ross suggests, but several details of her interpretation remain ambiguous. Did *all* of the students experience an almost reverential silence? Did some students, as I suspect, feel angry at Kübler-Ross for forcing them to confront their own mortality? Did anyone feel ambushed by her radical pedagogical experiment? She informs us that her students' thinking was "forever changed," but it is rare for a single lecture, however emotionally charged, to change irrevocably *everyone's* thinking. She credits Linda for teaching her students and herself about the reality of dying, but how did the young patient feel about the event? It's true that she had the opportunity, perhaps for the first time, to tell her story, but we would like to know more about how she felt after her talk. Instead, she drops out of Kübler-Ross's story.

I have never taught a class of medical students, but I know from decades of teaching self-disclosing writing courses that students must be prepared carefully to hear wrenching stories—and what can be more wrenching than to hear a young person talking about her impending death? Not everyone responds in the same way to emotionally charged essays. Many students may not know how or what to feel; it takes weeks or months to process an event like the one Kübler-Ross describes. She infers from her students' silence that they all react in the same way to Linda's story, but experience has taught me that silence is always difficult to interpret.

If Kübler-Ross were teaching today at a medical school and wanted to write about a dying patient—or, indeed, any patient—she would need the approval of the university Institutional Review Board (IRB), which oversees all human research. The psychiatrist would need the informed consent not only of the patient but the medical students as well. The IRB would carefully weigh the risks and benefits of the research and would require the researcher to report any research subject who became at risk. The IRB exists mainly to protect research subjects, but it also protects the researcher. Had Kübler-Ross received IRB approval, there would have been, almost certainly, less institutional controversy surrounding her work.

Kübler-Ross's failure to describe the individual differences among the medical students' responses to Linda's story repeats the same failure to describe the individual differences among the two hundred patients she interviewed for *On Death and Dying*. Given her radical pedagogical experiment with Linda, the psychiatrist might have anticipated that the medical students would display many of the emotions of the terminally ill. That is, some of the students would have responded to Linda's story with shock and denial, others with anger or depression, and still others with a degree of acceptance.

In *The Wheel of Life* Kübler-Ross acknowledges that her critics, including colleagues, accused her of exploitation. One can understand her anger and hurt, but one can also understand why her colleagues felt she was exploiting the dying. It is likely that some of the medical students who heard Linda speak shared their feelings with Kübler-Ross's colleagues. Forcing medical students to interview a dying young woman in the 1960s was sensationalistic, and some students, along with professors and administrators, were understandably troubled.

As a result of the interview with Linda, Kübler-Ross was unable to find colleagues who were willing to send their dying patients to her. Consequently, she began making house calls on cancer patients in surrounding neighborhoods. "I offered a mutually beneficial deal. In exchange for free bedside therapy, patients agreed to be interviewed at my seminars. This approach stirred up more controversy around the hospital, where my work was already called exploitative. Then it got worse. As patients and their families spoke publicly about how much they appreciated my work, the other doctors found another reason to resent me. I could not win" (*The Wheel of Life* 159). The controversy soon worsened. *On Death and Dying* was published around this time and became an international best seller. A favorable article about her work appeared in *Life* magazine on November 21, 1969. The article was based on Kübler-Ross's interview with a twenty-one-year-old woman, Eva, who was dying of leukemia. Eva had given her permission for the interview, but the hospital was not notified in advance. "One administrator criticized me for making the hospital famous for dying," Kübler-Ross reports in *The Wheel of Life* (167). Her patients were grateful for her work, but her medical colleagues and hospital administrators continued to believe she was guilty of exploitation, and in 1972 she resigned from Billings Hospital at the age of forty-six. Never would she work in another hospital.

What is striking about the hostility that Kübler-Ross's work provoked among physicians and hospital administrators is not that her work was controversial but that none of the criticisms came from her patients. Nowhere in *The Wheel of Life* does she report that any of her patients feels disappointed, exploited, or betrayed by her—an absence of criticism that strains credibility. She was a polarizing figure, and it is surprising that none of her patients were suspicious of her motives or methods.

There is little that is unusual about the five deaths that Kübler-Ross describes in the first half of *The Wheel of Life,* those of the porcelain angel, Suzy, the farmer, and Mr. and Mrs. Kübler. The reader can hardly disagree with the assumptions Kübler-Ross makes about these deaths: namely, that it is better to die in one's home, with sunlight streaming through the window, than in an impersonal institution; that it is better to die surrounded by one's relatives and friends than alone; that the dying should be accorded dignity and respect; that the wishes of the dying should be granted whenever possible; and that dying patients do not want their physicians and nurses to give up on them. Nor can one disagree with her insistence that the dying should receive sufficient pain medication and that sometimes the "best medicine of all is the simplest medicine"— meaning that the country doctor can help dying patients learn "self-love, self-forgiveness, compassion and understanding" (262). In an era of managed care, contemporary readers will almost certainly sympathize with her criticisms of physicians. How can one not approve of a physician who maintains that the "biggest help a doctor could give a patient was to be a good, caring, sensitive, loving human being" (104)?

Not all readers, however, will agree with Kübler-Ross's spiritual beliefs: "The more you go through, the more you learn and grow" (*The Wheel of Life* 17); "when you learn your lessons, the pain goes away" (18); "you may not get what you want, but God always gives you what you need" (111); and "life ends when you have learned everything you are supposed to learn" (157). Her belief in unconditional love is an impossible absolute for most people. We admire Kübler-Ross even when we realize that many of her generalizations about life as a process of positive growth are true only for incurable optimists like herself.

Kübler-Ross comes across in the first half of *The Wheel of Life* as a fiercely independent and tenacious woman who is not afraid to be a maverick in a profession that encourages conformity. She is a visionary with the courage of her convictions. She defied her rigid, authoritarian father who wanted her to be his secretary, patriarchal medical school teachers who believed that women should stay home and take care of their children, evasive physicians who failed to tell the truth to their dying patients, and hospital administrators who were concerned only with money. She is a woman with an unwavering belief in her destiny and calling. We may not believe in the existence of angels, but it is not hard to recognize that she is on the side of the angels by restoring dignity to the dying.

Life after Death

We trust most of Kübler-Ross's perceptions in the first half of *The Wheel of Life*, but in the second half she becomes an unreliable narrator, relating experiences to us that strain our belief. Indeed, much of the second half of *The Wheel of Life* reads like science fiction. Her work took a dramatic turn in the 1970s when she began offering workshops around the world. Whatever scientific caution existed in her while she was in a hospital setting, now disappeared. She describes, in the chapter entitled "Afterlife," the strange encounter with Mrs. Schwartz, who emerges at an opportune moment while the psychiatrist waits for an elevator with Pastor N., the man who was helping her teach the Death and Dying seminar. Kübler-Ross disliked Pastor N., who had replaced the Reverend Renford Gaines, with whom she had an excellent professional relationship. Just as she is about to tell Pastor N. that she no longer wishes to teach the seminar, Mrs. Schwartz appears and seems to hover in the air, as if she is transparent. After Pastor N. leaves, Mrs. Schwartz urges Kübler-Ross not to give up her pioneering work. There is nothing remarkable about Mrs. Schwartz's advice—except for the fact that she had died ten months earlier. "Was I having a psychotic episode?" Kübler-Ross asks herself. She is quick to rule out this possibility, but her readers may believe otherwise.

Not that Kübler-Ross is clinically psychotic. Rather, her belief that she has *scientific* proof in the existence of life after death undercuts her credibility as a physician. Her growing conviction in life after death results, predictably, in the growing skepticism of her family; her physician-husband, Emanuel Ross, "Manny"; and their two children, Kenneth and Barbara. Her discovery of the existence of a "flower fairy" fills her with excitement, despite her sadness that she cannot share this news with her family, from whom she feels increasingly estranged. Her involvement with Jay B., a shadowy man who founded the Church of Divinity in Escondido, California, further alienates her from her family. B. claims to have the ability to channel spirits from the "other side," an ability that Kübler-Ross believes demonstrates the existence of life after death. Through the channeler she meets her soul mate, Salem, who greets her as his beloved sister, Isabel. "Salem explained that in another lifetime, the time of Jesus, I had been a wise and respected teacher named Isabel. Together, we traveled back to a pleasant afternoon when I had sat on a hillside, listening to Jesus preach to a group of people" (203).

Kübler-Ross's family "sat with open mouths" when she narrated this experience to them. The family's disbelief turns into scorn as her involvement with this strange world deepens. "How can you believe that garbage?" her husband asks her, declaring that B. is taking advantage of her. She is stunned when her husband announces that he wants a divorce, and her description of saying good-bye to her family and home is startling for its lack of irony: "It was tough starting over at fifty years old, even for someone like me who had the answers to life's big questions" (205). Manny Ross's remark proves prophetic, as she discovers, to her dismay, but even when she ends her association with the sinister channeler, whom she acknowledges as a fraud, she never loses belief in her beloved spooks. By this time, many readers of *The Wheel of Life* have sided with Manny.

Kübler-Ross's experiences in the last seventy-five pages of *The Wheel of Life* become increasingly bizarre. A friend's husband, also a channeler, like the discredited B., conjures up a spirit who tells her that her work with death and dying is completed. "It's now time for you to begin your second assignment," informing the world that "death does not exist" (210). This message is reinforced by Salem, whom she can now summon without the help of B. She also beckons Pedro, her "favorite spook" (213), who carries her away in the palm of his hand and introduces her to a divine presence. "Millions of people in the world had mates, lovers, partners, and so on. But how many others had the thrill and comfort of being carried in the palm of His hand?" (213). She begins speaking on the next page with Jesus, a "mind-boggling" event that leads to her first out-of-body experience, which she had initially described in *On Life after Death*.

During the mid-1990s Kübler-Ross suffered a half dozen strokes, and she writes *The Wheel of Life* while sitting in her flower-filled living room in her home in Scottsdale, Arizona. The first indication of a serious health problem appears in 1988 when, during a typically stressful day, she suddenly loses consciousness while visiting her sister Eva in Switzerland. "I knew exactly what was happening . . . I was dying" (258). She welcomes the event. Exclaiming to her sister, "Eva, I'm dying," she gives her a "good-bye present," a firsthand account of what it feels like to die. A soothing numbness begins in her toes and moves up her body, past her waist. Far from experiencing anxiety or fear, she feels only pleasure, just as she had imagined death would be. Suddenly she is outside her body and tells her sister she has no regrets. She bids farewell to her children, wishes them "just love," and then feels as if she is on a ski slope, prepared to jump over the edge. Seeing a bright light, she positions her arms to fly straight into it. "'Here I come!' I screamed" (259). When she wakes up, alas, she finds herself lying across the table in her sister's kitchen. "She apologized for not calling an ambulance. 'Don't be a jerk,' I said. 'You don't have to call them. Obviously I didn't take off. I'm stuck here again'" (259).

Kübler-Ross narrates this event with wit and self-effacing irony, reporting that when she asked her sister to tell her what the account of death sounded like, Eva gave her a "weird look." It turns out that Eva heard her say only "I'm dying" and then "here I come." Everything between was a "complete blank"—except for the "crashing sound of dishes flying as I hit the table" (*The Wheel of Life* 259). What Kübler-Ross assumed was a coronary turned out to be only a slight fibrillation of her heart. She is disappointed that she is still alive, but the experience only strengthens her belief that death will be joyous and welcome when it comes.

Waiting for the End

There is nothing joyous, however, about Kübler-Ross's massive, brain stem stroke on May 13, 1995, which left her paralyzed on the left side. She describes her experience in a local hospital, where she receives CAT scans and an MRI, as torture, and she gives a karate chop to an insensitive nurse who exerts force to straighten a paralyzed arm. She acknowledges being a defiant and difficult patient, particularly while in the hospital. No surprise there. Her lifelong suspicion of hospitals has changed into active hostility. "The bureaucracy of the health-care system lived down to my expectations" (*The Wheel of Life* 279). As a physician she is "mortally offended" when faceless bureaucrats make decisions about her treatment. The physician who never charged a patient for treatment now finds herself denied medical care because of a "decision made by somebody in an office who'd never seen the patient" (280). Throughout 1996 she struggles with constant pain, dependent on twenty-four-hour care. "What kind of life is this?" she asks. "A miserable one." By January 1997, the time when she is completing the memoir, she is "anxious to graduate" (280). Despite her wish to die, she is still opposed to physician-assisted suicide. She must remind herself that, because she is stubborn and defiant, she must learn her final lessons the hard way, like everyone else.

Tellingly, Kübler-Ross never attempts to apply her stage theory of dying to her own situation. Has she forgotten about one of her major contributions to thanatology? We see anger, depression, and acceptance, but not denial or bargaining. In the penultimate chapter of *The Wheel of Life*, "The Butterfly," she yearns for death, which she remains convinced is a "wonderful and positive experience." Her faith in the process of growth remains unshaken. In the final chapter, "On Life and Living," she imagines herself dead and her family and friends attending her funeral, wishing her farewell.

Kübler-Ross's impatience to die is evident throughout the 2003 documentary, *Facing Death,* directed by Stefan Haupt. Ninety-eight minutes long, the film is based on conversations recorded in her isolated home in the Arizona desert. Sitting in a chair eighteen hours a day is "not living," Kübler-Ross remarks dolefully, "it's just vegetating." At one point she mentions feeling like a "zombie." She looks fatigued and frail, but an occasional smile reveals her old feistiness. She admits to being "wrong a few times" about the moment of her death. "Last year I said soon."

The documentary provides us with other information that doesn't appear in her writings or in Gill's biography. Friends, associates, and her two sisters offer their impressions of her past and present life. According to one of her sisters, Kübler-Ross's marriage broke up because she was a "workaholic," unwilling to spend more time at home with her husband. "If Beth had been a little bit smarter, she could have kept him. But she always left him alone." Kübler-Ross and her biographer claim that she resigned from the University of Chicago because of lack of support, but a colleague declares that her three-year appointment as an assistant professor of psychiatry was not renewed because she was not doing research. One of her assistants remarks that she has become "paranoid," though this is not evident in the film. Her paranoia is reality-based: her healing center in Virginia was burned down by arsonists who were incensed by her plan to care for children dying of AIDS. The documentary emphasizes her profound spiritual faith but remains silent about her out-of-body experiences and her involvement with occult phenomena.

Viewers of *Facing Death* have a keener understanding of Kübler-Ross's loneliness and despondency than readers of *The Wheel of Life,* largely because she is now closer to death, and because film is a more graphic medium than the written word. "I'm not used to such dependency," she confesses. She keeps the television on, without sound, to feel less lonely. She and her sister Erika Faust-Kübler express the wish to die together. The wish does not come true: Erika dies first. Books are piled near Kübler-Ross's chair, but she never mentions the consolation of reading or writing. Moving from bed to chair is exhausting: "I spend half an hour trying to consider whether to get up." The woman who helped shatter the taboo of not talking about death seems unable to manage her own death, not because of lack of effort, but because death follows its own mysterious script, impervious to human volition. For someone like Kübler-Ross who has undergone a radical transformation of personality, the inability to die in character—either as a medical scientist or as a mystic time-traveler—is particularly distressing.

Kübler-Ross refers to a new companion named Joseph who reminds her that she must learn to be patient, to put herself in the hands of God, and to "learn to love herself," to which she responds, "I really hated that. I can't sit here like an idiot and learn to love myself." Nor is it easy for her to follow his other injunction, to "learn surrender." Her dilemma is not that she has failed to accept death but that death has failed to accept her.

Dying Out of Character

Kübler-Ross is so impatient to die that she asks a friend to hasten her death. This revelation appears in Caroline Myss's foreword to the 2008 edition of *On Life after Death*. "During her last two years, as her health was failing, she phoned me three times: not to learn what she could do to help herself heal, but rather to find out what she could do to help herself die more quickly. She found living in a wheelchair, slowly waiting for death to come, an unbearable suffering. She fought with God until the very end, angry that she could not determine her time of death. Even Elisabeth, it seemed, had to walk through the famous stages of death and dying" (vii).

We cannot know how Kübler-Ross felt at the end of her life, but we would like to believe that the psychiatrist who spent her entire professional life helping thousands of patients and millions of readers prepare for their endings was able to achieve final peace. Her faith in a luminous afterlife never wavered. She shattered the long-standing silence surrounding dying and death, and for that we remain in her debt. *Facing Death* ends with Kübler-Ross's statement that she will soon "go dancing in the galaxies," and her many readers can only hope she was granted her wish.

CHAPTER 3

"With Autobiography There's Always Another Text, a Countertext"

Philip Roth and *Patrimony*

⌒◦

A "father's death," Freud contends in the preface to the second edition of *The Interpretation of Dreams,* is the "most important event, the most poignant loss, of a man's life" (xxvi). Although most psychoanalysts now believe that a mother's death has a greater impact on a son's or daughter's life, Philip Roth would agree with Freud. Roth's memoir *Patrimony* is a deeply moving account of his relationship with Herman Roth, who died in 1989 at the age of eighty-eight. Roth cared for his father in the final months of his life, when he struggled with a massive brain tumor. The memoir explores not only the father-son relationship and the problems arising from end-of-life care but also the ethics of disclosing painful and shameful experiences that the dying want to remain private. *Patrimony* also calls into question Roth's memory, including what he reveals and conceals about the biographical subject.

Patrimony has the ring of authenticity about it, largely because Roth insists that everything in it is true. Indeed, the subtitle emphasizes this: *A True Story.* On the cover of the paperback edition is the critical imprimatur from the *San Francisco Chronicle:* "A tough-minded, beautifully written memoir. . . . It smacks of honesty and truthfulness on every page." *Patrimony,* which won the National Book Critics Circle Award for biography, affirms the importance of remembrance and truth-telling.

Roth ends the story with the words, "You must not forget anything"—an injunction that becomes for the secular Roth a sacred if problematic commandment.

The Facts: *Roth's Autobiography?*

Given the many statements he has made throughout his long, prolific career that he is not an autobiographical writer, Roth's willingness to write openly and candidly about himself and his family, without disguises or evasiveness, is startlingly out of character. One of Roth's central paradoxes is that the more autobiographically transparent his fiction is, the more he denies he is writing about himself. Another paradox is that the more elusive he is in his nonfiction, the more he insists he is writing about himself. This is strikingly evident in his other memoir *The Facts: A Novelist's Autobiography*, in which he refers to the death of his mother and the fragile health of his father. Roth's discussion of his parents and childhood in *The Facts* prepares us for the more elegiac *Patrimony*. The two books complement and complicate each other.

Published in 1988, three years before the appearance of *Patrimony*, *The Facts* opens with Roth's letter to Nathan Zuckerman, his fictional alter ego who appears in several novels (including *The Counterlife*), to whom the novelist-turned-autobiographer offers his justification for writing about his real life. "If while writing I couldn't see exactly what I was up to, I do now: this manuscript embodies my counterlife, the antidote and answer to all those fictions that culminated in the fiction of you. If in one way *The Counterlife* can be read as fiction about structure, then this is the bare bones, the structure of a life without the fiction" (6).

Roth implies that he wrote *The Facts* partly because of his "exhaustion with masks, disguises, distortions, and lies" (6), and partly because he "needed clarification, as much of it as I could get—demythologizing to induce depathologizing" (7). The need to depathologize was particularly important to him because of a breakdown he suffered in 1987, "at the height of a ten-year period of creativity." What should have been minor surgery turned into a "prolonged physical ordeal that led to an extreme depression that carried me right to the edge of emotional and mental dissolution" (5). Another reason he wrote *The Facts* was "as a palliative for the loss of a mother who still, in my mind, seems to have died inextricably—at seventy-seven in 1981—as well as to hearten me as I come closer and closer and closer to an eighty-six-year-old father viewing the end of his life as a thing as near to his face as the mirror he shaves in" (8–9).

Roth's father was diagnosed with a brain tumor in 1988, and though it was not malignant, its size made surgery risky. The brain tumor may not have been evident when Roth was completing *The Facts,* but he nevertheless anticipated his father's impending death. "After nearly forty years of living far from home, I'm equipped at last to be the most loving of sons— just, however, when he has another agenda. He is trying to die" (*The Facts* 17). The last sentence is ambiguous, and Roth is anxious to avoid being misunderstood. "Trying to die isn't like trying to commit suicide—it may actually be harder, because what you are trying to do is what you least want to have happen; you dread it but there it is and it must be done, and by no one but you." Ironically, Roth, who was fifty-five when he published *The Facts,* seems more obsessed with dying and death than his father. This obsession is no less apparent in *Patrimony,* where his father seldom refers to his approaching death.

Throughout *The Facts* and *Patrimony* Roth depicts his father as a larger-than-life hero of mythological proportions. Noting that his father had only an eighth grade education, Roth tells us in *The Facts* that he achieved in the insurance business a "remarkable success for a man with his social and educational handicaps" (18). What made this success even more unusual, Roth adds, is that the family shoe store his father opened shortly after getting married went bankrupt, forcing him to take several low-paying jobs without a future. Nor was this Herman Roth's only business failure. In the middle 1940s, he invested all of his money in a frozen-food distribution company that also failed. He lost not only his own money but also the eight thousand dollars he had borrowed from his relatives. And so just as Roth and his older brother, Sandy, were entering college, their father was still trying to pay off debts incurred from his two bankruptcies. Significantly, there is not a word of reproach from Roth for these business failures. He admires his father's persistence, indomitable spirit, heroic work ethic, and familial loyalty. Herman Roth's entrepreneurial failures did not prevent him from working dutifully for Metropolitan Life Insurance Company, where he rose through the ranks until he became a district manager.

Roth's pride in his father also appears in *Reading Myself and Others,* where he elaborates upon his halcyon childhood. "'The weight of paternal power,' in its traditional oppressive or restraining guises, was something I had hardly to contend with in adolescence. My father had little aside from peccadilloes to quarrel with me about, and if anything weighed upon me, it was not dogmatism, unswervingness, or the like, but his limitless pride in me" (5). Herman Roth's "stubborn determination and reserves of strength" following his grave financial setbacks transformed him into a "figure of considerable pathos and heroism, [a] cross of a kind between Captain Ahab and Willy Loman" (5).

There are hints throughout *The Facts* of a conflicted father-son relationship, but we are given few specific details—certainly nothing that would suggest a stormy relationship. One of Roth's few "terrible" fights with his father occurred when he came home during his first midyear vacation from Bucknell. Refusing to explain to his father his "weekend whereabouts after midnight," Roth spent two days of "histrionic shouting and bitter silence." He negotiated a "fragile truce" with his father and then returned to college, "freshly evacuated from the Oedipal battlefield" (47)—a psychoanalytic interpretation upon which he refuses to elaborate.

The chapter in *The Facts* called "Now Vee May Perhaps to Begin" alludes to the last sentence in Roth's most famous novel, when Alex Portnoy's hitherto silent psychoanalyst, Dr. Otto Spielvogel, signals the real beginning of his analysand's therapy. Roth implies in *The Facts* that Alex's "comical counteranalysis" (156) in *Portnoy's Complaint* bears little relationship to his own psychoanalysis from 1962 to 1969. He has curiously little to say about psychoanalysis or the novel that brought him so much notoriety.

Roth's family drops out of the second half of *The Facts,* which is devoted to his explosive relationship with a woman who tricks him into marriage by pretending that she is pregnant and then refuses to divorce him. He refers to her as Josephine Jensen, "Josie," a pseudonym he uses, he admits in the prologue, to avoid exposing the identities of those characters who might not appreciate the violation of their privacy. But there was no need to disguise the name of his wife, Margaret Martinson Williams, whom he married in 1959, when he was twenty-six years old, and who died in 1968 in an automobile accident in Manhattan's Central Park during a time when Roth's marital woes were making national headlines. The marriage was a disaster from the beginning. Roth found himself so confused and shaken by this relationship, so demoralized and devastated, so unnerved and unmanned by Josie's duplicity, histrionics, and "botched" suicide attempts, that he began to fall victim to self-hatred, a phenomenon that he says he had never before experienced. Roth entered psychoanalysis to understand the meaning of this self-hatred. He could not fathom how his history as the "gorged beneficiary of overdevotion, overprotection, and oversurveillance within an irreproachably respectable Jewish household" (93) led him to become involved with a woman like Josie. He writes about this experience in his novel *My Life as a Man,* the most autobiographical of his fiction.

Roth has only praise for his parents during this dark period in his early and midtwenties. They sensed, far before their son did, that the marriage was doomed to fail. Roth is particularly grateful to his father, who acted toward Josie with "extreme diplomacy, with a display of gentlemanly finesse that revealed to me, maybe for the first time in my life, the managerial skills for which he was paid by the Metropolitan Life" (*The Facts* 106). Roth insists that his near-perfect childhood had nothing to do with his attraction to Josie, and that there was, therefore, no connection between his past and present. He thus rejects one of the central tenets of psychoanalysis, that the past shapes our present and future. He mentions only fleetingly his intense psychoanalysis, which was undertaken "to stitch back together the confidence shredded to bits in my marriage" (137).

"Where's the Anger?"

Roth's discussion of autobiographical facts is fascinating but not entirely convincing, as Nathan Zuckerman points out in the final thirty-five pages of the book. In a taunting, adversarial voice, Zuckerman challenges Roth on every major issue in *The Facts*, including the relationship with his parents. "Don't publish—you are far better off writing about me than 'accurately' reporting your own life," Zuckerman exclaims (161). He accuses Roth of being "kind, discreet, careful" (162), a criticism few of Roth's detractors have expressed. Zuckerman accuses Roth of selective memory, of excluding painful truths about his parents, of idealizing the past—in short, of writing out of character. "There's an awful lot of loving gentleness in those opening chapters of yours, a tone of reconciliation that strikes me as suspiciously unsubstantiated and so unlike what you usually do" (165).

Zuckerman cannot believe that the author of the wildly satirical novel *Portnoy's Complaint*, filled with the hero's endless accusations, rage, resentment, shame, and hostility, could have come from a nurturing home.

Zuckerman's prosecutorial voice seems far more authorial than Roth's, particularly when he sarcastically compliments his creator on being such a dutiful son—the opposite of Alex Portnoy. "Where's the anger?" Zuckerman impatiently demands—and never receives an answer. Pointing out that "Roth" is the least developed character in *The Facts*, Zuckerman declares, "You are not an autobiographer, you're a personificator" (162). He raises other questions about the self-disclosures in *The Facts*. "Your psycho-analysis you present in barely more than a sentence. I wonder why. Don't you remember, or are the themes too embarrassing? I'm not saying you are Portnoy any more than I'm saying you are me or I am Carnovsky; but come on, what did you and the doctor talk about for seven years?" (169). In what is perhaps his most stinging accusation, Zuckerman maintains that even if 99 percent of *The Facts* is true, the missing 1 percent changes the meaning of the story. "With autobiography there's always another text, a counter-text, if you will, to the one presented. It's probably the most manipulative of all literary forms" (172).

Zuckerman is a formidable fictional countervoice in *The Facts*. Through him, Roth expresses many of his driving obsessions without worrying excessively about disclosing autobiographical truth. He is the central char-acter in the "Zuckerman" novels, including those Roth wrote before and after *Patrimony*. Tellingly, the embattled father-son relationship is a central theme in these stories. Seeking to be the spiritual—or artistic—son of the celebrated novelist E. I. Lonoff, Zuckerman admits in the beginning of *The Ghost Writer* that "I had a loving father of my own, whom I could ask the world of any day of the week, but my father was a foot doctor and not an artist, and lately we had been having serious trouble in the family because of a new story of mine" (9–10). The trouble began when Zuckerman gave his father the manuscript of a story based on a family feud in which the latter tried unsuccessfully to play the role of peacemaker. "I was naive enough to expect nothing more than the usual encouragement for a story that borrowed from our family history instances of what my exemplary father took to be the most shameful and disreputable transgressions of fam-ily decency and trust" (81).

In *Zuckerman Unbound*, Roth's alter ego has written a Portnoyesque novel, *Carnovsky*, which is the object of frenzied media attention and ridi-cule. One Sunday morning Zuckerman "watched three therapists sitting in lounge chairs on Channel 5 analyzing his castration complex with the program host. They all agreed that Zuckerman had a lulu" (128). Zuckerman insists vainly that he is a novelist, not an autobiographer, but his father is so upset with his son's autobiographically transparent stories that he has a stroke and dies. Nathan fears that his father's last word, "Bastard," "barely audible, but painstakingly pronounced" (193), refers to himself. Nathan's older brother accuses him of patricide, the result of his failure to believe that writing about people has real consequences.

In the next Zuckerman novel, *The Counterlife,* Nathan's brother repeats the accusation, one from which Zuckerman can never entirely free himself, notwithstanding his protests to the contrary. And protest he does repeatedly throughout the story, arguing insistently, "I can only exhibit myself in disguise. All my audacity derives from masks" (275). Zuckerman continues to brood over his father in *I Married a Communist,* fearing that he fatally wounded him with the publication of the novel and, in the process, gravely wounded himself. Nor is it only in the Zuckerman novels that Roth reflects on a father similar to his own. The fear of a father's death appears in the 1977 novel *The Professor of Desire,* where David Kepesh often finds himself lost in reverie about his father. Twice in the story Kepesh imagines his father dead. In *Deception,* Roth's next novel after *The Facts,* an American novelist living in England named "Philip" writes about his elderly father, "Herm," in a way that seems autobiographical. "My old father still lives at the boil. He's got an opinion about everything and often it's not mine. I sometimes have to suppress being a fourteen-year-old with my father. Rather than waiting to die, sitting with my father I sometimes feel as though I'm waiting for life to begin" (81).

The father-son relationship lies at the heart of many of Roth's novels. He spends far more time analyzing this relationship than others equally complex, be they father-daughter, mother-son, or mother-daughter. In *The Anatomy Lesson,* a character asks Zuckerman why he spends so much time reading psychoanalytic studies about the father: "I look through these books on your shelves, your Freud, your Erikson, your Bettelheim, your Reich, and every single line about a father is underlined" (104–5). One suspects that the reason Zuckerman underlines every sentence about the father is to understand the relationship with his own father, a relationship that is endlessly complicated and problematic.

Roth characteristically has it both ways when he ends *The Facts* with Zuckerman's skepticism over the author's truth claims. It is not only

Zuckerman's voice that seems more authentic than his creator's but also his shrewd literary criticism. Zuckerman offers some of the most perceptive observations found anywhere about the nature of Roth's creativity. "*The things that wear you down are also the things that nurture your talent.* Yes, there is mystery upon mystery to be uncovered once you abandon the disguises of autobiography and hand *The Facts* over for imagination to work on. And no, the distortion called fidelity is *not* your métier—you are simply too real to outface full disclosure. It's through *dis*simulation that you find your freedom from the falsifying requisites of 'candor'" (184). Zuckerman's statements faithfully echo Roth's pronouncements in many of his books, including the interviews appearing in *Conversations with Philip Roth*. "To label books like mine 'autobiographical' or 'confessional' is not only to falsify their suppositional nature but, if I may say so, to slight whatever artfulness leads some readers to think that they must be autobiographical" (122). The novelist compares himself to a ventriloquist who "speaks so that his voice appears to proceed from someone at a distance from himself." The writer's art, Roth adds, "consists of being present *and* absent; he's most himself by simultaneously being someone else, neither of whom he 'is' once the curtain is down" (167).

How factual, then, is *The Facts*? Do we believe Roth—or his interrogator, Zuckerman? Significantly, Zuckerman does not identify any specific countertexts to *The Facts*. His accusations remain, finally, unsubstantiated and theoretical, thus allowing Roth the opportunity to maintain a dignified silence. Nevertheless, these accusations linger long after we have finished reading *The Facts*. Is Roth idealizing his parents? Is he falsifying his childhood and adolescence? Is he omitting shameful incidents of the past? What is the 1 percent of the truth that does not appear in *The Facts*? Where are the nonfiction countertexts? Roth addresses none of these questions in *Patrimony*, where his voice is similar to that of the autobiographer in *The Facts*. There is no "Zuckerman" voice in the memoir about his father, no countervoices or countertexts, no effort to undercut or qualify the truthfulness of the story.

"An Enfeebled Old Man"

Dedicated to "our family, the living and the dead," *Patrimony* opens with an elegantly crafted sentence that highlights Herman Roth's rapidly failing health: "My father had lost much of the sight in his right eye by the time he reached eighty-six, but otherwise he seemed in phenomenal health for a man his age when he came down with what the Florida doctor diagnosed, incorrectly, as Bell's palsy, a viral infection that causes paralysis, usually temporary, to one side of the face" (9). Roth has always been adept in diagnosing his fictional characters' physical and psychological disorders, and he writes here with characteristic clinical precision about his father's deteriorating health. The next sentence is also noteworthy: Roth tells us that his father had become "romantically involved" with a seventy-year-old retired bookkeeper, Lillian Beloff, a year after the novelist's mother died in 1981. Many people in Roth's situation would have felt ambivalent about an elderly parent beginning a relationship so quickly after the other parent's death, but Roth never intimates this. Within two pages Roth returns to present tense—1987—and describes how his father has turned into an "enfeebled old man" (12). His speech begins to slur, his vision fails, his appetite disappears. An MRI indicates the grim news: his father has a "massive tumor." Roth is understandably horrified because the disease strikes at the center of his father's identity. Viewing the MRI images, Roth begins to cry—"not because I could readily identify the tumor invading the brain but simply because it *was* his brain, my father's brain, which prompted him to think the blunt way he thought, speak the emphatic way he spoke, reason the emotional way he reasoned, decide the impulsive way he decided. This was the tissue that had manufactured his set of endless worries and sustained for more than eight decades his stubborn self-discipline, the source of everything that had so frustrated me as his adolescent son, the thing that had ruled our fate back when he was all-powerful" (16).

In an eerie example of life imitating art, Alex Portnoy often worries about his father's persistent headaches, fearing they are symptomatic of brain cancer. "My father has been 'going' for this tumor test for nearly as long as I can remember" (25), Alex confides to his silent psychoanalyst, Dr. Spielvogel, and he imagines his father's skull "splitting open from a malignancy" (26). No less than David Kepesh in *The Professor of Desire* or Nathan Zuckerman in several novels, Alex is preoccupied with his father's death. "I never get a telegram, never get a phone call after midnight, that I do not feel my own stomach empty out like a washbasin, and say aloud—aloud!—'He's dead.' Because apparently I believe it too, believe that I can somehow save him from annihilation—can, and must!" (118). In *The Anatomy Lesson* Zuckerman's mother dies of brain cancer, though Roth gives us no concrete details of her dying or death.

Most sons in Roth's fictional world suffer from "anticipatory grief." The term was coined by Erich Lindemann in his classic 1944 article "Symptomatology and Management of Acute Grief" and later developed by Therese A. Rando in several books. According to Rando, ambivalence is one of the key features of this phenomenon. "Ambivalence is viewed as having a special impact on anticipatory grief because the target of ambivalent feelings, that is, the dying patient, is not only still alive but is potentially vulnerable, balanced between life and death. This vulnerability makes any hostility or death wish appear particularly potent and dangerous and may contribute to the clinical impression that anticipatory grief appears to be more readily denied than conventional grief" (9). Robert Fulton has called into question the validity of this clinical concept, suggesting that "there is no certainty as to whether 'anticipatory grief' is functional or dysfunctional for the individual or the family. There is also uncertainty as to its implications for caregivers" (349). Nevertheless, it is striking to see how Roth's fictional sons are filled with anticipatory grief over the thought of the death of their aging fathers.

Roth's fictional sons, regardless of whether they are adolescent or middle-aged, brood endlessly over their fathers' health and approval. Nor is this a generalized fear of all parental loss: it is only Roth's fictional sons, not his fictional daughters, who worry about their fathers'—not their mothers'—deaths and approval. The more the sons are estranged from their fathers, the more they worry over their fathers' deaths. Alex cannot prevent himself from analyzing the meaning of his endless fear over his father's health, and he is honest enough to admit the darker implications of his worry. As he leaves for Europe with his girlfriend, the "Monkey," for an orgiastic vacation, he hears his father ask where he can be reached for the next month, and when Alex refuses to give him the address, the father exclaims, "What if I die?" Alex finds these words so unsettling that he later wonders aloud to his analyst whether he has only imagined them.

With each new story, Roth has become more preoccupied with death. While driving to see his father at the beginning of *Patrimony,* he makes an "accidental" turn on the New Jersey Turnpike and finds himself at the cemetery where his mother is buried, a place he has visited only twice.

He decides to leave his car and visit her grave. Significantly, he doesn't feel closer to her, as many people do when they visit their deceased loved ones. Nor does he find much value in meditating on the dead. Later he observes that the inadvertent visit to the cemetery had not brought him comfort or consolation. Nevertheless, the visit was "*narratively* right: paradoxically, it had the feel of an event *not* entirely random and unpredictable and, in that way at least, offered a strange relief from the impact of all that was frighteningly unseen" (74).

Roth's rejection of religion has remained one of the constants throughout his life, and nothing that happens in *Patrimony* causes him to waver from this disbelief. There are moments in *Patrimony* when Roth refers to God, but these moments are always ironic, as when he tells us, while he is looking at the pictures of his father's brain, that the mystery of human creation emanates from a tiny organ. "God's will erupted out of a burning bush and, no less miraculously, Herman Roth's had issued forth all these years from this bulbous organ. I had seen my father's brain, and everything and nothing was revealed" (17). Roth is always aware of what Kübler-Ross calls "life's big questions," but unlike her, he believes they will always remain unfathomable.

Presumably, Herman Roth shares his son's religious disbelief, though at one point he wryly observes to his doctor, "I've got a lot of people waiting for me on the other side" (*Patrimony* 164). Roth is surprised when his father agrees without hesitation to sign a living will, but they never engage in religious, spiritual, or existential discussions of dying or death. Nor do we see Herman Roth's actual dying or death. Roth succeeds in encouraging his father to reminisce over the highlights of his life, but Herman Roth never offers any final statements about life or expresses farewell to his children or grandchildren.

Why these omissions in *Patrimony*? Roth may not have felt it was necessary to talk about religion, given his unyielding views on the subject. Because he never informs his father that he is dying, the writer may have felt that a discussion of death would be too painful, both for him and his father. Nor do we learn whether anyone else in the family, such as Roth's brother, Sandy, or Lillian Beloff, discussed these issues with Herman Roth. If none of these discussions took place, one can infer that it was partly because of the fierce cultural taboo surrounding dying and death, a taboo that can be seen, paradoxically, in a memoir devoted precisely to dying and death. Few novelists and memoirists have written more about death than Roth, but there is surprisingly little discussion in his stories between the living and the dying.

The cultural taboo over death may also explain Herman Roth's decision to dispose of his wife's possessions immediately following her death. Even Roth is shocked when he discovers that his father has thrown out some of his son's college possessions, including the Phi Beta Kappa key that the writer had given to his mother years earlier. He interprets his father's behavior as "simply doing what he had done all his life: the next difficult job" (*Patrimony* 31). Herman Roth's "primitivism" stuns his son. "Standing all alone emptying her drawers and her closets, he seemed driven by some instinct that might be natural to a wild beast or an aboriginal tribesman but ran counter to just about every mourning rite that had evolved in civilized societies to mitigate the sense of loss among those who survive the death of a loved one" (32). And yet Roth adds that there was "something almost admirable in this pitilessly realistic determination to acknowledge, instantaneously, that he was now an old man living alone" (32–33).

Roth offers a loving and memorable portrait of his father while at the same time revealing that he was a difficult, at times impossible person. The comparison in *Reading Myself and Others* of Herman Roth with Ahab and Willy Loman is puzzling: unlike Melville's Ahab, Roth's father is never monomaniacal, and unlike Arthur Miller's Willy Loman, he is never broken-spirited or suicidal. And yet Herman Roth is an overworked insurance salesman whose entire life has been spent pursuing the American dream for his family. Linda Loman's statement about her husband also applies to Roth's father: "He's a human being, and a terrible thing is happening to him. So attention must be paid. He's not to be allowed to fall into his grave like an old dog. Attention, attention must be finally paid to such a person" (A. Miller 56).

Roth pays attention to the many formidable aspects of his father's personality, including his "reigning biases" that have grown worse in old age. Roth implies that because his father had little to do in retirement, he found himself dependent on his wife: "'You know what I am now?' he told me sadly on his sixty-fifth birthday. 'I'm Bessie's husband'" (*Patrimony* 37). Uninterested in developing new hobbies or doing volunteer work, Herman Roth "settled down to become Bessie's boss—only my mother happened not to need a boss, having been her own since her single-handed establishment of a first-class domestic-management and mothering company back in 1927, when my brother was born" (37). Bess Roth's determination to divorce her husband shocks her son. A year later she died of a massive coronary while at a restaurant with her husband. Roth later learns that on the evening of her death, his father "had fled from her corpse" at the hospital, where she was declared dead (33). Roth speculates that his father may have felt guilty over her death because he had pushed her to walk beyond her endurance on the day she died.

Herman Roth appears dazed and depressed after the death of his wife, and his son describes his effort to encourage his father to take care of himself and remain connected to the world. Alone in his apartment, the father is bereft and helpless; outside, he resumes his former talkative, gregarious self. Roth appears tender and solicitous both as a son and as a caregiver. Always masterful in his use of dialogue, he captures his father's mannerisms and characteristic perceptions of the world. Roth's questions, especially during the middle sections of *Patrimony*, encourage his father to speak joyfully about the past; both father and son are engaging storytellers.

Roth's affection for his father is one of the most affecting aspects of *Patrimony*. Gazing upon his father's aged body, Roth concedes that only his eyes remained "beautiful." That Herman Roth's eyes could remain beautiful throughout the obstacle course of life is no less noteworthy than the memoirist's awareness of the crushing nature of life, which takes its relentless toll on everyone.

"Will I be a zombie?" Herman Roth asks his son about the result of brain surgery (68). Roth responds evasively to this daunting question, assuring his father that the tumor is not likely to be cancer while at the same time withholding information about its massive size. Roth speaks to several physicians about his father's illness, and he tries to reassure his father that the situation is not hopeless. He takes his father from physician to physician, checks on the credentials of the surgeons, explains to his father the nature of the surgery, and helps to manage his father's fears—and his own. Indeed, his own fears are overwhelming, and he finds himself often weeping, depressed, and unable to write.

Throughout *Patrimony* Roth comes across as deferential to his father without endorsing the latter's harsh judgments of other people. Herman Roth is relentlessly hypercritical of his female companion, who, along with one of her stepsons, moved into his apartment a year after Bess Roth's death. He attacks Lil's docility and excessive weight, a criticism that Roth attempts to soften by observing that "eating was her only revenge, and like the tumor, it was something he could not stop no matter how he railed against it" (79). Roth succeeds in remaining sympathetic here to both his father and his companion. "He could never understand," Roth writes empathically, "that a capacity for renunciation and iron self-discipline like his own was extraordinary and not an endowment shared by all" (79). The capacity for renunciation and iron self-discipline characterizes the son as well. So, too, does Roth share his father's penchant for "hocking," a Yiddishism that he defines colorfully as "to badger, to bludgeon, to hammer with warnings and edicts and pleas—in short, to drill a hole in somebody's head with words" (80). It is the same quality that one sees in Alex's unceasing torrent of accusations against his parents in *Portnoy's Complaint*.

"All Sons Leave Their Fathers"

Why did Roth write a memoir about his father's death but not his mother's? The obvious answer is that Roth was a caregiver for his father, who died slowly, unlike his mother, who died suddenly, when Roth was living in England. Apart from this, the father-son relationship has always been more fraught than the mother-son relationship in Roth's fictional world. Sons separate themselves from their fathers at an early age in Roth's stories and cannot imagine returning home. In Roth's first novel, *Letting Go*, Gabe Wallach's dentist father watches helplessly as his wife dies from leukemia, and he then reflects sadly and angrily on his son's failure to console or care for him. "What kind of son was it, anyway, who left his aging father!"—a statement that is exclamatory rather than interrogatory. Dr. Wallach then follows it up with a statement that is a universal truth in Roth's world: "All sons. All sons leave their fathers. Of course. He considered himself a student of psychology and he was not naive about certain facts of life." Dr. Wallach knows what Philip Roth knows: "he had known in his heart that a boy does not become a man living in his father's house." In Roth's stories, "children grow up and go away. This was one of life's laws to which he and his son could not expect to be made exceptions" (487).

It is also one of life's laws in *Patrimony*. Roth left his parents' home at an early age, never to return, and they inhabit different worlds—different culturally, intellectually, and artistically. Throughout the story Roth appears as a loving son and a responsible caregiver, but it is evident that he feels out of place when he visits his father in a South Florida retirement community immediately following his mother's death. Roth devotes several pages to a musical program he attends with his father at the "Galahad Hall Social Club" (53). Following the chairwoman's announcements of the "Matzoh Fund Drive," Roth describes sympathetically what he would have satirized mercilessly in *Goodbye, Columbus*. A stranger to this culture, Roth inserts himself easily and amiably into his father's world, one that is so different from his own. It is surely remarkable that Roth can be nonjudgmental about his father's friends and acquaintances. He acts with exemplary caution and solicitude when he asks his father whether he has had another fight with Lil, and when his father recites a litany of complaints, Roth says, tactfully, "It's not my business to butt in . . . but is this really a good time to start an argument?" (*Patrimony* 82). His words help to defuse his father's anger, and a few moments later he describes how the three of them walk, arm-in-arm, to the drugstore, the crisis resolved. The image of the father, his new romantic relationship, and the son walking together hints at an Oedipal situation, with Lil replacing the son's deceased mother. Roth heightens the significance of this event by telling us that "it was the same walk on which my mother had overextended herself on the day she died" (83), but he never expresses any reservations about his father's new companion.

Later in the story, an old friend named Joanna Clark remarks on Roth's changed relationship with his father: "You've forgiven him. You've forgiven him that relentlessness and that tactfulness, that wanting to make everybody over in the same mold. All children pay a price, and the forgiveness entails forgiveness also for the price you paid. You talk about him in a very reconciled way" (*Patrimony* 127). Roth immediately agrees and then makes a revealing comment: "Since my mother died, I've got awfully close to him. It would have been easier the other way" (127). Did Roth become closer to his father, more forgiving, because of his father's increased vulnerability without his wife of fifty-five years? Or did Roth's relationship with his mother somehow prevent him from becoming closer to his father while she was still alive.

And yet if the latter possibility is true, how do we explain the fact that *all* of Roth's comments about his mother in *Patrimony* are uniformly positive? For years Herman Roth had believed he was "married to perfection, and for years he wasn't far wrong—my mother was one of those devoted daughters of Jewish immigrants who raised housekeeping in America to a great art" (36–37). Adroit in the "skills of nurturing domesticity," Bess Roth was a wife and mother of "wizardly proficiency" (38). The more Herman Roth devalues Lil ("she can't even buy a cantaloupe"), the more he idealizes his deceased wife: "Mother did everything right" (193). Why would he idealize his deceased wife if she wanted to divorce him shortly before her death? No hint of a dark or difficult side to Bess Roth appears in *Patrimony,* where she embodies the virtues of "modesty, humility, loyalty, bravery, efficiency, dependability" (63). Janice Winchester Nadeau calls this form of idealization "sanctification of the deceased," which occurs "when the person who has died is described by the bereaved as saintlike or other-worldly" (145). Bess Roth's saintly virtues must have been tested throughout her long marriage to a man who seemed so overbearing. Why, then, would Roth remain distant from his father while his mother was still alive, unless his idealization of her betokens unconscious ambivalence?

Totem and Taboo

Patrimony suggests that Roth had an easy, unconflicted relationship with his mother, one that could not be more different from Alex Portnoy's tempestuous relationship with his mother. The theme of Oedipal desire, so striking in *Portnoy's Complaint*, hardly appears in *Patrimony*. And yet there is a moment when Roth raises the specter of incestuous love. In one of the most curious scenes in *Patrimony*, Roth hails a cab in Manhattan to take him to the hospital where his father is having a biopsy of the tumor. Roth is speaking to the wife of an old friend as the cab approaches, and a few minutes later the cabdriver asks him whether he has "fucked" her. Looking into the rearview mirror, Roth sees a pair of eyes "whose truculent glare was even more startling than the question." "As a matter of fact, no," the anxious passenger replies. "One of my friends does. She's his wife." When the cabdriver responds cynically, "What difference does that make? He'd fuck your wife," Roth rejoins, "No, this particular friend wouldn't, though I understand it happens." Roth then confides to the reader, "I understood because I'd done it myself on a few occasions, but, unlike the driver, I wasn't putting all my cards on the table right off" (154). The cabdriver's menacing aura is matched by his menacing actions; he confesses proudly that he had knocked his father's four front teeth out: "My old man's in his grave now without his four front teeth. I knocked 'em out of his fucking mouth for him" (156). As the conversation continues, Roth studies this man with a "professional interest," fascinated by his transparent misogyny, paranoia, and patricidal fury, and when the driver asks him whether he's a "doctor," Roth pretends he's a psychiatrist in order to defuse the cabdriver's homicidal rage. Noting wryly the "positive transference" in their relationship, Roth offers an interpretation of the cabdriver that combines classic psychoanalytic theory and his own version of cultural studies:

> He is of the primal horde of sons who, as Freud liked to surmise, have it in them to nullify the father by force—who hate and fear him and, after overcoming him, honor him by devouring him. And I'm from the horde that can't throw a punch. We aren't like that and we can't do it, to our fathers or to anyone else. We're the sons appalled by violence, with no capacity for inflicting physical pain, useless at beating and clubbing, unfit to pulverize even the most deserving enemy, though not necessarily without turbulence, temper, even ferocity. We have teeth as the cannibals do, but they are there, imbedded in our jaws, the better to help us articulate. When we lay waste, when we efface, it isn't with raging fists or ruthless schemes or insane sprawling violence but with our words, our brains, with mentality, with all the stuff that produced the poignant abyss between our fathers and us and that they themselves broke their backs to give us. (*Patrimony* 159)

In this extraordinary passage Roth invokes *Totem and Taboo*, Freud's far-ranging contribution to social anthropology in which he analyzes the "horror of incest" and speculates that civilization arises from the suppression of aggressive and sexual instinct. Subtitled *Some Points of Agreement between the Mental Lives of Savages and Neurotics*, *Totem and Taboo* offers Freud's most compelling definition of ambivalence, a word he borrowed from the Swiss psychiatrist Eugen Bleuler. "It appears wherever, in addition to a predominant feeling of affection, there is also a contrary, but unconscious, current of hostility—a state of affairs which represents a typical instance of an ambivalent emotional attitude. The hostility is then shouted down, as it were, by an excessive intensification of the affection, which is expressed as solicitude and becomes compulsive, because it might otherwise be inadequate to perform its task of keeping the unconscious contrary current of feeling under repression" (49). Freud then suggests that this "solicitous over-affection" is found in the "most unlikely circumstances," especially in "attachments between a mother and a child or between a devoted married couple" (49).

Many of the ideas in *Totem and Taboo* resonate in Roth's world, beginning with Freud's 1934 preface to the Hebrew edition, with which Roth would surely identify: "No reader of this book will find it easy to put himself in the emotional position of an author who is ignorant of the language of holy writ, who is completely estranged from the religion of his fathers—as well as from every other religion—and who cannot take a share in nationalist ideals, but who has yet never repudiated his people, who feels that he is in his essential nature a Jew and who has no desire to alter that nature" (xv). No contemporary writer is more alert to the nuances of ambivalence than Roth or more attuned to the ways in which fear and desire, hate and love are locked into irresolvable conflict in relationships, be they familial, marital, or extramarital. And no writer is more inclined to agree with the following passage from *Totem and Taboo* than Roth, a passage that reflects the age-old battles between fathers and sons: "Psycho-analysis has revealed that the totem animal is in reality a substitute for the father; and this tallies with the contradictory fact that, though the killing of the animal is as a rule forbidden, yet its killing is a festive occasion—with the fact that it is killed and yet mourned. The ambivalent emotional attitude, which to this day characterizes the father-complex in our children and which often persists into adult life, seems to extend to the totem animal in its capacity as substitute for the father" (141).

Why does Roth include the scene with the "parricidal driver" in *Patrimony* (161)? Why the allusion to *Totem and Taboo*? Several explanations come to mind, beginning with Roth's efforts both to confirm and disconfirm Freud's theory of the primal father. Herman Roth may not seem, on the surface, emblematic of the violent and jealous father who awakens so much ambivalence in his sons, the primal horde, and who must, therefore, be slain for the sons to incorporate his totemic power. Nevertheless, Roth describes his father as "all-powerful" (*Patrimony* 16), a man "on whom the claims of family were so emotionally tyrannical" (91), who was "obdurate, resolute" (104), and whose strength continues to "amaze" his son (123), Herman Roth embodies for his son the qualities of "survivorship, survivorhood, survivalism" (125), and while Roth uses "totemic" (108) to describe his father's friends, clearly the word describes his own father as well. "He wasn't just any father," Roth writes, "he was *the* father, with everything there is to hate in a father and everything there is to love" (180).

Throughout *Patrimony* we see Roth's abiding love for his father, along with devotion and admiration. Metropolitan Life should have "beatified Herman Roth, as the Church beatifies martyrs who suffer for its causes" (180). Roth recognizes that his love for his father borders on idealization, and he anticipates his readers' skepticism here. "You can say that it doesn't mean much for a son to be tenderly protective of a father once the father is powerless and nearly destroyed" (180). He concedes that when he was growing up, he was in conflict with his father—conflict that caused the son to smack his forehead and howl in despair. Repudiating his father's authority became an "oppressive conflict, as laden with grief as it was with scorn" (180).

We can see the son's love for his father in *Patrimony* and, at worst, normal ambivalence, but we do not see hatred—except in the portrait of the patricidal cabdriver, who represents murderous Oedipal rage. This helps to explain Roth's inclusion of this scene in the memoir. The psychological defense mechanism of "splitting" comes into play here. The cabdriver is the bad son, part of the murderous horde who annihilates the father, while Roth is the good son, one of those who, appalled by insane violence, settles scores through his words and brain. In Freud's vision of the primal horde, the sons castrate the father and steal his magical potency; in Roth's vision in *Patrimony,* the good son looks at his father's penis without any feeling of ambivalence or Oedipal rivalry. " 'Good for him,' I thought. 'If it gave some pleasure to him and my mother, all the better' " (177).

Roth never minimizes the "poignant abyss" that separates him from his father, an abyss created, in large part, by language. Nowhere is the abyss more striking than in a letter Herman Roth wrote to his older son.

Roth contextualizes the letter by telling us that his brother had cautioned their father, "for the sake of domestic peace," to be less critical of Lil and of Sandy's son Jonathan, who was just beginning his career. The letter is filled with misspellings of simple words—"liveing room," "smokeing," "safed" (instead of "saved"), and "diceplin" (which he also spells "disaplin"). The misspellings demonstrate, perhaps too starkly, the father's eighth grade education. The letter also reveals Herman Roth's tendency to see the world in terms of black and white, as can be seen in the first paragraph: "I think there are two type's of (among people) Philosophies. People who care, and those that don't, People who *do* and people who Procrastinate and never *do* or *help*" (*Patrimony* 80). The father views himself as a person who both cares and does, and who went out of his way to pay for the surgeries of his wife and his younger son. He knows he is hocking—indeed, he signs the letter "The Hocker"—but he can't help himself, especially when he gives unsolicited advice to his grandson to save money: "A Penny saved is a penny earned." Apologizing for sounding overbearing, he admits that he has "many battles with my concience, but I fight my wronge thoughts. I *care,* for people in *my way*" (81).

There's nothing particularly shocking about Herman Roth's spoken words in *Patrimony,* but it is shocking to see how primitive his written language is. It's also startling to see how he can be so domineering in the name of "caring." The letter enables us to understand how difficult it must have been for everyone in the Roth family to live with him. From this point of view, Roth's decision to include the letter in *Patrimony* is narratively right—the father's words reveal a great deal about his personality. Roth could have told us what his father was like, but instead he *shows* us. He could have summarized his father's letter, but instead he *quotes* it word for word. As narratively right as the letter is, however, it raises a privacy issue: almost certainly the father never authorized the appearance of this letter in a story about his dying and death. This is the first but not the last problematic privacy issue raised in *Patrimony.*

A Broken Promise

The far more troubling privacy issue occurs later in *Patrimony* when Herman Roth, constipated for four days as a result of his worsening health, explosively evacuates his bowels when stepping out of a shower in his son's Connecticut house. Roth foreshadows this scene by telling us that a day before the incident, while passing the bathroom, he could see his father was "sitting on the toilet holding his head in his hands" (167)—one of the most poignant moments in the story. The accident occurs the next day. Almost bursting into tears, the father confesses, in a "voice as forlorn as any I had ever heard, from him or anyone, . . . I beshat myself" (172). Roth immediately cleans up his father and then the bathroom. Repeating that he "beshat" himself—an archaic word for anyone to use, especially someone with a limited vocabulary—the father, filled with shame, then makes the following request:

> "Don't tell the children," he said, looking up at me from the bed with his one sighted eye.
> "I won't tell anyone," I said. "I'll say you're taking a rest."
> "Don't tell Claire."
> "Nobody," I said. "Don't worry about it. It could have happened to anyone. Just forget about it and get a good rest." (173)

This remains the single most powerful and disturbing scene in *Patrimony*, one that raises many troubling questions. Roth not only breaks this promise but also refuses to explain or defend his actions. Nor does he express guilt, remorse, or regret over the broken promise. Surely he knows that many readers will be angered, perhaps appalled, by the decision to violate his father's privacy. Roth is honest enough to include this dialogue in the story—no one would have known about the broken promise had he not called attention to it—and yet he refuses to defend himself. How do we interpret his silence here? As an admission of guilt? As an expression of defiance of conventional morality? As an acknowledgment that this is what writers do—betray the people to whom they have promised confidentiality? In an interview published in *Conversations with Philip Roth*, the writer responded evasively to the question of how his father would have reacted to the broken promise. " 'I think about [that question] too,' he says. 'One doesn't want to be sentimental answering it. Well, I don't know what things he might not have liked so much. I don't know, he might not have liked some things. Who could?' he asks. 'Who could? But he's dead. So we needn't speculate' " (272).

Writing about a parent's or spouse's incontinence must be one of the most wrenching decisions for a memoirist, and it is instructive to contrast

Roth with other writers. John Bayley penned three memoirs about his wife, Iris Murdoch, who developed Alzheimer's disease. In the middle volume, *Iris and Her Friends*, Bayley writes lovingly—and comically—about his wife's increasingly unpredictable toilet habits. "Sometimes she will go to the right place, even though she makes a mess of it. More often, she will do it on the carpet outside, or in another room. Then she lays the results, as if with care, on a neighbouring chair or bookshelf. I don't mind a bit cleaning up, an operation which seems mildly to amuse her. I can make a joke of it, too, and we can laugh about it together. A small domestic challenge I can easily meet, and Iris seems to enjoy seeing me do it" (185–86). Bayley's comic vision of death and dying, his cheerful acceptance of being his wife's caregiver, is world's apart from Roth's tragic vision. For Bayley, there is no shame about being in his wife's situation, and, therefore, no guilt in writing about it. In the ironically entitled *A Very Easy Death*, Simone de Beauvoir writes about her shock when her mother, dying of cancer, decides not to "bother about" a bedpan. "And Maman, who had lived a life bristling with proud sensitivities, felt no shame. In this prim and spiritualistic woman it was also a form of courage to take on our animality with so much decision" (64). All three memoirists write about a loved one's incontinence, but only Roth has broken a promise to remain silent.

After commenting on the soiled bathroom, Roth compares the daunting task of cleaning the bathroom to the process of writing a book: "I have no idea where to begin" (*Patrimony* 173). It's an odd simile, since unlike writing a novel or memoir, cleaning a bathroom involves no betrayal of trust or confidentiality. A couple of pages later, Roth reflects on the meaning of his father's humiliating experience. "You clean up your father's shit because it has to be cleaned up, but in the aftermath of cleaning it up, everything that's there to feel is felt as it never was before" (175). This leads to the central epiphany of the memoir: cleaning up his father's shit turns out to be the son's patrimony. "And not because cleaning it up was symbolic of something else but because it wasn't, because it was nothing less or more than the lived reality that it was." The son's patrimony, in other words, is not the father's money or material possessions but "the shit" (176).

Only by breaking his father's promise, then, can Roth obey what he believes is a higher ethical imperative, verbally bringing back to life the man who has bequeathed him this legacy. Roth's devotion to art trumps his allegiance to life—or, perhaps we should say, as he might, that only a total commitment to art can do justice to capturing the complexity of life. Central to the novelist and memoirist is the injunction to remember everything, good and bad. It is the vow on which he ends *Patrimony:* "You must not forget anything" (238).

Roth's belief that art depends upon betrayal may also be seen in Art Spiegelman's two stories about his parents' experiences during the Holocaust, *Maus* and *Maus II.* "Artie," the narrator who is a writer/cartoonist, promises his father, Vladek, not to write about his affair with a woman whom he later casts off to marry another person. "I don't want you should write this story in your book," Vladek tells his son, because "it has nothing to do with Hitler, with the Holocaust." Artie protests, declaring that "it's great material, it makes everything seem more *real,* more human," adding, "I want to tell *your* story the way it really happened" (*Maus* 23). The father responds, "But this isn't so *proper,* so respectful. I can tell you *other* stories, but such *private* things, I don't *want* you should mention." Artie reluctantly agrees to the promise—and then breaks it. In *Maus II,* Artie has become an unlikely celebrity over the spectacular success of the first *Maus* volume and confesses his guilt to a therapist, Pavel, who, playing devil's advocate, wonders whether it's better not to write any more stories about the Holocaust. Artie appears to agree, citing Samuel Beckett's observation that "every word is like an unnecessary stain on silence and nothingness." But then Artie immediately qualifies himself: "On the other hand, he SAID it." Pavel agrees: "He was right. Maybe you can include it in your book" (*Maus II* 45).

Patrimony and the two *Maus* stories both suggest that writers must sometimes disclose dark secrets that they have sworn not to reveal because they are essential to understanding shameful experiences. Only by casting light on shame, Roth and Spiegelman imply, can it be detoxified. These shameful events are a central part of the fathers' burdensome legacies to their sons. Writing becomes a countershame technique—for the writers, not for their fathers. Significantly, the sons' betrayals occur only after their fathers have died. Both fathers are tough, blunt, and obdurate, formidable figures whose gifts for survival are bequeathed to their sons. Both Roth and Spiegelman reveal "mixed motives" in writing about their fathers, as Andrew Gordon has pointed out: "On the one hand, to memorialize the father and to record family history; on the other hand, to expose the father and to triumph over him through art."

Several literary critics have commented on the problematic nature of the bathroom scene in *Patrimony*. "Although in many ways *Patrimony* is the attempt to rewrite the father in a more powerful light," Hana Wirth-Nesher suggests, Roth's inclusion of the bathroom scene is also an "exercise of power over the father who had always wielded authority over him" (166). Nancy K. Miller argues that the bathroom scene is central to the memoir. "To shut the door on the bathroom would mean not only *not* writing the book but forgetting that writing in some way always begins just there, in the spectacular but nonetheless ordinary mess of human life. So a writer has to remember the bathroom and return there in memory because that is where the material is" (25). *Patrimony* "gets written in the space between two contradictory injunctions," Miller contends: "not to forget and not to tell" (28). One does not need to conclude, as Miller does, that the "betrayal of secrets is a requirement of the autobiographical act" (124) to agree with her that this betrayal is strikingly evident in *Patrimony*.

Similar betrayals may be seen in many of Roth's novels, where he writes about his family, friends, and acquaintances, often without changing their names. Claire Bloom, who was married to Roth, reports in her memoir *Leaving a Doll's House* her anger and dismay when she read the manuscript of *Deception,* in which Roth writes openly about being married to a woman named "Claire" while having an affair with another woman. "What left me speechless—though not for long," writes Bloom, "was that he would paint a picture of me as a jealous wife who is betrayed over and over again. I found the portrait nasty and insulting, and his use of my name completely unacceptable" (183).

While writing *Leaving a Doll's House,* Bloom struggled with the question of how much about her relationship with Roth she was willing to disclose. A passage from her memoir captures the ethical dilemma of transmuting a real person into art: "It is both shameful and courageous to take a record from life and use it as a means to an end. The painter Claude Monet, to his own shame, looking at his adored young wife on her deathbed, could not help recording the changing color of her skin and the dissolution of her once-beautiful face. But he went on to use this image in his work" (131–32).

Roth surely struggled with this dilemma in *Patrimony,* and he had no trouble remembering—and recording—the many adversities his father encountered in his work. The need to remember compelled Roth to write a letter to the *New York Times Book Review* in which he expressed indignation over the widespread anti-Semitism in the insurance industry. The letter, which appears in the opening chapter of *The Facts,* provoked a response from John Creedon, the president and CEO of Metropolitan Life, who pointed out that Herman Roth had never complained about anti-Semitism while working for the company. Roth recounts how he then spent several afternoons working in the archives of the American Jewish Committee to document this history of discrimination, and he quotes part of the letter he subsequently wrote to Creedon. Herman Roth agrees with his son's conclusions but nevertheless asks him not to write any more letters. "'Do me a favor, will you? After this,' he said, holding up my letter, 'that's enough.'" The response surprises his son, who adds, "Well, *this* was new—my father expressing chagrin over something I had written. In my Zuckerman novels, I had given Nathan Zuckerman a father who could not stand his writer son's depiction of Jewish characters, whereas fate had given me a fiercely loyal and devoted father who had never found a thing in my books to criticize" (*Patrimony* 187–88). This claim is repeated in an early interview published in *Conversations with Philip Roth,* in which Roth states that when some of the sections of *Portnoy's Complaint* appeared in a literary magazine, Herman Roth "gave out copies to friends, while Mrs. Roth, jokingly, declared that when the book appears, she will leave the country" (19–20).

Roth has long insisted that his parents were never critical of his novels, and that they loyally defended him against the charge of Jewish anti-Semitism that surrounded the furor over the publication of *Portnoy's Complaint.* Nevertheless, Roth has forgotten something important that he wrote about his parents decades earlier. Recall Zuckerman's criticisms of "Roth's" selective memory of his parents in *The Facts,* the omission of painful and shameful feelings, the tone of reconciliation and "loving kindness" that is even more pronounced in *Patrimony.* There is indeed a countertext that changes our understanding of both *The Facts* and *Patrimony,* a countertext that reveals the ways in which Roth's presentation of his father is out of character.

"The Angry Act"

Zuckerman's question, "Where's the anger?" leads us, ironically, to Hans J. Kleinschmidt's psychiatric case study "The Angry Act: The Role of Aggression in Creativity." In Roth's world, "nothing is never ironic," as Alex

Portnoy observes. As it turns out, "The Angry Act" is the major counter-text for both *The Facts* and *Patrimony*. As I discuss in *The Talking Cure*, Roth was writing *Portnoy's Complaint* when he was in analysis with Dr. Kleinschmidt in the mid-1960s. Roth revealed to him an embarrassing experience involving his parents when he was eleven years old. His mother and father take him to his uncle's clothing store to buy a bathing suit, and he feels intense shame when they fail to realize the kind of suit he wants. The following passage is from *Portnoy's Complaint*. "'I don't want that kind of suit any more,' and oh, I can smell humiliation in the wind, hear it rumbling in the distance—any minute now it is going to crash upon my prepubescent head. 'Why not?' my father asks. 'Didn't you hear your uncle, this is the best—' 'I want one with a jockstrap in it!' Yes, sir, this just breaks my mother up. 'For your little thing?' she asks, with an amused smile. Yes mother, imagine: for my little thing" (51). Kleinschmidt relates the same incident in his psychiatric case study. "He was eleven years old when he went with his mother to a store to buy a bathing suit. While trying on several of them, he voiced his desire for bathing trunks with a jock strap. To his great embarrassment his mother said in the presence of the saleslady: 'You don't need one. You have such a little one that it makes no difference.' He felt ashamed, angry, betrayed and utterly helpless" (124).

Roth and Kleinschmidt did not realize that the other was writing about the same incident, the former in a novel, the latter in a journal devoted to the relationship between psychoanalysis and art. Roth was furious when he discovered that his analyst had written about him without permission, rightly fearing that anyone who read his novel and Kleinschmidt's article would realize that he was the analyst's patient. Roth writes about this experience in *My Life as a Man*, where his autobiographical projection, the novelist Peter Tarnopol, recounts the bitter argument with *his* analyst, Otto Spielvogel, whose breach of confidentiality and reductive psychoanalytic interpretation infuriate Tarnopol—and Roth. Tarnopol is particularly incensed by Spielvogel's refusal to accept responsibility for the violation of confidentiality. Spielvogel tries to defend himself by dismissing Tarnopol's reaction as a result of "narcissistic" defenses, further enraging his analysand.

It's possible though unlikely that one could discover the link between *Portnoy's Complaint* and "The Angry Act" simply by accident. I made the connection only after reading *My Life as a Man*, where Roth leaves all the clues necessary to find the psychoanalytic article. I debated with myself whether to publish my discovery—I did not want to participate in another violation of the novelist's privacy, as the psychoanalyst had done. I finally justified the decision to include the chapter on Roth in *The Talking Cure* because it was Roth's words in *My Life as a Man,* not Kleinschmidt's words in "The Angry Act," that led to my discovery. If Roth did not want anyone to invade his privacy again, he would not have revealed to us that Tarnopol's analyst published his case study in a special issue of a psychoanalytic journal in the mid-1960s exploring "the riddle of creativity." Forty years ago there were fewer psychoanalytic journals than there are today, and when I began to search for the existence of the real article, I found it.

Before submitting *The Talking Cure* for publication, I sent my chapter on Roth to Kleinschmidt, to see if he wanted to comment on the chapter. The analyst at first angrily denied I had proven anything and insisted that he would file a law suit against me if I attempted to publish the Roth chapter. He backed off his threats when I pointed out that I was dealing not with confidential material or with hearsay but with a published novel and a published psychiatric case study. Kleinschmidt authenticated my discovery and spoke about Roth's anger toward him over the publication of "The Angry Act"—a title that could not be more prophetically self-fulfilling. In "Revisiting Philip Roth's Psychoanalysts," published in *The Cambridge Companion to Philip Roth,* I discuss my 1980 interview with Dr. Kleinschmidt, when I understood for the first time how Peter Tarnopol felt in *My Life as a Man* when he reveals, with begrudging admiration, his psychoanalyst's "immunity to criticism" (259).

Several of Kleinschmidt's observations about his patient in "The Angry Act" are almost identical to Roth's observations in *Portnoy's Complaint* and *My Life as a Man.* Kleinschmidt's discussion of his patient's symptomatology—"practices of voyeurism, exhibitionism and fetishism abound" (125)—becomes the clinical definition of "*Portnoy's Complaint,*" which Roth uses as the frontispiece of the novel: "Acts of exhibitionism, voyeurism, fetishism, auto-eroticism, and oral coitus are plentiful." Kleinschmidt's characterization of his patient resembles Spielvogel's characterization of Peter Tarnopol. "A successful Southern playwright in his early forties illustrates the interplay of narcissism and aggression while his points of fixation are later [than those of another patient] and his conflicts oedipal rather than pre-oedipal. He came into therapy because of anxiety states experienced as a result of his tremendous ambivalence about leaving his wife, three years his senior," observes Kleinschmidt in "The Angry Act" (123). "A successful Italian-American poet in his early forties entered into therapy because of anxiety states experienced as a result of his enormous ambivalence about leaving his wife," observes Spielvogel in *My Life as a Man* (239). Castration anxiety appears in both "The Angry Act" and *My Life as a Man*. "It soon became apparent that his main problem was his castration anxiety vis-à-vis a phallic mother figure," declares Kleinschmidt (124); "It soon became clear that the poet's central problem here as elsewhere was his castration anxiety vis-à-vis a phallic mother figure," declares Spielvogel (240–41). So, too, is the characterization of the father identical. "His father was ineffectual and submissive to the mother," Kleinschmidt notes (124). "His father was a harassed man, ineffectual and submissive to his mother," observes Spielvogel (241).

Roth's decision to base Alex Portnoy's parents closely on his own parents calls into question his idealization of his mother and father in *The Facts* and *Patrimony*. Roth imagines himself as the "bad son" in *Portnoy's Complaint*, the transgressive son who rails against his castrating mother and ineffectual and submissive father; he imagines himself as the "good son" in *The Facts* and *Patrimony*, the devoted son who honors his parents and defends them from attack by others. Roth's parents do not change dramatically over the years, but his attitude toward them does.

Roth's Fictional and Real Parents

Sophie and Jack Portnoy are satirical portraits of Bess and Herman Roth, and despite the novelist's deliberate exaggeration and distortion of them for comic effect, Alex's parents are recognizably Roth's parents. Sophie Portnoy's positive qualities appear in *The Facts* and *Patrimony* but not her negative qualities. In *Portnoy's Complaint* she is a smother-mother, identified with a "castrating" bread knife that evokes anger and dread in Alex. She points this knife at her young son when he refuses to eat, a scene that he later discloses bitterly to his analyst: "Doctor, why, why oh why oh why oh why does a mother pull a knife on her own son? I am six, seven years old, how do I know she really wouldn't use it? What am I supposed to do, try bluffing her out, at seven?" (16). Alex cannot exorcise the image of the maternal knife from his imagination, and he is enraged that none of her friends who hear the complaints about her disobedient son find the threat excessive: "*Alex is suddenly such a bad eater I have to stand over him with a knife* (43).

Alex's anger is also directed at his passive father for failing to defend him. "And why doesn't my father stop her?" (17). Ironically, the castrating knife in Alex's family is wielded not by his father but by his mother, something he has difficulty understanding and accepting. It's not that Jack Portnoy lacks sexual organs; in a scene that anticipates Roth's description in *Patrimony* of his father's penis, Alex remarks approvingly of his father's sexual equipment. "Oh, thank God! Thank God! At least he had the cock and the balls!" (42). To Alex, the father's wounded masculinity arises not from a physical but a psychological problem, namely, a wife whose authority and discipline remain unchallenged.

If Roth associates Sophie Portnoy with a castrating knife, he associates Jack Portnoy with blocked bowels—another quality that eerily foreshadows the portrait of Herman Roth in *Patrimony*. There are more than half a dozen references in *Portnoy's Complaint* to the father's "blockaded body" (5). Most of these references are comic, but others are disturbing. The most poignant reference occurs when Alex observes that he used to find his father "in the morning fast asleep on the toilet bowl, his pajamas around his knees and his chin hanging onto his chest. Up at quarter to six in the morning, so as to give himself a full uninterrupted hour on the can, in the fervent hope that if he is so kind and thoughtful as this to his bowels, they will relent and give in" (114). Sometimes Jack Portnoy finds mordant humor in the situation, as when he whispers to Alex, "I ought to stick a hand grenade up my ass" (115), but mostly he is tormented by his blocked bowels.

Like Herman Roth, Jack Portnoy works a brutally long day for a giant insurance company that never appreciates his commitment and years of service to them. Also like Herman Roth, Jack Portnoy has an eighth grade education. But whereas Roth honors in *Patrimony* his father's heroic work ethic and indomitable energy, Alex mocks his father's ignorance and lack of success. "Don't be dumb like your father," Jack tells his son, and though he says this "lovingly" (5), Alex grows up feeling ashamed of his father's lack of formal education. Alex recalls an incident when he was a freshman in college and tried to educate his father by ordering a subscription for him of the *Partisan Review*. As the thirty-three-year-old Alex discloses to his analyst, when he arrived home from college the magazine was nowhere to be found. "Thrown out unopened—I thought in my arrogance and heartbreak—discarded unread, considered *junk*-mail by this schmuck, this moron, this Philistine father of mine!" (9). Alex knows he is being judgmental here, but he can't forgive his father for his lack of culture and education. "No money, no schooling, no language, no learning, curiosity without culture, drive without opportunity, experience without wisdom. . . . How easily his inadequacies can move me to tears. As easily as they move me to anger!" (26). Alex's attitude toward his father is more complicated than Kleinschmidt implies in "The Angry Act," but there is little doubt that Alex regards his father as ineffectual and submissive.

Truth—or Kvetching?

Alex admires his mother more than his father, partly because she is more powerful and successful. She is, for Alex, a force of nature, and she achieves perfection in whatever she does. Alex is his mother's child in many ways: he is smart, energetic, and successful. His father is also a hard worker, but he is *not* successful. And yet for all of Alex's criticisms of his father, he resembles him in one crucial way: they are both hockers. "I hear myself indulging in the kind of ritualized bellyaching that is just what gives psychoanalytic patients such a bad name with the general public. Could I really have detested this childhood and resented these poor parents of mine to the same degree then as I seem to now, looking backward upon what I was from the vantage point of what I am—and am not? Is this truth I'm delivering up, or is it just plain *kvetching*?" (94).

The answer, no doubt, to this last question is both: Alex delivers up the truth through his complaints, which are simultaneously funny, sad, and serious. *Portnoy's Complaint* is both an astonishingly original novel and a fascinating psychiatric case study, one that has been analyzed (and overanalyzed) by countless literary and psychological critics. Published when Roth was in his midthirties, *Portnoy's Complaint* confirms many of Kleinschmidt's observations in "The Angry Act," including the ways in which aggression can be the driving force behind artistic creativity. "It may be the prime mover or the unconscious motivating force for a creative push; it can find poetic, literary, graphic or musical expression and thus channel and dissipate that which otherwise might be intolerable to the ego" (125). But aggression is only one of the motivations behind creativity; the need for reparation is no less important. Roth's parents were in their sixties when he published *Portnoy's Complaint*. There are moments when Alex fears his father's death (significantly, he doesn't fear his mother's death), but Sophie and Jack Portnoy are still alive and in good health. Alex never worries about becoming a caretaker. This is not the case in *Patrimony*, in which the prevailing tone is elegiac.

Having devalued his father throughout the 1960s, when he was in psychoanalysis and writing *Portnoy's Complaint*, Roth sought to repair the broken father-son relationship in the 1980s before it was too late. He did not want to become another Nathan Zuckerman, who remained estranged from a father who died cursing him. Writing *Patrimony* allowed Roth to repudiate "The Angry Act" and honor the father who, for all of his imperfections, remained proud of his son's vast achievements. Roth's need to heal the relationship with *both* parents may be seen in his novel *The Plot against America*, where he lovingly brings Herman and Bess Roth back to life and portrays them as thoughtful and articulate, able to foresee the rising menace of fascism long before other, better educated, people. Despite the limitations of Kleinschmidt's theory of artistic creativity, which emphasizes aggression but ignores reparation, he is right when he concludes that art "signifies the triumph of Eros over Thanatos; it is the triumph of libido over aggression" (127).

"I read *Patrimony*," Roth's impersonator proclaims in *Operation Shylock*. "Warmhearted but tough. You've been through the wringer" (380). *Patrimony* is certainly warmhearted, and no one can deny that Roth has been through the wringer, but the memoir suffers from the omission of dark countertexts and countervoices. We can now begin to understand the meaning of Zuckerman's assertion in *The Facts* that there is "something in the romance of your childhood that you're not permitting yourself to talk about, though without it the rest of the book makes no sense" (168–69). The gaps and silences in *The Facts* and *Patrimony* point in the direction of "The Angry Act."

One of the curious coincidences in *Patrimony* is that around the time Herman Roth was dying of a brain tumor, his son almost died of a heart attack. Roth needed emergency quintuple bypass surgery when he was fifty-six years old. After the surgery, he felt "reborn—at once reborn and as though I had given birth" (225). Roth's close encounter with death heightened his identification with *both* of his parents to such a degree that he imagined merging with them. These paternal and maternal identifications during his brush with death, which occur only a dozen pages before the end of *Patrimony*, testify to Roth's internalization of his parents. He is intrigued by the startling coincidence of his need for emergency bypass surgery during the time his father was dying. Nadeau coins the term "coinci*dancing*" to "capture the action of grieving people as they used coincidences to construct meanings. The *dancing* part of the term is intended as a play on the active and interactive nature of using coincidences to make sense of a death" (126).

We learn in the remaining pages of *Patrimony* about Herman Roth's deteriorating health and the agonized decision not to use "extraordinary measures" to prolong his life. "Dad, I'm going to have to let you go." The final revelation in *Patrimony* occurs when Roth tells us in the last paragraph that, "in keeping with the unseemliness of my profession" (237), he has been writing a book about his father's dying and death, a book that he has concealed from his father. Roth implies that his father died in character during a "twelve-hour ordeal" in which he "fought for every breath with an awesome eruption, a final display of his lifelong tenacity. It was something to see" (231–32). Roth adds that dying is "work" and that his father was a "worker." Afterward, Roth dreams that he has dressed his father in the wrong burial clothes. As *Patrimony* closes, Roth confesses his fear that he will live perennially as his father's "little son, with the conscience of a little son, just as he would remain alive there not only as my father but as *the* father, sitting in judgment on whatever I do" (237–38)—a fear that may indicate guilt over the broken promise to remain silent about his father's patrimony.

Rehearsing Death

After writing good-bye to his father in *Patrimony*, Roth continued his prodigious literary productivity, and many of his more recent novels seem to be rehearsals for his own farewell. Death appears to be his constant companion in these stories, the muse behind his imagination. "Whatever catastrophe turns up," he states in *The Human Stain*, "he transforms into writing. Catastrophe is cannon fodder for him" (170). The eponymous hero in *Sabbath's Theater* reads "book after book about death, graves, burial, cremation, funerals, funerary architecture, funeral inscriptions, about attitudes toward death over the centuries, and how-to books dating back to Marcus Aurelius about the art of dying. That very evening he read about *la mort de toi,* something with which he had already a share of familiarity and with which he was destined to have more" (88). Sabbath discovers what Roth has known for a long time: "everyone learns sooner or later about loss: the absence of a presence can crush the strongest people" (138).

"Can you imagine old age?" Roth asks in his aptly named novel *The Dying Animal.* "Of course you can't. I didn't. I had no idea what it was like. Not even a false image—no image. And nobody wants anything else. Nobody wants to face any of this before he has to. How is it all going to turn out? Obtuseness is de rigueur" (35). Roth's dark vision grows darker with each novel; "old age isn't a battle," he opines in *Everyman,* "old age is a massacre" (156). Roth's fear of the loss of his artistic creativity shows up in a variety of his characters, including the aging actor in *The Humbling,* who suddenly finds that he is no longer able to act. Devastated by the loss of his magical power and spurned by the woman with whom he has been having an affair, he takes his own life, no longer able to work or love. And in *Exit Ghost* Roth kills off a cynical and embittered Nathan Zuckerman, who rails at literary critics, journalists, and scandal mongers whom he views as responsible for the poisoning of literature and the destruction of the country's greatest writers. Nor does Zuckerman derive comfort from the possibility of a posterity self, literary immortality. The "retribution of biographical inquisition" (275), he predicts, will deflect attention away from the stories themselves, wrought in the writer's imagination, to the writer's life, which, Zuckerman implies, with Roth's approval, can never explain the mystery of creativity.

Roth need not fear that the creative process will one day be explained, either his own creativity or anyone else's. "Before the problem of the creative artist," Freud admits at the beginning of his essay "Dostoevsky and Parricide," "analysis must, alas, lay down its arms" (177). No Freudian, Roth would nevertheless surely agree with that statement, just as he would agree with Freud's observation that a father's death is the most poignant loss in a man's life. It is hard to imagine a more moving portrait of the father-son relationship than *Patrimony,* and whatever biographical secrets about Roth may come to light in the future, whatever countertexts and countervoices may appear, the memoir will surely remain an eloquent statement about the power of writing to honor both the living and the dead.

CHAPTER 4

"Death Confers a Certain Beauty on One's Hours"
Harold Brodkey and *This Wild Darkness*

⟋⟍⟋⟍

"*D*epend upon it, sir," Dr. Johnson remarked sardonically to Boswell, "when a man knows he is to be hanged in a fortnight, it concentrates his mind wonderfully." Nowhere is this more evident than in Harold Brodkey's astounding memoir *This Wild Darkness,* written while he was dying from AIDS. Concentration and clarity describe Brodkey's story, a contrast to the loquacity of his earlier works. *This Wild Darkness* opens in the spring of 1992 with the stark sentence, "I have AIDS," and it takes us on a portentous journey that ends in the late fall of 1995, when he is close to death. Only 177 pages long, *This Wild Darkness* remains one of the most arresting accounts of a writer's attempt to describe the transition between life and death. "This is how my life ended. And my dying began" (4), Brodkey observes mordantly in the beginning of the story as he is wheeled through his apartment into an ambulance. His life changes irrevocably from this moment, and yet much about it stays the same.

Brodkey was always an autobiographical writer, even when he was writing fiction. Early in his career he struggled with writer's block, prompting Harold Bloom to state in *Time* magazine that he was an American Proust: "If he's ever able to solve his publishing problems, he'll be seen as one of the great writers of his day" (November 25, 1991). The first sentence of his obituary in the *New York Times* evokes his incomplete legacy: "Harold

Brodkey, a novelist, short-story writer and essayist known almost as much for his failure to publish as for the books he eventually did publish, died yesterday at his home in Manhattan" (January 27, 1996).

Brodkey's writer's block was well known—and sometimes lampooned—in literary circles. He had a contract with Random House in 1964 to publish a novel called *A Party of Animals,* but it took him twenty-seven years to complete the massive 835-page tome, renamed *The Runaway Soul,* which received mixed critical reviews. During that time Brodkey changed publishers twice; published three books of short stories, some of which appeared in the *New Yorker;* taught creative writing at Cornell; and acquired a reputation as a writer with enormous talent and an equally prodigious ego. Jay McInerney savagely caricatured him in the character Victor Propp in the novel *Brightness Falls.* The pompous Propp has been working on a novel for twenty years, "the deadline for delivery receding gradually into a semi-mythical future. In this unfinished condition it, and its author, had become a local literary legend" (21–22). Later we learn that Propp "had entered an almost purely theoretical realm in which, as someone once said of E. M. Forster, his reputation grew with each book he failed to publish. The word 'genius' was increasingly appended to his name" (73). Brodkey claimed in *New York* magazine that John Updike based the character of the Devil in *The Witches of Eastwick* on him. Brodkey was referring to the bizarre character Darryl Van Horne, a self-proclaimed inventor, musician, and art fancier with an encyclopedic mind and a voracious sexual appetite for women, whom he "demanded" call him "king" (*The Witches of Eastwick* 118). Though Updike denied the charge, Brodkey spends much time in *This Wild Darkness* inveighing against his many critics.

Megalomaniac or Genius?

Controversy swirled around Brodkey in life and in death. April Bernard describes *This Wild Darkness* in *Slate* as an "agonizing production of willful beauty" that "gives the lie to the implicitly posed question about Brodkey: megalomaniac or genius? Because he was both" (October 22, 1996). *This Wild Darkness* abounds in assertions of the author's literary superiority. "I felt too conceited to have this death," Brodkey confesses early in the story (6); later he declares, oxymoronically, "I have a number of kinds of humility, but I am arrogant" (36). Near the close of the book he admits that he is "enormously conceited" about his writing (175). Brodkey was a polarizing figure in literary circles, largely because of his colossal ego. He told the *Washington Post* in 1986 that "to be possibly not only the best living writer in English, but somebody who could be the rough equivalent of a Wordsworth or a Milton, is not a role that a half-way educated Jew from St. Louis is prepared to play" (www.robotwisdom.com/jorn/brodkey.html). Richard Howard argues in the *Nation* that Brodkey's public announcement in the *New Yorker* that he had AIDS was a "matter of manipulative hucksterism, of mendacious self-propaganda and cruel assertion of artistic privilege, whereby death is made a matter of public relations" (cited in the *New York Times* obituary).

Published in 1996, *This Wild Darkness* recounts many of the autobiographical events that Brodkey elaborated upon in greater detail in his earlier short story collections and novels, including *First Love and Other Sorrows, Women and Angels, Stories in an Almost Classical Mode,* and *The Runaway Soul.* In the posthumously published *Sea Battles on Dry Land,* he observes, "For twenty years now, I have been writing in the voice and persona of a character named Wiley Silenowicz, who was adopted at the age of two, greatly damaged, ill, silent, beaten, semiautistic, starved" (69). Wiley Silenowicz's family is virtually indistinguishable from Brodkey's adoptive family—sometimes the only difference lies in their names. In *Women and Angels,* for example, he writes: "The Silenowiczes were a family that disasters had pretty completely broken" (31); the same sentence appears in *Stories in an Almost Classical Mode,* except for the name: "The Brodkeys were a family that disasters had pretty completely broken" (222).

The Trauma of Everyday Life

Significantly, Brodkey replays in *This Wild Darkness* the traumatic events of his childhood that he had written about earlier under the nearly transparent cloak of fiction. The body of his writings suggests that catastrophe was never far from his daily life. The earliest trauma was losing his biological mother before the age of two and then his biological father not long afterward. Harold Brodkey was born Aaron Roy Weintraub in 1930 in Staunton, Illinois. His mother, Ceil, died after much suffering, "either of peritonitis from a bungled abortion or from cancer, depending on who related the story" (*This Wild Darkness* 94). His father, Max Weintraub, was an "illiterate local junk man, a semipro prizefighter in his youth and unhealably violent" (21). The writer lamented his biological mother's loss for the rest of his life. He describes this disappearance as gradual—and also as a "mystery" (147), which remains his final word about maternal loss.

Brodkey felt intense guilt over his biological mother's death, partly because of the guilt instilled in him by his adoptive mother, whom he calls a "Daisy Buchanan type, though Jewish" (*This Wild Darkness* 50). "I was told that Doris took me once to the hospital to see my mother, who smelled of infection and medicines and that I refused her embrace, clinging instead to the perfumed Doris; the rescued child was apparently without memory of the dying mother" (94–95). Brodkey then suggests that the "crime" of abandoning his mother has remained with him his entire life.

After the death of Brodkey's biological mother, his father "sold" him to distant relatives for three hundred dollars. Joe and Doris Brodkey were ill throughout their adoptive son's childhood, and death was a lurking presence. He notes in *Stories in an Almost Classical Mode* that his stepparents "had not been kind in the essential ways to me—they were perhaps too egocentric to be kind enough to anyone, even to each other" (224). In *This Wild Darkness* he describes his adoptive mother as a cold, bitter woman "who had cancer and told all those around her that *they were getting on her nerves*" (38). "Doris said to me a number of times," he reveals in *Stories in an Almost Classical Mode,* "'Don't ever tell anybody what goes on in this house: they won't give you any sympathy; they don't know how—all *they* know is how to run away. . . . Take my advice and lie, say we're all happy, lie a lot if you want to have any kind of life'" (228). She also tried to convince him that he was capable of neither loving nor being loved. "You don't love anyone, you never loved anyone. You didn't even mourn when your real mother died, you don't ever think about her. I'll tell you what you are: you're filth" (*Stories in an Almost Classical Mode* 234). While his stepmother was dying, her sister accuses Brodkey of "killing Doris by leaving her," an accusation to which he responds sarcastically, "It's time you lived with her if you care so goddamn much" (*This Wild Darkness* 146).

As traumatic as these events were, the sexual abuse he endured from his adoptive father was more damaging, as he recounts in *This Wild Darkness:*

> Anyway, the major drama of my adolescence was that my adoptive father, Joe Brodkey, who was ill with heart trouble (a handsome invalid, as one would write in pornography) assailed me every day for two years, sexually—twice a day, every morning and every evening, when I was twelve and thirteen. He had nothing else to do, really. He was ill. We were not the same blood. I am being very shy. He never succeeded in entering me, but it was somewhat scary and sweaty. Except that there was the pathos of his dying. And there was my long history of boring irresistibility. And my mind, which was watching all of it. His blood pressure was fragilely high. I was too strong, too frozen, for very much to happen, for the drama to develop. (58)

This remains one of the most curious passages in *This Wild Darkness.* The colloquialisms "anyway" and "really" render this self-disclosure less startling than we might otherwise expect, along with the qualifier "somewhat." It's as if Brodkey can't decide whether this "drama" was traumatic, as one would almost certainly conclude, or sensationalistic, the stuff of melodrama or tragicomedy. The third-to-last sentence implies he may have been in a state of dissociation during this ordeal, suggestive of a psychic defense against pain, yet he begins the next paragraph with the assertion, "I am lying," telling us he *did* notice his adoptive father was "heartsick" for him, "clearly in *love*, in a way" (58).

"The Myth of My Irresistibility"

Brodkey never makes the comparison, but he resembles a female Lolita abused by a pedophiliac stepfather who cannot live without him. Unlike Lolita, Brodkey succeeds in fending off his stepfather's sexual advances, but the experience had a formative influence on him, contributing to what he calls the "myth of my *irresistibility*" (*This Wild Darkness* 52), which not only made him enticing to others, men and women alike, but also led to his lifelong vulnerability culminating in AIDS. In a passage that reads like a psychiatric case study, he observes, "Really, one sees people cursed with irresistibility as being finally interesting for how they fail.

For how they can be hurt. For how they retreat, become scarred, or obese, or dead. When I am attacked, it reminds me of my childhood. Spite and the desire to humble you combine uncertainly in an angry way to make you laugh with shock and secret recognition. Sanity becomes very pronounced in you, as a defense. Every touch verges on abuse, on recruitment" (56).

The myth of irresistibility is fraught with irony. Cyril Connolly's assertion that "whom the gods wish to destroy they first call promising" applies to Brodkey's life. More of a curse than a blessing, irresistibility produces, in his situation, intense feelings of guilt, perhaps because irresistibility stems from a young boy's efforts to live with having been repeatedly sexually molested by his stepfather. He admits that he "confessed nothing" and "complained to no one" about his stepfather's daily assaults. At times Brodkey maintains a double point of view, his stepfather's and his own, as when he writes in *The World Is the Home of Love and Death*, "Daddy is a man and is suffering. I'm a kid and I want to live" (219). Usually, however, he explores the traumatized child's point of view, for this is his own experience. His dying adoptive mother seemed to realize what was happening, for she warned him, oracularly, "If I were you, I'd learn to keep my mouth shut" (*This Wild Darkness* 59)—a warning that he disregarded years later when he became a writer. Anger toward his father and rejection of his father's sexual advances deepened Brodkey's patricidal feelings. "Then, I killed Joe Brodkey. But I didn't know—scientifically—it would kill him to talk to him with intelligence and finality. I stood up and leaned against the bureau and he lay on my bed, and I said he could not touch me anymore at all, not even a handshake, unless he *behaved*" (141).

As Einat Avrahami suggests, *This Wild Darkness* is organized around two major confessional plots: "The confession of the discovery of the disease and the ensuing struggle with it in the narrative present, and the confession of having been sexually abused by his stepfather for a period of two years at age twelve and thirteen." Both confessions are causally connected, Avrahami contends, "so that the extended period of incestuous abuse and the conditions that effected and terminated it are presented as an explanation of—indeed as a trigger for—the eventual contraction of HIV much later in his life" (170).

The myth of irresistibility led to Brodkey's relationships with other males. He implies in *The Runaway Soul* that his attraction to men may have been an effort to escape from women, particularly his adoptive mother. "I was ill off and on for a year after her death and then I resumed my life. I experimented with homosexuality—partly because I could not bear the sadness of women or the memories in trying to be strong and to be a partner, partly because I couldn't bear to saddle them with me or with my thoughts; and the silence then when I was with them suffocated me and made me cruel—and evasive" (631). He feels no anger toward the man from whom he suspects he contracted AIDS. A schoolteacher, Charles Yordy was ten or twelve years younger than Brodkey when they met at a homosexual bath in 1970. On the last day of his life, he telephoned Brodkey and, "instead of saying good-bye or anything like that, he said, 'I'm as smart as you are now'" (*This Wild Darkness* 144), dying words on which Brodkey does not elaborate.

Brodkey implies in *This Wild Darkness* that there was enough childhood guilt to last a lifetime. His "endless family story of woe and horror" only deepened the "mood of being accursed" arising from his AIDS diagnosis (95). Given his biological parents' disappearance from his life, his adoptive parents' mistreatment of him, and his matricidal and patricidal guilt, it is noteworthy that he was able to love deeply later in life. A character in *Profane Friendship* remarks, perhaps prophetically, "I doubt that anyone loves enough. The fact of love as love actually exists—well, perhaps only grief brings you face to face with real love: as in a waking dream, alone" (338).

"I Don't Want to Be Shut Up in a Coffin"

Brodkey was preoccupied with death long before his AIDS diagnosis in 1993, at the age of sixty-three, perhaps because of the early deaths of his biological and adoptive parents. Writing about his stepparents in his earlier stories foreshadows his meditations on death in *This Wild Darkness*. "It seemed to me to be wrong to argue that I should have had a happier home and parents who weren't dying," he confesses in *Stories in an Almost Classical Mode* (226), and he then describes his catch-22 situation: "If I said, 'Hello, Mamma, how is your pain?' she would shriek, 'You fool, I don't want to think about it! It was all right for a moment! Look what you've done—you've brought it back. . . . *I don't want to be reminded of my pain all the time!*'" (233). By remaining silent, however, he enraged her, for sometimes she would yell at him, "You'll die in misery, too—help me now and maybe God will be good to you." Or she'd say, "You'll end like me if you don't help me" (234). She implores him not to leave her for Exeter, as he wanted to do; he remains at home to care for her, but she continues to rail at him, calling him heartless.

In what is perhaps the most unnerving moment in *Stories in an Almost Classical Mode,* Brodkey evokes his stepmother's greatest terror: "I remembered Doris saying, 'I don't want to be shut up in a coffin.' That was fear and drama: it didn't explain anything. But it did if she wasn't dead yet: I mean I thought that maybe the question was *dying. Dying.* Going toward a coffin." He then recalls an earlier experience when he found a horizontal door in the grass next to a house. Opening the door, he finds himself descending into the earth as if he is burying himself alive, and he feels his identity disappearing: "your skin, your name dissolved; you were turned into an openness, into being a mere listening and feeling; the stillness, the damp, the aloneness, the walls of earth, of moist, white-washed plaster, soaked you up, blurred you; you did not have to answer when anyone called you" (236).

In *Stories in an Almost Classical Mode* Brodkey depicts in graphic detail the events leading to his adoptive mother's death. "I'm going to die soon," Doris tells him, adding that she doesn't want him to grieve for her. Her only request is to ask for his forgiveness, to which he responds, "I will if you give me your forgiveness, Momma" (264). The dialogue between them becomes unexpectedly tender, though she scolds him for his egotism: "You never thought you were conceited but you were—that's always the part of the story you leave out" (264)—an omission he now corrects for his readers. Toward the end she professes her love for him, once again asks for forgiveness, and dies. The death scene is peaceful, in stark contrast to the interminable suffering of the last months of her life and to the suffering she inflicted on him. "I listened to her breathing grow irregular. I said to myself, 'Die, Momma. On this breath. I don't want you to live anymore. Her breath changed again. It began to be very loud, rackety. I began to count her breaths. I counted fifteen and then neither her breath nor her actual voice was ever heard again" (265). After her death Brodkey states that he had a "nervous breakdown," in part because he couldn't believe how much he missed her. He doesn't give us the details of this breakdown, nor does he tell us how long it lasted or what, if anything, he learned from it. He closes this section of *Stories in an Almost Classical Mode* with an unusual apostrophe to the reader: "Make what use of this you like" (265).

What should we make of this death scene? Despite Brodkey's observation in *Sea Battles on Dry Land* that death scenes are "out of style" (438), and his statement in *This Wild Darkness* that he "can't bear death scenes in movies" (32), the one he sketches in *Stories in an Almost Classical Mode* is evocative and haunting. Doris's death does not have any particular "meaning," unlike most fictional deaths, which, as Garrett Stewart suggests in *Death Sentences,* are bent on meaning. "Art alone may be counted on to take us out of ourselves long enough to entertain with vision the end of ourselves. In fiction, therefore, death is alive with meaning, for its heroes on saving occasions, for us forever" (48). Doris Brodkey's death may not have the kind of meaning we would expect in a fictional story, but it does have significance. *Stories in an Almost Classical Mode* leaves us with a heightened understanding of the lonely and unsharable nature of death, the conviction, as Brodkey states in *The Runaway Soul,* that "Death is undergone singly—it is KNOWABLE ONLY as specific to one person . . . to each of us. All our data comes from that" (54).

Brodkey's stepmother's dying and death prove to be a rehearsal for his own. He knew that there are not many accounts of dying writers, and he was prepared to be as personal as necessary. "I don't see the point of privacy," he wrote in June 1993. "Or rather, I don't see the point of leaving testimony in the hands or mouths of others." The remark serves as the epilogue to *This Wild Darkness.* He is prepared to accept the charge of exhibitionism. "I do get the feeling I am a bit on show, or rather my death and moods are," he admits early in the story. "But so what?" (13). Later he acknowledges that he is "prejudiced toward a nakedness in print—toward embodiment" (30). He feels little reluctance to self-disclose to his readers, but he is wary of confiding his AIDS diagnosis to relatives and friends. "I did not want to invite trespass" (73). He implies toward the end of *This Wild Darkness* that because of the fierce controversy surrounding the early acknowledgment of his illness, he must bide his time before he is ready to share his personal life with the public, including details of his marriage to Ellen Schwamm. "But the real story of my death, the real nature of Ellen's and my relationship is private, is not to be historicized, not to be noted. Not yet" (131).

As the author of the story of his own dying, Brodkey leaves little to chance. Throughout the memoir he offers his own point of view, yet he also tries to capture his wife's and physician's viewpoints as well. He tells us in *This Wild Darkness* that he has never lied to his wife about his sexual past. Nor has he allowed false hope to undermine his story, even if a lie or concealment would prolong his life. He admits, however, that "telling the truth is never wholly recommended," especially if one has AIDS. "You might live longer with AIDS than you're supposed to, medically speaking, by not telling anyone you have it" (114). Nevertheless, he writes openly and publicly about his illness, despite his physician's recommendation to remain silent about it. "I'd rather be open about AIDS and scoff at public humiliation than feel the real humiliation of lying" (115). He never mentions Elisabeth Kübler-Ross, but his insistence on dying patients' right to know the truth supports her many statements. He also recognizes that self-disclosure strengthens relationships: "Having secrets and confessing them is what *deep* attachments are about" (114).

And yet toward the end of *This Wild Darkness,* when his illness has become more severe, Brodkey makes an odd qualification about the truthfulness of art. He decides not to give verbal sketches of those people, including his wife, who traveled to Venice to honor his literary creativity. "I don't think sketches of actual people can be managed by the ill," he confesses, fearful that the sketches would be too disturbing and cruel. "I think it would be an extraordinary intrusion, a trespass, to describe a real face coldly and what I see written there, death or triumph, hatred and disappointment, madness or escape from madness, curiosity, hidden, lonely love, appetite, and ferocity and wit, or blindness." Is he afraid that sketches of actual people would be perceived by them as betrayals of their trust? We cannot be certain. Nor can we be certain whether he is describing the ways in which the living project their horror onto the dying person or projecting his own dark emotions onto the living. One can imagine a dying person seeing facial expressions mainly of compassion and concern, love and acceptance, in which case a verbal description would not be disturbing or cruel. For the remainder of the story Brodkey prefers "to be truthful and clear-eyed about imaginary faces. Or ones belonging to the dead" (139).

Until this moment in *This Wild Darkness,* Brodkey never fears intruding or trespassing on his wife's privacy. Throughout the story Ellen

Schwamm embodies love, support, and acceptance. He pays her the ultimate compliment when he observes that "I have never been so trustingly
close to anyone since my real mother died" (116). He dedicates the book
to her—"For Ellen, my light"—a light that never flickers.

"I Am Psychologically Foreign to Her"

It is an ironic light, however, that Brodkey casts on her. A novelist herself,
Ellen Schwamm may have winced when she read some of Brodkey's
descriptions of her in *This Wild Darkness*. His first reference to her sets
the tone for his later remarks about her. Admitting that for the first time
in his life he began to feel uneasy about death, he observes, "Ellen was
treating me with an unyielding attention and a kind of sweetness, without any noticeable flicker of independence or irony. She had never once
been like that with me, even sexually. You'd have to know her to know
how rare any state other than autonomy is for her" (3). After he learns
that he has AIDS, she assumes she must also be infected, but she does not
immediately confide her fear to him. "She is often indirect; she frequently
lies to me because I bully her in a lot of ways; she is quick, tactically
quick" (7). A few pages later he reports her reactions to his grim diagnosis. "She does not steadily believe that I love her—it is one of her least
endearing traits to expect proof at unreasonable intervals. And what is
love? My measure of it is that I should have died to spare her. Her measure is for us to be together longer" (10–11). In one passage he refers to her
as a "fine-boned tyrant" (8), in another as "rebelliously saintly" (35).

Later, Brodkey notes that like his physician, Ellen feels it is a mistake
for him not to grieve over his death sentence. "I am psychologically foreign to her. I feel she does not have a grasp of what is happening, of what
my dying means, and how people will act" (65). Some of his statements
contain mocking irony that is directed toward both of them, as when he
summarizes their history of opposition and disagreement: "Ellen believes
in my judgment only perhaps by ignoring it much of the time" (70). He
calls her an "ass and a dolt" for loving him in his condition (80); two
pages later he describes with a mixture of awe and disbelief her devotion
to him: "It is really quite terrifying, a good woman, a sexual one, offering
and giving you fragments of motherhood that you have never had." In his
most disparaging comment, he discloses that she "hates herself, I think,

for not being an earner or a fighter in the world. She tends to have no mercy on herself." He then adds that she "wants to be rescued by another person" (116).

Ellen Schwamm plays a double role in *This Wild Darkness,* wishing to rescue her husband from illness and, when that fails, wishing to die with him. She is so devoted to him that she expresses the wish to be infected with AIDS herself. "I want to have it, too" she exclaims early in the story. "An emotional remark," he says to the reader. "A bit of a marital lie, of marital manipulation. But true enough in that if I decided to kill myself she was still determined, so she said, to kill herself too. She wanted to die of what I was going to die of" (34–35). And yet it seems more than a marital manipulation, for she voices the same urge a number of times. Early in the story he tells us that she wanted the two of them to commit suicide together, "in a few months, when everything was in order" (8). He recalls how, years earlier, when he confessed to her that he hated the "idea of solitude in a coffin" (81), a fear that may have been instilled in him by his dying adoptive mother, Ellen replied, "Well, we can be buried in the same coffin, a double coffin" (81).

How seriously should we take Ellen Schwamm's desire to commit suicide with her husband? How does she feel about suicide as a response to grief and loss? How does she regard her husband's passion for truth telling? And how does she respond to Brodkey's irresistibility? For a clue to the answers to these questions, we may turn to her two novels, *Adjacent Lives* and *How He Saved Her.* Both novels offer us insight into the woman who married Brodkey in 1981 (each had been married once before) and who remained with him until the end of his life. These novels are, to use Philip Roth's terms, countertexts and countervoices, heightening our understanding of *This Wild Darkness.*

Written before Ellen Schwamm met Brodkey, *Adjacent Lives* focuses on a sympathetic heroine who finds herself in an agonizing midlife crisis. Natalie Barnes is an accomplished translator and linguist who is married and has two children. She is drawn to a charming but self-absorbed art critic, has a brief affair with him, feels guilty and remorseful, and decides in the end that family is more important than passion. What's interesting about *Adjacent Lives* is not the novel's predictable affirmation of home and hearth but its probing examination of the dynamics of grief and bereavement. Natalie's response to the suicide of her uncle Laszlo, who throws himself out of his elderly mother's window after her death, reveals much about the novelist's own sensibility. Horrified by the suicide, Natalie does not react the way her friends do to the shocking event. "Where was Laszlo's courage, they are asking one another. They are deeply scandalized by his suicide, by his cowardice" (211). Natalie, however, empathizes with Laszlo's suicide, understanding the loneliness and grief that overcame him. She understands that suicide is not only a personal but also an interpersonal act, threatening the fabric of society. And yet, surprisingly, Schwamm tells us that Natalie agrees with Laszlo that suicide is justified under certain conditions. "She has experienced these conditions but only for short periods, periods too brief to permit the suspicion to harden into a certainty" (212). The novel ends with a qualified affirmation of life, but Natalie leaves open the possibility of justifiable suicide.

Brodkey never tells us in *This Wild Darkness* why he rules out suicide, nor does he speculate on how his death will affect his wife's life. Despite his protectiveness of her, he never takes seriously her suicidal threats. His last reference to suicide occurs when he admits thinking about it "a lot because it is so boring to be ill," then adds, mischievously, that suicide is "like being trapped in an Updike novel" (152). Toward the end of *This Wild Darkness* he remarks poignantly, "I can't live without pain, and the strength I draw on throughout the day is Ellen's" (172)

How He Saved Her *in Fiction and Life*

Their devotion to each other is evident in Ellen Schwamm's second novel, which contains a fascinating portrait of a man who bears an uncanny resemblance to Brodkey. A title like *How He Saved Her* is more appropriate for pulp fiction than for a serious novel, and yet one senses that the title is not ironic. The shadowy hero of the story, a man named Lautner, comes across as unabashedly messianic—at least to Nora Ingarden, a forty-year-old woman married to a wealthy tax lawyer and living in a fashionable Manhattan house in the seventies off Fifth Avenue. Lautner's arrival shatters Nora's comfortable world, and she soon discovers that her life has been empty and false. We never learn Lautner's age, background, ethnicity, religion, or profession. He is the only character in the story without a first name. Nor do we have a clear image of his appearance. "His face was extremely powerful in spite of nothing in it working properly: the nose was hardly Roman, the eyes were vastly intelligent but not well formed" (208). He appears and disappears mysteriously, as if he is an alien presence. Several times Nora imagines that he is the devil, a fallen angel, though she never seriously believes that he is evil or that he will lead her astray. He seems to be allied to a higher intelligence and power that she both fears and craves. He strikes her as a person who has reflected on life and death, love and loss, and he speaks with the authority of one who has read widely and deeply. He often sounds like Brodkey, as when he suggests to Nora, "Nothing is ever finished for the living. Even the fact of death isn't final. There's always memory. There are no endings except in books" (210).

Lautner is a Lawrentian figure, preaching not the resurrection of the body, as Mellors does in *Lady Chatterley's Lover*, but the art of living truthfully. Lautner tells Nora that he can give her "the gift of being open about what you will," and when she asks his name, he responds with a non sequitur, "trust your intuition" (76). Lautner is irresistible to Nora but to no other character in the novel. Few contemporary readers would find him a sympathetic figure. Throughout the novel he comes across as blunt to the point of rudeness. "I'll say this once and only once, Nora. Poses bore me and I don't choose to be bored. Furthermore, I am not enchanted by modesty, and still less by fake vulnerability" (78). Many readers would find a man like this to be boorish, not to mention misogynistic, but Schwamm doesn't. Instead, she struggles to capture his mysterious essence with imperfect language, concluding that it is an impossible task: "Since there was no way to present him in speech, no way that would not simultaneously raise and decide the issue of her sanity, she was forced to conclude that he was simply not a linguistic possibility" (88).

Notwithstanding these novelistic musings, Schwamm does her best to portray Lautner's ambiguous character. Too often he appears oracular, however, and there is something off-putting about the certainty of his convictions: "He had an infant's immunity to self-doubt. He was certainty itself, a Stalin of certainty" (93). Lautner ultimately rescues Nora from a dead marriage and a superficial existence, and she tries to find a way to reciprocate. "Her dream had always been to attach herself to a man of immense gifts and incorruptibility and power (they would be attached to each other with her as his indispensable tenant), to find a tortured genius, someone exhausted by inner greatness, and rescue him,

elevate him, crown him" (99). Lautner would be a more interesting character if we saw the ways in which he was tortured or exhausted. He warns
Nora that he has all the disciples he wants, but she becomes another one,
with the novelist's blessing.

Just as Connie Chatterley begins to recite Mellors's credos, so does
Nora echo Lautner's pronouncements, including the belief that art is the
soul's bridge. Again like Connie, Nora's symbolic death and rebirth occur
during the moment of sexual intercourse, when her female will surren-
ders to male sovereignty. There are hints of Lautner's sexual sadism, as
when she describes his voice "that was arching over her body like a whip"
(257). At the end of the novel, Nora gives up everyone and everything—
her hateful husband, two children, parents, friends, and Manhattan resi-
dence—to be with Lautner. Like Connie, she has also given up her neurotic self: her self-consciousness, self-pity, self-love, and self-righteousness.
Though neither she nor Lautner is religious in a conventional sense, she
achieves salvation in the end, with Lautner as her savior.

How He Saved Her begins with a first person frame narrator who refers
to Nora in the third person and ends with the narrator revealing herself as
Nora herself, after her salvation. She tells us that although she has "never
loved a mortal qua mortal, only as an immortal soul," she would, under
certain circumstances, "die for love" (266), a statement that recalls Brodkey's characterizations of Ellen Schwamm in *This Wild Darkness*. Nora
then reassures us that she has made the right choice to give up her old
world to be with Lautner. By choosing Lautner, however, she finds herself
estranged from family and friends. He has also made the right choice:
"The cards say I can rule the world as long as I have you" (269). Nora tells
us, without elaboration, that she wrote this story for him—though she
doesn't tell us how he responds to it. She ends the novel by reaffirming his
goodness and generosity, vowing to do everything possible to create an
"earthly salvation" in which he does not entirely believe (274).

How He Saved Her is not a roman à clef, but its autobiographical
implications are undeniable. Brodkey hints in *This Wild Darkness* at the
price his wife paid for marrying him. "She left her husband for me. She
walked out on everything. No one backed her but her children. We have
had fifteen years together so far. Some of those years were quite tense,
with public attacks that were a bit on the vicious side" (14). Lautner's
messianic complex highlights Brodkey's implacable self-confidence. The

heroines of Schwamm's two novels, Natalie and Nora, are both anchored to their families, one securely, the other, not; both resemble Brodkey's description of his wife in *This Wild Darkness:* "She has an identity, of the real, familied sort. (She has written two novels, both of which illustrate this)" (35). Lautner bullies Nora, just as Brodkey bullies his wife; both women have an "appetite for submission" (*How He Saved Her* 158). Both women are criticized for their optimism. "I'm a hopeful person," Nora tells Lautner, who eerily predicts that if he ever finds himself in a crisis, he will embrace not hope but pride (91). In *This Wild Darkness* Brodkey dismisses hope and optimism as an "American ad pitch" (46), preferring instead the unvarnished truth of AIDS as a death sentence. As in *Adjacent Lives,* the heroine of *How He Saved Her* talks about suicide. Nora concedes on the first page that although she is not a romantic, "I know that if he dies I will die. I'm ashamed of this." Later she admits to Lautner her suicidal thoughts. I suppose if I fell below a level of autonomy in the way you're describing, I'd have no choice but to contemplate suicide. I can't see myself leaning on anyone" (92).

Brodkey doesn't indicate in *This Wild Darkness* that he is the model for the hero of *How He Saved Her,* perhaps because he didn't wish to identify himself with a fictional character who is "pretentious and absurd," as Christopher Lehmann-Haupt complained in his review of the novel in the *New York Times* (June 21, 1983). Perhaps Brodkey did not want to appropriate *How He Saved Her* for himself. Perhaps the idea of being the source of a fictional savior was no longer appealing to him. And perhaps he didn't want readers to know that each borrowed from the other's writings. Schwamm's characters echo and sometimes foreshadow Brodkey's characters, as when a psychoanalyst named Tromp tells Nora, "The fact is, nobody loves anybody enough" (*How He Saved Her* 227), which anticipates a statement in *Profane Friendship:* "I doubt that anyone loves anyone enough" (338). For whatever reason, Brodkey limits his commentary on his wife's two novels to one parenthetical sentence. To my knowledge, no one has commented publicly on the link between Ellen Schwamm and Nora Ingarden, Brodkey and Lautner, or on the extent to which husband and wife figure in each other's books. Ironically, Brodkey is a more sympathetic complex character in *This Wild Darkness* than Lautner is in *How He Saved Her,* largely because the former is attuned to his inner contradictions and failings.

Brodkey completed the last draft of his Venice book, *Profane Friendship*, before starting *This Wild Darkness,* and a comment he expresses in the former, on memory, also applies to the latter. "Memory uses dramatic discontinuity as dreams do, and as stories do. Memory is as mad and maimed and bureaucratic and lazy and corrupt as the grotesque masks and figures of carnival and of mocking paintings show dreams to be" (53). Memory is equally discontinuous in *This Wild Darkness* as the memoirist goes backward and forward in time, using free association rather than chronology to hold together the story. *This Wild Darkness* consists of seven extended diary entries ending in the late fall of 1995, just months before his death. The diaristic form enables Brodkey to record his thoughts in real time as they occur to him, in no particular order. It also allows him to continue writing without worrying unduly that he cannot know at the beginning of the story how and when it will end.

Writing This Wild Darkness

While dying, Brodkey resigned himself to a future without himself, but he rarely doubted that his books would enjoy a long life. Despite a momentary fear in *This Wild Darkness* that he cannot find anything in his life of which he is proud, including his writing, his faith in his work is constant. In a moment of startling candor, he admits, parenthetically, that he is jealous of his own reputation: "I am Harold Brodkey. (I am jealous even of my own name now, of the literal letters in print; it is a mild jealousy but it sweeps through me and, for a second or two, I don't know quite what to do with the rhythmic heat of it.)" (111). It is a minor jealousy, however, and Brodkey's unpublished writings are never threatened by the equivalent of authorial infanticide. Toward the end of *This Wild Darkness,* when he feels death overtaking him, he states, "I cannot be bothered with my death except as it concerns my books" (175). One senses his sincerity here even though earlier he has admitted his "mania for brave talk" (20). On the penultimate page of the memoir he makes the most astonishing admission found anywhere in his writings, one that I imagine few other writers would make: "I can't change the past, and I don't think I would. I don't expect to be understood. I like what I've written, the stories and the two novels. If I had to give up what I've written in order to be clear of this disease, I wouldn't do it" (176). Brodkey reverses

Kübler-Ross's idea of bargaining: rather than bargaining with death to stay alive, he is willing to die as long as his writings live.

Throughout *This Wild Darkness* Brodkey draws strength and comfort from his writing. He remains devoted to the process and craft of his art. He never seriously doubts whether he is up to the challenge of writing, though he must have wondered how much of the story he would be able to narrate before death intervened. The writer's block that plagued him most of his life did not surface this time; he knew he did not have time to procrastinate. He is the consummate storyteller, allowing nothing to interfere with his writing except death itself. Like Scheherazade, he tells his story to stave off death, except that in his case, death is the subject of his story. Whereas most writers would be unable or unwilling to narrate their illness and impending death, the idea of death emboldens him, heightening his creativity.

Why does Brodkey write the story of his death? Why write at all? Writing serves many purposes for him. To begin with, writing is a form of resistance and rebellion, a way to defy and defer death. As he suggests early in *This Wild Darkness,* writing is his "defiant gesture at AIDS" (14). "Is death other than silence and nothingness?" he asks rhetorically (23). Because silence is a form of death, the writer must keep writing. Writing also functions as a meaning-making activity, helping Brodkey comprehend the incomprehensible. However difficult it is for him to write, it is more difficult for him *not* to write. Writing is often a lonely and solitary experience, but it is also, paradoxically, a way to *overcome* loneliness and isolation. Writing is an assertion of one's life and death, of one's unique identity and history, of one's efforts to connect with the past and the future. Brodkey also writes to create a posterity self, the survival not of the artist but of the art. "I know I am working, fighting, enduring—the verbs change every few minutes—for the temporary survival of a part of myself, and that until now nothing was ever life-and-death for me, nothing that I can recall" (64).

Given Brodkey's faith in the importance of his own writings, his belief, however qualified, in his literary immortality, it is not surprising that he expresses so much anger toward the critics who have disparaged his books. He cannot let go of this anger, even as he approaches death. In *Sea Battles on Dry Land,* he comments dryly, if not grandiosely, on his status as a writer: "My reputation, when it surfaced, was partly like Moby Dick coming up for air and vengeance. And a little bit like King Kong waddling in a papier-mache jungle and fated to die on the Chrysler Building—in love not with Fay Wray but with Anna Karenina and the American public" (152). Only a pedant, one might add, would point out that King Kong dies on the Empire State Building.

Brodkey repeatedly defends his books in *This Wild Darkness,* making no attempt to conceal his exasperation. "I think my work will live. And I am tired of defending it, tired of giving my life to it. I have been a figure of aesthetic and literary controversy, the object of media savagery and ridicule, also at times of praise" (19–20). A few pages later he notes how the public views him: "great artist here, fool there, major writer, minor fake, villain, virtuoso, jerk, hero" (25). His determination to write never falters, even on those days when he is too ill to write, days when he would cry or lie in bed with his eyes closed thinking about his work. Writing both energizes and exhausts him; he refers to writing as an "anodyne, the glancing and faintly radiant immediacy of the language" (110). He never wavers in his belief that writing is a form of truth-telling, necessary for life. He tells the physician who advised him not to disclose the diagnosis of AIDS that "it was therapeutic not to lie," that "truth is a form of caress."

Brodkey implies that the writer is a hero, often a tragic hero who finds himself required to make the ultimate sacrifice. He asserts early in *This Wild Darkness* that before he suspects he is ill from AIDS, he thought the illness was "literary exhaustion," the "death-urgency brought on by finishing a book," in this case, *Profane Friendship.* Later he adds that he assumed finishing the novel would "kill" him (25). He never doubts the necessity of such a death if it is required to complete a book. And yet if Brodkey sees himself, messianically, as a martyr to art, at other times he pokes fun at himself, using humor that is not entirely dark or macabre. Describing his return home from the hospital as an "awful parody, honeymoonlike," he reports that his wife exclaims, "No one would believe that this was one of the happiest times of my life." In response to this, he says, "I roared with laughter, which hurt my stiff lung and made me choke. And I came alive again, for a little while. Well, why not? When the other things are over and done with, when savagery and silence are the impolite, real thing, you're not alone. You still pass as human among humans" (98). There are moments when they are both giddy with marital joy, with the pleasure of being alive. "I feel really shitty," he tells his wife, "but actually—uh, you understand? I haven't often been this happy" (120).

"I Have Liked My Life"

One of the surprises of *This Wild Darkness* is that one may experience moments of overwhelming happiness and contentment amid the tortures of death. This would not surprise Kübler-Ross, though it would Philip Roth. Brodkey shows how dying heightens the experience of living, and how one learns to appreciate every moment, good and bad. *This Wild Darkness* represents, in Kübler-Ross's term, a life review, and Brodkey has few regrets. "I have liked my life," he tells us; he even likes his life "at present, being ill" (20). He is also grateful for being alive. There are startlingly few complaints in the story. While he would like to live longer, he realizes he has lived long enough to have a fulfilling existence. "I don't feel I am being whisked off the stage or murdered and stuffed in a laundry hamper while my life is incomplete. It's my turn to die" (20). He and his wife have put illness to good use. "We haven't had time to be this innocent with each other since I began publishing books. We haven't had a time with so little ugliness in it" (119).

There is nothing forced or Pollyannaish about this happiness, nothing to make us feel that he is whistling in the dark. On the contrary: it is the happiness born from courage and lucidity, not self-deception. "We are quite happy today, really," he avers in the summer of 1994. "It's an hour-by-hour thing" (*This Wild Darkness* 151). And near the end of the memoir he again confides that he is "happy, even overexcited, quite foolish. But *happy.* It seems very strange to think one could enjoy one's death. Ellen has begun to laugh at this phenomenon. We know we are absurd, but what can we do? We are happy" (176).

Just as William Styron's *Darkness Visible* calls attention to clinical depression, and Joan Didion's *The Year of Magical Thinking* highlights the grief arising from sudden spousal loss, Harold Brodkey's *This Wild Darkness* illuminates the process of dying. Each of these landmark memoirs is original and groundbreaking. If *This Wild Darkness* is less well known than *Darkness Visible* and *The Year of Magical Thinking,* it may be because Brodkey did not live long enough to publicize it. The story of protracted death usually involves both depression and grief, and this is one reason

Brodkey's task was more challenging than Styron's or Didion's. They could revise their stories; Brodkey could not. They could get other readers' opinions and judgments; Brodkey could not. They could read the latest research on mood disorders or bereavement; Brodkey could not. They could begin writing after the clinical depression lifted or the year of magical thinking ended; Brodkey could not. Dying writers cannot pen their own deaths. Brodkey knew that his death sentence from AIDS could be postponed but not averted. It is the rawness of *This Wild Darkness*, the sense that it was written in present time, without the possibility of prolonged reflection or revision, that makes it a tour de force.

Brodkey narrates two intersecting stories in *This Wild Darkness*, an inner story of his fluctuating moods, states of mind, perceptions, and revenant memories, and an outer story of the events surrounding his illness and treatment. In the beginning, the outer story dominates, but as the illness progresses, the inner story takes over. Many of his most striking observations focus on the feeling of derealization and dehumanization arising from his AIDS diagnosis, along with the sense of "being suffocated second by second" (11). This feeling of suffocation is both a cause and effect of his loss of composure. "I had an extremely stable baseline of mood and mind, of mental *landscape*. Well, that's gone; it's entirely gone" (16). He also feels a growing sense of disembodiment. At one point he remarks that his body "is like a crippled rabbit that I don't want to pet" (30); at another point he feels like the protagonist in *The Metamorphosis*: "I am like a cockroach, perhaps—with vanity, now with AIDS, with a cowardice much greater than that of Kafka's Samsa" (35). Midway through the story he feels so physically ill that he disowns his body, which was "mostly pain and odors, halting speech and a sick man's glances" (97). Near the end he finds it difficult to remember that he was once fully alive. "I am in an adolescence in reverse, as mysterious as the first," concluding, "I do not really understand this erasure" (172).

Throughout *This Wild Darkness* Brodkey uses relatively short and simple sentences that are far different from the labyrinthine sentences in his fictions, and for which McInerney lampooned him in *Brightness Falls* as a "rococo goldsmith" who crafted "bibelot sentences" (22). The ordinariness of death requires language that is equally quotidian, stripped of the linguistic excesses that we see in his fictional stories. He writes about himself in first, second, and third person, as if he is trying to describe as many subject positions as possible. He realizes that memory is often deceptive, even treacherous, but he never worries that he will fail to present truthfully the story of his dying. Nor does he worry that his readers will disbelieve him. It is often difficult for him to grasp his physical deterioration and psychological shock, yet he never loses control of either his language or point of view. Readers can easily locate themselves in time and space in his memoir in ways that they cannot in his novels, where he uses an impressionistic technique designed to evoke confusion. There are no dull moments in *This Wild Darkness,* no passages in which one's attention wanders.

Brodkey reports and analyzes a myriad of emotions and moods in *This Wild Darkness,* but he tells us almost nothing about the actual writing of the book. Did he know at the beginning the major outlines of the book, or did he, as seems more likely, record the story as it was happening? Did he have a plan of composition—or improvise? Much of the story appears written in real time, but sometimes he summarizes events that happened weeks earlier. How much revision, if any, did he have time to do? How much assistance did Ellen Schwamm provide in the writing and revision of the memoir? "I hadn't the strength to finish a thought without her help," he remarks in the middle of the story (71), yet he never explains precisely her role in the memoir. Did they agree or disagree about what the memoir would include or exclude? As a professional writer herself, she could have written an epilogue in which she narrated the events between his last written words and his death a couple of months later. She could have written the actual death scene herself if she was present.

"I Am Not Crushed by This Final Sentence of Death"

What does *This Wild Darkness* teach us about dying? To begin with, we learn that some people may not be devastated by the news of terminal illness. "I am not crushed by this final sentence of death," Brodkey states at the beginning of the story, adding the qualification, "at least not yet, and I don't think it's denial" (19). This qualification never requires additional modification. He never breaks down, never grieves, at least not in the way his physician anticipates. "He shakes his head at my refusal to grieve—from what I can tell, he distrusts both one's denial of a private Utopianism and one's denial of death. 'This is how I handle things,' I tell him. Ellen is on Barry's side; she thinks I should give in and grieve" (65). Just as living has its rhythms, so does dying, at times slowing and at other times quickening. Brodkey is attuned to these changes. The story of his dying reveals some of the emotions that Kübler-Ross discusses, though not in a definite sequential order. We are not present during his death, but his dying is in character, with a pen in his hand, recording the roller coaster of emotions that constitute life. He doesn't look forward to death, as Kübler-Ross does, but he never dreads it.

Perhaps because he is a writer, Brodkey has a heightened awareness of his own and others' emotions. He tells us early in the story that Ellen was "scared shitless," "deep into her bravery tactic—almost trembling with it" (*This Wild Darkness* 7). He says this with a degree of annoyance, but later he confesses to the same tactic, that he was "only pretending to be brave, after all" (78). Reflecting on his friends who died of AIDS, he remarks on their "air of nervous pretense, like guarded actors"; they played their role with "inverted brio" (67). At times he is stoic and tough-minded, at other times cranky and snobbish. He presents many faces and voices to us; all are a part of his complex personality. Sometimes he plays the role of comic, telling his physician, "grandly," that he's OK: "Look, it's only death. It's not like losing your hair or all your money. I don't have to live with this" (9). He knows from the experience of having been a trauma-tized child that "one who recovers, as I did, has a wall between him and pain and despair, between him and grief, between himself and beshitting himself" (9–10).

Brodkey strives throughout the memoir to knock down this wall, allowing us to see his many moods and emotions, including his fear, humiliation, and rage. His flair for the dramatic sometimes verges on the melodramatic, as when he declares, "I am dying . . . Venice is dying . . . The century is dying . . . The imbecile certitudes of the last three-quarters century are dying" (131). Brodkey often recycles his writings, and some of his statements in *This Wild Darkness* also appear in *My Venice*, published three years after his death. One of his most startling statements about dying appears in *My Venice* but not in *This Wild Darkness*: "I see eternity-in-reverse now, welling up as reality, a reality which is particularly Vene-tian and which is mine, no part of which is eternal, my Venetian reality in a modern moment" (8).

Toward the end of *This Wild Darkness*, on October 25, 1994, his sixty-fifth birthday, Brodkey informs us about the "strange alterations of self," including an irrational hope for a cure for AIDS (159). He doesn't know that he has less than three months to live, but he does know that the "less luck one has, the stronger is one's new conviction in one's luck" (159). Since he has already critiqued the American way of living and dying, which he believes is based on utopianism, he knows that such hope is illusory. Having lived with AIDS for two years, longer than most of its victims during the mid-1990s, he senses that, literally and figuratively, the "book is always closing" (152).

One of these strange alterations of self is the sense of an inner observer who witnesses the other part of the self in action. "I awake with a not entirely sickened knowledge that I am merely young again and in a funny way at peace, an observer who is aware of time's chariot, aware that the last metamorphosis has occurred" (172). This internal observer recalls the "second self" that William Styron discusses in *Darkness Visible*, a "wraithlike observer who, not sharing the dementia of his double, is able to watch with dispassionate curiosity as his companion struggles against the oncoming disaster, or decides to embrace it" (64). Brodkey's internal observer, part of his writer's equipment, allows him to monitor his shifting moods and, in Styron's terms, watch with dispassionate curiosity as the other part of the self struggles against approaching death. I suspect Brodkey would identify with Styron's perception of a "sense of melodrama" preparing for one's extinction: "a melodrama in which I, the victim-to-be of self-murder, was both the solitary actor and lone member of the audience" (*Darkness Visible* 64–65).

For a writer who is so self-disclosing, Brodkey is surprisingly ambivalent toward his readers. Several times in the story he addresses his comments to "you," that is, to his readers, whom he senses are preying upon or exploiting the artist. Here Brodkey resembles Sylvia Plath, who in her poem "Lady Lazarus" accuses her readers of being part of the "Peanut crunching crowd / [who] Shoves in to see / Them unwrap me hand and foot" (246). Brodkey's vision of art is not as sadomasochistic as Plath's, but he implies that his readers derive voyeuristic pleasure from witnessing the writer's suffering. There are moments when he can scarcely control or conceal the depth of his anger and fear, as when he admits that "underneath the sentimentality and obstinacy of my attitudes are, as you might expect, a quite severe rage and a vast, a truly extensive terror, anchored in contempt for you and for life and for everything" (*This Wild Darkness* 31). He is mistrustful of sympathy and empathy, fearing that they lead to vulnerability and victimization. "A woman I know who died a few years back spoke of the inescapable sympathy for weakness. She hated it. I don't want to talk about my dying to everyone, or over and over. Is my attitude only vanity—and more vanity—in the end?" (26). A few pages later he asks to be spared "predatory sympathy" (49).

As Brodkey withdraws from the world, turning inward to the self, he becomes less and less involved with people. "I like to be alone, me and the walls. I like what I do, I think what I think, and to hell with the rest of it, the rest of you; you don't actually exist for me anymore—you're all myths in my head" (153). Is he becoming more cynical here or describing the dying person's loss of interest in the outside world? Is this the "preparatory depression" that Kübler-Ross writes about in *On Death and Dying,* the grief that one experiences in undertaking the final separation from life? He loses not only his "sense of people" but also the need to be admired by the outside world (153). Earlier in the story he has taken comfort from the knowledge that he is not alone, and that people like his wife and physician are connected to him; now he dismisses connection with the outside world. "I don't want any human gesture of solidarity" (153).

In one of the most extraordinary moments of *This Wild Darkness,* Brodkey remarks that he finds the "silence of God to be very beautiful, even when the silence is directed at me" (153). One might have expected him to feel existential estrangement and loneliness here, but he feels a strange comfort from this silence—a silence that is unmistakably spiritual.

Unmoored

But Brodkey is not yet ready to embrace silence. However disconnected he is from the human community, he continues to write feverishly. Writing helps him maintain his tenuous identity even as death approaches, allowing him to remain connected with a world that seems to be rapidly withdrawing from him, or he from it. In the last paragraph he evokes movement away from life, using a word, *unmoored,* that suggests the beginning of a journey across uncharted waters: "But in the pliable water, under the sky, unmoored, I am traveling now and hearing myself laugh, at first with nerves and then with genuine amazement. It is all around me" (177).

In *Sea Battles on Dry Land* Brodkey tells us that in *The Death of Ivan Ilych* Tolstoy "makes the coming of death a spiritual judgment and the actuality of death a possible moment of illumination" (438), but the ending of *This Wild Darkness* conjures up a different kind of spiritual experience, one in which darkness is not transformed into light, as we see at the close of Tolstoy's story. Ivan Ilych's darkness ends in a moment of blinding illumination; Brodkey's darkness reveals no epiphany, only mystery and uncertainty. One cannot imagine Ivan Ilych asserting his happiness at the end of his life, as Brodkey does, or declaring that one can enjoy one's death. There are other differences in the stories' portrayals of dying and death. Ivan Ilych has never reflected on his life before his illness. Brodkey has. Ivan Ilych has been content with his conventional life, unwilling to do anything that might incur the disapproval of society. Brodkey's life has been unconventional in nearly every way, risky and dangerous. Still another difference lies in the authors' attitudes toward suffering. Ivan Ilych is tortured physically and psychologically by unrelenting pain, and death comes as a merciful release for this reason. Brodkey describes moments of acute suffering, but pain does not dominate his waking and sleeping life. Death is not a release from pain, as it is for so many other writers, but a journey into the unknown. The ending of *This Wild Darkness* has little in common with *Anna Karenina,* Willa Cather's *Death Comes for the Archbishop,* Patrick White's *Eye of the Storm,* or Andre Gide's *Symphonie Pastorale,* stories that Brodkey mentions briefly in his memoir.

The ending of *This Wild Darkness* conveys Brodkey's awe and wonder as he experiences his identity beginning to merge into the universe. This merger is not exactly the "oceanic feeling," the psychological term coined by Romain Rolland and popularized by Freud to signify unity or oneness. Brodkey is not a mystical writer, and we don't see a communion with nature or God. Nor does the ending evoke the "death instinct" that Freud defines in *Beyond the Pleasure Principle* as the "*urge inherent in organic life to restore an earlier state of things* which the living entity has been obliged to abandon under the pressure of external disturbing forces" (36). Rather, *This Wild Darkness* leaves us with a sense of identity diffuseness and dissolution. Martin Decoud's suicide on the Golfo Placido in Joseph Conrad's majestic novel *Nostromo* conjures up a similar sense of identity loss. As Decoud floats on the gulf's quiescent waters, the "enormous stillness, without light or sound," seemed to affect his senses "like a powerful drug. He didn't even know at times whether he was asleep or awake" (262). Brodkey, too, finds his consciousness dissolving as he begins drifting away. The unmoored raft on which he stands in the last paragraph suggests the beginning of a new and final voyage into the unknown.

There is no leave taking at the end of *This Wild Darkness,* no formal or informal expression of farewell to the people who have meant the most to him. Brodkey's last reference to his wife suggests they are "happy," with no hint of an impending separation. As Tom Ratekin points out in his Lacanian study, until the end of the memoir Ellen Schwamm appears in *This Wild Darkness* as her husband's "tether to the world, the person who is able to organize people and situations" (96). There is no mention of his wife in the last paragraph of the story, suggesting he is now untethered from her.

Whatever Brodkey experiences at the end of *This Wild Darkness* is profoundly solitary and unfathomable. The ending recalls Keats's "Negative Capability": "When man is capable of being in uncertainties, Mysteries, doubts, without any irritable reaching after fact and reason" (261). We cannot know for sure the meaning of the "laugh" at the end of *This Wild Darkness,* just as we can never know for sure the dying person's last thought. The menacing indefinite pronoun of the final sentence heightens the mystery of Brodkey's ending: "It is all around me." How far can a dying person go in telling the story of his or her own death? Susanna Egan raises this provocative question in *Mirror Talk* (195). The answer, in Brodkey's case, is close to the writer's actual death, to the point where his separation from life is nearly complete.

Brodkey never had the pleasure of seeing the publication of *This Wild Darkness,* but his satisfaction came from his attachment to writing, which remained secure to the end. Impending death concentrated his mind wonderfully, in Dr. Johnson's words, and despite Brodkey's threats of suicide, writing gave him a reason to live as long as possible. Dying of AIDS was not too high a price to pay for writing *This Wild Darkness,* the most stunning book of Brodkey's career.

CHAPTER 5

"I Have Never Been Tempted to Write about My Own Life"

Susan Sontag, David Rieff, and *Swimming in a Sea of Death*

⌒

"There is a Jewish saying," David Rieff observes ruefully in *Swimming in a Sea of Death,* his 2008 memoir about the death of his mother, Susan Sontag, "just as it is an obligation to tell someone what is acceptable, it is an obligation not to say what is not acceptable" (104). The meaning of this paradoxical proverb reverberates throughout the memoir, containing more disturbing ironies than Rieff grasps. *Swimming in a Sea of Death* reveals the striking continuities and discontinuities of Sontag's life—and of Rieff's as well. The memoir also raises a crucial question for the dying and their caregivers: "Is information, or knowing, power or is it cruelty?" (53). The "loved one's dilemma" (21) confronts Rieff everywhere. Should he have told his mother what she wanted to hear, namely, that she was not dying of cancer, or what she did not want to hear—that death was imminent? He tortures himself over the choice he made, and he asks his readers what they would do in his situation.

"One cannot use the life to interpret the work," Sontag writes in *Under the Sign of Saturn.* "But one can use the work to interpret the life" (111). Modifying this injunction, we can try to understand how her life and art influenced each other—and how Rieff's memoir casts further light on both. Suspicious of autobiographical writing, Sontag nevertheless discloses much about herself in her novels and criticism. These writings serve as countertexts to *Swimming in a Sea of Death*, offering us a fuller portrait of Sontag's life. Rieff does not share his mother's mistrust of autobiography, but his memoir is intriguing for what it reveals and what it conceals about their lives.

Susan Sontag, the "Dark Lady of American Letters," was one of the most influential American intellectuals of her age. Novelist, playwright, filmmaker, and fashion trendsetter, she was best known for her polemical essays. "Sontag's great form was the essay," Nancy K. Miller declares. "The essay gave her purchase on the world of interpretations: a world she wanted to explore, describe—and correct" ("Regarding Susan Sontag" 833). Sontag's celebrated *Against Interpretation* asserted boldly that a literary text's style is more important than its content. *On Photography*, which received the National Book Critics Circle Award, remains arguably the most authoritative statement on the subject, despite the fact that she later recanted many of her beliefs in *Regarding the Pain of Others*. Sontag received many prestigious literary and humanitarian awards as well as a MacArthur Fellowship, the so-called genius grant. In the opening paragraph of their 2000 biography, Carl Rollyson and Lisa Paddock note that Sontag has appeared as one of fifty great living Americans in Marquis's *Who's Who* and that she is number sixty-one on *Life's* list of "Women Who Shook the World" (xi).

An iconic figure, Sontag made a cameo appearance in Woody Allen's mockumentary *Zelig*, and she was a media cult celebrity despite her disapproval of popular culture (she appeared in an advertisement for Absolut Vodka). She was one of the few intellectuals who avoided academic teaching and supported herself through her writing. An activist who traveled to Hanoi to protest the Vietnam War, she directed Beckett's *Waiting for Godot* in Sarajevo to protest the Bosnian War. She often sparked fierce controversy not only for her radical intellectual and political views but also for her reluctance to acknowledge the open secret of her relationships with other women, including with the photographer Annie Leibovitz, who visually documented the last years of her life.

Sontag was a seventeen-year-old freshman at the University of Chicago, where she had transferred after one semester at the University of California at Berkeley, when she married one of her professors, Philip Rieff, in late 1950 after a ten-day courtship. She collaborated with him in the writing of a book that later became a classic study of psychoanalysis,

Freud: The Mind of the Moralist. The marriage produced one child, David Rieff, before it ended in bitter divorce in 1958. One of the terms of the divorce was that Sontag had to give up her claim of coauthorship of the Freud book; Philip Rieff didn't acknowledge her help in writing the book. Sontag never remarried, and she raised her son on her own. David Rieff is a distinguished investigative journalist and political analyst who has written cultural studies of Miami, Los Angeles, and the Bosnian war.

Sontag was diagnosed with advanced breast cancer in 1975, at the age of forty-two, and she was given only a 10 percent chance of survival at the time of her diagnosis. But survive she did, and she argues in *Illness as Metaphor* that recovery can be influenced, positively or negatively, by the ways in which patients use language to describe their disease. A decade later she published *AIDS and Its Metaphors,* a continuation of *Illness as a Metaphor* (the two books were reprinted in the same volume). In the late 1990s she developed uterine sarcoma and once again recovered. Sontag came to believe that survival from serious illnesses such as cancer depended on both excellent medical care and a heroic will to live. In March 2004 she developed myelodysplastic syndrome, a blood disease that is a precursor of leukemia. According to Siddhartha Mukherjee, who discusses Sontag briefly in *The Emperor of All Maladies,* her myelodysplasia was caused by the high-dose chemotherapy she had received for her earlier cancer treatments (306). Despite a harrowing bone marrow transplant at the Fred Hutchinson Cancer Research Center in Seattle, Washington, she died on December 28, 2004, two weeks short of her seventy-second birthday.

Self-Revelatory Diaries

Four years after his mother's death David Rieff published *Reborn,* the first volume of a projected three-volume selection of Sontag's journals and notebooks. He acknowledges in the preface his ambivalence over the project. Sontag had sold her papers to the University of California at Los Angeles library; according to the terms of the agreement she signed, all of her papers, including her private writings, would be open to the public after her death. Rieff, the executor of her estate, was given the choice of editing these papers for publication or allowing someone else to do so. Filled with misgivings, he made his decision: "My mother was not in any way a self-revealing person. In particular, she avoided to the extent she could, without denying it, any discussion of her own homosexuality or any acknowledgment of her own ambition. So my decision certainly violates her privacy" (*Reborn* ix–x).

Sontag's diaries and notebooks are a treasure trove for anyone who is interested in learning more about her life and the ways in which she transmuted private feelings into art. *Reborn* reveals her early death anxiety, her belief that her marriage was a "sequence of alternating self-immolations" for both husband and wife (207), the uncertainty over her emotional world, the shame she felt about her homosexuality, her dark vision of love, and the many conflicts with her mother. Above all, *Reborn* affirms her lifelong belief that writing is her way to "define myself—an act of self-creation—part of [the] process of becoming" (295). Quoting the French symbolist poet Remy de Gourmont, she remarks that "to write is to exist, to be one's self" (220). *Reborn* demonstrates, in short, Sontag's love for writing, the only love in her life that never failed or disappointed her.

David Rieff is conflicted about editing his mother's diaries, but he is clearly grief stricken about writing *Swimming in a Sea of Death*. Throughout the memoir he is filled with guilt because of his fear that he failed his mother by encouraging her denial of death. If his decision to publish her diaries violates her privacy, how did he feel about his decision to write a memoir about her? Curiously, he never raises this question, nor does he speculate how his mother would have felt if she knew he intended to write a book about her death. And he never tells us what, if anything, he might have done differently to comfort her—and himself. Much of his grief is tinged with regret and guilt, complicating his bereavement. The portrait of Sontag that emerges from *Reborn* and *Swimming in a Sea of Death* is strikingly different from the image she projected in her other writings. There were, almost certainly, more contradictions in her life and art than in most writers'.

"I have never been tempted to write about my own life," Sontag admits in an interview in *Conversations with Susan Sontag*. Acknowledging her "temperamental revulsion" against using real people in her stories, she adds that nothing she has written or portrayed in film is autobiographical in the sense that it was taken from her life (46). The "model of writing as self-expression is much too crude," she insists. "If I thought that what I'm doing when I write is expressing myself, I'd junk my typewriter. It wouldn't be liveable with. Writing is a much more complicated activity than that" (55). To another interviewer she asserted, "I take for granted that what happens in art is the transcendence of the personal. There are things in my work which are autobiographical. But the point is not to express oneself. The point is to make something wonderful" (198). She was no more interested in a writer's biography than in the writer's psychology: she mistrusted both biographical and psychological criticism.

And yet despite these public rejections of the personal element in her writing, Sontag's diaries convey a different story. She embraces self-disclosing writing in a November 19, 1958, entry in *Reborn*. "I cannot write until I find my ego," she states. "The only kind of writer [I] could be is the kind who exposes himself" (*Reborn* 218). She was nearly twenty-six when she wrote this entry, old enough to realize that writing requires both courage and risk taking. Notwithstanding this diary entry, Sontag learned to be more discreet in her public writings. Throughout her essays she consistently voices her mistrust of personal writing, and she gives few personal details even when she writes about her own illness. As Barbara Ching points out, Sontag wrote *Illness as Metaphor* "without mentioning that her father had died of tuberculosis and that she herself was suffering from cancer, the two diseases discussed at length in the book" (52).

Sontag does allow herself to speak personally in *AIDS and Its Metaphors*. "Twelve years ago, when I became a cancer patient, what particularly enraged me—and distracted me from my own terror and despair at my doctors' gloomy prognosis—was seeing how much the very reputation of this illness added to the suffering of those who have it." Her fellow patients also "evinced disgust at their disease and a kind of shame." These patients seemed to be "in the grip of fantasies about their illness by which I was quite unseduced" (100). Sontag doesn't elaborate on how she was able to remain "unseduced" by the shame of her disease, but she does reveal that she decided to write about the dangerous "mystifications surrounding cancer," adding, "I didn't think it would be useful—and I wanted to be useful—to tell yet one more story in the first person of how someone learned that she or he had cancer, wept, struggled, was comforted, suffered, took courage . . . though mine was also that story. A narrative, it seemed to me, would be less useful than an idea" (101).

Why a gifted novelist and storyteller would believe that it isn't "useful" to write about her own experience of cancer is puzzling. Did she believe that a personal story about her struggle with cancer would be too self-disclosing, formulaic, or mawkish? She might have heeded Arthur Frank's insight in *The Wounded Storyteller:* "Stories repair the damage that illness has done to the ill person's sense of where she is in life and where she may be going" (53). Sontag implies that stories about cancer should be not autobiographical but fictional, such as Tolstoy's *The Death of Ivan Ilych,* Arnold Bennett's *Riceyman Steps,* and Georges Bernano's *The Diary of a Country Priest.* There were, to be sure, nonfiction stories about cancer, written by patients who survived the experience, but Sontag was not interested in becoming one of these writers. She gives us only a few more autobiographical revelations, as when she discloses that she wrote *Illness as Metaphor* quickly, "spurred by evangelical zeal as well as anxiety about how much time I had left to do any living or writing" (*AIDS and Its Metaphors* 101).

"Neurotic Anxiety about Death"

From her earliest writings to her last, Sontag was preoccupied with death. In a diary entry written in September 1950, she examines this fear. "The most reasonable answer to my current neurotic anxiety about death: it is annihilation—everything (organism, event, thought, etc.) has form, has a beginning and an end—death is as natural as birth—nothing lasts forever nor would we want to" (*Reborn* 67). She never doubts that death is the end of life and that there is nothing beyond or after death. The opening statement in her first diary entry, written on November 23, 1947, makes this clear: "there is no personal god or life after death" (3).

Sontag's fascination with death appears in much of her fiction and nonfiction. In her first novel, *The Benefactor,* Hippolyte, the first-person narrator, muses over the imagination's ability to resist or succumb to disease. After declaring that disease "attacks each man alone," Hippolyte comments on how his wife's terminal illness, leukemia, has a "modern character": "It was not communicable, so I was in no danger" (208). Hippolyte's wife receives the news of her fatal disease "bravely," and contrary to Sontag's responses to her three cancer diagnoses, she stoically accepts her fate: "As there was no cure, there was nothing for her to do but to go to bed and await the illness' development" (208). A professor delivers a sermon entitled "On the Death of a Virgin Soul" during the funeral service, admonishing Hippolyte not to grieve, which provokes his strong disagreement: "It is too easy to be resigned to a loss borne by someone else. Besides, I had determined to allow my grief" (216). Hippolyte then distinguishes between personal and communal grief, allowing himself to feel only the latter. "Any personal grief would have been inappropriate on my part, for my relationship in life to my wife was not a personal one, in the usual sense of the word. My relationship to her in death could hardly be different" (216). He makes a long list of the various ways of dying, from which he concludes, "Oh, how frail we are" (217). He remains as detached from the living as from the dying, and he implies that love always fails. Why? "Because it is at bottom the desire for incorporation. The lover does not seek a beloved, only a bigger self" (201).

We cannot automatically assume that Sontag endorses Hippolyte's vision of love, though the statements in her other writings tend to confirm his cynicism. Her fictional characters experience love tinged with hate, an ambivalence they rarely if ever resolve, as we see in Sontag's second novel, *Death Kit,* when Hester tries to verbalize her feelings for the suicidal Diddy: "At times, I love you deeply. I hate you sometimes; maybe most of the time. And then I pity you, and I'd like to help you. But whenever I think of what it would mean to help you, I become frightened. You have a powerful desire to destroy yourself. I'm afraid that if I really held out my hand to you, you'd pull me under, too" (249). A similar view of love appears in Sontag's essay on Cesare Pavese, where she states that love is always a mistake (*Against Interpretation* 45). Her disturbing conclusion is that "love dies because its birth was an error. However, the error remains a necessary one, so long as one sees the world, in Pavese's words, as a 'jungle of self-interest.' The isolated ego does not cease to suffer. 'Life is pain and the enjoyment of love is an anaesthetic'" (45–46).

According to Rieff, Sontag was far more successful in her work than in her many love affairs, all of which, finally, disappointed her. "Throughout her life, my mother oscillated between pride and regret over her sense of having sacrificed so much in the way of love and pleasure for her work or, as she almost invariably referred to it, *the* work" (*Swimming in a Sea of Death* 76). "*The* work had to be served," he adds, "and served at any price" (76). Sontag's diaries reveal her many disappointments in love, and they also confirm her painful vision of love, one that she identifies with sadomasochism. A January 3, 1951, entry betrays her marital fears: "I marry Philip with full consciousness + fear of my will toward self-destructiveness" (*Reborn* 62). These fears have come true by the end of her marriage. "Sadism, hostility an essential element in love," she writes on February 25, 1958: "Therefore it's important that love be a *transaction* of hostilities" (193). A later entry, written on September 15, 1962, records her fear that love involves a loss of self, something she vows to avoid: "Love as incorporation, being incorporated. I must resist that" (305).

"I Don't Know What My Real Feelings Are"

Sontag's ambivalence toward love is symptomatic of a larger suspicion of emotion. "I don't know what my real feelings are," she admits in a 1961 diary entry, "so I look to other people (the other person) to tell me. Then the other person tells me what he or she would like my feelings to be. This is ok with me, since I don't know what my feelings are anyway" (*Reborn* 245). This diary entry is followed by another, on April 23, 1961, in which she expands on the role of emotions:

> Problem of the emotions is essentially one of drainage.
> The emotional life is a complex sewer system.
> Have to shit every day or it gets blocked up.
> Need 28 years of shitting to overcome 28 years of constipation.
> Emotional constipation the source of Reich's "character armor."
> Where to begin? Psychoanalysis says: by an inventory of the shit.
> It dissolves under continued—eventually humorous—gaze. (*Reborn* 266–67)

Where to begin indeed? One may characterize psychoanalysis as an "inventory of shit," but therapy is more than evacuation. Does Sontag believe that emotions are *only* a complex sewer system? That emotions are *only* negative feelings that must be purged daily lest they become toxic? That the only emotions are dark ones? The answer to the last question appears to be in the affirmative, since she views love as inseparable from hate. Seeking to understand why she believes emotions are dangerous, she recalls her early childhood. "I wasn't my mother's child," she writes in March 3, 1962, one of her most revealing diary entries, "I was her subject (subject, companion, friend, consort. I sacrificed my childhood—my honesty—to please her). My habit of 'holding back'—which makes all my activities and identities seem somewhat unreal to me—is loyalty to my mother. My intellectualism reinforces this—is an instrument for the detachment from my own feelings which I practice in the service of my mother" (*Reborn* 300).

Continuing her self-analysis, Sontag suggests that her fear of growing up, of becoming an adult, arises from the fact that she was never allowed to be a child. She blames her mother for this. Sontag could not live up to her mother's impossible expectations, could not please a woman who demanded complete control over her daughter's life. "Behind 'I'm so good that it hurts' lies: 'I'm trying to be good. Don't you see how hard it is. Be patient with me'" (*Reborn* 301). Surprisingly, Sontag never offers a feminist analysis of her matrophobia. Nor does she analyze her feelings toward her biological father, Jack Rosenblatt, who died of tuberculosis in 1938, when she was five years old, or her stepfather, Nat Sontag, a World War II hero whom her mother married in 1946. But Sontag does analyze a "will to failure" that sabotages her many talents. Only by remaining completely honest can she break this pattern of self-devaluation—which helps to explain one of her central beliefs, which she declares in her first diary entry, on December 23, 1947: "The most desirable thing in the world is freedom to be true to oneself, i.e., Honesty" (*Reborn* 3).

But honesty is difficult for a young woman growing up in the 1950s who realizes that her sexuality is different from the cultural norm. Sontag's desire to write, she discloses in a December 14, 1959, entry, "is connected with my homosexuality. I need the identity as a weapon, to match the weapon that society has against me." Two sentences later she concedes that she is "just becoming aware of how guilty I feel about being queer" (*Reborn* 221). "Being queer," she continues, "makes me feel more vulnerable. It increases my wish to hide, to be invisible—which I've always felt anyway" (221). Sontag never disclosed her lesbian relationships, not even when she was criticized by feminists who candidly admitted their own sexuality. At times she was disingenuous, as with the following statement about Paul Goodman: "I admired his courage, which showed itself in so many ways—one of the most admirable being his honesty about his homosexuality in *Five Years,* for which he was much criticized by his straight friends in the New York intellectual world; that was six years ago, before the advent of Gay Liberation made coming out of the closet chic" (*Under the Sign of Saturn* 9). Sontag implies, in the word *chic,* that coming out of the closet now is fashionable, easy, an act that does not require courage—and yet she remained in the closet her entire life.

Given her self-analysis in *Reborn,* one might expect Sontag to be more sympathetic to psychoanalysis, with its optimistic goals of self-analysis and self-healing, but her few references to the talking cure are unambiguously unsympathetic. "All Freud's heroes are heroes of repression (Moses, Dostoyevsky, Leonardo); that's what being heroic is for him," she writes in a September 1962 diary entry. "That's why he appealed to Philip." She grants that Freud was "brilliant about motives," but she regards him as a "tremendous champion of the self-mutilating 'heroic' will" (*Reborn* 304). In *Against Interpretation* she suggests that psychoanalysis encourages conformity, returning us to the world without changing it. "Psychoanalysis is understood as anti-Utopian and anti-political—a desperate, but fundamentally pessimistic, attempt to safeguard the individual against the oppressive but inevitable claims of society" (258).

Sontag was initially attracted to the early psychoanalytic maverick Wilhelm Reich. Rieff suggests in *Swimming in a Sea of Death* that when she was diagnosed with breast cancer, she believed, not intellectually but emotionally, Reich's claim that cancer is caused by sexual repression. " 'I feel my body has let me down,' she wrote. 'And my mind, too. For somewhere, I believe the Reichian verdict. I'm responsible for my cancer. I lived as a coward, repressing my desire, my rage' " (36). She publicly rejected Reichian theory only after her breast cancer treatments.

All of Sontag's later statements about psychoanalysis—and the psychologizing of illness—are negative. "Psychiatry," she asserts in her essay on the French writer Antonin Artaud, "draws a clear line between art (a 'normal' psychological phenomenon, manifesting objective aesthetic limits) and symptomatology: the very boundary that Artaud contests" (*Under the Sign of Saturn* 63). Like Artaud, Sontag affirms the autonomy of art: regardless of the artist's pathology, the poem can exist on its own. Rejecting biographical and, what is for her worse, psychobiographical studies of the artist, Sontag argues that readers can appreciate art without knowing anything about the artist. She is no less insistent that patients should not psychologize their illnesses—though she is silent about her own tendency to do so. "Psychological theories of illness are a powerful means of placing the blame on the ill," she declares in *Illness as Metaphor.* "Patients who are instructed that they have, unwittingly, caused their disease are also being made to feel that they have deserved it" (57).

"Dueling with Depression"

And yet given this suspicion of psychology and (to use Joyce Carol Oates's word) pathography, it is surprising how much Sontag has to say about the melancholy artist. She was "almost always dueling with depression," Rieff admits in *Swimming in a Sea of Death* (139), though she would not concede this. She doesn't include herself as a melancholy writer in *Under the Sign of Saturn*, but one reaches this conclusion after reading her essays and diaries. "Dissimulation, secretiveness appear a necessity to the melancholic," she writes about Walter Benjamin. "He has complex, often veiled relations with others. These feelings of inferiority, of inadequacy, of baffled feeling, of not being able to get what one wants, or even name it properly (or consistently) to oneself—these can be, it is felt they ought to be, masked by friendliness, or the most scrupulous manipulation" (*Under the Sign of Saturn* 118). Change the masculine pronoun to the feminine, and you have a portrait of Sontag herself.

Sontag emphasizes the power of the "will" to create one's life and overcome illness. The illness of which she speaks, and to which she returns again and again, is found in the "Saturnine temperament." She uses *Saturnine* as a synonym for melancholy, the poetic word for depression. (Ironically, Mukherjee uses the same word to describe her cancer: "A moody, saturnine leukemia eventually volcanoed out of Sontag's marrow" [306–7].) To engage in work is to engage in self-creation, one of the most important themes in her diaries. Noting dryly in her posthumous book *At the Same Time* that hyperproductivity is "not as well regarded as it used to be" (59), she herself was hyperproductive, though in her more self-disparaging moments she felt she should have accomplished more than she did.

Sontag identified with those artists who were willing to work hard to craft stories and, in the process, achieve not self-expression but self-transcendence, by which she means an escaping from oneself. She articulates this view in *At the Same Time* and in *Where the Stress Falls*, where she also implies that writers do not have agency: "It feels true only in a trivial sense to say I make my books. What I really feel is that they are made, through me, by literature; and I'm their (literature's) servant" (259). She also rules out the therapeutic possibility of artistic creation: "My books are not a means of discovering or expressing who I am, either; I've never fancied the ideology of writing as therapy or self-expression" (260).

Many of the authors Sontag wrote about were, like her, haunted by death. As early as 1966 she suggests, in the essay on Pavese, that the writer is the "exemplary sufferer because he has found both the deepest level of suffering and also a professional means to sublimate (in the literal, not the Freudian, sense of sublimate) his suffering" (*Against Interpretation* 42). She admired Elias Canetti, the Bulgarian-born novelist who won the Nobel Prize for Literature in 1981, because of his defiance of death. Sontag's essay on Canetti, according to David Rieff, is "disguised autobiography," and what she "most cherished" about his work was his "fear of death" (*Swimming in a Sea of Death* 12). Canetti is "one of the great death-haters of literature," she states in *Under the Sign of Saturn,* and then she explains how all of his work—and, as it transpires, her own—aims at a refutation of death. "Canetti insists that death is really unacceptable; unassimilable, because it is what is outside life; unjust, because it limits ambition and insults it" (192). In *Illness as Metaphor* Sontag makes a similar observation about death-denying writers: "For those who live neither with religious consolations about death nor with a sense of death (or of anything else) as natural, death is the obscene mystery, the ultimate affront, the thing that cannot be controlled. It can only be denied" (55). To "accept" death, in Kübler-Ross's terms, would be unthinkable to her.

Bearing Witness to Pain

Sontag's most significant books are those in which she confronts the problems of suffering and death: *Illness as Metaphor, AIDS and Its Metaphors*, and *Regarding the Pain of Others.* These books are not personal: David Rieff calls *Illness as Metaphor* and *AIDS and Its Metaphors* "almost anti-autobiographical—intentionally so" (*Swimming in a Sea of Death* 28). In these books Sontag displays not only her characteristic insight but also her sympathy and empathy, qualities not always evident in her other works. She offers in these three books a paradigm of how we should look at suffering and bear witness to the pain of others.

Sontag speculates on this "looking" in her most famous book, *On Photography,* but much of her theorizing is problematic. "To photograph is to appropriate the thing photographed," she states categorically at the beginning of the book (4), and a few pages later she makes an even more sweeping generalization: "To photograph people is to violate them, by seeing them as they never see themselves, by having knowledge of them they never can have; it turns people into objects that can be symbolically possessed" (14–15). Curiously, it does not matter to her whether a person wants to be photographed or not. Nor is she interested in the photographer's motives to document a subject. Many of her statements are overstatements, as when she writes, "Photography implies that we know about the world if we accept it as the camera records it. But this is the opposite of understanding, which starts from *not* accepting the world as it looks" (23). This may be true for some photographers, but not for those who realize that a photograph is, at best, a surface image. Sontag follows this with a sentence that admits to no exceptions: "The knowledge gained through still photographs will always be some kind of sentimentalism, whether cynical or humanist" (24). The word *sentimentalism* abounds in her writings, from the beginning of her career to the end, and always with a pejorative meaning, implying something superficial, naive, or dishonest. Asserting that photography is an "elegiac art" and that "all photographs are *memento mori*" (15), Sontag opines that insofar as photographs are a reminder of death, they are an "invitation to sentimentality" (171).

Sontag's generalizations are bold, startling, aphoristic, and memorable. They demand to be taken seriously, but they also produce counterstatements that are equally valid. She characteristically takes extreme positions without qualifying them. *On Photography* would be a more nuanced book if she admitted that she was talking about one person's point of view, her own, rather than generalizing for all people, photographers and nonphotographers alike. One of the ironies surrounding the book is that Sontag never owned a camera, never took a photo herself.

There is only one personal moment in *On Photography,* when Sontag describes her experience looking for the first time at photographs of Nazi concentrations camp victims. "Nothing I have seen—in photographs or in real life—ever cut me as sharply, deeply, instantaneously. Indeed, it seems plausible to me to divide my life into two parts, before I saw those photographs (I was twelve) and after, though it was several years before I understood fully what they were about" (20). Apart from the misleading word *fully*—how can any photo capture the horror of the Holocaust?—Sontag tells us that something "broke" when she looked at those photographs in a California bookstore in 1945. "Some limit had been reached, and not only that of horror; I felt irrevocably grieved, wounded, but a part of my feelings started to tighten; something went dead; something is still crying" (20). Sontag's sympathy and empathy in *On Photography* seem precarious, easily exhausted, and she remains skeptical of photographers who do not believe they are practitioners of a "predatory" art. She privileges photographers like Henri Cartier-Bresson and Richard Avedon who talk "honestly (if ruefully) about the exploitative aspect of the photographer's activities," while she dismisses other photographers whose claims of "innocence" are mere "verbiage" (123).

"Illness Is the Night-Side of Life"

Sontag's next book, *Illness as Metaphor,* hits much closer to home, and though she does not speak about her own struggle with breast cancer, she writes more compassionately and movingly, probably because she is so close to her subject. "Reading 'Against Interpretation' followed by *Illness as Metaphor* and *AIDS and Its Metaphors*," Jay Prosser remarks, "we see how a posturing polemic in an essay by someone at the start of her writing career is carried in the two illness books to a sincere and a compassionate plea for confronting the failures of the body, the limits of life, and the reality of death" (189). Sontag opens *Illness as Metaphor* with two of her most startling sentences—"Illness is the night-side of life, a more onerous citizenship. Everyone who is born holds dual citizenship, in the kingdom of the well and in the kingdom of the sick" (3). These sentences conjure up a sense of myth, and yet, paradoxically, she does everything she can to demythicize and demetaphorize the nature of illness. "My point is," she states, sounding more like a lecturer than a storyteller, "that illness is *not* a metaphor, and that the most truthful way of regarding illness—and the healthiest way of being ill—is one most purified of, most resistant to, metaphoric thinking" (3). Whereas elsewhere Sontag identifies with those writers like Canetti who deny death, now she decries those who deny telling the truth to dying cancer patients. "The policy of equivocating about the nature of their disease with cancer patients reflects the conviction that dying people are best spared the news that they are dying, and that the good death is the sudden one, best of all if it happens while we're unconscious or asleep. Yet the modern denial of death does not explain the extent of the lying and the wish to be lied to; it does not touch the deepest dread" (8).

As Carl Rollyson points out, Sontag revealed in several interviews the nature of her dread as well as her tendency to blame herself for the disease. "To interviewers she admitted that her first reaction to the disease had been terror. She thought of it as a death sentence, a curse, and wondered, 'What did I do in my life that brought this on?'" Rollyson adds that in the early weeks of her recovery from the mastectomy she "tortured herself with the idea that one could get cancer from holding in one's grief" (115).

Sontag noted in a 1978 interview that she experienced not only "the most acute kind of animal panic" but also, unexpectedly, "moments of elation. A tremendous intensity. I felt as if I had embarked on a great adventure. It was the adventure of being ill and probably dying. And, I don't want to say it was a positive experience, because that sounds cheap, but of course it did have a positive side" (*Conversations with Susan Sontag* 109). Sontag sounds here like Harold Brodkey, though it would be many years before he wrote *This Wild Darkness*. She also sounds, oddly enough, like Kübler-Ross, who waxed poetic about death as a wonderful and positive experience. Unlike Kübler-Ross, however, Sontag never believed in God, life after death, or reunion with the dead. Nor is there any evidence that these moments of elation occurred when Sontag was actually dying from blood cancer.

If *Illness as Metaphor* does not touch the deepest dread or evoke moments of elation during Sontag's struggle with breast cancer, it nevertheless argues persuasively for a change of attitude toward serious illness. We cannot avoid metaphors when we write and speak about illness, dying, and death, as Sontag urges us to do; but we can choose our metaphors carefully and wisely so that patients are not blamed (and do not blame themselves) for their illnesses. "Nothing is more punitive than to give a disease a meaning," she writes (58), observing correctly that cancer is "multi-determined" (60). She is right when she warns us that to compare cancer to a "war" is to attach moralistic significance both to the disease and the patient. "The people who have the real disease are also hardly helped by hearing their disease's name constantly being dropped as the epitome of evil. Only in the most limited sense is any historical event or problem like an illness. And the cancer metaphor is particularly crass" (85). She might have added, with a touch of humility, that she had used crass cancer metaphors twice herself, first in *Against Interpretation,* when she observes that "*Saint Genet* is a cancer of a book, grotesquely verbose"

(93), and then in *Styles of Radical Will,* when she states that "the white race *is* the cancer of human history" (203).

Reading *Illness as Metaphor* with the knowledge of Sontag's death, one sees a cruel irony of which she remained unaware at the time. "Leukemia is the only part of the cancer metaphor pulling toward romantic values," she writes. "It is the one form of cancer—just the most well-known one—that isn't associated with the tumor. There's no operation you can perform for it. And there's not this idea of mutilation and amputation that's connected with the fear of cancer" (*Conversations with Susan Sontag* 113). She makes a similar observation in a revealing parenthesis in *Illness as Metaphor.* After describing the ways in which writers have romanticized tuberculosis, she remarks: "The heroine of Erich Segal's *Love Story* dies of leukemia—the 'white' or TB-like form of the disease, for which no mutilating surgery can be proposed—not of stomach or breast cancer" (18). Only toward the end of her life did she discover that leukemia and other blood cancers have their own special tortures.

Sontag admits in the first paragraph of *AIDS and Its Metaphors* that "one cannot think without metaphors" (93), a concession that was not obvious to her in *Illness as Metaphor.* One of her most personal books, *AIDS and Its Metaphors* reveals her state of mind as a breast cancer patient—or at least how she recalls the experience twelve years later. She now embraces the idea of writing as healing, admitting that she wrote *Illness as Metaphor* "to calm the imagination" (260). She takes pleasure in pointing out in *AIDS and Its Metaphors* that being cured of cancer has had the effect of "confounding my doctors' pessimism," and she praises the "new candor about cancer" (103). She makes two predictions in *AIDS and Its Metaphors* that have not come true: that AIDS will be renamed and that the new disease has "banalized" cancer.

AIDS and Its Metaphors, as well as Sontag's fictional story "The Way We Live Now," published in the *New Yorker* in 1987, had a profound impact on readers. The novelist David Leavitt read "The Way We Live Now" and immediately felt "a sense of enormous and long-withheld release. Up to that point, reading fiction about AIDS had seemed to me akin to being shown a brick wall somewhere in the distance and then, at full speed, being hurled into it. Sontag, however, had written a story that transcended horror and grief, and which was therefore redemptive, if not of AIDS itself, then at least of the processes by which people cope with it" (1470). For Leavitt, "The Way We Live Now" succeeded "primarily because it offered a possibility of catharsis, and at that time, catharsis was something we all badly needed" (1471).

Surviving breast cancer and then uterine sarcoma inevitably changed Sontag's life, and though she doesn't discuss these two experiences in *Regarding the Pain of Others,* published only one year before her death, the book reveals several changes in her thinking. To be sure, some of the statements early in the book are consistent with those appearing in *On Photography,* as when she states that "there is shame as well as shock in looking at the close-up of a real horror." Now, however, she qualifies herself in a way that she does not in the earlier book: "Perhaps the only people with the right to look at images of suffering of this extreme order are those who could do something to alleviate it—say, the surgeons at the military hospital where the photograph was taken—or those who could learn from it. The rest of us are voyeurs, whether or not we mean to be" (*Regarding the Pain of Others* 42). Notwithstanding the last sentence, Sontag acknowledges, late in the book, that some of the essays she published decades earlier in *On Photography* no longer strike her as true. She disagrees specifically with her earlier claim that repeated exposure to photographs makes them appear less real. "As much as they create sympathy, I wrote, photographs shrivel sympathy. Is this true? I thought it was when I wrote it. I'm not so sure now" (105). In an extended footnote, she discusses how photographs can mobilize public opinion against the atrocities of war. After singling out images of barbarity during the Spanish Civil War, World War I, World War II, and Iraq, she then cites the work of David Rieff, though she doesn't identify him as her son.

"Remembering Is *an Ethical Act"*

Sontag maintains that compassion is an "unstable emotion" and that it "needs to be translated into action, or it withers" (101), but the emphasis in *Regarding the Pain of Others* is that sympathy sensitizes us to the suffering of others. Toward the close of her book she makes one of her most prescient statements, one that applies as much to writers as to photographers: "Remembering is an ethical act, has ethical value in and of itself. Memory is, achingly, the only relation we can have with the dead" (115.

David Rieff never discloses his reasons for writing *Swimming in a Sea of Death,* but presumably one of the motives was to bear witness to his mother's life and death. Like Sontag, he is a freelance intellectual, and he shares her belief that remembering is an ethical act—and that memory is, achingly, the only relation we can have with the dead.

A graduate of Princeton University, Rieff worked from 1978 to 1989 as a senior editor at Farrar, Straus, and Giroux, his mother's exclusive publisher, and then served on the boards of several humanitarian organizations. He is now a contributing editor to the *New York Times Magazine.* In his first book, *Going to Miami,* he remarks that "home has always been for me an idea as difficult as it is beguiling. Part of this feeling, I have no doubt, comes from the biographical fact that I don't so much come from a nuclear family as from a sub-atomic one" (91). Before editing *Reborn* and writing *Swimming in a Sea of Death,* he wrote occasionally about Susan Sontag, not always identifying her as his mother. A student of literature, he has read widely and deeply, and he often cites the same writers that his mother does, including Friedrich Nietzsche, Franz Kafka, George Orwell, Walter Benjamin, Herbert Marcuse, Albert Camus, Simone de Beauvoir, and Elias Canetti. At the end of *Los Angeles: Capital of the Third World,* he reports a conversation with a friend in which he remarks, without attribution, "We must love one another or die," to which the friend responds, correcting him, "We must love one another and die" (259). Few readers will catch the allusion to Auden's poem "September 1, 1939" or realize that the poet later changed "or die" to "and die," a change that makes a world of difference in the poem's meaning.

Rieff shares many of Sontag's assumptions about art, politics, and history. He claims in the acknowledgments of *The Exile* that "all writing, but particularly the kind of non-fiction that laps at the borders of several genres that I tend to write, is both predatory and appropriative" (209), echoing his mother's pronouncement that photography is a predatory art. Some of his assertions in *Los Angeles* about Americans in general apply to his mother in particular, as when he remarks that Americans, like Fitzgerald's Gatsby, "continue to cast their biographies as one long drama of breaking free" (47). He contends in *Slaughterhouse: Bosnia and the Failure of the West* that knowledge "is not power" (40), a theme that pervades *Swimming in a Sea of Death,* and he also uses the same Talmudic proverb that he uses in the memoir—"It is your obligation to tell people things they can hear; it is your obligation not to tell people things they cannot hear" (41). He writes in *A Bed for the Night: Humanitarianism in Crisis* that "war and not peace has been the norm" (332), similar to Sontag's observation in *Regarding the Pain of Others* that "war has been the norm and peace the exception" (74).

Like Sontag, Rieff anatomizes the contradictions of American culture and art. Both mother and son are progressive thinkers who are not afraid to critique left-wing politics. They are both suspicious of emotions, and they often use the word *sentimentality* as a criticism of insincerity and inauthenticity. And both have dedicated books to the other: Sontag dedicated *The Volcano Lover* to "David, beloved son, colleague," and Rieff dedicated *At the Point of a Gun* to "my mother, Susan Sontag."

If photography is, as Sontag famously declares, an "elegiac art," and if "all photographs are *memento mori*" (*On Photography* 15), then what shall we say about end-of-life memoirs? They are, literally and metaphorically, inventories of mortality, invested with, as Sontag once sardonically observed about herself, posthumous reality.

Rieff portrays Sontag in *Swimming in a Sea of Death* as a woman who loved life and who lived "as if stocking a library, or materializing her longings—many of them unchanged since lonely girlhood" (15). She wrote about herself, in one of her unpublished diaries, as an "eternal student" (15); her "avidity" for life was endless. He notes that she spoke with increasing frequency of wanting to live to be a hundred. Her goal in life, survival, never changed "from the moment of diagnosis almost to the hour of her death" (82). Her belief that she was "special" seemed to be both the cause and effect of surviving two aggressive forms of cancer, but when she developed leukemia, which rarely is curable in adults, she believed she would once again prevail. She "died as she had lived: unreconciled to mortality, even after suffering such pain—and God, what pain she suffered!" (13). Rieff's invocation to God is ironic, since he tells us in the next sentence that like Elias Canetti, the poet Philip Larkin, and himself, she disdained religious consolation.

The Denial of Death

Rieff's portrayal of his mother's prodigious energy and insatiable desire for life will surprise none of her many admirers. Nor should one be surprised by her shock upon hearing of her diagnosis of incurable blood cancer or her feeling of being dazed, disoriented, and depressed before, during, and after her treatment. Nor is the depth of her anger during the final months of life surprising. What is surprising is that Sontag's faith in medical science—the possibility that a cure for the most aggressive cancers might be just around the corner—approached "religiosity" (*Swimming in a Sea of Death* 31). "Contemptuous of the false optimism of the age—something she associated with the deep America she came from and which she both feared and despised—my mother nonetheless shared it, if only unconsciously, where the question of illness was concerned" (88). Rieff is never sure whether her denial of death to the last days of her life was helpful or harmful. She "pushed away the grimmer news" about cancer and employed what he calls "positive denial" that now, in retrospect, was "the denial of death itself" (92). Her "faith" in science, according to Rieff, became a "scientism" that contradicted her otherwise cool, intellectually skeptical view of reality (94). "My mother had always thought of herself as someone whose hunger for truth was absolute. After her diagnosis, the hunger remained, but it was life and not truth that she was desperate for" (102).

Rieff's description of his mother's behavior after her diagnosis is also startling. "In the immediate aftermath of her diagnosis, my mother at times seemed to oscillate between a hollowed-out somnolence and a sharp, manic busyness that occasionally edged into hysteria, and at other times seemed almost incongruously rational and calm" (*Swimming in a Sea of Death* 65). Hysteria? Surely he is aware of the word's ancient association with misogyny. He uses the adjectival form of the word later in the book when he describes himself as emotionally retreating from his mother as she approaches death, but he is quick to add that, unlike her, he has *not* become "hysterical" (99). *Hysterical* is a strange word for a feminist-friendly writer to use to describe Susan Sontag, one of the feminist icons of her age. The word not only contradicts her lifelong championing of feminist causes but also endorses the stereotype of weak, irrational women.

The evocative title of Rieff's memoir implies that the son finds himself swimming in the same sea of death as his mother—and that he feels like he is drowning while trying to be with her. Many caretakers feel that they are overwhelmed by their responsibilities, but Rieff's dread of being dragged under is different. Though it appears unlikely from his comments that he was his mother's primary caregiver, her illness appears to paralyze him. Boundaries between mother and son become problematic;

he cannot locate a distance where he can *safely* care for her or simply be with her. "In being in some sense part of my mother's emotional life support, I found *myself* to be on emotional life support" (*Swimming in a Sea of Death* 101). He seems particularly susceptible to emotional contagion, the "spreading" of emotions to other people.

Unable to observe his mother's suffering without suffering himself, Rieff is angry with those physicians who, through arrogance or insensitivity, "infantilize" his mother (a criticism Mukherjee also makes of one of Sontag's oncologists), but he too seems infantilized by these doctors as well as by his mother's terror of death. He opens his story by referring to the sword of Damocles that hangs over his mother's head beginning with her breast cancer diagnosis in 1975, then refers to it later when it seems to be touching her throat, but it is never far from his own throat as well. He remarks that people thought his mother "had gone mad" (*Swimming in a Sea of Death* 81), adding that he wondered whether he too was going mad. He finds himself at sea even after her death. "As she died, we swam alongside her, in the sea of her own death, watching her die. Then she did die. And speaking for myself, I find that I am still swimming in that sea" (161–62).

Rieff implies that his mother's refusal to hear—and accept—the truth of her medical condition did not, finally, serve her well. He cannot be sure, because she never spoke to anyone about this. But there is little doubt that her need for false reassurance did not serve *him* well. Twice he refers to folie à deux (*Swimming in a Sea of Death* 73, 113), madness shared by two people. After her breast cancer diagnosis there were "no go" areas about illness (42), one of many subjects that became "off-limits" (53). Death became the forbidden topic: "Almost until the moment she died, we talked of her survival, of her struggle with cancer, never about her dying. I was not going to raise the subject unless she did. It was her death, not mine. And she did not raise it. To have done so would have been to concede that she might die and what she wanted was survival, not extinction—survival on any terms. To go on living: perhaps that was her way of dying" (17).

Rieff never mentions Kübler-Ross's writings, but he would have found many of her insights illuminating. If Sontag was among the 1 percent of the population who, in the psychiatrist's words, "desperately need denial of their illness," Rieff might have felt less guilty that he did not try to express the truth she was unwilling to hear. Kübler-Ross would not have denied Sontag the hope that she would survive, however unlikely this hope might be.

"I Became Her Accomplice"

Rieff's self-doubts intensify as he narrates the story of his mother's dying and death. "The questions tumble out, in wakefulness and in dreams. At least, more than two years after her death, they continue to for me: Did I do the right thing? Could I have done more? Or proposed an alternative? Or been more supportive? Or forced the issue of death to the fore? Or concealed it better?" He never resolves these questions, concluding only that they are the "unanswerable questions of a survivor" (21). He recalls the Scylla/Charybdis decision he was forced to make decades earlier. "I remember pacing the corridors of the breast cancer floor at Memorial Hospital wondering what to tell my mother and what not to tell her. To do so seemed like sadism. But not to do so seemed like betrayal. In the end, I did nothing" (26). He tortures himself for having done nothing at the time. "I became her accomplice, albeit with the guiltiest of consciences" (43).

Why does Rieff feel so guilty? Part of his feeling may be survivor guilt, a phenomenon that Sontag's fictional characters know well. "Survivors always feel guilty," one character in her film script *Brother Carl* observes, to which another responds, "They're right. To survive *is* to be guilty" (152). Rieff's self-lacerations in *Swimming in a Sea of Death,* however, go beyond normal survivor guilt. Part of the difficulty is that mother and son are unable to talk about their fears, anxieties, and worries. Rieff cannot empathize with his mother without feeling burdened by her dark emotions. He begins the memoir by telling us that while telephoning her from Heathrow Airport in London on March 28, 2004, half way home from a long trip abroad, he hears her say that a blood test she has recently taken "doesn't seem so good" (2). Her anxiety immediately infects him. "I'm ashamed to say that I was relieved when we rang off" (4). Seeing her the next morning, he remains calm, but in retrospect, "I wish I'd hugged her close or held her hand. But neither of us had ever been physically demonstrative with the other, and while much has been said and written about how people transcend their pettier sides in crises, in my experience, at least, what actually happens is that more often we reveal what lies beneath the waterline of what we essentially are" (5). He implies here and elsewhere that mother and son have been neither emotionally open nor demonstrative with each other. While hearing her weep, Rieff thinks to himself, "say something" (96), but he can think of nothing to say, not even a simple declaration of love. "I said nothing. My mind was a doleful blank" (96).

At one point Rieff mentions his mother's anger toward her own mother, "whose coldness and withholding nature (my mother's words, again), so haunted her" (24). This description also seems to apply to Susan Sontag as a mother. People become understandably self-absorbed during illness, especially terminal illness, but it's revealing that Rieff never reports his mother attempting to comfort *him*. She was in an "emotional freefall" (42). So was he, but she seems unaware of his own crisis. Never does she ask how he is feeling or express concern about his life. Several times Rieff intimates that he is psychologically unprepared to deal with his mother's dying, and on one occasion he suggests that this may have been due to his upbringing. "The biographical irony of the fact that, from childhood, I was formed—or do I mean deformed?—by my readiness to form opinions and stick to them was not lost on me" (123–24). Deformed? What does he imply here? That his childhood was devoid of genuine love? That he came from a family that privileged ideas over feelings? That his parents did not respect his autonomy and otherness? If he was, as he says, deformed in his childhood, does that make him emotionally abused? Sontag's statement in *Reborn* about sacrificing her childhood and her honesty to please *her* mother seems to be equally true of Rieff, who is never able to express the truth to *his* mother. The sins of the mother seem to haunt Sontag's life, both as daughter and mother, suggesting unresolved intergenerational conflicts. In the end, her faith in reason is unable to provide her with any comfort or strength as death approaches, and the son appears to be no less emotionally bereft. He reveals that expressions of love never comforted her. "If love was stable, the case for survival was volatile" (132). He *tells* us about the stability of his love for his mother but *shows* us its instability.

Survivor Guilt

Near the end of his memoir, Rieff suggests that there was tension in his relationship with his mother, but he doesn't elaborate on it. "I have preferred to write as little as possible of my relations with my mother in the last decade of her life, but suffice it to say that they were often strained and at times very difficult" (160). It is a crucial revelation, or nonrevelation, one that shapes every aspect of his story. Unprepared to disclose these tensions, he implies that somehow he was an unworthy or undutiful son. This may explain, in part, the depth of his survivor guilt. All he can say is that "there are times when I wish I could have died in her place" (159). Realizing that this last statement is melodramatic, he nonetheless cannot express his feelings in any other way. Emotions are dangerous for them both; nowhere is Rieff more his mother's son than in his dismissal of feelings as "sentimental." Sontag's statement that "intellectualism" is an "instrument for the detachment from my feelings in the service of my mother" (*Reborn* 300) seems to be true of Rieff as well. There is never a moment when mother or son expresses love for the other. Sontag's last words to him, "I want to tell you . . . ," remain hauntingly incomplete (162).

In one of his most disturbing speculations, Rieff tells us that he does not believe his mother "could love a world without herself, much as the moralist in her would have despised herself for not doing so" (168). If this is true, then he must have realized that his mother's terror of death overwhelmed her love for him. Erik H. Erikson talks about the final stage of the life cycle that produces, in some people, "generativity," the "concern for establishing and guiding the next generation" (138). Generativity seems to be sadly lacking at the end of Sontag's life.

Rieff confesses that he did not know how to behave toward his mother as she lay dying. "Mostly, I felt at sea" (103), perhaps punning on the title of his memoir. Criticizing himself for his "clumsiness and coldness," he wishes he could have been a better person, then pauses, criticizing his self-criticisms: "But even to put my own failings at the center of this is a species of vanity" (103). Why is it vanity, however, to understand how his fraught relationship with his mother shapes his perception and narration of the story of her death? *Swimming in a Sea of Death* is as much about his life as it is about hers, and if he had a better understanding of his ambivalence toward her, he might not have been so guilt-ridden about her death. Sontag's demands during her illness may have been impossible for anyone to obey, for what she required, at the end, was nothing less than immortality.

Early in the memoir Rieff speaks about his mother's wish to "absorb" and her refusal to be "absorbed—and certainly not to be absorbed into eternity, into nothingness" (15). He implies that she wished to absorb him too—and that unless he distanced himself from her, he would be absorbed. According to biographers Carl Rollyson and Lisa Paddock, Rieff told a journalist that he had a "symbiotic" relationship with his mother. "In the end, separation was difficult and probably took too long" (55). Sigrid Nunez confirms this impression in her memoir *Sempre Susan,* suggesting that many people felt Sontag was too close to her son, never allowing him to have an independent existence. This helps to explain Rieff's struggle to care for his mother without losing his identity. She expected everyone to "buoy her up" (*Swimming in a Sea of Death* 124), and she became furious when they could not. Without using the word, Rieff alludes to his mother's sense of entitlement. "That neither I nor anyone else in her circle had any right to an opinion that, to the contrary, our factual opinions were quite literally valueless, never seems to have occurred to her" (129). Nor does Rieff use the word *narcissistic,* but that's how she comes across to him even before her illness. "My mother came to being ill imbued with a profound sense of being the exception to every rule" (144).

One of Rieff's most curious admissions is that during his mother's illness he decided to take no notes. "Perhaps no writer can escape the sliver of ice in the heart that is one of the professional deformations of their craft, but to the extent I could, I wanted no 'writerly' distance to separate or protect me emotionally from the reality of what was going on" (*Swimming in a Sea of Death* 106–7). Tellingly, the "deformations" that he associates with the profession of writing may be linked to being "deformed" by his childhood, implying that being the child of two professional writers who could not live with or respect each other somehow damaged his heart, the metaphorical center of his affective world. Notice how the meaning of the first part of Rieff's sentence has little logical connection to the second part. The "sliver of ice in the heart" may suggest the fear that writing about his mother's life and death will be "predatory and appropriative," the words he uses in *Los Angeles* to describe the kind of nonfiction he writes. Sontag viewed the writer, as well as the photographer, as predatory. If this is what Rieff means, he never questions how his mother would have felt if she knew he was planning to write a book about her.

Indeed, one of the most conspicuous questions Rieff fails to address is how he feels about writing a personal memoir of a writer who denounced autobiography. Would she have regarded the memoir as a betrayal of her privacy? The second part of Rieff's sentence, wanting "no writerly distance" to protect him emotionally, shifts the meaning away from his mother and onto himself. If he is metaphorically *Swimming in a Sea of Death*, feeling as if he is drowning, wouldn't he want writerly distance? Wouldn't his mother want her beloved son and colleague to remain strong, if only so he could care for her? He never tells us how he feels about writing the memoir. Is *Swimming in a Sea of Death* Rieff's "angry act"? Or is it, more positively, an act of reparation? Does Rieff believe, with Philip Roth, that in keeping with the "unseemliness" of the writer's profession, autobiography always involves breaking promises and betraying secrets? What exactly is Susan Sontag's legacy to her son?

While writing *Swimming in a Sea of Death*, Rieff was researching other books on death, but these readings apparently were not useful to him. "As I have written this memoir, I have been reading what other writers have said about death and it seems to me that few of them were any more resigned to extinction than my mother was" (153). His criticism here resembles his mother's complaint that literature offers no consolation for death. He cites Joan Didion several times, repeating her well-known line, "We tell ourselves stories in order to live" (38, 43). Unlike Didion, he doesn't emphasize the ways in which writing leads to meaning-making and self-understanding. Rieff remains skeptical about the value of knowledge, implying that nothing he read—or wrote—helped him.

Complicated Grief

Swimming in a Sea of Death reveals what clinicians call "complicated" (as opposed to "uncomplicated") grief, which is usually symptomatic of intense ambivalence toward the deceased. Pathological grief, according to Mardi Horowitz and his colleagues, is the "intensification of grief to the level where the person is overwhelmed, resorts to maladaptive behavior, or remains interminably in the state of grief without progression of the mourning process towards completion" (1157). What seems pathological, Horowitz contends, is not the "emotional or ideational content of a state but its intensity or prolongation" (1159). Rieff is never so overwhelmed that he cannot function or write, but he constantly second-guesses himself, worrying about what he did or did not do for his mother. *Swimming in a Sea of Death* is filled with self-doubt, self-recrimination, and self-reproach. The word *guilt*, which is repeated more than a dozen times, becomes a leitmotif; guilt, Rieff admits, is the "default position of the survivor" (177).

Rieff cites Simone de Beauvoir's 1964 memoir *A Very Easy Death*, though he misses an essential part of its meaning. Mme Beauvoir's physicians and family told her, even when she was close to death, that she had peritonitis instead of terminal cancer. Rieff recognizes that medical ethics have changed, and that physicians do not usually lie to their patients, as they did a few decades ago; nevertheless, he seems nostalgic about the past. "In some ways things were easier back in the days when doctors routinely lied to their patients about their prognoses, and sometimes about the actual nature of their illnesses as well, and when there was no Internet for a patient or a loved one to turn to in order to uncover the bad news for themselves" (124). Rieff would sympathize with many of de Beauvoir's responses to her mother's illness, including the assertion, "I was astonished at the violence of my distress" (25). He would also understand the daughter's feeling that she was also dying: "And I too had a cancer eating into me—remorse" (67). Like Sontag, Mme de Beauvoir did not want to die, even when racked with pain, and both mother and daughter experience the same rebellion against death. "Religion could do no more for my mother than the hope of posthumous success could do for me," de Beauvoir writes. "Whether you think of it as heavenly or as earthly, if you love life immortality is no consolation for death" (106). Despite these similarities, there is a striking difference between *Swimming in a Sea of Death* and *A Very Easy Death:* There is no doubt in de Beauvoir's mind that she should have told her mother the truth of her illness. "Because she had always been deceived, gulled, I found this ultimate deception revolting" (122). The irony is that unlike Mme de Beauvoir, Susan Sontag's entire life was a quest for truth, thus adding to Rieff's guilt over deceiving her.

Reframing Hope

Throughout *Swimming in a Sea of Death* Rieff spends much time debating with himself the meaning of hope, especially the kind of hope that should or should not be offered to the dying person. He usually contrasts hope not with its opposite, hopelessness, but with *truth*. He then mentions, only to reject it, a new meaning of the word *hope* that is not antithetical to *truth*. "Doctors who specialize in caring for the dying often use the expression 'reframing hope,' by which they mean helping mortally ill people find a way to shift from hoping to live to connecting in some final, profound way with their loved ones—saying what they had never said, asking what they had never dared ask" (152). Rieff doubts whether reframing comforts many terminally ill people. "I assume some are strengthened by it, though even in such cases I can't help feeling that 'hope' is far too strong and sentimental a word" (152). Hope becomes, in a revealing metaphor, a "poisoned chalice" (169).

Rieff doesn't mention by name any of the physicians who engage in reframing, but one example who comes to mind is Sherwin B. Nuland, whose gripping book *How We Die* is anything but sentimental. Nuland, who taught surgery at Yale, speaks about the hope that can exist even when rescue is impossible: "The greatest dignity to be found in death is the dignity of the life that preceded it. This is a form of hope we can all achieve, and it is the most abiding of all. Hope resides in the meaning of what our lives have been" (242). The reframing of hope also appears in *Signs of Life,* Tim Brookes's memoir about his experience volunteering at a hospice while his mother was dying from pancreatic cancer. "Hope invites clichés," he concedes, but he then asks us to go beyond platitudes. Once we let go of the long-term future, Brookes suggests, we can still hope for manageable joys: "A visit from an estranged son, the luxury of a guilt-free cigarette, some quiet afternoons dozing in a deck chair. Accepting finality can bring not only such quiet hopes but, in an unexpected way, a kind of truth, of freedom. Life, in fact" (33).

One can counter, cynically, that it is easy to offer hope if one is not dying. And yet there are writers who knew they were dying but who nevertheless affirmed the kind of hope that does not depend upon recovery. Anatole Broyard, the noted American literary critic and book reviewer for the *New York Times,* is one of these writers. Broyard admired *AIDS and Its Metaphors* and predicted that it would become a classic study of illness narratives. Broyard himself wrote *Intoxicated by My Illness,* which has become a classic. Broyard developed an aggressive form of prostate cancer in 1989 and died a year later at the age of seventy. In the book he describes storytelling as a "natural reaction to illness: People bleed stories, and I've become a blood bank of them" (20). Broyard calls stories "antibodies against illness and pain," and then, speaking personally, observes that "when various doctors shoved scopes up my urethral canal, I found that it helped a lot when they gave me a narrative of what they were doing. Their talking translated or humanized the procedure. It prepared, strengthened, and somehow consoled me. Anything is better than an awful silent suffering" (20).

Broyard had never been seriously ill before developing cancer, and his response to hearing the diagnosis of terminal illness was the opposite of most patients', including Sontag's. "I've been feeling exalted since I heard the diagnosis. A critical illness is like a great permission, an authorization or absolving" (23). Broyard had Sontag's illness books in mind when he wrote about the importance of style to the patient. "The illness genre ought to have a literary critic—in addition to or in reply to Susan Sontag—to talk about the therapeutic value of style, for it seems to me that every seriously ill person needs to develop a style for his illness. I think that only by insisting on your style can you keep from falling out of love with yourself as the illness attempts to diminish or disfigure you" (25). Unlike Sontag, who asserts in *Illness and Its Metaphor* that one should reject the belief that one is responsible for cancer, Broyard argues, counterintuitively, the opposite position: "If you reflect that you probably helped to bring your illness on yourself by self-indulgence or by living intensely, then the illness becomes yours, you own up to it, instead of blaming something vague and unsatisfactory" (29). The patient is then back in the driver's seat. Broyard's most startling injunction occurs when he refers to the British psychoanalyst D. W. Winnicott's unfinished autobiography. "The first paragraph simply says, 'I died.' In the fifth paragraph he writes, 'Let me see. What was happening when I died? My prayer had been answered. I was alive when I died. That was all I had asked and I had got it.' Though he never finished the book, he gave the best reason in the world for writing one, and that's why I want to write mine—to make sure I'll be alive when I die" (29–30).

Sontag and Rieff were surely familiar with *Intoxicated by My Illness,* since all three of them wrote for the *New Yorker* and were part of the New York literary establishment. It's surprising that Rieff does not mention another writer who was energized by the approach of death, Harold Brodkey, who also wrote for the *New Yorker.* Rieff refers to Bertolt Brecht, who affirms the "solace of art" in the presence of death, but he then denies the consolation of artistic immortality, the creation of a posterity self, for writers like his mother. The next-to-last paragraph of *Swimming in a Sea of Death* reveals Rieff's bitter disappointment with art, which is less a solace than a "mendacity" for him and his mother. "Art had always been my mother's solace, too. But not the least of the cruelties of her death was that what had sustained, inspired, and informed her life made it so much harder for her to die" (170).

Premeditation of Death

Swimming in a Sea of Death is filled with disturbing ironies and paradoxes. In the epilogue Rieff tells us about his mother's interest in memento mori, including a human skull she kept on her desk for decades alongside photos of her favorite writers. The skull may have been a counterphobic symbol of the need to keep death safely at bay, but it didn't work in her case. "Premeditation of death is premeditation of freedom," Montaigne wrote, and yet Sontag never achieved freedom from abject terror.

This is all the more surprising in light of Sontag's extraordinary artistic and intellectual achievements. She seems to be atypical here. In *Death and the Creative Life,* the psychologist Lisl Marburg Goodman argues that, based on her interviews with more than three hundred people, artists and scientists of high achievement tend to be less terrified of death than those of lower achievement. "With very few exceptions," she concludes, "both scientists and artists seem relatively at ease with their lives, including the prospect of death. Not only did their responses indicate a much higher level of having come to terms with death than those given by the majority of individuals in every other group; on a nonverbal level as well there emerges an unmistakable quality of ego-syntony, a feeling that one is in harmony with oneself and with one's environment. This sharply contradicts the stereotyped image of the complex, high-strung tense, highly creative individual" (127). Those people in Goodman's study who felt fulfilled in life were more accepting of death than those who felt unfulfilled. "But even more important, to know that one is doing all that one is equipped to do, to experience life as meaningful while one is still in the midst of it, may well take the sting out of death and liberate us from the fear that inhibits most people to strive toward self-actualization in the first place" (157). Goodman ends her book by quoting George Bernard Shaw's wry remark, "All is well that ends" (164).

What shall we finally say about *Swimming in a Sea of Death*? It is an unusual memoir, in many ways, an antimemoir. Rieff writes little about his relationship with his mother, his growth and development as a writer, his feelings about his absent father. Like his mother, he remains silent about many aspects of his life, which are off-limits to the reader. Unlike Philip Roth, he does not create a verbal portrait of a parent, either through dialogue or characterization. He never tells us what he and his mother hoped for or expected from each other. We learn almost nothing about how his mother felt toward him. Nor does he tell us how he felt writing a memoir about a woman who went out of her way to conceal her life from others. Did writing the memoir help him express a farewell to his mother, as Annie Leibovitz said about putting together a book of photographs of Sontag for her memorial service? "The project was important," Leibovitz writes, "because it made me feel close to her and helped me to begin to say good-bye."

What Rieff does tell us in *Swimming in a Sea of Death,* indeed, what he *shows* us on almost every page, is the striking disparity between Sontag's public and private lives. There's also a radical contrast between her living and dying. She was a great woman but a not-so-great mom. He offers details of her life that help us understand her complexity. Rieff remarks in *A Bed for the Night* that the "iconoclastic German Marxist Herbert Marcuse once quipped, 'If *The Facts* don't match the theory, so much the worse for *The Facts*'" (100). Rieff records many of these facts about his mother, no matter how unsettling they may be. Some critics, such as Jay Prosser, find these facts distressing. "What is most unbearable for the reader who turns from Sontag's work to her son's memoir is the gap between the ideals of her work and *The Facts* of her death" (202). And yet, more positively, Sontag comes across as a fascinating and contradictory figure who, like Jay Gatsby, was always trying to reinvent herself. "I consider myself somewhat posthumous," she observes ruefully (*Conversations with Susan Sontag* 151), perhaps anticipating her posterity self. She emerges, as Nietzsche might have observed, as human, all too human.

There is a striking disconnect between Sontag's writings and her life. She was not able to accept her death sentence as stoically as some of her fictional characters. During her breast cancer treatment, she claimed that she had "embarked on a great adventure," the "adventure of being ill and probably dying" (*Conversations with Susan Sontag* 109), but this was not true at the end of her life. She reminds herself in a 1950 diary entry that "death is as natural as birth—nothing lasts forever nor would we want to" (*Reborn* 67), yet she lost sight of this at the end.

Sontag's dying was both in and out of character. To the extent that she identifies with death-denying writers like Elias Canetti who found death unacceptable and unassimilable, her refusal to accept her terminal illness was in character. She died unreconciled to mortality. To the extent that she insists upon telling the truth to the terminally ill, her refusal to accept her terminal illness was out of character. As she writes in *Illness and Its Metaphors,* lying to the terminally ill, and the wish to be lied to, betokens the refusal to "touch the deepest dread" (8).

Rieff never mentions *Terra Infirma,* Rodger Kamenetz's memoir about his own mother's death, but he would have profited from reading it. There are many similarities between Rieff and Kamenetz: both are talented writers, the former a journalist, the latter a poet; both are secular Jews who cite the Talmud; both have difficulty separating from mothers who remained in denial about their terminal cancer; both feel they are dying while witnessing their mothers' deaths; both are haunted by loss and tortured by survivor guilt; both feel uncomfortable writing about dying, death, and bereavement; both cite poets and philosophers who have been obsessed with death; and both fear writing sentimental memoirs. "For what story is more sentimental than the death of a boy's mother," Kamenetz writes (2). The crucial difference between Rieff and Kamenetz is that the latter's mother finally accepted the reality of her illness, with positive consequences for both her and her son. "When the patient is forced to confront her own death, a dizzying perspective opens up; she stands on a cliff, and her loved ones stand beside her, looking down on the panorama of a life. It is breathtaking and produces a philosophical calm, as the Chinese sages knew who came to the mountains to die" (*Terra Infirma* 95).

Dread overwhelmed Sontag at the end of her life, and one wonders whether she would have been comforted not by a physician who was unable to cure her leukemia, but by a psychiatrist who could remind her that dread is part of the human condition. The existential psychiatrist Irvin Yalom has written about the primitive dread of death, "a dread that is part of the fabric of being, that is formed early in life before the development of precise, conceptual formulation, a dread that is chilling, uncanny, and inchoate, a dread that exists prior to and outside of language and image"

(45). Anne Harrington suggests that group therapy is often successful in helping terminally ill people confront the dread of death. Such therapy may not always extend the length of a patient's life, but it may increase the quality of life, helping them "live more authentically and fully, no matter how long or short the time they have remaining" (203–4). One cannot easily imagine Sontag in therapy, but Sigrid Nunez reports, unexpectedly, that in her early fifties Sontag began seeing a psychiatrist for depression: psychotherapy became one of her new enthusiasms.

After reading *Swimming in a Sea of Death,* we are left to ponder what should be revealed and concealed to the dying person. Are we, in fact, obligated not to speak about what is unacceptable, as the Talmudic proverb suggests? Should we seek to find a way to help the terminally ill hear what they probably already suspect? Is there somehow a middle position that involves neither lying nor telling the truth? Rieff never resolves the "loved one's dilemma," but his memoir is a cautionary tale about the problems caused by revealing too little. The memoir also shows what happens when, to use Broyard's words, the dying fall out of love with themselves.

In her play *Alice in Bed,* Sontag has Emily Dickinson observe, "One can't think about death steadily any more than one can stare at the sun. I think about it slant" (59). So, too, does Sontag think about death slant. When asked by a novelist, "What emotion do you write out of," Sontag replies, "Grief." Surprised by her answer, she adds, "I didn't know that's what I felt, but I realised that my writing comes out of a deep pessimism" (*Conversations with Susan Sontag* 219). And yet pessimism never prevented Susan Sontag from living intensely, and, until her final illness, she was able to swim in a sea of death with her characteristic courage, grace, and style.

CHAPTER 6

"Sleeplessness for Me Is a Cherished State"

Edward W. Said and *Out of Place*

⌒⌒⌒⌒⌒⌒⌒

ike Susan Sontag, Edward W. Said was one of the most influential literary theorists, culture critics, and public intellectuals
of his age. Born in West Jerusalem, Palestine, in 1935, he
attended prep school in Cairo and visited the United States for the first
time in 1948, during the Arab-Israeli War. An undergraduate at Princeton
and a graduate student at Harvard, he was appointed an assistant professor of English and comparative literature at Columbia in 1963, where he
was later promoted to University Professor, Columbia's most prestigious
position. His 1978 book *Orientalism* has become a foundational text in
postcolonial studies, revealing the long history of persistent Eurocentric
prejudice against the Middle East and Asia. Said was a polymath, fluent in English, French, and Arabic and conversant in several other languages; he was also an accomplished classical pianist and was the music
critic for the *Nation.* Academic superstar, prolific author, media celebrity,
and political activist, Said was the most visible and outspoken advocate
for the Palestinians, and from 1977 to 1991 he served on the Palestine
National Council, the PLO's parliament-in-exile. Among the most controversial American academics and activists in the last thirty years, he was
a polarizing figure inside and outside of academia.

Said was diagnosed with chronic lymphocytic leukemia in 1991, fourteen years before Sontag was diagnosed with blood cancer. Like her, he

was not known for personal writing. He preferred writing literary, cultural, political, and music criticism without revealing much about himself. Unlike Sontag, he never denied the seriousness of his illness; he knew that his leukemia was treatable but not curable. Terminal illness compelled him to write a life review in which he explored the psychological, moral, and cultural influences on his life. He began writing *Out of Place* in 1994 while recovering from three early rounds of chemotherapy. He remarks in the preface that his memory "proved crucial to my being able to function at all during periods of debilitating sickness, treatment, and anxiety," adding that his almost daily "rendezvous with this manuscript supplied me with a structure and a discipline at once pleasurable and demanding" (xi). Said completed the memoir in 1999 and died four years later at the age of sixty-seven.

Out of Place is a fascinating memoir, insightful, psychologically revealing, and startlingly honest. The book is not, strictly speaking, an end-of-life memoir, partly because it was not his last work, and partly because it ends in 1963, with the completion of his doctoral dissertation at Harvard. Said refers several times to his terminal illness, and his memoir is a record of his formative, or, as he would wryly describe it, his deformative years and the disease that will finally kill him. His major interest in *Out of Place* is not in describing illness but in showing how the events of his childhood and youth shaped his life and work. Unlike Harold Brodkey's *This Wild Darkness,* in which death is imminent, *Out of Place* portrays death as a future problem. Nevertheless, the memoir reveals the complex ways in which Said's heightened awareness of mortality influences his understanding of both past and present: his ambivalent relationships to his parents, both of whom died of cancer; his view of his own identity, or identities; his sense of dispossession, dislocation, and discontinuity; and his vision of literature and music, which he explored in a book aptly called *On Late Style,* published posthumously in 2006. Said died the way he lived, unable or unwilling to bring together the disparate elements of the self.

Said was sometimes confrontational in his political writings, but he was never an apologist for violence or terror. His loyalty to Palestine was never in question, but he often criticized Palestinian leaders for their political failures. He insisted that he was anti-Zionist but not anti-Semitic, not simply because Arabs are Semites but because he was opposed to all forms of prejudice. In 1999 he organized, with his close friend Daniel Barenboim, the West-Eastern Divan Orchestra, a summer workshop for young Arab and Israeli musicians. The acclaimed orchestra tours Europe, the Middle East, North America, and South America. "The name was derived," Rashid Khalidi points out, "from the poem by Goethe about the essential unity between East and West, and the Divan symbolized the ideas that Said always held about the essential humanity of both sides of this largely false dichotomy between East and West, and of both sides of the Palestinian-Israeli divide" (52).

Said remains a contradictory and paradoxical figure. He notes at the beginning of *Out of Place* the ambiguity of his name: his English name, Edward, and his Arabic surname, Said. Valerie Kennedy remarks in her critical study that Said is the "most significant but also the most contested figure in the domain of postcolonial theory" (147). In the beginning of his career he was associated with poststructural theory, but he gradually became critical of its antihumanist implications. He was one of the most honored and celebrated academics, lecturing at dozens of colleges and universities and receiving many prestigious literary prizes, but he always regarded himself as an outsider. He spent most of his life theorizing identity, and yet in an interview published in *Power, Politics, and Culture* he told Jacqueline Rose that he wanted to "reach out beyond identity to something else, whatever that is. It may be death. It may be an altered state of consciousness that puts you in touch with others more than one normally is. It may be just a state of forgetfulness which, at some point, I think is what we all need—to forget" (431). What makes this comment so puzzling is that Said spent most of his life theorizing identity; remained a secularist, interested in this life, not the next; and insisted in all his writings that one must never forget the past. What, then, did he mean about reaching out beyond identity?

Out of Place has been honored for its literary value, receiving the 1999 *New Yorker* Award for Nonfiction, but it has received little scholarly attention—perhaps because it is so personal. Edward Said scholarship has become a growth industry in the last three decades, occupying the attention of literary theorists, postcolonial scholars, culture critics, and political observers. And yet scholars have not explored the ways in which the specter of death changed Said's life and work.

"I Thought That My Days Were Numbered"

Said never hesitated to mention his medical situation, though few interviewers asked him for information about his health. He declared in a 1993 interview that he had a chronic blood disease—he did not specify it was leukemia—and that he feared he would not be able to complete *Culture and Imperialism.* "So, it was very important for me to finish, because for some months I thought (irrationally) I was going to die very soon. There was no objective evidence that I would die quickly, but I thought that my days were numbered, and they obviously are" (*Power, Politics, and Culture* 190). In a 1997 interview he stated that he was "quite ill and weak from the side effects of chemotherapy for leukemia" during his first visit to India. "But I was also exhilarated at the nonstop welcome that was everywhere in evidence, particularly among students, teachers, and journalists" (280). Work was the best therapy for Said, and he continued lecturing, teaching, writing, and traveling to the end of his life, dying in character.

Writing autobiographically while living with terminal illness allows a memoirist to make connections that might otherwise be impossible. These connections become sharper if one views life ironically, as Said does. "I recall with stunning clarity my father's early injunction against remaining in pajamas and dressing gown past the early-morning hours," he admits; "slippers in particular were objects of contempt. I still cannot spend any time at all lounging in a dressing gown: the combined feeling of time-wasting guilt and lazy impropriety simply overwhelms me" (*Out of Place* 105). How can a person who wrote two dozen books and who was a tireless political activist believe he is lazy? Few people accomplished as much as Said did. Nevertheless, he confesses that illness, "sometimes feigned, sometimes exaggerated" (105), helped him avoid the discipline demanded by his father.

As a youth Said worried excessively about his health. "I became the family joke for being especially gratified by, even soliciting, an unnecessary bandage on my finger, knee, or arm" (*Out of Place* 106). This observation occasions one of the most important insights in the memoir. "And now by some devilish irony I find myself with an intransigent, treacherous leukemia, which ostrichlike I try to banish from my mind entirely, attempting with reasonable success to live in my system of time, working, sensing lateness and deadlines and that feeling of insufficient accomplishment I learned fifty years ago and have so remarkably internalized" (106). Writing is a paradoxical act for Said, enabling him to call attention to death while simultaneously banishing the thought from his mind. Sometimes he wonders whether his single-minded devotion to work will help him triumph over cancer—though he knows this is wishful thinking.

Said was in London in early September 1991, attending a seminar he had convened of Palestinian intellectuals and activists, when he first learned about his diagnosis. His wife, Mariam, telephoned him from New York with the results of a blood test he had recently taken during his annual exam. Something in her voice alarmed him. He promptly telephoned his physician, who assured him that the results of the blood test could wait until he returned home. "I'm not a child, and I have a right to know," Said insisted. "With a whole set of demurrals—it's not serious, a hematologist can very easily take care of you, it's chronic after all— he told me that I had chronic lymphocytic leukemia (CLL), although it took me a week to fully absorb the initial impact of the diagnosis" (*Out of Place* 215). At the time he was asymptomatic, but after a New York City cancer center confirmed the diagnosis, Said reveals that it took him another month to understand "how thoroughly I was shaken by this 'sword of Damocles,' as one volubly callous doctor called it, hanging over me" (215). It is the same metaphor, we recall, that David Rieff uses in *Swimming in a Sea of Death*. A month after his diagnosis Said found himself in the middle of a letter he was writing to his mother. There was nothing unusual about writing to her—except that she had died eighteen months earlier.

Said writes to his deceased mother not because he believes they will be reunited in the next world—he is, as he often declared, a secularist— but because he felt a narrative impulse stirring in him. He contemplated several changes in his life, decided to remain living in New York City, and in 1992 took his family to his homeland, Palestine, which he had not visited in forty-five years. His oncologist, Dr. Kanti Ray, one of the two dedicatees of *Out of Place* (the other is Mariam Said), monitored him for more than a year without treatment, though he was told that sooner or later he would require chemotherapy. "By the time I began treatment in March 1994 I realized that I had at least entered, if not *the* final phase of my life, then the period—like Adam and Eve leaving the garden—from which there would be no return to my old life" (216). Two months later he began writing *Out of Place*.

Writing about Illness

Said admitted in an interview that he never planned to write a memoir and that he felt ambivalent about the genre. "I'm not a journal keeper," he remarks. "It was really something that both the disease and the death of my mother in 1990 sort of stimulated. Another purpose in doing it was that I wanted my children to have something to look at" (*Interviews* 179). Said knew, however, that he was writing for a much wider audience than simply his family. He was writing for himself, his family, and for future readers. He was creating, in short, a posterity self. Said's books are rigorously social, cultural, and political, including his studies of literature and music, but his primary focus in *Out of Place* is on the personal and psychological dimensions of his life, about which he was largely silent in his earlier books, including *After the Last Sky*, his 1986 memoir that documents Palestinian lives. The reader remains keenly aware throughout *Out of Place* that Said writes from the point of view of a cancer patient with a limited amount of time left.

Out of Place serves a double purpose for Said, allowing him to write about his life while at the same time grappling with the anxieties of cancer. Both tasks are similar, he suggests: "to write is to get from word to word, to suffer illness is to go through the infinitesimal steps that take you through from one state to another" (216). In his other work he went "across the illness" while in his memoir he was "borne along" it. He carried the manuscript with him wherever he went, so he could work on it during his treatments. The writing of the memoir and the phases of his illness "share exactly the same time, although most traces of the latter have been effaced in this story of my early life" (216). He writes about illness as both a patient and an observer. His body may be under siege, but his memory enables him to conjure up and analyze the distant past. He knows he must be "sharply alert, awake, avoiding dreamy somnolence." That's why he embraces sleeplessness. "I've thought in fact that this book in some fundamental way is all about sleeplessness, all about the silence of wakefulness and, in my case, the need for conscious recollection and articulation that have been a substitute for sleep" (217).

One of the most remarkable moments in *Out of Place* occurs when Said recalls the desperate homesickness he felt in 1952 when he traveled to the United State to study, leaving his mother, his room, and "Cairo's grace." He remembers suspending his feeling of "paralyzed solitude" to allow "another less sentimental, less incapacitated self to take over" (244). Tellingly, the ominous cancer diagnosis in the 1990s awakens the same feelings, paralyzed solitude, followed by the determination not to allow fear to incapacitate him:

> Forty years later a similar process occurred, when I had been diag-nosed with leukemia and discovered myself for a while almost com-pletely gripped by the grimmest thoughts of imminent suffering and death. My principal concern was how terrible it was to have to separate from my family and indeed from the whole edifice of my life, which in thinking about I realized I loved very much. Only when I saw that this dire scenario constituted a paralyzing block at the center of my consciousness could I begin to see its outlines, which helped me first to divine and then make out its limits. Soon I became conscious of being able to move this debilitating block off center, and then to focus, sometimes only very briefly, on other, much more concrete things, including enjoyment of an accomplish-ment, music, or a particular encounter with a friend. I have not lost the acute sense of vulnerability to illness and death I felt on discovering my condition, but it has become possible—so as with my early exile—to regard all the day's hours and activities (includ-ing my obsession with my illness) as altogether provisional. (244)

Past and present fuse suddenly here in a jarring epiphany worthy of a George Eliot novel or a Freudian case study. Just as Said was able to work through the paralyzing loss and separation of the 1950s, so does he resolve to live with the death sentence he received in the early 1990s. He doesn't invoke the repetition-compulsion principle, which Freud theorized in *Beyond the Pleasure Principle*, but we can see how Said attempts to master his fear by writing about it. He feels the same way about travel: he has, wherever he goes, a "secret but ineradicable fear of not returning," but he pushes himself to overcome anxiety. "What I've since discovered is that despite this fear I fabricate occasions for departure, thus giving rise to the fear voluntarily. The two seem absolutely necessary to my rhythm of life and have intensified dramatically during the period I've been ill" (217). One infers from all of his writings, including his first book, *Joseph Conrad and the Autobiography of Fiction*, that Said experienced life as "altogether provisional" from his earliest years. Terminal cancer only heightened this provisionality. We can also see that writing was for Said, as it was for Conrad, a way to overcome paralyzing solitude.

The Autobiography of Fiction and Criticism

Conrad was the writer with whom Said most strongly identified, and there were many similarities, temperamental and cultural, between them. Said does not discuss these commonalities in *Joseph Conrad and the Autobiography of Fiction*, but he does in his later books. The most obvious similarity is that both men lived their adult lives in exile, as Said suggests about Conrad in *Power, Politics, and Culture*. "He had this strange sort of exilic consciousness; he was always outside any situation he wrote about, and I feel that affinity with him" (246). So, too, does Said feel he is in exile, caught between the worlds of Palestine, Egypt, and the United States. Said is aware of the positive as well as the negative implications of being an outsider; in *Humanism and Democratic Criticism*, he argues that "only in that precarious exilic realm can one first truly grasp the difficulty of what cannot be grasped and then go forth to try anyway" (144). A second similarity between Said and Conrad is that they were inherently skeptical, questioning every aspect of reality. A third similarity is that they both wrote about the dark side of colonialism. And a fourth similarity is that both men turned to writing as self-rescue. "To Conrad, it seemed as if he had to *rescue himself*, and, not surprisingly, this is one of the themes of his short fiction" (*Joseph Conrad and the Autobiography of Fiction* 12). In *The World, the Text, and the Critic*, Said suggests that Conrad's writing "was a way of repeatedly confirming his authorship by refracting it in a variety of often contradictory and negative narrative and quasi-narrative contingencies" (109). Writing as rescue is one of Said's themes in *Out of Place*, as Linda Anderson realizes: loss "can be doubly abated through writing; as a form of reverie it is a psychic strategy to transcend the losses of the past, and to relieve the self of the unbearable anxiety of illness in the present" (168).

Many of Said's other statements about Conrad are also true about himself. "Conrad's inclination to look back with sorrow and shame at the course of his life" (*Joseph Conrad and the Fiction of Autobiography* 53), and his fear "that his rescue of himself would never come about directly as the result of one sustained effort" (62) also apply to Said, who keenly felt the Palestinians' sorrow and shame. The following observation also applies to Said: "as a Pole in Poland he would be irremediably lost, whereas in England, writing for the English, Conrad the foreigner would be forced to surmount his laziness and incompetence and to produce something" (62). This comment deepens our understanding of Said's observation in *Out of Place* about his "combined feeling of time-wasting guilt and lazy impropriety," a fear that remained with him his entire life.

In many ways *Joseph Conrad and the Autobiography of Fiction* is Said's own disguised autobiography. Consider, for example, this statement: "Writing and life were, for him, like journeys without maps, struggles to win over and then claim unknown ground. His personal struggle Conrad saw reflected in the political and historical developments around him. As the physical and moral geography of Europe changed, he changed too. And the cataclysm was just ahead" (63). Change Europe to Middle East and you have Said's situation. His dilemma was worse than Conrad's, for Said lived in an adopted country that refused to accept the Palestinians' homelessness and right to self-determination. Conrad never felt entirely at home in England and hated Russia for partitioning and ruling Poland, but Said was labeled the Professor of Terror by *Commentary* and was the target of death threats. Both men were racked by guilt and shame as a result of leaving their homelands. Said's shame was not only existential but, more significantly, political and cultural, watching helplessly as his friends were imprisoned or killed while defending their homeland. After the 1967 Middle East War, Said came to believe that, as a Palestinian, he and his people had suffered, almost inconceivably, at the hands of Israel and the United States. To resist their attempted submersion of his Palestinian identity became the guiding force for the rest of his life. Little wonder, then, that in his second book, *Beginnings* (1975), Said asserts that the literary critic is a "wanderer, going from place to place for his material, but remaining a man essentially *between* homes" (8). Said felt that he lived in a state of "in-betweenness," of perpetual rootlessness.

"She was Gertrude and Ophelia, I, Hamlet, Horatio, and Claudius"

Throughout *Out of Place* Said characterizes his mother, Hilda Said, as a beautiful and brilliant woman, fluent in several languages, who was "certainly my closest and most intimate companion for the first twenty-five years of my life." Even now, he feels "imprinted and guided by several of her long-standing perspectives and habits," including a "paralyzing anxiety about alternative courses of action" and a "chronic, mostly self-inflicted sleeplessness" (12). During his youth he was in an "enraptured state of precarious, highly provisional rapport" with her, which he attributes to her shifting feelings toward life and himself: "she had the most deep-seated and unresolved ambivalence toward the world, and me, I have ever known. Despite our affinities, my mother required my love and devotion, and gave them back doubled and redoubled; but she could also turn them away quite suddenly, producing in me a metaphysical panic I can still experience with considerable unpleasantness and even terror" (13). One moment empowering and the next moment intimidating, Hilda Said was the most formative personal influence on his life. "Later," Said adds sadly, "our relationship darkened a good deal" (13).

Hilda Said embodied conditional love. He allowed her moods to regulate his own, and he accepted her stern judgments of him. "No matter how close I was to her she could always reveal a mysterious reserve or objectivity that never fully explained itself but nevertheless exercised harsh judgment and was simultaneously dispiriting and maddening to me" (*Out of Place* 45). He could never understand as a youth what he and his siblings had done wrong when she made statements like "My children have all been a disappointment to me. All of them" (56). Nor can he understand as an adult. She was, in subtle ways, more dictatorial toward her children than her husband was. Said uses the word *manipulative* at least a half dozen times to characterize her. He also describes her as intrusive, inconsistent, and self-absorbed. She has a "controlling gaze" (178) that foreshadows, though Said does not make the connection, Foucauldian surveillance. Their relationship was always one-sided. "Yet as always there was something conditional about her wanting me with her, for not only was I to conform to her ideas about me, but I was to be for her while she might or might not, depending on her mood, be for me" (218).

Said remained deeply attached to her in his youth, and he implies that he was her favorite in the family. Because his father was much older than his mother and away much of the time, the mother-son bond became even more intense and problematic, like the one between Susan Sontag and David Rieff. Said describes in chapter three of *Out of Place* an event in early 1944 when the Shakespearean actor John Gielgud was coming to Cairo to perform *Hamlet*. Hilda Said suggested that she and her nine-year-old son read the play together before Gielgud's arrival. "She was Gertrude and Ophelia, I, Hamlet, Horatio, and Claudius" (51). "There must have been at least four, and perhaps even five or six, sessions when, sharing the book, we read and tried to make sense of the play, the two of us completely alone and together, for four afternoons after school, with Cairo, my sisters, and father totally shut out" (51–52). Said admits he "only half-consciously understood the lines" and that he had at the time no understanding of incest and adultery. He recalls that his mother's voice went up a pitch, acquiring a "bewitchingly flirtatious and calming tone" (52). Reading *Hamlet* with his mother "as an affirmation of my status in her eyes, not as someone devalued, which I had become in mine, was one of the great moments in my childhood" (52).

Curiously, Said doesn't comment on the Oedipal implications of the event, of which he surely must have been conscious while writing the memoir. Nor does he discuss the "family romance." Said knew a great deal about psychoanalysis, to which he was generally sympathetic; *Freud and the Non-European* is based on a 2001 lecture he delivered under the auspices of the Freud Museum in London. In *Beginnings* he makes an observation that highlights the Oedipal nature of the mother-son relationship. He tells us that Freud draws attention to a type of knowledge "so devastating as to be unbearable in one's sight, and only slightly more bearable as a subject of psychological interpretation." The act that produces this dark knowledge is incest, "which can be very correctly described as a tangling-up of the family sequence." Oedipus is not simply king, father, and husband but also "parricide, adulterous son, royal criminal, and national calamity." The "tangle of roles," Said continues, "resists ordinary sequential understanding, for the original author of the family line, the father, is murdered and his place usurped by the son." Oedipus is overwhelmed by the "burden of plural identities incapable of coexisting within one person." In such a case, Said concludes, "the image of a man conceals behind its facade multiple meanings and multiple determinations" (*Beginnings* 170).

Said did not kill his father, but he usurped his father's role in the family by becoming his mother's most intimate companion. However unaware he was of incest, literal or metaphorical, as a young boy, he was surely aware of it as a man, though he never explicitly admits the Oedipal nature of his relationship with his mother in *Out of Place*. To disclose that kind of knowledge publicly would be "unbearable." One way to avoid Oedipus's fate, Said generalizes in *Beginnings,* is through distance and detachment; another way is to acknowledge the plural identities of self-hood, including an "almost unbearably complex tangling of opposites" (170). Said uses both strategies in *Out of Place* to avoid Oedipus's fate.

Said closes chapter three of *Out of Place* by observing that it must have been the memory of those distant *Hamlet* afternoons in Cairo that made his mother become enthusiastic again during the last two or three years of her life, when she was suffering from cancer, to see *Antony and Cleopatra* with him in London. He recalls a passionate line from the play, "Eternity was in our lips and eyes, Bliss in our brows bent," and then he adds that they shared for the last time the "language and communion" despite the disparity in their ages and the fact that they were mother and son. "Eight months later she began her final descent into the disease that killed her" (*Out of Place* 53).

Hilda Said remains the most mysterious and elusive character in her son's life, as enigmatic in death as she was in life. He doesn't openly char-acterize her as emotionally unstable and fickle, but he implies this when he refers to her "fabulous capacity for letting you trust and believe in her, even though you knew that a moment later she could either turn on you with incomparable anger and scorn or draw you in with her radiant charm" (*Out of Place* 60). "But who was she really?" Said asks, then observes that unlike his impassive father, his mother was "energy itself, in everything, all over the house and our lives, ceaselessly probing, judging, sweeping all of us, plus our clothes, rooms, hidden vices, achievements, and problems into her always expanding orbit. But there was no common emotional space. Instead there were bilateral relationships with my mother, as colony to metropole, a constellation only she could see as a whole" (60).

Colony to metropole? How much significance should we attach to this metaphor? *Metropole,* from the Greek word metropolis, "mother city," implies a colonizing country. Said uses the word often in his writ-ings, particularly in *Culture and Imperialism,* where he observes that the "metropolis gets its authority to a considerable extent from the devaluation as well as the exploitation of the outlying colonial possession" (59). Comparing his mother to an imperialistic nation, and himself to a colony, is not something that Said would say lightly. In light of their conflicted mother-son relationship, it is reasonable to infer that his efforts to negotiate a safe distance from her, one that would not undermine his freedom, autonomy, and independence, contributed significantly to the direction of his future scholarship. *Orientalism* charts the West's construction of the East, the crude caricatures of the Islamic world; *Out of Place* explores the less obvious but no less significant tensions much closer to home, the fear that unless Said distanced himself from a potentially engulfing mother, his own identity would be overwhelmed.

And yet if it was necessary for Said to separate himself from his mother, he feared her separation from him. "As I look back over those years," he admits in the middle of *Out of Place,* "I can see the real anxiety induced in me by my mother's withdrawal, where the need to reconnect with her was kept alive paradoxically by the obstacles she placed before me. She had become a taskmaster whose injunctions I had to fulfill" (156). She was indeed a stern taskmaster, reminding him of his many failures and disappointments. Confessing to "some fairly obnoxious behavior" toward his sisters, he recalls his mother's anger toward him. "To her dying day my mother was a bilateralist; that is, she encouraged us to deal with each other through her" (173). He knew he needed to be more open to her, but also knew that it would make him more vulnerable to her manipulations.

Notwithstanding his efforts to the contrary, Said's interpretation of the mother-son relationship appears to be a product of adult thinking, influenced by his postcolonial theorizings. In a long interview he gave in 1992, later published in *Power, Politics, and Culture,* he was asked about the "autobiographical novel" he was writing about his youth, a novel that metamorphosed into *Out of Place.* His intention was to recreate the "Cairo-Jerusalem-Beirut axis" in which he grew up in a "pre-political way" (124–25). Whether he succeeded in avoiding this problem, however, is open to question. No matter how self-disciplined a writer may be, it's difficult if not impossible to think about early childhood experiences entirely from the child's point of view. Later experiences inevitably shape our recollection and understanding of the past.

Said has less to say about his mother in the second half of *Out of Place,* which is devoted to his education, but he returns to her in the last two pages of the memoir. She was racked by pain in the last few months of her life, when the cancer was spreading, and he supports her decision not to have chemotherapy, implying it was an act of courage. "Years later I was to have four wasting years of it with no success, but she never buckled, never gave in even to her doctor's importunings, never had chemotherapy" (294). This is one of the few times he is critical of his own medical treatment. During this time Hilda Said was unable to sleep despite sedatives, sleeping pills, and soothing drinks. "Help me to sleep, Edward," she once implored him with a "piteous trembling" in her voice that he can still remember. She slept all the time during the last six weeks of her life. "Waiting by her bed for her to awaken, with my sister Grace, was for me the most anguished and paradoxical of my experiences with her" (294). He doesn't suggest the possibility that his mother needed merciful sleep as a way to escape from irremediable pain and depression. In the last two paragraphs of *Out of Place* he mentions that his own inability to sleep may be her "last legacy to me, a counter to her struggle *for* sleep" (294). Equating sleep with death and loss of identity, he welcomes sleeplessness, which allows him to remain conscious of himself and existence. And though he doesn't explicitly state this, sleeplessness gives him the time to write.

"A Devastating Combination of Power and Authority"

Said's relationship with his father was conflicted for different reasons. "Whatever the actual historical facts were, my father came to represent a devastating combination of power and authority, rationalistic discipline, and repressed emotions; and all this, I later realized, has impinged on me my whole life, with some good, but also some inhibiting and even debilitating effects" (*Out of Place* 12). At the time of Said's birth, his father, Wadie, was at least forty, twenty years older than his wife. He taught his son the value of hard work, discipline, and persistence, qualities that allowed Wadie Said to succeed in the business world—he owned the largest office equipment and stationery business in the Middle East. In many ways he was a Horatio Alger figure, pursuing the dream of financial success: his motto was "never give up." But there was a more ominous side to the legacy the father bequeathed to his son. "I have no concept of leisure or relaxation and, more particularly, no sense of cumulative achievement" (12). The son often felt infantilized in the presence of his Kafkaesque father, stern, harsh, overbearing. "I called my father Daddy until his dying day, but I always sensed in the phrase how contingent it was, how potentially improper it was to think of myself as his son" (18).

Said's father embodied as many contradictions as his mother. "He managed to combine harshness, unreadable silence, and odd affection laced with surprising generosity which somehow never gave me enough to count on, and which until very recently I could neither dismiss as no longer threatening nor fully understand" (*Out of Place* 28). Wadie Said had at least two radically different personalities, one for home, the other for work; Said compares him to Wemmick in *Great Expectations*, another radically split character. Said never uses the word *traumatized* to characterize his childhood and youth, yet this is the impression we receive on page after page of *Out of Place*. He was not an orphan, like Pip in *Great Expectations*, but despite coming from a privileged family, he felt guilt and shame for his words and deeds. With his father's approval, his teachers shamed him for being an Arab and repeatedly caned him; he was made to feel inadequate and inferior wherever he went. He was constantly in a state of "disgrace," an "English word that hovered around me from the time I was seven" (58). He often felt like a coward because of his failure to confront his tormentors, particularly his father's massive authority.

In a scene that evokes Kafka's *Letter to His Father,* Said recalls his humiliation one chilly Sunday afternoon in 1949, at age fourteen, when he heard a loud knock on his bedroom door followed by his father's aggressive entry into his bedroom. "My father stood near the door for a moment; in his right hand he clutched my pajama bottoms distastefully, which I had despairingly remembered I had left in the bathroom that morning. I held out my hands to catch the offending article, expecting him as he had done once or twice before to scold me for leaving my things around." But the father's criticisms were worse than the son expected. " 'Your mother and I have noticed'—here he waved the pajama—'that you haven't had any wet dreams. That means you're abusing yourself' " (70). With his mother looking on in disgust, Said could only deny the accusation. "I was immediately seized with such terror, guilt, shame, and vulnerability that I have never forgotten this scene" (72). Later he reveals his parents' dissatisfaction with his body and the repeated physical "corrections" to which he was subjected. As late as 1957, when he graduated from Princeton, Said was forced by his father to wear a truss to correct his posture, one more humiliation he silently endured.

Wadie Said experienced serious medical crises in 1942 and 1948, and at a relatively early age his son feared the likelihood of his father's death. In 1961 Wadie Said had an operation to remove a mole that turned out to be melanoma; a biopsy revealed that it had metastasized. The diagnosis was devastating to Said, and he describes in detail imagining his father's body "being taken over by a dreadful, creeping invasion of malignant cells, his organs slowly devoured, his brain, eyes, ears, and throat torn asunder by this dreadful, almost miasmic, affliction" (257). Wadie Said's cancer was a turning point in his son's life, and he came to believe that his family's privacy had been permanently shattered. His assumptive world was also shattered, including his personal safety and well-being. He confronted a terror he had never experienced before, being utterly alone and defenseless. "It was as if the carefully constructed supports maintaining and nourishing my life were being suddenly knocked away, leaving me standing in a very dark void" (257).

Despite the fact that he "seemed to have died about half a dozen times" (258) during 1961, Wadie Said survived for another ten years. The illness affected the son almost as much as the father, for Said feared that he, too, was riddled with cancer and would suffer his father's fate. "Various dermal excrescences and lumps were self-diagnosed symptoms that the Harvard Health Service doctors routinely dismissed with marked exasperation. The overpowering depth of the link I felt to my father mystified me" (261). Said doesn't analyze his phobia here; surely he knew that cancer was not contagious. But cancer is contagious in another way: the fear and dread associated with cancer infect relatives, friends, and strangers alike. Said worried that his father's frightful fate would soon befall him. The fear must have been magnified years later when his mother developed and then succumbed to breast cancer.

Said's conflicted feelings toward his father, along with heightened awareness of his own mortality, provide the context for the first and only mention in his memoir of being in psychoanalysis. He reports experiencing an "epiphany" in a psychoanalytic session in which he complained about his father's attitude toward him. "I found myself shedding tears of sorrow and regret for both of us, and for the years of smoldering conflict in which his domineering truculence and inability to articulate any feeling at all combined with my self-pity and defensiveness kept us so far apart." Said was overwhelmed with emotion when in therapy he analyzed his feelings toward his father. "Perhaps, for oedipal reasons, I had blocked him, and perhaps my mother with her skill at manipulating ambivalence had undermined him." Twenty years after his father's death, Said "confronted with tears" his feelings about their stormy relationship, achieving in the therapist's office a "redemptive view" of the man who could never express his feelings toward him (*Out of Place* 261–62).

Said's brief discussion of psychoanalysis raises more questions than it answers. He doesn't tell us how long he was in psychoanalysis, the frequency of his analytic sessions, or the theoretical orientation of his analyst. Nor does he disclose whether psychoanalysis helped him understand other aspects of his life. His uncharacteristic use of the word *redemptive* suggests the magnitude of his forgiveness. From Said's chronology, it appears that he entered psychoanalysis around the time he learned about his own cancer diagnosis. He doesn't discuss whether psychoanalysis helped him cope with his terminal disease, nor does he reveal how he responded to his father's death in 1971.

In life Wadie Said often resembled a "marble statue," remaining silent when his son most needed help. His dying was sadly in character, Said implies, in a moving passage in which a childhood incident, when he was four years old, foreshadows the father's death. Said recalls "scampering along" behind his father, falling, scratching his hands and knees badly, and then instinctively calling out, "Daddy . . . please." His father stopped, turned around toward him, then resumed walking briskly, not saying a word. "That was all. It was also how he died, turning his face to the wall, without a sound. Had he, I wondered, ever really wanted to say more than he actually did?" (*Out of Place* 79). Said never answers the question, but he remains haunted by his father's death, which fills him with grief and guilt.

We learn in *After the Last Sky* that dispossession characterized Wadie Said's death as it had characterized his life. The family tried to honor his wish to be buried in Dhour el Shweir, the Lebanese mountain village that he had loved, but they could not buy a small plot in a local graveyard. The "still angry memory" prevents Said from describing the details of this "grotesque time." They were finally able to find a burial plot in a Christian Church, but even that fell through when the family received telephone bomb threats (172).

Writing *Out of Place* helped Said realize that he was split into two different people, the "Edward" who was a product of his parents' and teachers' upbringing, and the "non-Edward" who was in revolt. The non-Edward self is the one he identifies with his core, inner self. In his youth these two selves were separate and unintegrated, as if he were a multiple personality. "It was as if the integration and liberty I needed between my selves would have to be endlessly postponed, although I subliminally retained the belief that one day they would somehow be integrated" (202).

Said had a more positive relationship to his own children than his parents had to him, though tellingly, he uses the word *Oedipal* to describe his relationship with his son, Wadie E. Said. Perhaps the most controversial act in Said's life occurred when he threw a stone at an Israeli army post on the Lebanese border in the summer of 2000. Immediately prior to the incident, Said visited, with several other people, a deserted prison in which Arabs had been tortured. "The instruments of torture were still there, the electrical probes they used. And the place just reeked of human excrement and abuse. Words cannot express the horror, so much so that my daughter started crying, sobbing" (*Power, Politics, and Culture* 445). The group then traveled to the Lebanese border where there was a watchtower surrounded by barbed wire and concrete. His son and a few others in the group tried to see who could throw stones the farthest. "And since my son is a rather big fellow—he is an American who plays baseball—he threw furthest. My daughter said to me, 'Daddy, can you throw a stone as far as Wadie?' and that of course stirred the usual kind of Oedipal competition. So I picked up a stone and threw it" (446). The media distorted the significance of the event, which did little to dispel Said's reputation as an extremist.

"A Cluster of Flowing Currents"

At the close of *Out of Place* Said contrasts his mother's comalike sleep at the end of her life with his own sleeplessness, which for him is a "cherished state to be desired at almost any cost" (295). Shedding the "shadowy half-consciousness of a night's loss" is invigorating, not because of a fear of dying or death, but because sleeplessness is conducive to his creativity. He discloses in the penultimate paragraph that during his last chemotherapy treatment—a "twelve-week ordeal"—he fought bitterly the "induced somnolence" that he associates with being helpless and infantilized. "For me, sleep is death, as is any diminishment in awareness" (295). In the last paragraph he rejects the idea of a single, solid, unitary self and instead compares himself to a "cluster of flowing currents," a simile that suggests a postmodern theory of identity or personality—a kind of multiple personality. "These currents, like the themes of one's life, flow along during the waking hours, and at their best, they require no reconciling, no harmonizing" (295). This fluid, ever-shifting view of identity, always moving in different directions, like counterpoint in music, gives birth to a "form of freedom." He then adds the qualification that he would "like to believe" that this is indeed freedom though he is "far from being totally convinced" that it is. He ends the memoir with a sentence that captures perfectly the themes of cultural, psychological, geographical, musical, and medical dislocation: "With so many dissonances in my life I have learned actually to prefer being not quite right and out of place" (295).

Music

Classical music was always important to Said, never more so than at the end of his life. He loved to perform, listen to, and write about music. He penned four books entirely or largely about music: *Musical Elaborations, Parallels and Paradoxes: Explorations in Music and Society* (coauthored with Daniel Barenboim), *On Late Style: Music and Literature against the Grain*, and *Music at the Limits*. Said attributed his lifelong passion for music to his mother, to whom he dedicated *Musical Elaborations*, published in the year of her death. Mariam C. Said suggests in her preface to *Music at the Limits* that Glenn Gould's death in 1982 motivated her husband to write seriously about music. She offers several examples of how he sought out music when faced first with his mother's and then his own death. Sometimes the only way he could endure his mother's illness was to "drown himself in the sounds of magnificent, beautiful music—no doubt a reminder of his childhood with her" (xii). Music became his constant companion once he was diagnosed with cancer. He told his wife three months before his death the music he wanted to be played at his funeral. "I realized that he was telling me that this was the beginning of the end and that he was dying" (xiii).

Living with Terminal Illness

In a 1997 interview Said disclosed that although his health is "moderate to poor," he has learned to live with illness and not think about it all the time. "That is the great lesson: to be able to just focus on what one is doing and to live in a day, rather than to worry about tomorrow and say 'How will I be tomorrow? Can I do this tomorrow?'—that kind of thing. I've learned a new kind of discipline, which is necessary. So I feel optimistic most of the time. I don't feel depressed. I mean I'm going to die, but of course everyone dies. And to be able to face it provides a certain kind of calm" (*Interviews* 136). In a 1999 interview he spoke about having chemotherapy and radiation treatments in 1994 that "led to various kinds of infections and debilitating consequences which, during 1997 and 1998, were very, very difficult for me" (*Interviews* 177). In the mid-1990s he discovered that he had a rare form of blood cancer, refractory leukemia, which resists all the known chemotherapy treatments. In 1998 he had a twelve-week experimental treatment, involving a monoclonal antibody, which left him sick the entire time, but the treatment resulted in a temporary remission. In a 2000 interview Said commented on the irony of being a Palestinian treated at Long Island Jewish hospital by an Indian physician, an American Indian assistant, and Irish nurses. "It's lovely. I feel like a privileged person. I consider myself the longest serving inmate of that particular institution, having been in treatment for seven or eight years. They are very kind to me. I love being in their hands. I don't like being there. I wish I wasn't. But if one has to be there, that's a very good place to be" (*Culture and Resistance* 64). Said's wry humor and gratitude are striking.

Said could not wish away his illness, but there were times when it conferred certain benefits, as he discloses in a 2002 essay called "Slow Death: Punishment by Detail" that later appeared in *From Oslo to Iraq and the Road Map*. Amid the pain and discomfort of illness and treatment there are "intermittent passages of lucidity and reflection that sometimes give the mind a perspective on daily life that allows it to see things (without being able to do much about them) from a different perspective" (194). Illness confers one more benefit on Said: it released him from onerous political responsibilities. Soon after becoming ill, he telephoned Christopher Hitchens "quite happily" with the news that he had resigned his position on the Palestine National Council. "It was almost as if the

intimation of mortality had emancipated him from the everyday require-
ments of party-mindedness and tribal loyalty," Hitchens reports in his
memoir *Hitch-22*, adding, "I have sometimes noticed in other people
that a clear-eyed sense of impending extinction can have a paradoxically
liberating effect, as in: at least I don't have to do that anymore" (395).

After being diagnosed with leukemia, Said asked Hitchens whether he
thought it was a good idea to speak to Susan Sontag. "I thought definitely
yes, if only because they would have so much else to discuss" (Hitchens 395). Said and Sontag had dinner together, though Hitchens did not
know what they talked about. Sontag was diagnosed with blood cancer in
2004, a year after Said's death. Had she developed blood cancer around
the time that he did, we can only wonder whether his courage and forth-
rightness in acknowledging his terminal illness might have helped her
during the final months of her life.

Unlike most cancer patients, Said made few concessions to illness.
Nowhere in his published writings does he speak about making preparations for death, relinquishing his many scholarly responsibilities, making
major social and personal adjustments, or bidding farewell to family and
friends, activities that are common in the last year of life, as Allan Kellehear points out in *Dying of Cancer*. Leukemia became a chronic disease
that Said learned to live with, and while he mentions in several interviews
feeling sick from treatment, he was always able to resume work. But there
were certainly times when illness and treatment sharply limited his activities. William Spanos quotes two of Said's emails that convey exhaustion.
In the first email, dated May 23, 2002, Said writes about his willingness
to give the commencement address the following month at Mount Her-
mon, a prep school in Massachusetts from which he had graduated. "I'm
just coming out of the first cycle of a horrendously complicated and rigorous protocol that will go on through October. I won't bother you with
the details, but I can write and read, and have no energy now to do much
else" (Spanos 229). Illness did not prevent Said from asking Spanos about
his own health problems. By May 30, Said's health had dramatically
worsened, and he sent another email indicating he was too sick to deliver
the speech. This email conveys more graphically than any other published writing the depth of Said's physical and psychological suffering.
"I'm crushed, I was at the hospital yesterday since over Mem day I developed a very high fever, chills, shaking, etc. I now have pneumonia and
my state is very fragile. My doctor has grounded me till August at least, a

crushing blow, but since I've had three life-threatening pneumonias in the last three months, it's pretty ominous and has discouraged me for the first time since I began treatment 8 years ago" (Spanos 230).

And yet once again Said recovered and continued with his usual activities. Jacqueline Rose reports visiting Said in his apartment, in late September 2003, four days before his death, to give him some of her writings. "I will read them," he promised. The next day he was hospitalized. Referring to Said in the second person, Rose records her shock over his death. "I had held back in the blithe belief that our dialogue would be endless, that having defeated your illness so many, many times before, you would go on doing so forever" ("The Question of Zionism" 319).

Late Style: "Confronting the End"

Mortality hovers over *On Late Style*. At the time of his death Said was writing his book on artistic lateness and working on several other books as well: *Humanism and Democratic Criticism*, the last book he completed, and *From Oslo to Iraq* and the *Road Map*. The idea for *On Late Style* came to Said in the late 1980s before his cancer diagnosis. Editing the manuscript, Michael Wood observes that Said's interest in late style was never "merely autobiographical. Thoughts of his own death deepened his attachment to the question of late style; they didn't instigate it" (xvii). Nowhere in *On Late Style* does Said disclose his own ill health. Why? He may have felt that he had revealed everything he wanted to write on the subject in *Out of Place*, especially if he believed he had several more years ahead of him. He may have also feared that readers would be distracted by the autobiographical implications of his thesis. He does make one veiled comment, however, at the beginning of *On Late Style*: "I come finally to the last great problematic, which for obvious personal reasons is my subject here—the last or late period of life, the decay of the body, the onset of ill health or other factors that even in a younger person bring on the possibility of an untimely end" (6).

What constitutes late style for Said? It's easier to say what he is not interested in. Defining himself in the beginning of the book as a "profoundly secular person" (*On Late Style* 4), he excludes from discussion religious, spiritual, or existential issues. Nor is he interested in how terminal illness and impending death shatter literary writers' and composers' assumptive worlds. Instead, he focuses on the artist's inability or unwillingness near the end of life to resolve, reconcile, or harmonize inner tensions. He concedes that some late works may reflect a new spirit of reconciliation or serenity not found in their earlier writings. This is one type of artistic lateness, but he is interested in a second type, one that involves a "nonharmonious, nonserene tension and above all, a sort of deliberately unproductive productiveness going against . . ." (7). Alluding to *King Lear*, Said suggests that the kind of late style in which he is interested does not produce the "serenity of 'ripeness is all' "—a strange example to cite, since the raging Lear is hardly serene. Rather, the late works he seeks to understand reveal "intransigence, difficulty, and unresolved contradiction" (7)—works that resemble, by implication, *Out of Place*.

Said discusses several composers, writers, and performers in *On Late Style*, including Mozart, Richard Strauss, Benjamin Britten, Jean Genet, the Italian novelist Giuseppe Tomasi di Lampedusa, the Greek Alexandrian poet Constantine Cavafy, and Glenn Gould, his favorite pianist. It is mainly the late Beethoven, however, who stimulates his interest in artistic lateness. Said turns to Theodor Adorno, the influential early twentieth-century German philosopher, for guidance. Adorno had used the phrase "late style" in an essay fragment on Beethoven, dated 1937, which was first published in a collection of music essays in 1946 and then published posthumously in a book on Beethoven in 1993. (Adorno died in 1969.) Said does not point out the irony of an essay on late style that came to the public's attention mainly in a posthumous book—an irony that applies to Said's own posthumous book.

Said embraces Adorno's view of late Beethoven, whose last compositions constitute an event in the history of modern culture: "a moment when the artist who is fully in command of his medium nevertheless abandons communication with the established social order of which he is a part and achieves a contradictory, alienated relationship with it. His late works constitute a form of exile" (*On Late Style* 7–8). Said agrees with Adorno that we see not only heroism but also intransigence in Beethoven's third and final period, an intransigence that cannot be explained biographically. Late style is what happens if art does not "abdicate" its rights in favor of reality. Said then quotes approvingly a passage from Adorno's essay on Beethoven, including the observation that "Death is imposed only on created beings, not on works of art, and thus it has appeared in art only in a refracted mode, as allegory" (9).

The late artist, in Said's view, rejects or defies the reader's or audience's expectations and thus chooses not to die in character, at least not in his or her art. Late art, then, is neither denial or acceptance, in Kübler-Ross's terms, but defiance. Said's endorsement of late style reveals a highly romantic view of artistic creativity in which the artist heroically defies the inevitability of death. For Said and Adorno, Beethoven's late works "communicate a tragic sense in spite of their irascibility" (*On Late Style* 11). There is no acceptance or transcendence in this vision of artistic lateness, no coming to terms with death. Rather, there is an "inherent tension in late style that abjures mere bourgeois aging and that insists on the increasing sense of apartness and exile and anachronism, which late style expresses and, more importantly, uses to formally sustain itself" (17).

Perhaps only a musicologist can evaluate the accuracy of Said's and Adorno's interpretation of late Beethoven, but we can see a parallel between Said's belief that Beethoven refuses to resolve conflicts and contradictions in his late compositions and Said's similar refusal to resolve conflicts and contradictions in his late-work memoir, *Out of Place*. Both Beethoven and Said refuse to let death into their musical and literary works, respectively. The two men know they are going to die—resistance to or denial of death is ultimately futile—but they try to keep alive inner tensions. There are other parallels between Said's interpretation of late Beethoven and his own vision of life. "Beethoven's late works remain unreconciled, uncoopted by a higher synthesis: they do not fit any scheme, and they cannot be reconciled or resolved, since their irresolution and unsynthesized fragmentariness are constitutive, neither ornamental nor symbolic of something else" (*On Late Style* 12). Said never resolves the "cluster of flowing currents" of his life that "require[s] no reconciling, no harmonizing" at the end of his memoir. The "increasing sense of apartness and exile and anachronism" in late Beethoven appears throughout *Out of Place*. Dying in character requires Said to reject any attempt to seek comfort in art. No less than the late artist, the late critic and theorist, in his view, seek discomfort. Quoting Adorno, Said ends *On Late Style* with the observation that in the "history of art late works are the catastrophes" (160). Whether Said regarded his own late writings as catastrophes is impossible to say, but there is little doubt that he viewed himself at the end as unreconciled to the inevitability of death, forever in exile and out of place.

"Writing Becomes a Place to Live"

The one place Said always feels at home is in his writing. "For a man who no longer has a homeland," he declares in *Reflections on Exile and Other Essays*, "writing becomes a place to live" (568). For Said, writing is both a place and a process. Writing *Out of Place* allows him to tell the story of his early life and to make sense of that life in ways that his earlier writings failed to do. "It wasn't until the early fall of 1991, when an ugly medical diagnosis suddenly revealed to me the mortality I should have known about before, that I found myself trying to make sense of my own life as its end seemed alarmingly nearer" (*Reflections on Exile and Other Essays* 555–56). Though he was, by his own admission, a "compulsive worker," he had never tried to put the "whole jumble" of his life together. Writing *Out of Place* helps him do that.

Out of Place leaves us with many perplexing questions. How was it possible for Said, victimized in so many ways by his parents, to become a champion for the displaced other? It would have been far more likely for him to turn out like his parents, fighting to maintain their embattled privileged position. How did he achieve such insight into the ambiguous legacy they bequeathed to him? How was he able to overcome decades of anger and bitterness toward his mother and father to write about them with such clarity and compassion? From where did his forgiveness arise? How was he able to prevent the hypochondria he experienced as an adolescent and college student, or the terror arising over his father's cancer diagnosis, from resurfacing after his own cancer diagnosis? How was it possible for Said to hold together the warring antinomies of his self without suffering a major psychological breakdown, as his father did early in his career?

Surely there must have been times when these warring antinomies threatened to fragment. Even Said recognized the need for self-integration. He admits in *Reflections on Exile and Other Essays* that in 1972, after he spent a sabbatical year in Beirut studying Arabic philosophy and literature for the first time, he felt that he had allowed the "disparity between my acquired identity and the culture into which I was born, and from which I had been removed, to become too great." He concludes that there was an "existential as well as a felt political need to bring one self into harmony with the other" (561).

And yet inner harmony proved elusive to Said. In the afterword to

From Oslo to Iraq and the Road Map, Wadie E. Said reports that his dying father remained haunted by Palestine. "Indeed, it still pains me to remember that in his last full day of consciousness and alertness, prior to succumbing to his illness, my father was overcome by emotion because he felt that he had not done enough for the Palestinians. All present at this extraordinary scene were dumbfounded: if Edward Said had not done enough for Palestine, then what have we done?" (302).

Said remains in death as controversial as he was in life. Even his burial place remains paradoxical, as Ella Shohat suggests. "That Said's final resting place is in Broummana, Lebanon, rather than either New York, where he lived for decades, or Jerusalem, where he was born, provides a suitably troubled and inconclusive allegory to the equally ruptured voyages of his ideas across national borders" (41). There is no doubt that Said's ideas, however ruptured, have spread across national borders. Tony Judt, not given to extravagant praise, begins his foreword to *From Oslo to Iraq and the Road Map* with a striking assessment of Said's achievement: "When Edward Said died in September 2003, after a decade-long battle against leukemia, he was probably the best-known intellectual in the world" (vii).

Out of Place celebrates not only the irreconcilable elements of Said's character but also his capacity for self-reflection, self-criticism, and self-affirmation. In reaching out "beyond identity," as he told Jacqueline Rose in *Power, Politics, and Culture,* he sought to discover the psychic disruptions and dissonances between the individual and society that can never be resolved. Nothing is out of place in his masterful memoir. Though he didn't know how much time he had left in writing his story, he cut no corners. Before his diagnosis he wrote about fictional and historical characters; after his diagnosis he wrote about his own evolving character. The story of his own life is as intriguing and improbable as that in any novel. He achieves in the memoir a unique voice that is extraordinarily sensitive to the complexities of life, his own and others as well. Had he been more ideological, his memoir would have been less compelling. He examines his life with an unflinching honesty and candor that never fail to impress the reader, and he never allows terminal illness to darken his story. *Out of Place* is an impassioned account of a groundbreaking scholar-activist whose pursuit of truth and social justice continued to the end of his life.

CHAPTER 7

"There Is More Than One Sort of Luck"
Tony Judt and *The Memory Chalet*

*I*t might be thought the height of poor taste to ascribe good fortune to a healthy man with a young family struck down at the age of sixty by an incurable degenerative disorder from which he must shortly die." Judt's sardonic observation in *The Memory Chalet* cannot fail to startle us. How can anyone feel fortunate to be in his situation? The answer, he explains, is that there is more than one sort of luck. "To fall prey to a motor neuron disease is surely to have offended the Gods at some point, and there is nothing more to be said. But if you must suffer thus, better to have a well-stocked head: full of recyclable and multipurpose pieces of serviceable recollection, readily available to an analytically disposed mind" (13–14).

As it turns out, Judt has much more to say, and it is all fascinating to read. Most people in his situation would hardly refer to themselves as the beneficiary of good luck. If a person has the "good fortune" to suffer from amyotrophic lateral sclerosis (ALS), Lou Gehrig's disease, unable to walk, talk, write, or even move, what would bad fortune involve? Judt doesn't exactly raise this question, but he would probably say that bad luck means losing the ability to think, remember, imagine—and write. He truly had the good fortune to remain creative to the end of his life. And his good fortune is also ours.

Born in London in 1948 to Jewish parents, Judt was the first person in his family to complete secondary school, much less attend college, and he was proud of his roots—or rootlessness, since he lived in so many places on both sides of the Atlantic. Diagnosed with ALS in 2008, when he was sixty years old, he began writing his end-of-life memoir a few months into the disease. It was in character for him to write during the last two years of his life, for he had spent his entire career reading, writing, and teaching. Educated at King's College, Cambridge, and the École normale supérieure, Paris, Judt taught at Cambridge, Oxford, and Berkeley before being appointed the Erich Maria Remarque Professor of European Studies at New York University, where he served as the chair of the History Department and as Humanities dean. The author or editor of fourteen books, Judt wrote on a wide variety of subjects spanning history, politics, Marxism, French intellectuals, social justice, and current events. He was a frequent contributor to the *New York Review of Books, The Times Literary Supplement,* the *New York Times,* and the *New Republic.* A historian rather than a creative writer, Judt had never written autobiographically. He knew he had no time to waste in writing his story. His disease progressed quickly, and he completed *The Memory Chalet* in 2010, the year of his death.

Judt tells us in the opening chapter of *The Memory Chalet* that soon after his diagnosis he began writing entire stories in his head during the course of the night. "Doubtless I was seeking oblivion, replacing galumphing sheep with narrative complexity to comparable effect. But in the course of these little exercises, I realized that I was reconstructing—LEGO-like—interwoven segments of my own past which I had never previously thought of as related" (5–6). Toward the end of *The Memory Chalet* he refers to his friend Edward Said. Judt doesn't mention *Out of Place,* but like Said, he put to good use his many sleepless nights.

The "Memory Chalet"

Beyond telling us that he dictated *The Memory Chalet,* Judt doesn't elaborate on the physical challenges of writing while paralyzed, but he does reveal how he uses a unique storage and filing system to help him recall the experiences and descriptions contained in the story. As he explains, the word *chalet* evokes the small *pensione* that he and his family visited during winter vacations in the Villars ski region in Switzerland in the late 1950s. These vacations occurred more than fifty years ago, but he still recalls nostalgically the many happy details of the hotel, its rooms, bar, dining room, lounge, furniture, and even random collection of books. Long fascinated by the mnemonic devices used by travelers to recall their odysseys, he remembers reading Jonathan Spence's *The Memory Palace of Matteo Ricci*, an account of an Italian traveler to medieval China. Judt has no interest in constructing in his head an imposing palace, but he is intrigued by the possibility of using the Swiss *pensione* of his childhood as a memory chalet to write his life story:

> The advantage of a chalet lay not only in the fact that I could envisage it in very considerable and realistic detail—from the snow rail by the doorstep to the inner window keeping the Valaisan winds at bay—but that it was a place I would want to visit again and again. In order for a memory palace to work as a storehouse of infinitely reorganized and regrouped recollections, it needs to be a building of extraordinary appeal, if only for one person. Each night, for days, weeks, months, and now well over a year, I have returned to that chalet. I have passed through its familiar short corridors with their worn stone steps and settled into one of two or perhaps three armchairs—conveniently unoccupied by others. And thence, the wish fathering the thought with reasonably unerring reliability, I have conjured up, sorted out, and ordered a story or an argument or an example that I plan to use in something I shall write the following day. (*The Memory Chalet* 6–7)

The Memory Chalet consists of twenty-five feuilletons, or installments, each reflecting on a chapter or aspect of Judt's life. The twenty-five essays arise from the "nocturnal visits" to his memory chalet. The most intriguing essays are the first one, "The Memory Chalet," which describes how he arranges his thoughts at night so that he can retrieve them in the morning; "Night," in which we learn about the circumstances of his writing (or dictating); "Mimetic Desire," where he expounds on the romance of trains; "Joe," an account of his life on an Israeli kibbutz where he practiced "muscular Judaism"; "Revolutionaries," a discussion of his brief enchantment with the utopian clichés of the late 1960s; "Meritocrats," in which he reveals his controversial views on higher education; "Words," where he conveys his faith in articulate prose; "Midlife Crisis," where he discloses how his decision to learn Czech transformed his teaching and scholarship; "Girls, Girls, Girls," am amusing account of his rejection of political correctness and gender politics; and "Edge People," where he describes his suspicion of identity politics.

The book jacket accurately refers to *The Memory Chalet* as a "memoir unlike any you have ever read," but oddly enough, Judt never uses the word *memoir*. He admits in the first essay that he doesn't know how to describe the "sort of genre" of the book: the feuilletons convey an impressionistic effect. "The little histories that take shape in my head as I lie sheathed in nocturnal gloom are unlike anything I have written before" (11). That may be true, but being a historian of the postwar world has given him the training and practice to interrogate the events of his life. Rereading *The Memory Chalet,* he is struck by the person he never became—until now. "Many decades ago I was advised to study literature; history, it was suggested to me by a wise schoolmaster, would play too readily towards the grain of my instincts—allowing me to do what came easiest. Literature—poetry in particular—would force me to find within myself unfamiliar words and styles to which I might yet discover a certain affinity. I can hardly say that I regret not following this advice: my conservative intellectual habits have served me well enough. But I think something was lost" (12).

"A Modern-Day Mummy"

Judt saw himself as a historian, not a creative writer, committed to objective rather than subjective truth. In his last book, *Thinking the Twentieth Century*, a series of conversations with his close friend and fellow historian Timothy Snyder, Judt makes a colorful distinction between memory and history. "Memory is younger and more attractive, much more disposed to seduce and be seduced—and therefore she makes many more friends. History is the older sibling: somewhat gaunt, plain and serious, disposed to retreat rather than engage in idle chit-chat. And therefore she is a political wallflower—a book left on the shelf" (276–77). Despite this distinction, he melds memory *and* personal history in an engaging book that is not likely to be left on the shelf.

By writing literature, Judt gains a personal voice attuned to the expected and unexpected challenges of writing under nearly impossible conditions. His intelligence, wit, and grit never fail him, even as he chronicles his body's increasing failure. "ALS constitutes progressive imprisonment without parole," he informs us at the beginning of the second chapter, "Night." Showing instead of telling, he helps us to visualize his death sentence. "Having no use of my arms, I cannot scratch an itch, adjust my spectacles, remove food particles from my teeth, or anything else that—as a moment's reflection will confirm—we all do dozens of times a day" (*The Memory Chalet* 16). Being prepared for bed each night is like being prepared for death. He is first rolled into the bedroom in the wheelchair in which he has spent the last eighteen hours, then maneuvered into his cot and wedged into place with folded towels and pillows. His left leg is "turned out ballet-like" to prevent it from collapsing inward. The entire process requires concentration. "If I allow a stray limb to be misplaced, or fail to insist on having my midriff carefully aligned with legs and head, I shall suffer the agonies of the damned later in the night." He's covered, his hands placed outside the blanket but nevertheless wrapped because they are always cold, and then he is offered a "final scratch on any of a dozen itchy spots from hairline to toe." A breathing tube is carefully placed in his nose, and his glasses are removed. And there he lies: "trussed, myopic, and motionless like a modern-day mummy, alone in my corporeal prison, accompanied for the rest of the night only by my thoughts" (17–18).

Judt's thoughts about his cockroach-like existence remind him of Kafka's story *The Metamorphosis*. Like Gregor Samsa, he realizes that even his closest relatives and friends are unable to understand his isolation and imprisonment. "Helplessness is humiliating even in a passing crisis" (20). Judt never seriously contemplates suicide, but he cannot banish the possibility from his mind, as he hints at parenthetically. "Imagine the mind's response to the knowledge that the peculiarly humiliating helplessness of ALS is a life sentence (we speak blithely of death sentences in this connection, but actually the latter would be a relief)" (20). Nietzsche's wry consolation—"the thought of suicide can get one through many a long night"—is not an option for Judt, since he is physically unable to end his life.

Judt's nights are worse than his days because he has no one to speak to when he cannot sleep. Writing at night helps to pass the time, but it would be wrong, he cautions, to overstate the pleasure. He has little patience for the well-meaning who try to rationalize his death-in-life existence. "That way lies futility. Loss is loss, and nothing is gained by calling it a nicer name. My nights are intriguing; but I could do without them" (21). Nevertheless, the idea of writing remains a lifeline for him, a solace, a way of getting through the day and night.

Judt never sugarcoats his situation, but the sensation of horror and dread appears only momentarily in *The Memory Chalet,* and it is not the dominant mood of the story. We don't know whether he has decided not to brood over the horror of his situation—that way lies madness—or whether his memory and imagination enable him to transcend horror. Do those who, like Judt, find themselves physically paralyzed regard their body as the repository of the self, or are they able to separate self from body? Judt never dwells on this age-old philosophical question, but there is no doubt that he regards his memory and mind as intact and trustworthy, able to function despite the nightmare of paralysis.

In a race against time, Judt finds himself losing control of his words. "They still form with impeccable discipline and unreduced range in the silence of my thoughts—the view from inside is as rich as ever—but I can no longer convey them with ease" (*The Memory Chalet* 153). Vowels and consonants slide out of his mouth, inaudible even to the person who is trying to capture his words. Communication, once his strongest asset, is now his weakest. Soon he shall be confined to the "rhetorical landscape of my interior reflections" (154). Ironically, the more he loses the power of speech, the more critical he is of those who use garbled language. Like George Orwell, whose essay "Politics and the English Language" he cites approvingly, Judt recognizes that clear speech reflects clear thinking, both of which are necessary in a democracy. Whereas Orwell believed that people misuse language to deceive or mystify, Judt maintains that shoddy prose is now symptomatic of intellectual insecurity: "we speak and write badly because we don't feel confident in what we think and are reluctant to assert it unambiguously" (153). His hope for the future depends on an educated citizenry who will not retreat into mystification or obfuscation. "No longer free to exercise it myself, I appreciate more than ever how vital communication is to the republic: not just the means by which we live together but part of what living together means" (154).

Tony Judt and Edward Said

There are many parallels between Tony Judt and Edward Said. Like Said, Judt hated school, partly because he was treated like a member of an inferior minority—he was one of only about ten Jewish students in a school of more than one thousand. Both lived the major part of their lives in their adopted country, the United States, in which they never felt entirely at home or comfortable. Both became superstar academics and influential public intellectuals who devoted their lives to teaching and to writing books, articles, and reviews spanning a wide range of subjects and disciplines, including literature, history, politics, and culture. Many of Judt's characterizations of Said, in the foreword to *From Oslo to Iraq and the Road Map*, apply equally well to himself. Like Said, Judt continues to "generate irritation, veneration, and imitation," is a "very public intellectual, adored or execrated with equal intensity" by many readers, is mistrustful of younger scholars' "over familiarity with 'theory' at the expense of the art of close textual reading," and enjoys intellectual disagreement, "seeing the toleration of dissent and even discord within the scholarly community as the necessary condition for the latter's survival" (vii–viii). As an example of the importance of intellectual disagreement, Judt points out that his criticism of the "core thesis" of Said's *Orientalism* was no impediment to their friendship. Judt's book *Postwar: A History of Europe since 1945* received nearly the same scholarly acclaim as *Orientalism*. A magisterial 897-page tome, *Postwar* was a runner-up for the 2006 Pulitzer Prize for General Nonfiction and later named by the *Toronto Star* as the decade's best historical book.

Both Judt and Said were scholar-critics who made others uncomfortable, including those who were their political allies. No less than the Arab Said, the Jewish Judt was, to an "American Jewish community suffused with symbols of victimhood," a "provocatively articulate remembrancer of Israel's very own victims" (*From Oslo to Iraq and the Road Map* x–xi). Judt's articles about Israel's treatment of Palestine provoked angry letters from pro-Israeli writers and organizations, which only furthered his resolve to speak out. As Steven J. Zipperstein observed in "The Two Tony Judts," "it remains ironic that he became one of the world's most indispensable intellectuals at just the moment that he made his case for Jews as perpetual outsiders" (12).

Both Judt and Said were known for their intimidating erudition, ana-lytic intelligence, and acerbic wit. Writing generally in the third person, they did not use these gifts, before their illnesses, to probe the ironies, ambiguities, contradictions, and paradoxes of their private lives. Except for Said's brief memoir *After the Last Sky,* neither had written autobio-graphically before being diagnosed with terminal illness. Judt does not regret becoming a historian and culture critic, but illness gives him the opportunity and freedom—however ironic that word is when describing someone in the throes of ALS—to write personally.

A Solitary Traveler

Judt uses this newfound opportunity and freedom to write the story of his life. Like Said, he lived in many places and regarded himself as home-less and deracinated, but unlike Said, he writes about his early homes affectionately: "nostalgia makes a very satisfactory second home" (*The Memory Chalet* 56). He writes about the pleasure of solitude—another irony in that the unsettling solitude occurs at night, when he is walled off from the world. One of his most pleasant memories appears in the chap-ter entitled "Mimetic Desire" when he writes about being "loved" by a train:

> What does it mean to be loved by a train? Love, it seems to me, is that condition in which one is contentedly oneself. If this sounds paradoxical, remember Rilke's admonition: love consists in leaving the loved one space to be themselves while providing the security within which that self may flourish. As a child, I always felt uneasy and a little constrained around people, my family in particular. Solitude was bliss, but not easily obtained. *Being* always felt stress-ful—wherever I was there was something to do, someone to please, a duty to be completed, a role inadequately fulfilled: something amiss. *Becoming,* on the other hand, was relief. I was never so happy as when I was going somewhere on my own, and the longer it took to get there, the better. Walking was pleasurable, cycling enjoyable, bus journeys fun. But the train was very heaven. (65–66)

Recalling his experiences as a solitary traveler, Judt reflects on how he entertained himself by riding on trains, a guilty pleasure he never shared with anyone. Enthralled by the romance of solitude, he rode as a twelve-year-old late at night and into the early morning. The Waterloo train station inspires him the way country churches and baroque cathedrals inspire poets and artists. Train stations continue to enchant him, as the opening sentence in *Postwar* reveals: "I first decided to write this book while changing trains at the Westbahnhof, Vienna's main railway terminus" (1). In *The Memory Chalet* he is struck by the paradox of experiencing these train rides as an opportunity for solitude, since trains were designed in the nineteenth century to provide collective transportation. He then comments authoritatively on the sociological implications of public transportation. "The railways effectively invented social classes in their modern form, by naming and classifying different levels of comfort, facility and service: as any illustration can reveal, trains were for many decades crowded and uncomfortable except for those fortunate enough to travel first-class" (69). The knowledge that he will never again ride the trains weighs on him like a "leaden blanket," driving him further and further into the gloom of terminal illness, the recognition that he will never travel again. He ends the chapter plaintively: "No more Waterloo, no more rural country halts, no more solitude: no more becoming, just interminable being" (71).

Judt's personal loss reflects a larger cultural loss, and in *Ill Fares the Land*, written during the early stages of ALS, he warns of the calamitous implications of abandoning or privatizing railways. "If we cannot see the case for expending our collective resources on trains, it will not just be because we have all joined gated communities and no longer need anything but private cars to move around between them. It will be because we have become gated individuals who do not know how to share public space to common advantage" (216).

Seeing America

As an outsider, Judt sees Americans in ways that they do not see themselves; at times he resembles a modern Alexis de Tocqueville. While in North Platte, Nebraska, he experiences a negative epiphany: "In the middle of nowhere, hundreds of miles from anything resembling a city and thousands of miles from the nearest salt water: if *I* felt cut off, surrounded by eight-foot-high fields of corn, what must it be like to live in such a place? No wonder most Americans are profoundly uninterested in what the rest of the world is doing or what it thinks of them. Middle Kingdom? The Chinese didn't know half of it" (*The Memory Chalet* 161). His conclusion? "Everywhere is somewhere else's nowhere" (164). He sees us as still puritanical: "Americans assiduously avoid anything that might smack of harassment, even at the risk of foregoing promising friendships and the joys of flirtation" (187).

Judt has much to say, positively and negatively, about the United States, praising American public universities for their outstanding libraries; delighting in New York City, which, though it may be in its twilight, remains a world class city; but criticizing cities like Houston, Phoenix, and Charlotte, whose office buildings bustle from nine to five before dying at dusk. "Ozymandias-like, such exurbations will sink back into the marshland or desert whence they arose once the water runs out and gasoline prices them out of existence" (*The Memory Chalet* 160). A paradoxicalist, he remarks that he feels most European when he is in the United States.

"A Believer"

In his quest for truth, Just is never afraid to acknowledge the perils of dogmatic belief, including the misguided political commitments of his youth. "I knew what it meant to be a 'believer'—but I also knew what sort of price one pays for such intensity of identification and unquestioning allegiance. Before even turning twenty I had become, been, and ceased to be a Zionist, a Marxist, and a communitarian settler: no mean achievement for a south London teenager" (*The Memory Chalet* 98). He tells us ruefully that like so many baby boomers in the 1960s, he conformed in his nonconformity. His memoir abounds in anecdotes about his activist past, as when, demonstrating outside the American embassy in London against the Vietnam War, he found himself squeezed between a bored police horse and a park railing. "I felt a warm, wet sensation down my leg. Incontinence? A bloody wound? No such luck. A red paint bomb that I had intended to throw in the direction of the embassy had burst in my pocket" (120). Despite the fact that he was by birth, temperament, and training a student of western European history, he "missed the boat" when it came to the cataclysmic events in Poland and Czechoslovakia, when communism was crumbling. "For all our grandstanding theories of history, then, we failed to notice one of its seminal turning points" (125).

An early advocate for and then critic of identity politics, Judt developed an immunity for intellectual and political movements, skewering the political left and right with equal conviction. He remains, from beginning to end, a teacher, committed to an educational philosophy based on meritocracy, giving everyone an equal chance and then selecting those who are most talented. "Liberalism and tolerance, indifference to external opinion, a prideful sense of distinction accompanying progressive political allegiances: these are manageable contradictions, but only in an institution unafraid to assert its particular form of elitism" (*The Memory Chalet* 145). Like Edward Said, Judt has the courage of his convictions, but he also has an ironic sensibility, skeptical of all positions, his own included. Though he is regarded as a public intellectual associated with the political left, many of his university colleagues regard him as a "reactionary dinosaur" (205). He remains, again like Said, out of place in many ways, aware of the dangers of fierce unconditional loyalties to a country, a religion, or a set of ideas. "The thin veneer of civilization rests upon what may well be an illusory faith in our common humanity. But illusory or not, we would do well to cling to it" (207).

Judt remarks in the preface to *The Memory Chalet* that he never intended the essays for book publication: "I started writing them for my own satisfaction" (xiii). Were it not for the enthusiastic support of one of his literary agents, as well as the encouragement of Robert Silvers, the editor of the *New York Review of Books,* where several of the essays were first published, *The Memory Chalet* would not have appeared. The book deserves a wide audience. Judt might have quoted a statement from *The Memory Palace of Matteo Ricci* where Spence's eponymous Christian missionary, who taught the Chinese how to build a memory palace, told his publisher in 1606, "The whole point of writing something down is that your voice will then carry for thousands of miles, whereas in direct conversation it fades at a hundred paces" (22). By the time he dictated *The Memory Chalet,* Judt's voice could hardly be heard, but his words will carry far.

In the preface Judt admits that he was troubled by an "ethical question" as soon as he made the decision to publish the essays in *The Memory Chalet.* "Because I did not write them with the view to immediate publication, these short pieces never benefitted from an internal editor—or, more precisely, a private censor. Where they spoke of my parents or my childhood, of ex-wives and present colleagues, I let them speak. This has the merit of directness; I hope it will not cause offense" (xiii–xiv). The fear is unwarranted: nothing he says about his parents, ex-wives, colleagues, or friends is likely to cause offense. Unlike Said's withering critique of his parents in *Out of Place,* Judt has no criticisms of his parents in *The Memory Chalet*—and there is no mention of his colleagues or friends. Judt never searches for comfort or consolation about approaching death, but had he done so, he would have found apt passages in Spence's book, where Ricci reflects on how writers from antiquity thought about death. "From Seneca, Ricci quoted the thought that he had no regrets for his dead friends, since he had anticipated their loss while they lived and remembered them as still living after they had died" (Spence 150). Judt recounts some of the mistakes of his life, but he has, like Ricci, few regrets. He ended up doing what he wanted to do—teach and write—and getting paid for it. He remains in love with the life.

We read *The Memory Chalet* not to learn anything about dying or death but to see what one is capable of achieving in a near-impossible situation. And we read *The Memory Chalet* for Judt's insights on the continuities and discontinuities between past and present. He castigates those who believe we cannot learn from the past, as he points out trenchantly in *Reappraisals.* "Not only did we fail to learn very much from the past—this would hardly have been remarkable. But we have become stridently insistent—in our economic calculations, our political practices, our international strategies, even our educational priorities—that *the past has nothing of interest to teach us*" (2). In *Ill Fares the Land* he ends with the hope that he has provided some guidance to those, especially the young, who sense the problems with contemporary life. "As citizens of a free society, we have a duty to look critically at our world. But if we think we know what is wrong, we must *act* upon that knowledge. Philosophers, it was famously observed, have hitherto only interpreted the world in various ways; the point is to change it" (237).

Responsibility

Words never fail Judt. We never see him strain to make himself heard; *The Memory Chalet* has an easy spontaneity and seamlessness that belie the conditions under which it was written. He never has difficulty maintaining emotional control. Judt does not disclose his wife's and children's reactions to his terminal illness, but one suspects that unlike Susan Sontag, his recognition of the seriousness of his disease, along with its inevitable outcome, spares his family, however grief-stricken, from the perception that they, too, are swimming in a sea of death. Few of the emotions Kübler-Ross describes in her stage theory of death appear in *The Memory Chalet*: shock, denial, anger, and depression are strangely absent from the narrative. Nor do these dark emotions appear in *Ill Fares the Land,* also written when he was dying. Instead, we see in both late books acceptance, but of a more active type than Kübler-Ross has suggested, one closer to what Lois and Arthur Jaffe have described: "A sixth stage of dying, responsibility, may well follow Kübler-Ross's fifth stage of acceptance. Acceptance conveys passive assent, whereas responsibility implies an active state of doing something about one's situation" (210).

Responsibility is a crucial value for Judt in all his writings, as we can see in *The Burden of Responsibility* (1998), a study of three prominent twentieth-century French intellectuals, where he reveals the same commitment to humanistic values that appears in *The Memory Chalet*. Léon Blum, Albert Camus, and Raymond Aron are compelling to Judt because of their "shared quality of moral (and, as it happened, physical) courage, their willingness to take a stand not against their political or intellectual opponents—everyone did that, all too often—but against their 'own' side" (20). Judt's admiration for Camus, as a moralist, for thinking and writing "against the grain of his times in distinctive ways, all of which help account for his difficulty in finding a home in this century" (122), applies equally well to himself (and Edward Said). So, too, does Judt's characterization of Camus as a rootless cosmopolitan apply to himself (and Said): "And like other rootless cosmopolitans he sought throughout his life to ground himself in something firm, knowing all the while that it was a hopeless exercise and that to be in exile just *was* his true condition" (104). In *Past Imperfect,* Judt's study of French intellectuals, he criticizes those thinkers who refuse to accept responsibility for their past actions or words. "Because intellectuals write, and thereby leave a record of their former opinions that cannot easily be erased, they are constrained in later years to admit that yes, they did say and do those absurd things. But it is not sufficient to draw a veil over those years and claim to have grown beyond the foolishness of youth. Even though we may not be the person we were, in a certain philosophical sense, we alone can take responsibility for the deeds of that former self" (5).

History and memory are Judt's lifelong passions, as he demonstrates in *Postwar* and *The Memory Chalet,* respectively. He writes about history in *Postwar* with a nondogmatic progressive point of view, always on the side of social democracy, but never succumbing to utopian thinking. As he observes from his own experience, "for all its political applications, History is a discipline peculiarly impervious to high theoretical specula-tion: the more Theory intrudes, the farther History recedes" (*Postwar* 399). In the epilogue to *Postwar* he writes that the "instrument of recall" of the past is history, in both its meanings: "as the passage of time and as the professional study of the past—the latter above all." History, he argues, "contributes to the disenchantment of the world," but it needs to be learned—"and periodically re-learned" (830). In its encyclopedic presentation of European events of the last half century, *Postwar* reminds Europeans of the lessons Europe needs to learn, and relearn, if it is to avoid the terrible conflicts of the past.

What Judt offers in *The Memory Chalet* is not mainly the history of the last fifty years but the memory of one man's lifetime. If world his-tory disenchants, Judt's memory will enchant his readers, recalling an age filled with nostalgic recollections of happier days. Even as it rapidly approaches its own extinction, Judt's memory recalls experiences with a clarity that never shows signs of aging or dimming. Neither self-serving nor self-promoting, he avoids memorializing himself. He realizes that memory is inevitably contentious and partisan, that we tend to present ourselves as the infallible heroes of our own life stories. Throughout *The Memory Chalet* we sense that Judt's memory is alert to the ironies, ambi-guities, and contradictions of *lived* experience, and that, therefore, we can trust his memory.

Aware of his profound debt to the past and his commitment to a future when he will no longer be alive, Judt writes *The Memory Chalet* partly because of his ongoing responsibility. He tells us early in the story about the unproductive nights when he lies in bed staring at empty space, unable to write a single word. He realizes that he shouldn't be too hard on himself: simply getting through the night with his sanity intact is an achievement. And yet he feels guilty when he cannot write, saying to himself, "who could do any better in the circumstances?" The question is not rhetorical, for he immediately offers a surprising answer: "a better me" (10). Presumably he invokes his better self whenever he confronts the dark night of the soul, when the "alm uncle," his "perennially dissatisfied alter ego" (10), rules. Both Said and Judt struggle to their dying breath to fulfill their responsibility to themselves and to the world; both fear, at the end, that they have come up short. Said's better self excoriates him on his deathbed for not doing enough for the Palestinians; Judt's better self cruelly reminds him of the horror of his present situation. And yet no one can fault Judt for not using his remaining time creatively, for he completes his memoir shortly before he dies. *The Memory Chalet* bears witness to a remarkable age and to a remarkable person.

The Memory Chalet contains an understandably elegiac mood, but it leaves us with the conviction of a deeply passionate and fulfilled life. Judt's end-of-life memoir is not only an eloquent review of his own life but also a portrait of an age unparalleled in its accomplishments and calamities. He ends the book, appropriately, by recalling his visit with his family in 2002 to Mürren, the idyllic village in the Swiss Alps that remains his idea of paradise. "We cannot choose where we start out in life, but we may finish where we will. I know where I shall be: going nowhere in particular on that little train, forever and ever" (226). In its insights, wit, and range, *The Memory Chalet* would be impressive even if the author were not dying. That Judt writes it while almost completely paralyzed makes it even more remarkable. He remains alive, in his imagination, to the end, dying in character at the height of his creativity.

CHAPTER 8

"I Never Realized Dying Could Be So Much Fun"

Art Buchwald and *Too Soon to Say Goodbye*

⟶

*A*rt Buchwald, one of America's most beloved humorists, wrote three memoirs, including *Too Soon to Say Goodbye,* which he began while waiting to die in a Washington, D.C., hospice. He entered Washington Home and Hospice in mid-March 2006 after the decision to end dialysis following the amputation of the lower part of his right leg due to poor circulation. He expected to die in a few weeks, but then, to his doctors' amazement, his kidneys started to function again. Hundreds of visitors, celebrities and strangers alike, came to pay tribute to him, and he received nearly three thousand letters. In hospice he indulged in his lifelong passions of eating, holding court, being with friends, and writing. After five months, he checked himself out of hospice, returned to his home in Martha's Vineyard, completed *Too Soon to Say Goodbye,* and then died quietly in January 2007 at the age of eighty-one.

Buchwald became a media sensation while he was dying, but he was already known to millions of Americans for his long-running, nationally syndicated column in the *Washington Post* and for his dozens of books, fiction and nonfiction, lampooning every aspect of American society. Described as a "Will Rogers with chutzpah," he had a droll wit that was playful and light-hearted. Nevertheless, early maternal loss darkened his vision, scarring him with lifelong feelings of anger, guilt, and abandonment. *Too Soon to Say Goodbye* touches lightly on these emotions, but before examining the ways in which he writes goodbye to his readers, it is instructive to look at his two earlier memoirs, *Leaving Home* and *I'll Always Have Paris.*

Life as an Orphan

Buchwald never saw his mother, who was institutionalized immediately after his birth. She spent the remaining thirty-five years in a state psychiatric hospital, where she died at the age of sixty-five. He later admitted that like many children who never knew their mothers, he spent his entire life searching for someone to replace her. As a young boy he was placed in a foundling home because he had rickets. Though he was Jewish, he was then sent to a boarding school run by Seventh-Day Adventists, where he was subjected to anti-Semitism and religious indoctrination. "For many years I had dreams from that period," he confesses in *Leaving Home.* "A blurred likeness of the devil kept popping up, and it wasn't one of those friendly devils you see on canned ham salad—he was one mean son of a bitch" (29).

When Buchwald was five, he and his three sisters were placed in the Hebrew Orphan Asylum in New York City by his immigrant father, who could not afford to raise them during the Depression. "Except for the shame of being in an 'orphanage,' the home could have been considered a very proper prep school" (*Leaving Home* 48–49). Although he was well cared for in the orphanage, he felt lonely and unwanted, feelings that haunted him for the rest of his life. After the Hebrew Orphan Asylum, Buchwald lived in a series of foster homes, none of which seemed like a real home. His sisters were finally allowed to move in with their father, but he was forced to remain in the foster home, a decision that angered and saddened him. By the time he turned fifteen, he was allowed to rejoin his family, but the reunion was hardly joyous: "I began to look back on my foster homes with nostalgia" (107).

Buchwald's childhood was not entirely Dickensian, but it was traumatic enough, and he was never able to forget growing up without a mother and a father. The nomadic existence left him feeling parentless, homeless, and rootless. Like the bereft Pip in *Great Expectations,* he learned to parent himself, a difficult process because of the lack of role models. He ran away from home when he was sixteen, lied about his age, and enlisted in the U.S. Marines during World War II. Following the war, he studied at the

University of Southern California but was unable to graduate because he had never completed high school. In 1993 the university awarded him an Honorary Doctor of Letters, an irony he couldn't resist sharing with the thirty-two thousand people who heard him deliver the commencement address that year: "I told the students about my failure to get a diploma and pointed out that since USC had seen fit to give me a doctorate all these years later, all of them wasted their time" (*Leaving Home* 231).

In 1948 Buchwald moved to Paris on the GI Bill; he lived there for fourteen years before returning permanently to the United States. He began his professional career as a columnist for the European edition of the *New York Herald Tribune*. He was the only American journalist writing a regular column in Europe at the time, a position that gave him access to well-known Americans living abroad. His trademark political and social satire appeared in such books as *Have I Ever Lied to You?; "I Am Not a Crook"; Washington Is Leaking; While Reagan Slept; "You Can Fool All of the People All the Time"; Lighten Up, George; We'll Laugh Again;* and *Beating around the Bush.* He received the Pulitzer Prize for Outstanding Commentary in 1982 and in 1986 was elected to the American Academy and Institute of Arts and Letters.

As Buchwald gained international fame and literary success, however, he struggled with mental illness. Like his mother, he suffered from severe depression and manic depression, and twice he was hospitalized for suicidal feelings, which he later wrote about in his three memoirs.

In 1949 Buchwald met a young Irish American woman who had recently arrived in Paris. Born and raised in a small Pennsylvania town, Ann McGarry began her career as a salesperson, but through a series of lucky breaks and persistence, she soon became the publicity director for one of Paris's most influential clothes designers. She and Buchwald dated for more than two years before he agreed hesitantly to marry her. The story of their life together in Europe appears in *I'll Always Have Paris* and in her memoir, *Seems Like Yesterday* (1980). Her book is unusual in that she is always being "interrupted" by her husband's commentary, which at times confirms but at other times disconfirms her point of view. *Seems Like Yesterday* is revealing in the ways in which husband and wife disagree with each other. He is the "famous writer" whose need to have the last word, and sometimes the first word, does not always seem funny. He acknowledges that Ann did not always find his articles amusing. "She said I was destroying any chance of making it in the newspaper world and she didn't want to have anything to do with someone who made a spectacle of himself" (*Seems Like Yesterday* 30).

Buchwald's success was due to his ability to make a spectacle of himself. He rarely jokes, however, about his fear of emotional commitment. He is silent about this issue at the beginning of *Seems Like Yesterday*, implying that his desire to date as many women as possible during his early years in Paris was due to his devotion to writing. "How can someone write the Great American Novel if he has to worry about meeting the same girl every night for dinner?" (34). As time progressed, his wife became increasingly frustrated. "I yearned to hear Art say, 'I love you,' but he refused as adamantly as if I'd asked him to change his name. 'I have never said those words to anyone, and I don't think I ever will'" (46). Later in the memoir Buchwald addresses his fear of emotional commitment, tracing it to his early life as an orphan. The idea of settling down with a woman was so upsetting that he would find himself frequently throwing up in the bathroom. "Years later when I went into analysis my psychiatrist and I figured out that it was my way of trying to say something" (105).

Buchwald's commitment phobia also appears in *I'll Always Have Paris,* where he relates it to his need for constant approval from his readers.

> Because of my foster-home background and being deprived of a normal family existence, the idea of having a family of my own was as frightening as anything I could imagine. I saw myself as an uncle, but not as a husband and father. This was my way of avoiding pain. And the more I thought about the responsibility and taking on such alien emotions as love, the more I upchucked and wanted to escape. What I planned to do was spend my life entertaining the crowd. I needed constant applause. I would go from one gathering to another, making new friends and new fans. Childhood wounds were too deep, and I was fearful of letting anyone get too close to me. I was a mess. (93)

Spousal Loss and Guilt

Seems Like Yesterday ends in 1963, when the Buchwalds decide to return to the United States. The memoir closes with Buchwald's telling admission in his last interruption: "My conclusion is that like most people who spent so much time in Paris, we have tended to romanticize our lives and remember the good things, blotting out the bad ones" (219). Some of the "bad" things emerge in *Too Soon To Say Goodbye*, where he comments cryptically on their long marriage. "We were married for forty years. It was a happy marriage if you don't count the unhappiness" (40).

Hints of the conflicted marriage appear briefly in *I'll Always Have Paris*. After revealing his reluctance to marry, he skips over most of their life together and then comments on how they grew apart after their children left home. Estrangement turned into anger and bitterness—and then tragedy struck. "Before the divorce proceedings were started, she contracted lung cancer, which spread. The doctors pronounced her illness terminal and she spent one year suffering, much of it in bed. Joel, our son, quit his job to take care of her" (98). Buchwald was not a caregiver, and he never discloses what, if anything, he learned from his wife's terminal illness. A priest was instrumental in their reconciliation, and during Buchwald's last visits with her, "we revived some of the magic of our marriage" (99).

Ann Buchwald died in 1994, and in *Too Soon to Say Goodbye* he reveals additional details of her final days. "She coped by turning her anger against me, to the point where I felt it best for both of us if I left home. Still, we remained very close" (40). He then elaborates on the dark emotions he felt after her death, speaking with a seriousness unmediated by his legendary humor. "When a loved one dies, you carry around a lot of guilt. I still do. And even now, I hurt when I think about her. In an odd way, my days here in the hospice are somehow connected with her death. I think of her [buried] on Martha's Vineyard and dream that I'll be with her soon" (40).

Exorcising Ghosts

Grief is not always a laughing matter for Buchwald, and his three memoirs reveal the extent to which he struggled against mental illness. He became obsessed with his absent mother, seeking her everywhere. She remained the mysterious source of much of his sorrow. "In 1963, I had a severe depression myself and was hospitalized. In my darkest moments in my room, I would cry, 'I want my mommy, I want my mommy.'" Nor was his psychiatrist surprised to hear about these dreams: "I had gagged up a whole lifetime of maternal deprivation" (*Leaving Home* 15). Buch-wald did not attend his mother's funeral, but he recalls writing a eulogy based on what he thought her to be like. He imagined her showering all of her love on him, her only son, and he dreamed of becoming a doc-tor, lawyer, or accountant to please her. He then refers to the advice he received from a physician about the tendency toward self-blame after a relative's death: "A psychiatrist told me that when you grieve you think of all the things you didn't do for your loved one and not the things you did do. I should have become a rabbi, which would have pleased my mother very much. I should have married a nice Jewish girl rather than a nice Catholic girl. When I left home I should have called her every day" (*Too Soon to Say Goodbye* 43).

Buchwald never eulogized his mother's death, but writing about her in *Leaving Home* brought therapeutic relief. "I never told anyone about my eulogy, but it always made me feel better" (43). Many years after her death he and his siblings decided to visit her grave, but no one knew where it was located. After much difficulty they located the cemetery and found her gravestone, at which they stared in silence. "I felt I was at the end of a long journey and the circle had now been closed" (45). He finds a mother surrogate in his hospice nurse, Jackie Lindsey, his "chief Ball Breaker." She bathes and dresses him every day and sometimes causes him pain when she touches his "family jewels." Nevertheless, he refers to her as the "mother I never had. She gives me hope, love, and encourage-ment. She listens to all my stories and I listen to all of hers" (*Too Soon to Say Goodbye* 26).

Buchwald knew his father, but the relationship between them was largely nonexistent. He describes him as a "Sunday father" because none of his children lived with him. "He used to say, 'You dasn't do this,' and 'You dasn't do that.' I didn't argue. I just did as I pleased. I was his only son and I hurt him—first when I refused to be bar mitzvahed, then when I ran away from home and joined the Marines, and finally when I moved to Paris. He couldn't understand why I wanted to become a writer" (*Too Soon to Say Goodbye* 46). Buchwald attended his father's funeral and mourned his death, "mainly for the lonely life he led after my mother was put away, living in one room in the Bronx. I still talk to him and I tell him, 'I am sorry that I wasn't bar mitzvahed, Pop'" (47).

Additional information about Buchwald's difficult childhood and its impact on his later life appears in *Leaving Home*. "I am new at writing memoirs," he announces in the introduction. "It's probably the most egotistical project a person can undertake, but it does provide an opportunity to sum up the few years I've spent on earth in my own words" (7). The experience of writing a life review helped him come to terms with maternal loss. "Early in life I had to explain her absence to strangers, as did my sisters. The easiest thing was to say she died giving birth to me. I don't know how many times I told this lie, but apparently every time I did I committed a form of matricide. She was dead as far as friends and strangers were concerned, but she was very much alive to me—sequestered away in a distant place I had never seen. The story was credible—but for most of my life I have lived in fear that someone would unearth my dirty secret and I would be severely punished for not having disclosed it" (12). Writing about shame, paradoxically, was a countershame technique, freeing him from the fear of exposure. Writing about shame also helped Buchwald come to terms with his own death. It is rare in our death-denying culture to write humorously about death—and even rarer to write humorously about one's *own* impending death.

Writing as Rescue

Buchwald also writes about the strained relationships with his children, whom he neglected in his pursuit of fame. In *I'll Always Have Paris* he acknowledges that in his role as a "hot-shot columnist" he missed his children's birthday parties. He doesn't trace the neglect of his children to his father's neglect of him, which a psychobiographical interpretation would suggest, nor does he disclose his children's reactions to reading his stories about his family. But he implies that writing was a form of reparation, a way to repair past relationships and work through guilt and anger. Indeed, writing was a form of self-analysis and self-therapy, enabling Buchwald to understand a lifetime of anger, guilt, sadness, and confusion. Writing, particularly his inimitable satirical writing, helped him to express his fury. "My anger was buried deep behind the humor. I have always had trouble with anger. I have swallowed it, and it's come back later to give me the shakes. As a child, I vowed never to show it, no matter how upset I became—because if I did, everybody would discover that I wasn't a nice person. My heroes in this world are those who can get rid of their anger and not feel bad about it." When asked what he tried to do with his humor, his response is immediate: "I'm getting even. I am constantly avenging hurts from the past. . . . For me being funny is the best revenge" (*I'll Always Have Paris* 80).

Writing is also a way for Buchwald to confront his fear of death. "For a humorist, I think a lot about death. During both my depressions, I contemplated suicide." Depressions are cruel, he points out, and if a person "is egotistical enough and in a suicidal frame of mind, he methodically plans his own funeral" (*Leaving Home* 100–101). Echoing Nietzsche, he implies that anything that doesn't kill you makes you stronger. "Things were so bad at first I was even placed in a psychiatric ward. I was certain I would never laugh again. But a funny thing can happen to you in a depression. If you don't hurt yourself, you can gain tremendous insights and empathy, find inner strengths and hidden talents. It's a mysterious process, but if you hold on, you become a wiser and better person" (101). Writing about death was a counterphobic act, a way to master his fears and defy death. He could not have known while penning *Leaving Home* that writing was also a way to rehearse and celebrate his own death, as we see in his end-of-life memoir.

Poster Boy for Death

Too Soon to Say Goodbye begins with a preface written in July 2006. The first sentence, "What started out the worst of times ended up the best of times," echoes the opening of *A Tale of Two Cities*. How can dying be the best of times? Buchwald's daunting challenge lies in answering this question.

Buchwald became a "media star" by accident when he spoke on Diane Rehm's radio show. "I figured, what the heck, I had nothing to do. I went on and talked about hospice, about not taking dialysis, and about what it was like to die. I had a feeling Diane's listeners would want to know what I had told my children, and I discussed how they were reacting to my decision. The interview produced 150 letters and e-mails, the majority of which were sympathetic" (*Too Soon to Say Goodbye* 20). He expected to die in a few weeks and decided to make the best of the situation, eating whatever he wanted—including McDonald's milkshakes and hamburgers. He entertained a constant flow of visitors, some of them famous, such as Ethel Kennedy, John Glenn, Tom Brokaw, and Russell Baker, others ordinary people who wished to pay their last respects. He took delight in holding court in the hospice living room, which he called his "salon." Following his interview with Diane Rehm, he appeared on George Stephanopoulos's program *This Week* and became the subject of a long article in the Sunday *New York Times.* He also appeared on Jim Lehrer's *NewsHour,* CNN, and the *Today* show. He had truly become a media star for death.

Buchwald shatters one taboo after another by speaking and writing about the termination of life. To begin with, he doesn't use euphemisms like "pass away." Instead, he speaks openly and honestly about death—and the euphemisms he uses, such as "big sleep" and "dirt nap," poke fun at linguistic evasiveness. Far from withdrawing into loneliness, silence, and depression, as many people do in his situation, he relishes his new role as "hospice poster boy." He loves being the center of attention, and he uses this position to educate the public about the importance of hospice, for which he becomes an eloquent advocate. "The hospice volunteers play a vital role. Many first learned about the hospice program when a family member or loved one received hospice care. They too are drawn by a desire to comfort those at the end of their lives. Some volunteers see the work as a way of confronting their own mortality" (*Too Soon To Say Goodbye* 23). He gives his readers a brief history of hospice, describes what it's like living there, offers information about hospice of which the public may be unaware, and expresses gratitude to the many staff members and volunteers who help him. "The nice thing about a hospice," he writes, "is we can talk about death openly. Most people are afraid that if they even mention it, they will bring bad karma on themselves" (29).

Buchwald's public endorsement of hospice is also, indirectly, an endorsement of Kübler-Ross's pioneering research on death and dying. His response, however, to the many get-well cards sent to him in hospice could not be more different from her reaction to the get-well cards sent to one of her dying patients. "I shared with him," she writes in *Questions and Answers on Death and Dying,* " my own gut reactions of rage and anger at the wall covered with phony get-well-soon cards when everybody who sent him a card obviously knew he was in the final stages of his life and totally unlikely ever to recover" (25). Her ability to empathize with her patient's anger proves to be helpful to both of them, but Buchwald's response is no less appropriate and effective: he gently chides the many strangers who send him get well cards: "Even now, some people just haven't figured out what I'm doing here" (*Too Soon to Say Goodbye* 95). He remains optimistic that people will talk about death if they are allowed to do so. He encourages the hospice residents and their families to talk about death, and he gives readers permission to think about their own mortality.

In a health article published in the *New York Times* on January 23, 2007, shortly after Buchwald's death, Jane E. Brody noted that the humorist hoped to make "hospice" a household word. Brody herself is an advocate for hospice. She points out that the average patient is in hospice for less than three weeks before dying. "The most common report from families after a loved one's death is regret that hospice had not been called in sooner," Brody states. "In a study of 275 patients, families that benefitted from hospice thought three months would have been optimal and that less than three weeks was too short." Though Buchwald died not in hospice but in his home, Brody declares that he was a "living testimonial to the benefits of hospice care." In another *New York Times* article on August 23, 2010, Brody reports on a study appearing in the *New England Journal of Medicine* that confirms the many benefits of palliative care associated with the hospice movement. Patients with metastatic lung cancer who received palliative care as well as standard cancer therapy "had a better quality of life, experienced less depression, were less likely to receive aggressive end-of-life care and lived nearly three months longer than those who received cancer treatment alone."

One of Buchwald's most endearing qualities is his humility in the face of death. "What's beautiful about death," he tells us, "is you can say anything you want to, as long as you don't lord it over others, pretending to know something they don't" (*Too Soon to Say Goodbye* 30). He prepares for death while focusing on life, reminding his readers that the "big question we still have to ask is not where we're going, but what we were doing here in the first place" (30). Sometimes his tone becomes acerbic, as when he declares, "I have no idea where I am going and no one else knows. And if they claim they know, they don't know what the hell they are talking about" (11).

Both Buchwald and Kübler-Ross accept death but for strikingly different reasons. Buchwald appreciates the life he has been privileged to enjoy, and what he finds "beautiful" about death is its great mystery. By contrast, Kübler-Ross remains convinced that life *after* death is a "wonderful and powerful experience" because of God's unconditional love. He is in no rush to leave the life he loves; she cannot wait to leave a life of frustration and begin the final journey. These differences should not obscure their many agreements over death and dying. Like Kübler-Ross, Buchwald considers dying an important part of life, and he is gratified that hospice, an institution Kübler-Ross is credited with bringing to the United States, enables people to receive compassionate care. Like her, he knows that people appreciate those who can speak honestly and openly about death.

It does not take long for Buchwald to become a hospice superstar. Believing he was put on earth to make people laugh, he finds humor everywhere. Thus he uses the couch in the family room for "therapy sessions" with friends. Instead of crying over his amputated leg, he boasts about having a handicapped parking permit to attend athletic events. "Goodbye, leg. I didn't need you as much as I thought" (*Too Soon to Say Goodbye* 138). He takes pleasure in revenging himself on those who have victimized him, as when he portrays himself as David waging war against the Goliath film company Paramount, which stole his idea for a film later starring Eddie Murphy. Recalling an incident of racial hatred in boot camp, he reaches a distinctly non-Christian conclusion: "You can hate someone forever even if you don't know his name" (126).

Buchwald would agree with Anatole Broyard and D. W. Winnicott that one should be alive when one dies. One of the oddities of dying, Geoffrey Scarre points out, is that it is not the opposite of living, as death is the opposite of life. "*Dying is a form or phase of living,* Scarre suggests. "We need to be alive to be dying, and only when we are dead are we finished with dying" (149). Scarre reminds us that the dying person "may still have many things to do." Buchwald's dying, as he describes it in his end-of-life memoir, is an intensification of his living.

The Blues Brothers

Too Soon To Say Goodbye urges a more compassionate attitude toward mental illness. Again Buchwald speaks from personal experience. One of the most powerful sections in the memoir is the four-page chapter entitled "Depression," which opens with a startling observation: "Many people thought I was having or would have a depression when I lost my leg and entered the hospice. I was depressed, but that was nothing compared to the episodes I experienced in 1963 and 1987" (36). Losing a leg turned out to be less traumatic than losing his mind. In 1997 he and Mike Wallace disclosed on *Larry King Live* their long histories of depression. Hearing that Buchwald had two serious bouts with depression, his friend William Styron, a fellow sufferer, told him that he would be inducted into the "Bipolar Hall of Fame" if he became depressed again (38). Tipper Gore gave Buchwald a "Lifetime Achievement Award for Depression" for his mantra, "Don't commit suicide, because you might change your mind two weeks later" (37).

One of the "blues brothers," Buchwald used humor to make fun of the scars of childhood, but the pain did not go away, and the depression turned into anger toward others and himself. Twice he was hospitalized for suicidal feelings, severely depressed during the first episode and manic during the second. "No one recognized my manic phase because people thought I was being funny" (*Too Soon to Say Goodbye* 38). Then came the crash, when he was both suicidal and homicidal. His physician talked him out of his plan to throw himself out of the window of a skyscraper, and soon he admitted himself to the psychiatric ward of Georgetown University Hospital, where he was treated successfully with lithium.

The Man Who Would Not Die

Buchwald credits his humor for allowing him to enjoy the final months of his life, but it was also his profound gratitude that is evident throughout *Too Soon to Say Goodbye*. He is grateful for his family, friends, colleagues, physicians, hospice workers, readers—and for life itself. Gratitude is one of the "positive" emotions, along with joy, hope, admiration, pride, and love. Gratitude is, as Robert C. Roberts suggests, a "deeply social emotion relating persons to persons in quite particular ways" (65). Gratitude is generally viewed as a positive counterpart to vengeance. Gratitude "tends to bind us together in relationships of friendly and affectionate reciprocity, whereas resentment tends to repel us from one another, only to bind us in relationships of bitter and hostile reciprocity" (Roberts 68). Buchwald enjoys revenging himself on his enemies in *Too Soon To Say Goodbye*, but gratitude is the dominant emotion. Sometimes people express gratitude to ingratiate themselves with others, as La Rochefoucauld claimed: "Our virtues are most frequently but vices in disguise. The gratitude of most men is merely a secret desire to receive greater benefits" (quoted in Buck 100). Buchwald's gratitude, however, is genuine, reflecting his belief that life is a gift to be shared with others.

Too Soon to Say Goodbye is a crowd pleaser, affirming the importance of gratitude, good works, memory, and self-fulfillment. Buchwald affirms joy without glossing over sorrow, and there is no subject on which he is unwilling to write, including life's inevitable regrets and disappointments. The pen never fails him: everything is grist for his writerly mill. *Too Soon to Say Goodbye* is not a literary masterpiece, as Philip Roth's *Patrimony* is, nor is it an intellectually powerful memoir, as Edward Said's *Out of Place* and Tony Judt's *The Memory Chalet* are. Unlike Kübler-Ross's *The Wheel of Life*, *Too Soon to Say Goodbye* does not read like a science fiction thriller; unlike Harold Brodkey's *This Wild Darkness* and David Rieff's *Swimming in a Sea of Death,* it lacks narrative suspense. Nevertheless, *Too Soon to Say Goodbye* remains a remarkably optimistic account of a man's love affair with life. And it is genuinely groundbreaking in shattering one taboo after another about dying and death.

"The Man Who Would Not Die," as Buchwald wryly calls himself, wrote *Too Soon to Say Goodbye* in a few months, and then he left hospice to spend the remaining time with his family. He wrote the afterword at his home on Martha's Vineyard, after living almost five months in hospice. Nor did death, when it finally came, silence his voice. The day after his death the *New York Times* posted a video obituary in which he declared, "Hi. I'm Art Buchwald, and I just died" (www.nytimes.com/packages/html/obituaries/BUCHWALD_FEATURE/blocker.html).

We don't see a death or dying scene in *Too Soon to Say Goodbye,* nor do we see a transition from life to death. Buchwald never describes the process by which he accepts the inevitability of death. Instead, we see a writer whose body is no longer intact but whose imagination has never been more creative. If his decision not to spend the rest of his life on dialysis indicates his wish to live and die on his own terms, the extra nine months he was granted is a tribute to his indomitable spirit. He led a storied life that he chronicled in dozens of accounts, fictional and nonfictional, and he wrote about deferred death with unsurpassed verve.

Too Soon to Say Goodbye defies much of the conventional wisdom about dying and death. Buchwald never portrays himself as isolated, alienated, confused, frightened, angry, or depressed about his impending death. Nor does he portray death as ugly or menacing; death is not the Grim Reaper but simply the biological end of life. Nothing about his dying is shameful or off-limits to his satirical imagination. He demonstrates the possibility not only of a good but an entertaining death. His "dying trajectory," a concept first suggested by Barney Glaser and Anselm Strauss in *Awareness of Dying,* was longer than anyone expected, and he put the extra time to good use.

Scripting Death

Buchwald's experience in hospice, where he defied everyone's prediction about imminent death, turned out to be even more fantastic than the one he had imagined nearly forty years earlier. In *Shadow Box*, George Plimpton asked several of his writer-friends, including Buchwald, how they imagined their own endings. Plimpton gave the writers the example of Jean Borotra, the French tennis star who imagined dying as he served an ace on center court at Wimbledon. In Plimpton's words, "Art Buchwald, like Borotra, fancied himself dropping dead on the center court at Wimbledon during the men's final—at the age of ninety-three" (287). In Philip Roth's *Exit Ghost*, Nathan Zuckerman cites Buchwald's fantasy, adding that it "must have seemed a lark of an assignment [for Plimpton] to ask other writers to tell him how they imagined themselves meeting death—scenarios that, as he recounts them, were invariably comical or dramatic or bizarre" (264). Buchwald refers to this fantasy briefly in *Too Soon to Say Goodbye*: "I insist that my obituary not say, 'He died after a long illness.' I want it to read, 'He died at the age of 98 on a private tennis court, just after he aced Andre Agassi'" (52).

Buchwald states in the afterword to *Too Soon to Say Goodbye,* upon leaving hospice and returning to Martha's Vineyard, that he "never realized dying could be so much fun" (145). Few of us may agree with him about that or rival his experience as a hospice superstar, but it doesn't matter. He was fortunate to experience the good death that he did, as his physician notes in one of the eulogies in the epilogue. "When Art died, it was a good death. He was comfortable and understood that in his very good and extraordinary life he had achieved his goal of being loved, and that was the very best therapy" (168). Given his lifelong fantasies of scripting death, Buchwald died in character, affirming life to the end.

How did Buchwald feel about completing his end-of-life memoir? Did he experience a welcome sense of closure? In *Too Soon to Say Goodbye* he notes his long correspondence with William F. Buckley Jr., who, when he heard Buchwald was dying, wrote a sympathetic letter and mentioned that "Hertz might throw in six pallbearers for free" (92). Buckley died in 2008, and his son, Christopher Buckley, admits in his memoir *Losing Mum and Pup* that although most authors are "happy—thrilled, even, to the point of doing cartwheels—upon finishing a book," his father's depression deepened after completing what he suspected would be his last book (146). I suspect that Buchwald was delighted he was able to complete *Too Soon to Say Goodbye,* though he may have wished to write a sequel.

No one has written about dying with such feisty humor as Buchwald. He wanted the world to notice his life—and death. Thinking about his obituary in the *New York Times,* he says he doesn't want any head of state or Nobel Prize winner to die on the same day he does: "I don't want them to use up my space" (*Too Soon to Say Goodbye* 52). He knew he would be dead by the time his memoir was published, but he wanted one more opportunity for fame, immortality, and a posterity self. He also knew he would remain alive as long as his books are read. Sandra M. Gilbert calls this phenomenon "textual resurrection" and cites the following line from Walt Whitman's *Leaves of Grass*—"Who touches this book touches a man" (72). Simon Critchley observes in *The Book of Dead Philosophers* that "wherever a philosopher is read, he or she is not dead. If you want to communicate with the dead, then read a book" (243). The same is true of end-of-life memoirists. They remain alive to us as long as we remember them. Or as Critchley says, citing Jacques Derrida's belief in "impossible mourning," the "dead live on within us in a way that disturbs any self-satisfaction, but which troubles us and invites us to reflect on them further" (243).

We smile upon completing *Too Soon to Say Goodbye* because of Buchwald's ability to remain joyful despite or because of the many sorrows he has borne. "I've always been an upbeat person. It's the thing that has kept me going all my life. To the many people who wrote me, I mostly answered like this: 'Thanks for your letter. I'm writing as fast as I can. Love, Art'" (91).

"Love, Art" contains an unintended pun, a double entendre, for we love both the man and his art, the many irrepressible stories, funny and sad, satirical and poignant, that he penned for more than half a century. In devoting himself to his art, he managed to stave off death and helped countless readers endure their own losses. "Performing for laughs was my salvation," he writes in *Leaving Home*. "The other thing that helped me escape the reality of our lives was to concoct mysterious stories about myself" (61). His love for himself was, finally, inseparable from his love for art and fantasy. In *Too Soon to Say Goodbye* he transmutes what might otherwise be a story of suffering and sorrow into an affirmation of a joyful, fulfilling life. He found a way to make dying less lonely and frightening, first by holding court in hospice, then by appearing on radio and television programs, then by scripting his own funeral, and finally by writing *Too Soon to Say Goodbye,* which provides us with the pleasure of an earned happy ending.

CHAPTER 9

"Learn How to Live, and You'll Know How to Die"
Morrie Schwartz's *Letting Go* and Mitch Albom's *Tuesdays with Morrie*

⌒

*N*early everyone has heard of *Tuesdays with Morrie,* Mitch Albom's best-selling memoir about his relationship with his former Brandeis University sociology professor Morrie Schwartz, who succumbed to amyotrophic lateral sclerosis on November 4, 1995, a month short of his seventy-ninth birthday. Few people know, however, that a year before Albom published his book, Schwartz published his own end-of-life memoir, *Letting Go,* in which he offers his reflections on "living while dying." Curiously, *Tuesdays with Morrie* never refers to *Letting Go,* which offers a fascinating insight into Schwartz's life. Nor does Schwartz, who writes about reestablishing ties with people he had been out of touch with for years, "including former students who contacted me after hearing that I was ill" (*Letting Go* 70), mention Albom in *Letting Go.* The two memoirs complement and complicate each other.

A Research Sociologist

Long before he became known to millions of readers as Morrie, he was Morris S. Schwartz, the coauthor of three scholarly books on mental illness. Before developing ALS, Schwartz never wrote about death and dying, but much of what he wrote about mental illness helps us to understand his final years as a patient. After receiving his PhD in sociology from the University of Chicago in the 1950s, Schwartz worked for five years at Chestnut Lodge, a psychiatric institution in Rockville, Maryland. The experience influenced his later research and teaching.

In his first book, *The Mental Hospital,* coauthored with psychiatrist Alfred H. Stanton, Schwartz writes from the point of view of participant-observer, which subverts the position that "'the doctor knows best,' or that the sociologist, being free for scientific inquiry, 'knows best'" (435). Many of the authors' observations about mental patients have uncanny relevance to dying patients, including the recognition that they see the world as "unreal," live with the feeling "of restraint and being closed in, or suffocated," and experience "utter, desperate, and unrelieved loneliness, with no hope of change" (169). Stanton and Schwartz's empathy is striking, along with their knowledge that those who are ill or dying need to remain connected with others. Attachment theory, formulated by John Bowlby in his three-volume work *Attachment and Loss,* is central to Stanton and Schwartz's vision of psychiatry and sociology, respectively. Throughout *The Mental Hospital* they champion the value of human connectedness. Alienation, isolation, and stigmatization are as problematic for the dying patient as for the mentally ill patient. "To be a mental patient"—or a dying patient—"means to feel removed from the human race and to view oneself as not quite human" (169).

Schwartz's next book, *The Nurse and the Mental Patient,* coauthored with Emmy Lanning Shockley, a psychiatric nurse and former director of nursing education at Chestnut Lodge, explores the problem of "withdrawn" patients. The coauthors make a valuable distinction between solitude and withdrawal. "In solitude one takes time out to be alone, to think, to contemplate events that have occurred, or to become reacquainted with oneself and the changes that have happened in one's life. One temporarily removes oneself from relations with others. But in a withdrawn state the patient is constantly by himself and away from others. Only rarely does he associate with anyone on his own initiative" (91). The distinction between solitude and withdrawal is important not only for the mental patient but also for the dying patient. Solitude may be considered a preparation for dying, therefore, necessary, whereas withdrawal makes dying more difficult.

Morris Schwartz's final coauthored book, *Social Approaches to Mental Patient Care,* written with his wife, Charlotte Green Schwartz, discusses the "ancillary therapies" found in most mental hospitals, including occupational therapy, music therapy, recreational therapy, and bibliotherapy. The objective of these therapies is to allow patients to express themselves. These activities encourage patients to "discover unknown talents and desires and to develop deep and continuing interests in creative work" (123). The authors make several recommendations at the end of the book, including a revision of the role of the mental patient. "Genuine respect for the patient and for the dignity of his person, some privacy in living arrangements, and opportunities for the cultivation of self-esteem must be built into his role" (300).

A Participant-Observer of His Own Illness

Schwartz's extensive experience as a participant-observer serves him well when, dying of ALS, he pens his only single-author book, *Letting Go*. "When you're ill, you need to learn to be both a participant and an observer in whatever is happening to you. In my own case, I had developed this capacity over several years when I was a researcher at Chestnut Lodge Sanatorium, where I observed and analyzed patient-staff interactions for a project on mental illness" (*Letting Go* 99). Being a participant-observer enables him to write about himself with detachment, "watching what was happening, even though the events themselves were very, very moving emotionally. There came a time when I could almost simultaneously look at what was going on while I was experiencing it" (99).

Letting Go is written in a simple style that is never simplistic, pedantic, or condescending. One can fault Schwartz for his overuse of qualifiers like *very* and clichés like *the plague,* but it's unlikely he had the time or energy to revise the dictated chapters. The tone of *Letting Go* is upbeat and inspirational without being overly platitudinous. Throughout the book Schwartz speaks like a teacher, but he realizes that no one is an expert on death and dying. His humility is reflected in his self-effacing humor. "I've never been a very brave person in terms of dealing with physical pain. If I were in a torture chamber and my inquisitors wanted a confession, I probably would confess fast" (107). Some of his statements in *Letting Go* are obvious and unnecessary, such as, "get as much help as you can when you need it" (10). Other recommendations are easier to accept in theory than in practice: "Be hopeful but not foolishly hopeful" (106). And other statements contain understated irony: "Entertain the thought and feeling that the distance between life and death may not be as great as you think" (119).

Unlike other end-of-life memoirs such as Harold Brodkey's *This Wild Darkness,* Edward Said's *Out of Place,* Tony Judt's *The Memory Chalet,* and Art Buchwald's *Too Soon to Say Goodbye, Letting Go* describes in wrenching detail the relentless deterioration of the body. This is one of the memoir's strengths. Schwartz captures in a few pages the cruelty of the fatal, degenerative disease in which the mind remains alert as the body massively fails. Upon learning in 1994 that he has ALS, he asks himself, "Am I going to die, or am I going to live?" (3). He never doubts that he will soon succumb to the disease, but he vows not to withdraw from life, as many people in his situation would do. Remaining alive means observing the inexorable progression of the disease. He describes his difficulty swallowing and anticipates the loss of speech, remarking that people will need to "frame much of what they are saying as questions that I can answer in a yes-or-no code. That's the way I am approaching the coming loss of speech" (6). He urges those in his situation not to remain preoccupied with either their body or their illness. "Recognize that your body is not your total self, only part of it" (13).

Any disease, especially one like ALS, can rob patients of their dignity, but it is possible to create what Harvey Max Chochinov, a psychiatrist at the University of Manitoba, calls a model of "dignity-conserving" palliative care.

> Continuity of self refers to a sense that the essence of who one is remains intact, in spite of an advancing illness. *Role preservation* is the ability of patients to function or remain invested in their usual roles, as a way of maintaining congruence with a prior view of themselves. *Maintenance of pride* is the ability to maintain a positive sense of self-regard or self-respect. *Hopefulness* is seeing life as enduring, or as having sustained meaning or purpose. *Autonomy/control* is the ability to maintain a sense of control over one's life circumstances. *Generativity/legacy* is the solace or comfort of knowing that something of one's life will transcend death. *Acceptance* is an ability to accommodate to changing life circumstances. Finally, *resiliency/fighting* spirit is the mental determination exercised in an attempt to overcome illness or to optimize quality of life. (2256)

Significantly, all eight subthemes discussed by Chochinov appear in *Letting Go*. Schwartz never wavers in his continuity of self, and he clearly relishes his role as teacher and mentor. So, too, does his pride remain intact. His hopefulness arises not from his belief in a miraculous cure but from the conviction that his life has had enduring meaning and purpose. He demonstrates autonomy/control first by writing and then, when that is no longer possible, by dictating his book. His generativity/legacy is evident on every page of *Letting Go*. His acceptance of death coexists with his resiliency/fighting spirit as he continues to battle with life even as he prepares to let go.

Without deceiving himself about the challenges that await him, Schwartz interprets some of his losses as gains. He recognizes that he will soon lose the power of speech, but he knows he will be able to "take advantage of silence, because maybe that's the way to really hear yourself" (*Letting Go* 5). Anticipating the worst helps him, paradoxically, adapt to his deteriorating health. "Whatever powers you find yourself losing, be it walking or talking or being as mentally sharp as before, the more you can anticipate their impact, the easier your adjustment will be" (7). ALS may have shattered his assumptive world during the beginning of his illness, but he retains his belief in the goals that he has pursued since childhood: "to behave with courage, dignity, generosity, humor, love, openhearted-ness, patience, and self-respect" (12).

Schwartz's advice to his readers in *Letting Go* is consistent with the observations he makes in his three coauthored psychiatric books. The bedrock of his philosophy lies in the open expression of emotions, especially dark emotions: frustration, anger, bitterness, resentment, and shame. He has an abiding belief in the talking cure. He advocates talking honestly with those who will listen, and, when necessary, speaking with a therapist, particularly if one suffers from depression. He remains realistic about the value of speaking about one's illness. "The catharsis or relief you get doesn't mean your grief is all over and has been resolved or that crying has taken care of the situation. Rather, for the moment you come to some stasis, some sense of rest" (36). Abounding in philosophical and psychological insights, *Letting Go* reads like a contemporary version of the *ars moriendi,* the art of dying, a tradition that emerged in the fifteenth and sixteenth centuries. A secular *ars moriendi, Letting Go* provides useful advice for the dying and their caregivers: how to manage physical and psychological pain, how to accept the inevitability of death, how to cope with stressful situations, how to grieve, and how to achieve inner peace.

Schwartz is not afraid to mention that he cries—often. "I let the tears flow until they dry up. And then I start to think about what I'm crying about. I'm crying about my own death, my departure from people I love, the sense of unfinished business and of leaving this beautiful world. Crying has helped me gradually come to accept the end—the fact that all living things die" (*Letting Go* 30). His revelation is counter to the cultural bias that men should not cry. In *Men Don't Cry . . . Women Do,* Terry Martin and Kenneth Doka describe three distinct patterns of grief: intuitive, instrumental, and blended. Intuitive grievers convert their energy into the affective domain, while instrumental grievers convert their energy into the cognitive domain. Those with a blended pattern, which constitutes the majority of grievers, reflect a balance or symmetry in their affective and cognitive responses (32). Based on these classification, Schwartz lies midway between being an intuitive and blended griever. Without privileging the affective over the cognitive, he knows that terminal illness poses greater challenges to our emotional understanding rather than to our intellectual understanding.

Schwartz affirms the writing cure as well as the talking cure. After he became ill, he started to write "aphorisms for my own benefit" (*Letting Go* 66). Soon he shared his writings with family and friends, and then the aphorisms became the basis for an interview published in the *Boston Globe.* Few of these aphorisms are memorable or witty—Schwartz never rises to the level of the masters of the aphoristic genre, such as Michel de Montaigne, Blaise Pascal, Francois de La Rochefoucauld, Friedrich Nietzsche, Mark Twain, or Oscar Wilde—but collectively the aphorisms cast much light on love and loss, dying and death.

Schwartz mentions several writers in *Letting Go,* and it is instructive to see what he learns from each one. He acknowledges that George H. Mead's *Mind, Self, and Society* influenced him in graduate school. He singles out Mead's early emphasis on "taking the role of the other." Mead doesn't use the word *empathy* to describe taking the role of the other, but he implies this—and empathy is a key word throughout Schwartz's writings. Schwartz refers briefly to Martin Buber's *I and Thou,* published in German in 1923 and translated into English in 1937. Schwartz interprets the I-Thou relationship to mean that self and other are reciprocally related without a loss of individuality. Schwartz paraphrases Auden's celebrated line in his poem "September 1, 1939," "Love each other or die" (*Letting Go* 122), though he doesn't note, as David Rieff does in *Swimming in a Sea of Death,* that Auden changed the line to read "We must love one another and die." Schwartz also refers to Alexander Bowen's "useful" book *The Betrayal of the Body.* "His idea is that we think our body should be perfect or at least should be functioning at a high level all the time. When it does not, we feel betrayed by it as if there's some ordained commandment that we always will be healthy and our body always will be responsive" (*Letting Go* 7–8).

Elizabeth Kübler-Ross's Influence

Curiously, Schwartz does not cite the book that most influenced his thinking: Elisabeth Kübler-Ross's *On Death and Dying.* Most of his insights echo her statements. The subtitle of *Letting Go—Morrie's Reflections on Living while Dying*—reminds us of Kübler-Ross's observation in *Death Is of Vital Importance* that she is not the "death and dying lady" but the "life and living lady" (137). His emphasis on ventilation recalls her similar statements in *On Death and Dying.* Both writers urge the dying to express all of their emotions, positive and negative, and they encourage family and friends to listen patiently and empathically, without offering false hope or consolation. Additionally, they both argue that grieving, mourning, and crying are natural processes that help one to prepare for death. Like Kübler-Ross, Schwartz urges patients suffering from "reactive depression" to enter psychotherapy. Like her, he implicitly accepts Freud's theory of decathexis, of "letting go," though he affirms a relational vision where the dying remain connected to the living.

Perhaps most important of all, Schwartz knows, like Kübler-Ross, that the dying person experiences different and, often simultaneously, contradictory emotions. He does not refer to the stage theory of dying, but he writes about denial, anger, depression, and acceptance. He admits that he went "in and out of acceptance" shortly after learning he had ALS. There are other similarities, including Schwartz's emphasis on "life review," the exact term Kübler-Ross uses to describe how the deceased should reflect on their lives. Forgiveness lies at the heart of their writings.

Both Schwartz and Kübler-Ross are inspirational writers, conveying courage, strength, hope, humor, and dignity. And both affirm teaching and learning from the other. "They tell me they are learning from me," he observes in *Letting Go,* sounding like Kübler-Ross, "that watching me is an inspiration to them. And in return I feel that they're continuing to keep me alive because there's so much energy and good feeling, love, concern, and care that comes from these friends, as well as from my family. Since I'm so restricted in my movements, they bring the world in" (83). Schwartz's concluding exhortation in *Letting Go*—"Learn how to live, and you'll know how to die; learn how to die and you'll know how to live" (125)—could appear in any of Kübler-Ross's books.

If Kübler-Ross's spirit hovers over *Letting Go,* why, then, does Schwartz fail to express his indebtedness to her? It's unlikely that he experienced what Harold Bloom calls the "anxiety of influence," the belief that "precursor" writers intimidate living ones. It's more likely that Schwartz fails to mention Kübler-Ross because of his skepticism of her later ideas: her out-of-body experiences, her mysticism and occultism, her belief in reincarnation and communion with the dead, her conversations with Jesus, and her assertion that death is a wonderful and positive experience. The secular Schwartz was concerned with this life, not the next one, and nowhere do we see in *Letting Go,* as we do in *The Wheel of Life,* the desire to be on the "other side."

And yet, paradoxically, Schwartz acknowledges near the end of *Letting Go* his evolving spirituality. In the penultimate chapter, "Developing a Spiritual Connection," he discloses his early rejection of his father's Orthodox Jewish faith, his gradual dissatisfaction with his own agnosticism, his growing interest in Eastern meditation, and his ongoing search for spiritual truth. "The fact that you're seeking means you've already established a spiritual connection" (116). In his view, people are spiritual not because of the answers they reach but because of the questions they raise. In the last chapter, "Considering Death," Schwartz recounts an allegory, told to him by his meditation teacher, about a male wave who is terrified about crashing into the shore and being annihilated. A female wave responds, reassuringly, "You don't understand. You're not a wave; you're part of the ocean" (127). Schwartz ends with the assertion that though he will soon die, he will continue to live on. "In some other form? Who knows? But I believe that I am part of a larger whole" (127).

There are few regrets in *Letting Go,* apart from those events over which Schwartz had no control, such as the death of his mother when he was eight years old. The loss left him bereft his entire life. The experience "sensitized Morrie to loss and his need for other people," observes a former student, Paul Solman, in the introduction to *Letting Go* (xi). Maternal loss was the shaping event in Schwartz's life, as it was in Brodkey's and Buchwald's lives, influencing not only their choice of career but also their interest in mourning and bereavement. According to Solman, Schwartz stated that "Greenhouse," the low-fee psychotherapy organization he created in the 1960s, arose from his ability "to mourn loss, starting with his mother and ending with himself" (xv).

Letting Go is a personal account of Schwartz's battle with terminal illness, and in it he reveals his grief over his mother's death and his anger toward his father who refused to allow him to grieve. The book reveals nothing, however, about how his illness has affected his wife and two children. To this extent it resembles *The Wheel of Life, Out of Place, The Memory Chalet,* and *Too Soon to Say Goodbye.* Schwartz is also uncomfortable with his loss of privacy. "When you're sick, privacy becomes a valuable commodity because it's very hard to come by. As I get more and more dysfunctional, I have to suffer more invasion of my privacy" (91).

The Astonishing Popularity of Tuesdays with Morrie

This invasion of privacy for Schwartz and his family was nothing, however, compared to the publicity they received following the publication of Mitch Albom's *Tuesdays with Morrie.* The book soon reached the "number one" position on the *New York Times* bestseller list, where it remained for 205 weeks. *Tuesdays with Morrie* is one of the best-selling memoirs of all time, selling over 14 million copies. Translated into 41 languages, it was made into a television movie, produced by Oprah Winfrey and starring Jack Lemmon (in his last credited role) as Morrie and Hank Azaria as Mitch Albom. *Tuesdays with Morrie* was the most-watched TV movie of 1999 and won four Emmy Awards. The book is now taught in high schools and colleges throughout the world.

Albom, a professional sports columnist for the *Detroit Free Press,* had lost contact with his professor after graduation. Seeing the dying Schwartz interviewed by Ted Koppel on the ABC television program *Nightline,*

Albom decided to reconnect with him. Experiencing an early midlife crisis, Albom felt emotionally drawn to Schwartz, who quickly became a father figure to him. Albom flew to Massachusetts every week—on Tuesdays—to interview his former mentor, who lived in West Newton, a quiet suburb of Boston. A slim memoir that can be read in a few hours, *Tuesdays with Morrie* explores Schwartz's reflections on death, dying, and the meaning of life. The reflections prove transformative to his former student, who quickly becomes his teacher's disciple.

Albom's Acknowledged and Unacknowledged Indebtedness to Schwartz

The "Morrie" who appears in *Letting Go* is similar to the eponymous figure who reflects upon death in Albom's memoir. Most of Schwartz's observations in *Tuesdays with Morrie* echo those he makes in *Letting Go*, beginning with his statement to Ted Koppel, "when all this started, I asked myself, 'Am I going to withdraw from the world, like most people do, or am I going to live?' I decided I'm going to live—or at least try to live—the way I want, with dignity, with courage, with humor, with composure" (*Tuesdays with Morrie* 21). As in *Letting Go*, he emphasizes the importance of emotional self-expression, including crying. In both memoirs he affirms the need to remain connected with others, and he reaches out to a larger audience who may be interested in his story. The allegory of the wave appears in both *Letting Go* and *Tuesdays with Morrie*, along with the theme of (self-)forgiveness. Acceptance of death is central to both *Letting Go* and *Tuesdays with Morrie*. After stating, "once you learn how to die, you learn how to live" (82), Schwartz repeats the sentence, word for word, *three* times. As in *Letting Go*, his most essential advice in *Tuesdays with Morrie* is the need to love and be loved—and he then cites the same line from Auden's poem.

There are also differences between the two Morries. He's blunter and funnier in Albom's story. "Mitch, you are one of the good ones " (4), he tells his student, who has presented him with a briefcase with his initials on the front, immediately after graduation. It's an odd remark, implying that not all of Schwartz's students were good. Albom cites one of Schwartz's wry aphorisms that does not appear in *Letting Go:* "When you're in bed, you're dead" (131). Schwartz's abrasive side is evident in Albom's story. When Ted Koppel asks him for his impressions of *Nightline,* Schwartz pauses, then admits that he thought Koppel was a "narcissist" (21). He's also earthier, admitting to Koppel and Albom his fear that soon "someone's gonna have to wipe my ass" (22).

Albom expresses his gratitude to Schwartz for his help, but he never cites *Letting Go,* the precursor to *Tuesdays with Morrie.* Why the omission? Did Albom fear that Schwartz's self-characterization in *Letting Go* would lessen the originality of *Tuesdays with Morrie*? Was he apprehensive that Schwarz's reflections in *Letting Go* on "living while dying" might eliminate or diminish the need for his own story about "an old man, a young man, and life's greatest lesson"? Throughout *Tuesdays with Morrie* Albom focuses on the student-teacher relationship, yet the student seems remiss in documenting his reliance on his teacher's own book on death and dying.

Not that *Tuesdays with Morrie* fails to offer us new information about Schwartz. We learn that shortly after his diagnosis, Schwartz "hobbled" into the classroom to teach his final course. "My friends, I assume you are all here for the Social Psychology class. I have been teaching this course for twenty years, and this is the first time I can say there is a risk in taking it, because I have a fatal illness. I may not live to finish the semester" (9). I admire Schwartz's openness, his willingness to make risky self-disclosures. Death becomes his final research project, and he shares his conclusions with his students. I'm sympathetic to his decision to make death education a part of his college curriculum, but I wish that he had told us his students' reactions to their dying professor. Was he as life-affirming in the course as he is in *Letting Go*? Did anyone drop the course? Albom never discusses these questions though he quotes Henry Adams's observation that "a teacher affects eternity; he can never tell where his influence stops" (79).

"Our Final Thesis"

Tuesdays with Morrie raises another question. "I always wished I had done more with my work," Schwartz confesses to Albom toward the end of *Tuesdays with Morrie.* "I wished I had written more books. I used to beat myself up over it. Now I see that never did any good" (166–67). We never learn what those books might have been about or why he failed to write them. His three coauthored books were written early in his career. Published in a ten-year period and totaling more than eleven hundred pages in print, *The*

Mental Hospital, *The Nurse and the Mental Patient*, and *Social Approaches to Mental Patient Care* reveal that he was a prolific and speedy writer, bursting with ideas. The last of these books appeared in 1964, thirty years before he became ill. The publication gap is mystifying. Did Schwartz feel that he had nothing more to say after 1964? Did he lose the self-discipline that is essential for scholarship? Albom reveals in the conclusion to *Tuesdays with Morrie* that the book was "largely Morrie's idea. He called it our 'final thesis'" (191). If the book genuinely was a collaborative effort, did they consider the possibility of coauthorship? Nowhere in *Letting Go* or *Tuesdays with Morrie* does Schwartz express a desire for literary fame or immortality. Nevertheless, he wanted his story to be told, and by encouraging Albom to write about their time together, he affirms the need for a posterity self—though neither teacher nor student could imagine the astounding popularity of the end-of-life memoir.

Tuesdays with Morrie is a highly readable "thesis," but there are several gaps and omissions in it. We learn little about Schwartz's forty-four-year marriage. Albom refers occasionally to Charlotte Schwartz, always positively, but in both *Letting Go* and *Tuesdays with Morrie* Schwartz's wife is off-limits for discussion. Albom admits, in a candid passage, "Charlotte was a private person, different from Morrie, but I knew how much he respected her, because sometimes when we spoke, he would say, 'Charlotte might be uncomfortable with me revealing that,' and he would end the conversation. It was the only time Morrie held anything back" (148–49). The silence piques the reader's interest. How did Charlotte Schwartz, her husband's coauthor, feel about his need to surround himself with friends and students during the last months of his life? How did his illness affect her? How did she feel about the sudden media attention and the loss of privacy? Did she consider coauthoring *Letting Go* with him, discussing how a wife prepares for her husband's death?

Letting Go and *Tuesdays with Morrie* reveal the need to overcome shame associated with a disease like ALS. We learn in *Tuesdays with Morrie* that Schwartz depends upon others for nearly everything except for breathing and swallowing—and even these two body functions are compromised at the end. He speaks with characteristic honesty when he reveals acceptance of his situation. Some of his statements are counterintuitive, as when he admits enjoying his dependency. One reason he needs to remain connected with others is to manage his death anxiety; another reason is to overcome shame. One of his goals is to "shame shame," that is, to bring to light that which usually remains hidden. In the end we are powerless over death, but we can regard it as a natural process, without the shame and terror that often accompany it. A week before his death he tells Albom, in a raspy voice, "Death ends a life, not a relationship" (*Tuesdays with Morrie* 174).

During the fourteenth and final Tuesday, Albom admits that he doesn't know how to express farewell to his beloved teacher and "Coach," to which Schwartz responds, in a barely audible voice, "This . . . is how we say . . . goodbye . . ." (185). They express their love for each other and, for the first and only time in the story, Albom cries.

Schwartz dies calmly and serenely; dying is wrenching, but death is a welcome release. He dies when those attending him are momentarily out of the room, a phenomenon that occurs more often than not. Virginia Morris offers an explanation of this phenomenon. "I have been told that this happens because patients do not want their loved ones to see them go. They want to spare them that pain" (120–21). Albom does not cite Morris, but he endorses her explanation. "I believe he died this way on purpose. I believe he wanted no chilling moments, no one to witness his last breath and be haunted by it, the way he had been haunted by his mother's death-notice telegram or by his father's corpse in the city morgue" (*Tuesdays with Morrie* 187–88).

Schwartz appears not only at peace with himself throughout the story but also wise and benevolent. He acknowledges anger, frustration, sadness, and self-pity, but he always seems to act selflessly, as when he tells his sons, "Do not stop your lives. . . . Otherwise, this disease will have ruined three of us instead of one" (*Tuesdays with Morrie* 10). He consents cheerfully to be a research subject, a human textbook: *"Study me in my slow and patient demise. Watch what happens to me. Learn with me"* (10). His words evoke Tolstoy's Ivan Ilych, who wears a medallion with the words *respice finem* inscribed on his watch chain: "look to the end." Unlike Tolstoy's protagonist, who reaches a transformative epiphany only at the end of his life, Schwartz's death is consistent with his life: he dies in character.

To compare Albom to Tolstoy is not to imply that *Tuesdays with Morrie* has the literary power of *The Death of Ivan Ilych*. No story about mortality, fictional or nonfictional, rivals Tolstoy's masterpiece in its language, insights, and power of observation. Tolstoy's Olympian detachment and authorial omniscience remain unsurpassed. Albom shows the deterioration of Schwartz's body, but he doesn't capture, as Tolstoy does, the terror of mortality, including the lies, evasions, and self-deception surrounding death and dying. Nor do we experience in *Tuesdays with Morrie,* as we do in *The Death of Ivan Ilych,* a character's profound existential and spiritual despair. Albom succeeds, however, in showing how an insidious disease like ALS ravages Schwartz's body without weakening his indomitable spirit. One recalls Hemingway's observation in *The Old Man and the Sea:* "A man can be destroyed but not defeated."

"A Teacher to the Last"

Throughout *Tuesdays with Morrie* Schwartz embodies unconditional love. He is never angry or disappointed with his former student, never possessive or judgmental, never condescending or pedantic. He remains an idealized father figure from beginning to end. "If I could have had another son, I would have liked it to be you,", he remarks when he is close to death (168). There are times when he appears almost saintly. His physical suffering—his struggle to speak, swallow, and breathe—conjures up the image of martyrdom. Some readers may believe that Schwartz resembles, in his wisdom, compassion, and unimaginable physical suffering, Jesus, a comparison that helps to explain Albom's role as disciple.

Schwartz's blessing is important to Albom because for sixteen years the student feels guilty that he has neglected his former professor. As the story opens, Albom seems to be failing the "test" of life, and he cannot prevent himself from raising the question, *"What happened to me?"* (33). Thirty-seven years old when he reconnects with Schwartz, Albom portrays himself as a relentlessly driven person who, in his pursuit of fame and fortune, has lost touch with the meaning of life. Schwartz teaches him valuable life lessons: be prepared to reject a culture that promotes materialism and narcissism; remain connected with relatives, friends, and teachers; don't be afraid to express emotions, including the need to cry; experience emotions deeply and then let them go; never forget that love is the most important part of life; and accept the inevitability of change, including death. The words Schwartz wants inscribed on his tombstone—"A Teacher to the Last" (134)—characterize his lasting impact on Albom, who becomes a faithful follower by writing the story of their friendship.

Letting Go and *Tuesdays with Morrie* leave us with several ironies. Schwartz observes dryly to Albom, "Now that I'm dying, I've become much more interesting to people" (32). Albom becomes involved with Schwartz precisely at the time his mentor is in the process of detaching himself from life. Having forgiven himself for not writing more books, Schwartz writes one more book—two, if we count *Tuesdays with Morrie,* which reads like a coauthored work. Despite the fact that Schwartz had a long and respected career as a research sociologist and professor, few of us would know about the teacher were it not for his student. Albom constructs Schwartz into a national icon.

The cynical Albom becomes humanized—tenderized—as a result of his meetings with Schwartz. The teacher's influence on his student persists, as we can see from Albom's later writings. In *The Five People You Meet in Heaven,* a character declares that lost love is still love. "It takes a different form, that's all. You can't see their smile or bring them food or tousle their hair or move them around a dance floor. But when those senses weaken, another heightens. Memory. Memory becomes your partner" (173). Schwartz states at the end of Albom's story: "As long as we can love each other, and remember the feeling of love we had, we can die without ever really going away" (174). Albom reaffirms this belief in the epilogue to *For One More Day:* "Sharing tales of those we've lost is how we keep from really losing them" (197). *Tuesdays with Morrie* may not prove, as Henry Adams claimed, that a teacher affects eternity, but it does demonstrate that pedagogical wisdom may last a lifetime and affect countless people.

CHAPTER 10

"I'm Dying and I'm Having Fun"

Randy Pausch and *The Last Lecture*

~~~~~~

andy Pausch's *The Last Lecture* never refers to *Letting Go* or *Tuesdays with Morrie,* but the stories have much in common. Like Schwartz, Pausch was an academic who disclosed to his students that he was dying. Both believed in the inseparability of life education and death education. Both offered their advice—personal, psychological, philosophical, and educational—to readers, many of whom were college students, about achieving a good death. The two professors demonstrated that death is both private and communal.

There is no evidence that *Too Soon to Say Goodbye* is the inspiration behind *The Last Lecture,* but Art Buchwald and Randy Pausch also have much in common. Like Buchwald, Pausch was a media star for death, appearing on national radio and television programs. Buchwald was interviewed on *60 Minutes;* Pausch appeared on *The Oprah Winfrey Show* and then, shortly before his death from pancreatic cancer, on July 25, 2008, at age forty-seven, he was the subject of an hour-long Diane Sawyer feature on ABC. Buchwald's statement that he never knew dying could be so much "fun" is almost identical to Pausch's observation that "I'm dying and I'm having fun" (179). Having fun meant speaking to a large audience in which the dying men could tell their stories, convey the life lessons they learned and sought to pass along to others, and receive support from their readers. Having fun also meant refusing to allow impending death to darken their sunny vision of life. Like Buchwald, Pausch fantasizes about a heroic death, imagining his last lecture like the final scene in *The Natural*, "when the aging, bleeding ballplayer Roy Hobbes miraculously hits that towering home run" (7).

Both Buchwald and Pausch use gallows humor, jokes, anecdotes, and wisecracks in their stories, and both delight in shattering the conventional wisdom about dying and death. Both prove to be articulate advocates for worthwhile organizations, Buchwald for hospice, Pausch for the two organizations dedicated to fighting the disease that would soon kill him, the Pancreatic Cancer Action Network and the Lustgarten Foundation. (He also testified before Congress in support of additional money for pancreatic cancer research.) Pausch was never in remission long enough to become the man who would not die, nor did he live a long life, but he did everything he could to remain alive, and his memoir, no less than Buchwald's, is both upbeat and inspirational.

Being a media star has its ambiguities. "If death was 'medicalized' in the mid- to late twentieth century," Douglas J. Davies observes, "at the turn of the new millennium it became increasingly 'media-ized'" (74). He uses the neologism to describe the frequency with which corpses appear in detective or war films. "Seldom does any British murder-hunt forget to include at least one visit to the morgue where a post-mortem is under way" (73). Unlike corpses in real life that are unsettling to witness, those on television or in a film are "safe when viewed in comfort" (74). Davies does not comment on end-of-life memoirs that portray death as entertaining, but these, too, may be viewed as media-ized. By portraying dying as fun, Pausch takes the sting out of death, which helps to explain the popularity of *The Last Lecture*.

We cannot trace the development of Pausch's vision of death over the course of a lifetime, as we can with the other memoirists in my study. Nor can we see a shift in attitude toward death within the memoir itself: death remains safely in the distance, even at the end of the story. But *The Last Lecture* is notable, partly because it has become a publishing phenomenon on college campuses; partly because of Pausch's creation of a posterity self for a world in which he would no longer be alive; partly because his story is quintessentially American, the embodiment of the American dream; and partly because he wanted to die in character, expressing undying love and gratitude for a life in which nearly all of his aspirations came true.

"What Wisdom Would We Impart?"

Pausch was a professor of computer science and human-computer interaction at Carnegie Mellon University in Pittsburgh when he was diagnosed with pancreatic cancer in September 2006. Not long after the diagnosis, when he still hoped for a cure, Carnegie Mellon asked him to give a talk in their Last Lecture Series in which selected professors were asked to offer reflections on their professional and personal lives. "What wisdom would we impart to the world if we knew it was our last chance? If we had to vanish tomorrow, what would we want as our legacy?" (Pausch 3). These are challenging questions for anyone, but they become daunting for someone who has only a few months to live, as Pausch discovered in August 2007, one month before the scheduled lecture. Rather than canceling, he delivered the aptly titled "The Last Lecture" on September 18, 2007, to an audience of four hundred students and faculty. He then elaborated on the content of his talk in *The Last Lecture*, published in 2008. Pausch was reportedly paid $6.7 million for the rights to publish the book by the Disney-owned publisher Hyperion. *The Last Lecture* became a *New York Times* best-seller, and to date more than 4 million copies of the book have been sold in the United States alone.

Pausch remains vague about the composition of *The Last Lecture*. He tells us in the book's introduction that "under the ruse of giving an academic lecture, I was trying to put myself in a bottle that would one day wash up on the beach for my children" (x). He mentions asking *Wall Street Journal* reporter Jeffrey Zaslow, a Carnegie Mellon alumnus, for help. "On fifty-three long bike rides, I spoke to Jeff on my cell-phone headset. He then spent countless hours helping to turn my stories—I suppose we would call them fifty-three 'lectures'—into the book that follows" (x). He never tells us why Zaslow is not listed as a coauthor, nor do we learn how the two men decided what to include and what to omit. Did they have time to revise the manuscript, which is often the most important part of the writing process? What was Pausch's state of health when they completed the manuscript? How did he feel about the completed book?

Jeffrey Zaslow never had the opportunity to write his own life story, for he died on February 10, 2012, in a car accident in northern Michigan. He was fifty-three. After *The Last Lecture* he cowrote, with the pilot

Chesley B. "Sully" Sullenberger III, the book *Highest Duty: My Search for What Really Matters,* about the jet that landed safely in the Hudson River in 2009 with 150 passengers. He also cowrote *Gabby: A Story of Courage and Hope,* about Arizona congresswoman Gabrielle Giffords, who survived a gunshot wound to the head. Paul Vitello observed in an obituary published in the *New York Times* that Zaslow "was drawn to stories about people seeking meaning in their lives, often in the face of mortality." Nearly all the books Zaslow wrote or cowrote became bestsellers. "He was curious about everything, and interested in everything," his wife, Sherry Margolis, a news anchor for television station WJBK Fox 2 in Detroit, said in the obituary. "And he knew what would make a good story" (*New York Times,* February 10, 2012).

The Last Lecture combines several genres: memoir, medical case study, eulogy, caregiving manual, morality tale, college preparatory book, and motivational self-help guide. Pausch reveals how he made nearly all of his academic and personal dreams come true, how he was accepted into a doctoral program that first rejected him, how he used his academic skills to work as an Imagineer for Walt Disney, and how he refused to become depressed when being treated for pancreatic cancer. He remains startlingly positive throughout the story, avoiding the understandable impulse toward self-pity. *The Last Lecture* might be subtitled *Love Story,* but unlike Erich Segal's sentimental novel, Pausch tries to avoid tearing up his readers. Nevertheless, as Fran McInerney suggests, *The Last Lecture* fulfills readers' expectations about a heroic death. "Successful, handsome, articulate, father of three young children and with a rare fatal disease, Pausch embodies many of the dominant traits of the romantic genre" (227). And yet McInerney is understandably reluctant to dismiss *The Last Lecture,* for in many ways it remains a noteworthy book. Pausch's message is worth hearing even if it does not reflect, as McInerney points out, the " 'everyday' deaths of the old, the ugly, the poor, the outcast or the infirm" (227). Pausch ends by expressing optimism, hope, gratitude, and, implicitly, courage and strength, delivering a message that fairy tales are worth pursuing even if they don't always have happy endings.

The memoir begins dramatically, with Pausch acknowledging in the introduction that he has an "engineering" problem: "While for the most part I'm in terrific physical shape, I have ten tumors in my liver and I have only a few months left to live" (ix). He knows that most people will read the book because they have heard about his death. How does one write about death without exploiting it? How does one write a feel-good story about an illness that kills almost everyone who develops it? What makes *The Last Lecture* different from other end-of-life memoirs? How does a dying author avoid coming across as preachy or sanctimonious? These questions must have preoccupied Pausch and Zaslow. It is a tribute to their collaboration that they wrote a memoir that offers a unique perspective on death and dying.

Posterity Self

Pausch is forthright about his need to deliver a last lecture. "Why was this talk so important to me? Was it a way to remind me and everyone else that I was still very much alive? To prove I still had the fortitude to perform? Was it a limelight-lover's urge to show off one last time? The answer was yes on all fronts" (7–8). Pausch's wife, Jai, identifies probably the most important motive: "to leave a legacy for the kids" (9). Struggling to prepare the last lecture, Pausch hints at the rising tension with his wife because his work is taking precious time away from being with his family. Leaving a legacy for the family means, ironically, spending less time with them in the present. "I know Randy," Jai complains to their psychotherapist, whom they began seeing immediately after his diagnosis. "He's a workaholic. I know just what he'll be like when he starts putting the lecture together. It'll be all-consuming" (6).

However difficult the balance between work and family may have been for Pausch before his diagnosis, it becomes more difficult for him afterward. Nevertheless, preparing for the lecture energizes him, and though he knows that no one will blame him if he cancels the talk, he finds himself driven to tell his story. In one sense he is more fortunate than the other memoirists discussed in this book, who were not only working against time but also knew that no one would complete their story if they died prematurely. Recall Julian Barnes's sardonic question: "Would you rather die in the middle of a book, and have some bastard finish it for you, or leave behind a work in progress that not a single bastard in the whole world was remotely interested in finishing?" (109). Barnes never imagines the possibility of a coauthor finishing a deceased writer's book. Coauthor notwithstanding, Pausch writes like a man possessed, and he vows that nothing in his control will prevent him from delivering the lecture.

Pausch never seems uncomfortable about any of his self-disclosures; the idea of writing as betrayal, seen so vividly in Roth's *Patrimony*, would be foreign to him. Whereas Roth takes no comfort in his recent novels from the knowledge that his stories will live on long after his death, the existence of a posterity self is a consolation to Pausch. "I had started to view the talk as a vehicle for me to ride into the future I would never see" (8). Later he observes, about the teaching program he created called Alice, which allows introductory computing students to create animations for telling stories, "Through Alice, millions of kids are going to have incredible fun while learning something hard. They'll develop skills that could help them achieve their dreams. If I have to die, I am comforted by having Alice as a professional legacy" (128). During his talk he brings some of the large stuffed animals he has won at carnivals and invites the students in the audience to take them home, not as a souvenir but as a way for him to remain connected symbolically to other people. "Anybody who would like a piece of me at the end of this, feel free to come up and take a bear; first come, first served" (50).

The Last Lecture does not have a linear narrative, perhaps because Pausch did not know whether he would have enough time to sketch the movement from past to present. Instead, the book is anecdotal, moving forward and backward in time. There is no particular order in the sixty-one brief chapters or vignettes in the book. Once he learns that the cancer has spread to his liver, there is never any doubt about his fate. He focuses not on his impending death but on the rich and fulfilling life that precedes it. Carpe diem, or seize the day, is one of the themes of the story, and Pausch exhorts his readers to live in the moment even as they work to create their future.

Pausch offers few details about his illness or treatment, and almost nothing about the experience of dying. "Pancreatic cancer has the highest mortality rate of any cancer; half of those diagnosed with it die within six months, and 96 percent die within five years" (57). During his cancer treatment he can't help thinking about a line from *Star Trek II: The Wrath of Khan*. "In the film, Starfleet cadets are faced with a simulated training scenario where, no matter what they do, their entire crew is killed. The film explains that when Kirk was a cadet, he reprogrammed the simulation because 'he didn't believe in the no-win scenario'" (45). Pausch discovers that death is easier to avert in art than in life, and though he never gives up hope for a cure, he never falls back upon denial or hopelessness.

After his diagnosis, Pausch underwent the "Whipple" procedure, regarded as one of the most complicated and lengthy surgeries, in which part of his liver, gallbladder, a third of his pancreas, and several feet of his small intestine were removed. Only a small percentage of pancreatic cancer patients are eligible for the debilitating surgery. The surgery caused Pausch's weight to plunge from 182 to 138 pounds. Following surgery, he received chemotherapy and radiation therapy. For a time he appeared cancer-free, but as happens nearly always with pancreatic cancer, the disease soon returned with a vengeance. Pausch mentions how his wife fell into his arms when he breaks the bad news to her, but he doesn't dwell on their shock and sorrow. He *tells* us about their sadness, but he *shows* us his determination to remain focused on staying alive. "The whole horrible exchange was surreal for me. Yes, I felt stunned and bereft for myself and especially for Jai, who couldn't stop crying. But a strong part of me remained in Randy Scientist Mode, collecting facts and quizzing the doctor about options. At the same time, there was another part of me that was utterly engaged in the theater of the moment" (61). Once the cancer metastasizes, the only option is palliative treatment.

Pausch is candid about the help he received following his diagnosis. He finds psychotherapy unexpectedly valuable in helping him and his wife with depression. He also learned—not that he had ever forgotten— the value of remaining optimistic, which was an essential aspect of his character before his diagnosis. "If you're optimistic, you're better able to endure brutal chemo, or keep searching for late-breaking medical treatments" (183). He also remained connected with the many friends, colleagues, and well-wishers who became a part of his support system.

Teachers and Mentors

The Last Lecture allows Pausch to expound upon life, but he knows that "if you dispense your own wisdom, others often dismiss it" (23). Instead, he shrewdly quotes the wisdom of others. Pausch remains indebted to his father, a World War II hero, who died in 2006. His father "encouraged creativity just by smiling at you" (27). Pausch mentions "channeling" his father during the last lecture (23), but he speaks metaphorically; we don't see the literal channeling that Kübler-Ross discusses in *The Wheel of Life*. Pausch's mother was a high school English teacher with a wry sense of humor: "After I got my PhD, my mother took great relish in introducing me by saying: 'This is my son. He's a doctor, but not the kind who helps people'" (24).

Pausch's middle school football coach, Jim Graham, enforced a strong, no-nonsense work ethic and preached the value of learning the fundamentals. "That was a great gift Coach Graham gave us. Fundamentals, fundamentals, fundamentals. As a college instructor, I've seen this as one lesson so many kids ignore, always to their detriment: You've *got* to get the fundamentals down, because otherwise the fancy stuff is not going to work" (36). Andy van Dam, Brown University's legendary computer science professor, kept reminding Pausch that his strengths were also his weaknesses. He advised Pausch to get a PhD and then become a professor, offering an unusual pedagogical explanation: "Because you're such a good salesman, and if you go work for a company, they're going to use you as a salesman. If you're going to be a salesman, you might as well be selling something worthwhile, like education" (172).

Pausch is, in fact, an extraordinary salesman for higher education, in general, and for Carnegie Mellon University, in particular. One of the leaders in virtual technology, he shares his excitement over computer graphics. He encourages his students to use their academic skills in industry and film, citing the example of one undergraduate who was hired by George Lucas to work on a new *Star Trek* film. Pausch motivates his students by raising the bar for success, and he emphasizes the importance of team work, a leadership skill that academia does not always appreciate. Reportedly, Jared Cohon, Carnegie Mellon's president, was so moved by Pausch's interdisciplinary work and his devotion to teaching that the university pledged to name after him a pedestrian bridge linking the university's new computing building and the performing arts center. Pausch also proves to be an extraordinary salesman for Walt Disney Imagineers, the artists, writers, and programmers who design theme parks. He quotes approvingly Walt Disney's statement, "If you can dream it, you can do it" (16), which becomes Pausch's credo.

Pausch dispenses advice throughout *The Last Lecture,* but what prevents the story from becoming tiresome is his self-mocking wit. He tells us that he has given "some pretty good talks" during his career, but "being considered the best speaker in a computer science department is like being known as the tallest of the Seven Dwarfs" (6). Admitting his tendency to be arrogant and self-centered, he refers to himself as a "recovering jerk" (116). After disclosing that Carnegie Mellon initially rejected his application to its doctoral program, he adds, "It's interesting, the secrets you decide to reveal at the end of your life" (174). Some of Pausch's advice goes against conventional wisdom, such as his belief that too many children are coddled, knowing their rights but not their responsibilities. "I've heard so many people talk of a downward spiral in our educational system, and I think one key factor is that there is too much stroking and too little real feedback" (114).

Pausch has nothing kind to say about terminal cancer, which brings few epiphanies, but he is grateful for the time to prepare for the end and express his farewell. Approaching death, he mentions that now he has a "better understanding of the story of Moses, and how he got to see the Promised Land but never got to set foot in it" (128). It is a telling comparison, one that reveals not a little self-regard.

Preaching Virtue

The Last Lecture abounds in advice for those who, like Pausch, believe in working hard to make their childhood dreams come true. Many of his life lessons for personal and professional success recall the "thirteen virtues" Benjamin Franklin includes in his celebrated *Autobiography*. Published in 1809, almost twenty years after his death, Franklin's *Autobiography* is a shaping force behind *The Last Lecture*, not as a conscious or even unconscious literary influence, but as a cultural icon that continues to animate the American dream. There is no evidence that either Pausch or Zaslow read Franklin's *Autobiography*, but there are striking similarities between the two books. Both Franklin and Pausch consciously (and at times self-consciously) preach virtue as they themselves have embodied it in their own lives, and both hope that their admittedly didactic stories will instruct those who read them. Both Franklin and Pausch believe in self-education and self-improvement. Both write their autobiographies for their children: Franklin begins the *Autobiography* with the words "Dear Son," and Pausch is always citing his three children, whom he hopes will be guided by his words. And both Franklin and Pausch not only acknowledge their vanity but also appreciate its positive value. Pausch would almost certainly agree with Franklin's candid statement, in the first paragraph of the *Autobiography*, about one of the main motives for writing a life story. "Most people dislike vanity in others whatever share they have of it themselves, but I give it fair quarter wherever I meet with it, being persuaded that it is often productive of good to the possessor and to others who are within his sphere of action" (4).

Franklin originally conceived of twelve virtues, but he added a thirteenth, humility, in recognition that even pride has its limits. Each virtue includes a brief precept. Pausch endorses in *The Last Lecture,* explicitly or implicitly, *all* of Franklin's virtues. The first, temperance, is implicit: Pausch is fun-loving and irrepressible but always within reason. The second, silence ("speak not but what may benefit others or yourself"), appears in his heartfelt praise for those who have helped him in life, especially his parents, teachers, and mentors. The third, order, characterizes Pausch, a self-described efficiency freak. The fourth, resolution, describes his singular ability to complete the last lecture despite experiencing severe cramps, nausea, and diarrhea from chemotherapy. The fifth, frugality, appears in his recognition that "time must be explicitly managed, like money" (108). The sixth, industry, characterizes his entire life, a model of hard work, persistence, and boundless energy. The seventh, sincerity, characterizes his wife, from whom he learns "directness" and "honesty" (97). The eighth, justice, reflects Pausch's insistence on playing fairly and always telling the truth. The ninth, moderation, combines his work ethic and his ability to have a good time. The tenth, cleanliness, is a quality that the admittedly untidy Pausch learns from his wife. The eleventh, tranquility, may be seen in his calm acceptance of death. The twelfth, chastity, reflects Pausch's marital fidelity. And the thirteenth, humility, may be seen from what Pausch learns from his mentor Andy van Dam: "I was self-possessed to a fault; I was way too brash and I was an inflexible contrarian, always spouting opinions" (67).

Franklin and Pausch have other character traits in common, including their delight in making lists. "I'm a big believer in to-do lists," Pausch admits (108), which is precisely what Franklin does in his *Autobiography,* where he creates a calendar and then marks off the days when he breaks particular virtues. Pausch's fondness for proverbs, what his students call, while rolling their eyes, "Pauschisms" (108), recalls Franklin's pithy precepts. They are alike in another significant way: both were public-spirited inventors who turned down patents that would have made them wealthy. Franklin declined a patent on the famous stove he invented, declaring that "as we enjoy great advantages from the inventions of others, we should be glad of an opportunity to serve others by any invention of ours, and this we should do freely and generously" (143). So, too, did Pausch and Carnegie Mellon forgo a patent on their software Alice, offering it free so that millions of children could use it to create their own dreams.

Many of Pausch's recommendations for success are eminently practical and in the spirit of Franklin's *Autobiography,* including, "you can always change your plan, but only if you have one," "develop a good filing system," "rethink the telephone," "delegate," and "take a time out" (108–10). Some readers may find tips like these pedantic and trivial, especially in a book written at the end of the author's life; other readers may argue that these recommendations demonstrate Pausch's commitment to the future. He also offers timely medical advice that may help the dying and their caregivers, including the courage to endure treatments that have devastating side effects, the refusal to give up hope when confronted with terminal illness, and the ability to remain grateful when many others in the same situation might succumb to despair and bitterness.

Franklin wrote his *Autobiography* over many years, and it remained unfinished at his death. The *Autobiography* has a leisurely, disconnected quality that is different from the urgent tone of *The Last Lecture,* penned in a few months. Franklin's prescription for success, though admired by many readers, evoked the sharp satire first of Mark Twain and then of D. H. Lawrence, who in *Studies in Classic American Literature* railed against Franklin's virtues. "The perfectability of man, dear God! When every man as long as he remains alive is in himself a multitude of conflicting men. Which of these do you choose to perfect, at the expense of every other?" (9). The apocalyptic Lawrence would criticize *The Last Lecture* in the same way, exhorting Pausch to repudiate his "ideal self" and give voice to his "strange and fugitive self" that howls like a wolf or a coyote (9). Non-Lawrentian readers may criticize Pausch's prescription for success, particularly his endorsement of the American dream, which for too many people has remained unrealizable. Franklin has the time to characterize himself in great depth; he is a round, three-dimensional character, while Pausch is not. Franklin was one of the great geniuses of his age—of *any* age; Pausch, by contrast, though a computer science visionary, wisely refuses to compare himself to a genius.

Franklin and Pausch believed in self-education and self-improvement, but they did not have similar temperaments. In many ways they could not be more different. Part of Franklin's character was puritanical, a quality he never completely outgrew. Pausch is a product of the generation that created virtual reality, and he was never obsessed with guilt or with original sin. Franklin's industriousness and frugality compelled him to avoid all appearances to the contrary. "I dressed plain and was seen at no places of idle diversion" (*Autobiography* 82). The flashy Pausch admits that before his marriage he was a bachelor "who spent a lot of time dating around, having great fun, and then losing girlfriends who wanted to get more serious" (73). Many of the differences between Franklin and Pausch are cultural and historical as well as characterological. There are also unmistakable literary differences between *Autobiography* and *The Last Lecture.* Franklin's life story is one of the world's major autobiographies and perhaps the first great American literary classic. *The Last Lecture* does not aspire to be a literary masterpiece, but it is a compelling account of one man's struggle to use his remaining time wisely and courageously. In an age when cynicism and greed are rampant, where morality is honored in the breach, and where entitlement rules the day, the popularity of *The Last Lecture* derives from its affirmative message that the dying can teach the living how to follow their own dreams and enable the dreams of others.

Pausch's optimistic message is part of a long tradition of American popular self-education that begins with Franklin's *Autobiography.* The tradition is easy to criticize, as folklore scholar Sandra K. Dolby concedes in *Self-Help Books,* but self-help books are valuable both for writers and readers. "One latent function of self-help books is that they provide their authors with an opportunity to bear witness to their own transformation or conversion. This may go far in explaining why the expanded essay form is so popular among self-help authors. The intimate, personal tone of the essay permits the unabashed enthusiasm and sense of epiphany the writer is often required to keep subdued in more scholarly writing" (48). Dolby points out that although self-help books are formulaic and didactic, following a "basic pattern of critique and solution" (83), they provide people with the courage and conviction to improve their lives. "These accessible and engaging books of popular advice are a good thing," she concludes. "People read self-help books because they feel better for having read them. Accessible wisdom is essential in America's traditional ideal of an educated citizenry, and the self-help books that just keep filling the marketplace are evidence that most Americans are not dour and down in the mouth but instead hopeful and determined to improve themselves and meet life head on" (159). Dolby doesn't discuss end-of-life memoirs, but *The Last Lecture* falls into the tradition of American popular self-education. Death is not a "problem" that can be "solved," but books like *The Last Lecture* and *Tuesdays with Morrie*, written for a popular rather than a scholarly audience, may help readers achieve a more self-fulfilling life.

Dying in Character

After he learns he has cancer, the quirky Pausch buys a new convertible and has a vasectomy as a way to convince himself that he still has a future. Even after he learns he has only a few more months to live, he resolves to enjoy the rest of his life, in effect, to be alive when he dies. It is the same vow that Winnicott and Broyard make when they reach the end of life. I don't know whether Pausch would endorse Harold Brodkey's statement in *This Wild Darkness* that he does not want to be cured of AIDS if it means he must give up his writings, but there is no doubt that the computer scientist wanted to leave behind a body of work that would outlive him. Unlike Edward Said and Tony Judt, Pausch is not a public intellectual, but they all agree on the importance of rigorous academic standards and hard work. Like Buchwald, Pausch conveys his impending death with spirited humor and verve. He doesn't script his own funeral service, as Buchwald does, but millions of people have read *The Last Lecture* and have seen him on a popular YouTube video.

Early in *The Last Lecture* Pausch refers to himself as a "dying showman" (9), and he is always aware of the performative nature of lecturing and writing. He allows nothing to interfere with his story, neither the justifiable demands of his wife and children; the debilitating side effects of major surgery, chemotherapy, and radiation therapy, not to mention the relentless progression of his disease; nor whatever existential fears he may have about approaching death. His belief in the power of dreams,

Gatsby's green light, remains unshaken. He notes at the end of *The Last Lecture* that he has come full circle after completing his talk. "I had first made the list of my childhood dreams when I was eight years old. Now, thirty-eight years later, that very list had helped me say what I needed to say and carried me through" (204).

To remain optimistic about life with the knowledge that death is only a few months away requires what Jonathan Lear calls, in a slightly different context, radical hope, hope that is "directed toward a future goodness that transcends the current ability to understand what it is" (103). Pausch demonstrates this radical hope on every page of *The Last Lecture,* showing in the process that dreams can survive the dreamer's death.

CHAPTER II

"Now I Cultivate the Art of Simmering Memories"

Jean-Dominique Bauby and *The Diving Bell and the Butterfly*

*I*magine waking up to discover you are paralyzed from head to toe, unable to walk, talk, eat, drink, swallow, or breathe. Imagine finding yourself in this situation without preparation, warning, or explanation. You cannot move your hands, which feel as if they are burning hot or ice cold. Your arms and legs exist only to convey unrelenting pain. Your head weighs a ton, and the only movement of which you are capable is blinking your left eyelid, your only means of communicating with the world. You are imprisoned in a body that has become an oppressive diving bell. Imagine being in this torture chamber with full consciousness of what is happening—or not happening. The only escape from the diving bell is through your memory and imagination, which effortlessly take flight. Escape, however, is only momentary and partial. Now imagine being imprisoned in this diving bell for week after week, month after month. Is this nightmare the stuff of science fiction? A Kafkaesque penal colony? A gothic horror story? It is "locked-in syndrome," the world in which Jean-Dominique Bauby finds himself in his stunning memoir *The Diving Bell and the Butterfly*.

Bauby, the editor in chief of French *Elle,* suffered a massive stroke on December 8, 1995, when he was forty-three, which resulted in a rare neurological disorder that left him paralyzed. For twenty days he lay in a deep coma, and when he awoke he found himself in a naval hospital at Berck-sur-Mer, on the French Channel coast. In the past, a cerebro-vascular stroke in the brain stem, the link between the brain and spinal cord, resulted in merciful death, but now, in Bauby's droll words in the prologue, improved resuscitation techniques have "prolonged and refined the agony" (*The Diving Bell and the Butterfly* 4).

Blinking

The only way to communicate with the world is through blinking, which became Bauby's method of writing. "You read off the alphabet," not the ABC alphabet but one based on the frequency of a letter's use in the French language, "until, with a blink of my eye, I stop you at the letter to be noted. The maneuver is repeated for the letters that follow, so that fairly soon you have a whole word, and then fragments of more or less intelligible sentences" (*The Diving Bell and the Butterfly* 20). It is a "simple enough system," Bauby adds with mordant understatement, conceding that it works better in theory than in practice. It took him ten months, blinking four hours a day, to complete the memoir. The book reportedly took about two hundred thousand blinks to write; an average word took approximately two minutes. Comparisons are invidious, but unlike Tony Judt and Morrie Schwartz, who become disembodied voices, Bauby cannot even speak.

Writing a book under these circumstances is almost as unimaginable as suffering from locked-in syndrome. One problem with writing is that Bauby must depend upon the transcriber's patience and accuracy. "Crossword fans and Scrabble players have a head start. Girls manage better than boys. By dint of practice, some of them know the code by heart and no longer even turn to our special notebook—the one containing the order of the letters and in which all my words are set down like the Delphic oracle's (*The Diving Bell and the Butterfly* 20–21). "Meticulous people," he adds, "never go wrong: they scrupulously note down every letter and never seek to unravel the mystery of a sentence before it is complete" (22). Another problem with writing is the difficulty of revising. Writing is hard enough, but how do you have the fortitude to rewrite when you can only blink? Still another problem is that the communication system discourages repartee: "The keenest rapier grows dull and falls flat when it takes several minutes to thrust it home. By the time you strike, even you no longer understand what had seemed so witty before you started to dictate it, letter by letter" (71). And a fourth problem is the need to know in advance where you are heading in your narrative, since any pause or indecision would feel interminably long. Many writers can think only with a pen in the hand, or with fingers on a word processor. Bauby must know in advance exactly what he wants to write. "In my head I churn over every sentence ten times, delete a word, add an adjective, and learn my text by heart, paragraph by paragraph" (5–6).

Given the fiendish difficulty of composition, not to mention the nearly total paralysis of your body, it is remarkable that Bauby is able to write an account of the neurological catastrophe. Astonishingly, he remains in control of the story, never worrying whether he will have the time or energy to complete it. Nor is he worried that his artistic creativity will desert him. The words seem to pour out of him, each word aesthetically perfect, like a Mozart composition. There is never a moment when the narration becomes tedious, boring, or repetitive. One marvels at his unsurpassed powers of observation.

The Diving Bell and the Butterfly

One also marvels at Bauby's metaphorical language, beginning with the title of his story. The diving bell captures the sense of being locked in, confined, separated from the rest of the world. As a symbol, the diving bell generally has a positive meaning, allowing divers to descend to great depths that would be otherwise unreachable. Bauby's diving bell functions in this way, taking him into uncharted territory where he glimpses a strange, surreal world that remains unknown to those who dwell on the surface. The diving bell's negative meaning, however, predominates in Bauby's story. The diving bell is a claustrophobic prison from which there is no escape except through his imagination, which takes flight like a butterfly. Bauby's diving bell recalls *The Bell Jar*, Sylvia Plath's semiautobiographical novel in which Esther Greenwood finds herself imprisoned in a glass bell jar, stewing in her own sour air. Early in the story Bauby sees the "head of a man who seemed to have emerged from a vat of formaldehyde. His mouth was twisted, his nose damaged, his hair tousled, his gaze full of fear. One eye was sewn shut, the other goggled like the doomed eye of Cain. For a moment I stared at that dilated pupil, before I realized it was only mine" (25).

Bauby sustains these two metaphors, diving bell and butterfly, throughout the story. He tells us in the first paragraph that he feels "like a hermit crab dug into his rock" (3). The exhausting exercise of pronouncing the entire alphabet "more or less intelligibly" leaves him feeling "like a caveman discovering language for the first time" (41). He personifies the "chorus line" of his new alphabet, in which letters have a new order of importance. "That is why E dances proudly out in front, while W labors to hold on to last place. B resents being pushed back next to V, and haughty J—which begins so many sentences in French—is amazed to find itself so near the rear of the pack. Roly-poly G is annoyed to have to trade places with H, while T and U, the tender components of *tu,* rejoice that they have not been separated" (20). The act of blinking becomes the equivalent of weightlifting for him, and his daughter Céleste has turned into a "genuine acrobat" in understanding him (72). His friends are so horrified when they visit him in the hospital that they "are gasping for air like divers whose oxygen has failed them" (93).

Bauby doesn't describe the weeks of grogginess and somnolence as he slowly returned to consciousness from the long coma. At first he believes that he will quickly recover movement and speech. His active mind is busy with a thousand projects, including writing a novel and a play. The discovery that he is now a quadriplegic, confined to a wheelchair, is devastating. "In one flash I saw the frightening truth. It was as blinding as an atomic explosion, and keener than a guillotine blade" (*The Diving Bell and the Butterfly* 9). Forced to abandon his "grandiose" plans, he clings to the hope that he will be able to wiggle his toes in several years. There is also the possibility that in time he will be able to eat normally, breathe without a respirator, and perhaps have enough breath to make his silent vocal cords vibrate. Are these realistic hopes, or is he still in denial? For now, Bauby's goal is simply to swallow the overflow of saliva that floods his mouth. He never abandons hope for a partial recovery, never considers the possibility that he will remain imprisoned in his present condition. Nor does he worry about imminent death.

One of the many surprises of *The Diving Bell and the Butterfly* is how quickly Bauby adapts to his new situation. Completely dependent upon others for help, he finds himself infantilized, as we saw in Tony Judt's and Morrie Schwartz's end-of-life memoirs. Like Schwartz, who is thirty-three years older, Bauby has conflicting feelings about this dependency. "I can find it amusing, in my forty-fifth year, to be cleaned up and turned over, to have my bottom wiped and swaddled like a newborn's. I even derive a guilty pleasure from this total lapse into infancy. But the next day, the same procedure seems to me unbearably sad, and a tear rolls down through the lather a nurse's aide spreads over my cheeks. And my weekly bath plunges me simultaneously into distress and happiness" (16–17). Unlike Schwartz, who knows he will soon die, and who can remind himself that he has led a long and full life, Bauby has two young children who cannot fathom his situation. Nor can he.

Bauby's worst moment occurs when he is with his ten-year-old son, Théophile, who wishes to play hangman with his father. "I ache to tell him that I have enough on my plate playing quadriplegic" (*The Diving Bell and the Butterfly* 70–71). Grief surges over Bauby as he realizes he cannot adequately convey his love to Théophile. "There are no words to express it. My condition is monstrous, iniquitous, revolting, horrible. Suddenly I can take no more. Tears well and my throat emits a hoarse rattle that startles Théophile. Don't be scared, little man. I love you. Still engrossed in the game, he moves in for the kill. Two more letters: he has won and I have lost. On a corner of the page he completes his drawing of the gallows, the rope, and the condemned man" (71–72). Words fail Bauby as a father but not as a writer, and he allows his son's drawing of the gallows, the rope, and the condemned man to resonate with personal meaning.

Bauby believes in a future that he hopes will be better than the present, but he lives primarily in the past. How can one not live in the past when the present is unbearable and the future uncertain? Fortunately, Bauby's past is filled with rich memories that he is able to recall in extraordinary detail. A gastronome who can no longer eat or drink, he now cultivates the "art of simmering memories." The art never fails to provide him—and us—with aesthetic pleasure. "You can sit down to a meal at any hour, with no fuss or ceremony. If it's a restaurant, no need to call ahead. If I do the cooking, it is always a success. The *boeuf bourguignon* is tender, the *boeuf en gelée* translucent, the apricot pie possesses just the requisite tartness" (*The Diving Bell and the Butterfly* 36). Bauby's memory is so sharp, his prose style so evocative and sensuous, his wit so trenchant that we forget the writer is conjuring up imaginary delights. His loss is, paradoxically, the reader's gain. "At the outset of my protracted fast, deprivation sent me constantly to my imaginary larder" (37). Again and again the butterfly of his imagination breaks free from the diving bell of his imprisoned body to describe the garden of earthly delights surrounding him. And yet these joyful memories remind him of his present situation. "Rarely do I feel my condition so cruelly as when I am recalling such pleasures" (17). Bauby's old life still "burns" within him, but more and more of it is "reduced to the ashes of memory" (77).

The Count of Monte Cristo

In one of the most curious examples of life imitating art, Bauby recalls a mysterious character in Alexandre Dumas's *The Count of Monte Cristo* who eerily foreshadows his own situation. Dumas depicts the shadowy Noirtier de Villefort as the last person with whom one would wish to identify. "Described by Dumas as a living mummy," Bauby writes, "a man three-quarters of the way into the grave, this profoundly handicapped creature summons up not dreams but shudders. The mute and powerless possessor of the most terrible secrets, he spends his life slumped in a wheelchair, able to communicate only by blinking his eye: one blink means yes; two means no" (*The Diving Bell and the Butterfly* 47). Noirtier de Villefort turns out to be literature's first—and only—example of locked-in syndrome, although the medical term was not proposed until 1966, more than a century after the publication of Dumas's novel. Bauby had been reading Dumas's story before his stroke and planned to write a modern-day version of the novel, with vengeance as the driving force. Not for a moment did Bauby imagine that he would soon be in the identical situation of Dumas's haunting character.

Bauby devotes only two pages to *The Count of Monte Cristo*, a novel that is more than twelve hundred pages long. Reading Dumas's story after completing *The Diving Bell and the Butterfly*, I was struck by the many similarities between Monsieur Noirtier de Villefort and Bauby. The opening description of Noirtier, paralyzed from an apoplectic stroke, resembles Bauby in several ways: he was a "man of immense learning, unparalleled perception and a will as powerful as any can be when the soul is trapped in a body that no longer obeys its commands" (Dumas 654). Like Bauby, Noirtier is a corpse whose eyes disclose an inner life that "was like one of those distant lights which shine at night, to tell a traveller in the desert that another being watches in the silence and darkness"

(653). Just as Bauby is fiercely attached to his two children, so is Noirtier devoted to his beloved granddaughter, Valentine, who, with the help of a dictionary, is able to understand him. Often referred to as "the invalid," Noirtier is a "useless burden" in appearance, but his superior intelligence and implacable determination save his granddaughter from a prearranged marriage to a man to whom she is irrevocably opposed. Noirtier also saves her, and himself, from being poisoned by her stepmother. His silence seems to heighten the depth of his emotions, a phenomenon that is also true for Bauby. A look of infinite pain enters Noirtier's eyes when he is troubled; his eyes light up with joy when he is with Valentine. When he believes, incorrectly, that she is dead, his "motionless grief, his frozen despair and his noiseless tears were something terrible to behold" (1103). We never have access to Noirtier's thoughts, but he remains one of the most intriguing and admired characters in *The Count of Monte Cristo,* able to communicate, like Bauby, with those who listen to him. Dumas ends his novel with the words "wait" and hope," words that also reflect the ending of Bauby's story.

"The Vegetable"

In Bauby's sardonic words, the "gods of literature and neurology" prevented him from writing a revenge novel like *The Count of Monte Cristo* (48). And yet, ironically, revenge is one of the motives behind the writing of The *Diving Bell and the Butterfly.* In the chapter mordantly entitled "The Vegetable," Bauby mentions that six months have passed since his stroke, a period in which he has not responded to the many letters that were accumulating on his dresser. During this time many vicious rumors have circulated about Bauby. "The gossipers were as greedy as vultures who have just discovered a disemboweled antelope. 'Did you hear that Bauby is now a total vegetable?' said one. 'Yes, I heard. A complete vegetable,' came the reply" (82). Bauby decides to send a letter to sixty of his friends and associates informing them of his medical situation. "I would have to rely on myself if I wanted to prove that my IQ was still higher than a turnip's" (82). He sends out the collective letter every month, not only to remain in touch with those he loves but also to prove his enemies wrong. Bauby never sugarcoats the truth, and he admits that "to keep my mind sharp, to avoid descending into resigned indifference, I maintain a level of resentment and anger, neither too much nor too little, just as a pressure cooker has a safety valve to keep it from exploding" (55).

But it is love, not hate, that keeps Bauby alive. Letters to and from his friends enable him to remain connected with the world, an attachment that is essential to his health and well-being. He describes the ritual of having these letters opened, unfolded, and spread out before him as a "hushed and holy ceremony," and he then elaborates on the spiritual implications of reading each letter carefully. "Some of them are serious in tone, discussing the meaning of life, invoking the supremacy of the soul, the mystery of every existence. And by a curious reversal, the people who focus most closely on these fundamental questions tend to be people I had known only superficially. Their small talk had masked hidden depths. Had I been blind and deaf, or does it take the harsh light of disaster to show a person's true nature?" (83). Insights such as this abound in Bauby's story. Reading and writing allow him to maintain his personal and professional identity, his self-worth and self-esteem. Reading and writing also give him something to do to pass the time. He saves all the letters he receives, those discussing the meaning of life and others that simply relate the details of daily life: "roses picked at dusk, the laziness of a rainy Sunday, a child crying himself to sleep" (83). He hoards his letters "like treasure" and dreams of a day when he will be able to "fasten them end to end in a half-mile streamer, to float in the wind like a banner raised to the glory of friendship" (84). That streamer, celebrating the glory of friendship, the joy of everyday existence, and the power of resiliency, appears in the form of *The Diving Bell and the Butterfly,* forged from letters created blink by blink.

Sunday is the most difficult day of the week for Bauby because there is no mail, no physical therapist, no speech pathologist, no psychologist. On Sunday he feels totally locked in, especially if he is unfortunate enough to have no visitors. On Sunday he looks futilely at his books and realizes that no one will read them to him.

The Diving Bell and the Butterfly moves forward in time to the present, August 1996, when the story ends; but it also circles backward to that fateful December day in 1995 when life as Bauby knows it ends forever. In the penultimate chapter, "A Day in the Life," an allusion to a Beatles song, he recalls the ordinary events of the day of his stroke—shaving, dressing, drinking a hot chocolate—that now seem miraculous to him.

His memory becomes blurred as he describes the onset of the stroke, but not for a moment during that day does he suspect he is dying. "A Day in the Life" ends ominously, with the sentence "And then I sink into a coma" (127).

The final chapter, affirmatively entitled "Seasons of Renewal," records Bauby's new life sitting in a wheelchair in the hospital, making progress. "I can now grunt the little song about the kangaroo, musical testimony to my progress in speech therapy" (130). He refers to his transcriber, Claude, reading to him the pages of his book. "Some pages I am pleased to see again. Others are disappointing. Do they add up to a book?" (131). He never answers this question. He ends by raising three questions about the possibility of recovery followed by two brief sentences. "Does the cosmos contain keys for opening up my diving bell? A subway line with no terminus? A currency strong enough to buy my freedom back? We must keep looking. I'll be off now" (131–32).

Do Bauby's pages add up to a book? The French edition of *The Diving Bell and the Butterfly* went on to become a number one best seller across Europe, selling millions of copies. It was later made into a film, directed by Julian Schnabel, which was nominated for four Academy Awards in 2008. And Bauby's recovery? Two days after the publication of the book he died of pneumonia.

If we read *The Diving Bell and the Butterfly* biographically, the portentous penultimate chapter, which describes the transition from life to death, is a more fitting conclusion than the overly optimistic final chapter, which describes a recovery that never takes place. The unexpectedly jaunty closing line of the story, "I'll be off now," contains a dark irony suggestive of death. There is neither fear nor apprehension in Bauby's final words, only an odd, laconic farewell.

Bauby captures, both literally and figuratively, locked-in syndrome. *The Diving Bell and the Butterfly* is both an illness narrative and an end-of-life memoir. As an illness narrative, the story demonstrates the truth of Susan Sontag's statement at the opening of *Illness as Metaphor:* "Illness is the night-side of life, a more onerous citizenship" (3). Only a few unlucky people will find themselves in locked-in syndrome, but everyone has felt at times withdrawn, helpless, isolated, and misunderstood. If Bauby can find a way to communicate with the world, to make himself understood, so may those suffering from less extreme illnesses and injuries. Bauby is, in Arthur Frank's terms, the "wounded storyteller" who turns illness into story. "As wounded, people may be cared for, but as storytellers, they care for others. The ill, and all those who suffer, can also be healers. Their injuries become the source of the potency of their stories" (*The Wounded Storyteller* xii).

Throughout *The Diving Bell and the Butterfly* Bauby's voice, simultaneously clinical and poetic, remains ironic and at times cynical. He refers to the "sententious" tone of the neurologist who tells him that getting dressed is "good for the morale" (8). He describes the ophthalmologist who sews his right eyelid shut, to prevent the risk of an ulcerated cornea, as arrogant and brusque; when the physician asks him whether he sees double, Bauby feels like replying, "Yes, I see two assholes, not one" (55). He has nicknames for the hospital staff: Blue Eyes, Big Bird, David Bowie, Prof, Rambo, and Terminator, the last two of whom are "not exactly models of gentleness." He singles out Thermometer: "her dedication would be beyond reproach if she did not regularly forget the implement she thrusts under my armpit" (111). And yet by the end of the story he acknowledges his affection for everyone: "I realized that I was fond of all these torturers of mine" (111).

Final Dignity

Bauby died in character, using his available time to complete his story. Writing was one of his major adaptive strategies during his illness— probably the one he valued the most. The world of fashion magazines, with which he was familiar, seems worlds apart from the nightmare of locked-in syndrome, but he was able to bridge the gap through writing.

Bauby never succeeded in escaping from the diving bell of locked-in syndrome, but we remember him for the dazzling literary butterfly that was wrought with suffering. Elisabeth Kübler-Ross saw the butterfly as a symbol of the transition from death to life; just as a butterfly emerges from a cocoon, so does a dying person, in her view, escape from a body that is no longer needed. The butterfly symbolizes in literature, mythology, and folklore not only rebirth but also the soul. Bauby's butterfly affirms the power of the imagination to survive in the most harrowing circumstances. *The Diving Bell and the Butterfly* is never didactic. It teaches us nothing, and yet we learn much from it. Early in the story Bauby wonders "what conclusions anthropologists of the year 3000 will reach if they ever chance to leaf through these notebooks" (21). Only a person contemplating a posterity self would ask this question. If the anthropologists in the next millennium respond the way literary critics have responded in this millennium, they will recognize *The Diving Bell and the Butterfly* as a work of incomparable genius. A memoir of rare lyricism, beauty, and irony, *The Diving Bell and the Butterfly* explores deftly the heights and depths of human existence—and it shows how one's life can be changed with the blink of an eye.

CHAPTER 12

"I Live in My Suffering and That Makes Me Happy"
Roland Barthes and *Mourning Diary*

oland Barthes, one of the most influential writers, literary theorists, and semioticians of the late twentieth century, died in 1980 at the age of sixty-four, but he was back in the news in 2010 with the publication of *Mourning Diary*, written in response to his mother's death. Barthes is best known for his 1967 essay "The Death of the Author," which contends that the author is irrelevant in trying to understand a text. His structural and poststructural writings were often abstract and abstruse, but there was nothing theoretical about his searingly personal grief over maternal loss. Losing his father at the age of one, Barthes lived nearly his entire life with his mother, Henriette Barthes. Her death on October 25, 1977, at the age of eighty-four, was devastating to him. He wrote about her first in *Camera Lucida,* a meditation on photography, observing that during her six-month illness he "nursed her, held the bowl of tea she liked because it was easier to drink from than from a cup." She had become "my little girl, uniting for me with that essential child she was in her first photograph" (72). He experienced her as his "feminine child" and remarked on the irony that although he was childless, he had in her illness "engendered" her. Barthes began writing about her a month after her death, but it took his literary executors thirty years to publish *Mourning Diary,* partly because the book is so out of character for him.

"A Little Compilation" about His Mother

Barthes implies in *Camera Lucida* that after his mother's death he has no reason to live "unless, utopically, by writing, whose project henceforth would become the unique goal of my life" (72). That project, he declares, is a book about his mother: "What I wanted—as Valéry wanted, after his mother's death—was 'to write a little compilation about her, just for myself' (perhaps I shall write it one day, so that, printed, her memory will last at least the time of my own notoriety)" (63). The compilation he created was *Mourning Diary*, a loving tribute to her memory. The three hundred entries, brief handwritten jottings on scraps of typing paper, sometimes no more than a few words long, continue until September 15, 1979, six months before he died, at age sixty-four, of injuries and complications after being struck by a laundry van while walking in Paris. "In taking these notes," Barthes writes on October 29, 1977, "I'm trusting myself to the banality that is in me" (*Mourning Diary* 17). It's true that some of his entries are less insightful than others, but many are revelatory. His next entry, recorded on the same day, is characteristically thought-provoking. "A stupefying, though not distressing notion—that she has not been 'everything' for me. If she had, I wouldn't have written my *work*" (16).

Barthes needed his mother's security to write. Her prolonged illness shattered that security, leaving him bereft and mute. Her absence now compels him to write. In another entry penned on October 29, 1977, he denies anything positive can arise from her death, though he concedes that in time he may feel new desires awakening. One day later he discovers, to his surprise, that despite the crushing absence of his mother, he wants to live: "that this death fails to destroy me altogether means that I want to live wildly, madly, and that therefore the fear of my own death is always there, not displaced by a simple inch" (21). He vows to remain alive for as long as possible.

Mourning Diary charts the ebb and flow of Barthes's grief and reveals, in the process, the crucial role of writing in his recovery. He is never so grief-stricken that he cannot express and analyze his feelings. He writes not only to express his emotions but also to understand them. "Who knows? Maybe something valuable in these notes?" he asks himself in an October 27, 1977 entry (7). In another entry on the same day, he observes that bereavement, which he equates with depression, is different from sickness, implying it is not a condition that results in cure. He states in another entry written on the same day that it's impossible to "measure" the intensity of one's bereavement (10). And in yet another entry on October 27 he declares: "It is, here, the formal beginning of the big, long bereavement," adding that "for the first time in two days, the *acceptable* notion of my own death" (12). What does he mean in that last statement? That he cannot live without his mother? Or that he has no obligation to remain alive because she is no longer alive? I suspect he means the latter, not the former, for he observes three days later, "Many others still love me, but from now on my death would kill no one" (22), suggesting, perhaps, that his mother would not have survived his own death.

Barthes sounds like a linguist and a philosopher in some entries, as when he asks in an October 29, 1977, entry, "In the sentence 'She's no longer suffering,' to what, to whom does 'she' refer? What does that present tense mean?" (*Mourning Diary* 15). On November 1 he puzzles over the indeterminacy of the senses, wondering whether he feels too little or too much. There is nothing academic about his musings elsewhere, as when he declares on October 31 that he is back in his apartment for the first time since his mother's death. "How am I going to manage to live here all alone? And at the same time, it's clear there's no other place" (24). He admits in another entry on the same day that he is terrified when he experiences a "blank moment—a kind of numbness—which is not a moment of forgetfulness" (26). He appears bemused in a November 2 entry that he can be both a "devastated subject" and the "victim of *presence of mind*" (30).

In a November 3, 1977, entry Barthes refers to his mother as wanting "everything, total mourning," but he then realizes that he is the one "who is investing her with the demand for such a thing." Though deceased, she still "offers me lightness, life, as if she were still saying: 'but go on, go out, have a good time'" (32). He dreams of her for the first time on November 4: she is lying down but not ill. In another entry on the same day he appears riddled with guilt when making a cup of tea or writing a letter, activities that distress him—"as if, horribly enough, I *enjoyed* the now quite orderly apartment, 'all to myself,' but this enjoyment *adheres* to my despair" (35). On November 10 he is "embarrassed and almost guilty because sometimes I feel that my mourning is merely a susceptibility to emotion" (43). On November 12, his birthday, he writes about being sick and unable to tell his mother how he feels. Nine days later he complains about his ill health, sounding like a patient in psychoanalysis: "Since *maman's* death, a sort of digestive weakness—as if I were suffering precisely where she took the greatest care of me: food (though for months she no longer prepared it herself")" (61).

Crying

Barthes is unabashedly emotional in the months immediately following his mother's death. He cries repeatedly, sometimes without warning. On November 5, 1977, he hears a girl behind the counter in a bakery repeat a word that reminds him of his mother, "*Voilà* (*I'm here*, a word we used to each other all our lives)," which brings tears to his eyes: "I kept on crying quite a while back in the silent apartment" (37). November 11 is a horrible day: "More and more wretched. Crying" (45). He bursts into tears on November 12 when he hears a person sing "My heart is full of a terrible sadness" (47). He refers to a "violent crying jag" on December 27 while visiting Urt, the town where his brother and sister-in-law live, and where his mother is buried. On March 25, 1978, he has a nightmare in which his mother is lost: "I am overwhelmed, on the verge of tears" (107). On May 6 an aria from Handel's opera *Semele* makes him cry, and on June 12 an onset of grief results in tears. A day later he weeps when he looks at a photograph of his mother taken when she was a young girl in 1898, a photo that he later includes in *Camera Lucida*. His last reference to crying in *Mourning Diary* appears on August 13, 1979, when he mentions leaving Urt after a difficult visit, feeling in "desperate straits, tears over *maman's* death" (238).

What does crying mean for Barthes? In *A Lover's Discourse* he reflects on weeping, offering several explanations. "By weeping, I want to impress someone, to bring pressure to bear upon someone ('Look what you have done to me')." He makes himself cry "to prove to myself that my grief is not an illusion: tears are signs, not expressions." His tears tell a story, producing a "myth of grief." One tear "will say more" than many words (182).

Barthes's tears throughout *Mourning Diary* demonstrate the depth of his grief, telling the story of his bereavement over maternal loss. Tears are certainly signs, but they are also expressions of emotion, what Martha

Nussbaum calls "geological upheavals of thought" (90). Barthes's tears, like Morrie Schwartz's, reveal what Martin and Doka call a "blended pattern of grief," balanced between affective and cognitive responses. Barthes's tears never prevent him from trying to understand his emotional and intellectual responses to his mother's death. Crying is an example of attachment behavior, as Judith Kay Nelson suggests, "designed to signal those around us that we are in distress and in need of care and comfort" (137). Barthes's crying is unusual because of what Tom Lutz calls the "prohibition against male tears" that took "center stage in the middle of the twentieth century" (237). Barthes never regrets or apologizes for his crying, probably because it's easier for a man to cry in his private diary than in his public writings.

"My Heart Is Full of a Terrible Sadness"

The first four or five months following his mother's death are the most wrenching for Barthes, and it is during this time that he writes most frequently in his diary, penning several entries a day. His main emotion is intense sorrow bordering on despair. He knows that bereavement is not illness, yet he cannot avoid feeling ill, as he records on October 31, 1977. "Part of me keeps a sort of despairing vigil; and *at the same time* another part struggles to put my most trivial affairs into some kind of order. I experience this as a *sickness*" (*Mourning Diary* 25). People tell him to "keep your 'courage' up," he writes on November 10, not realizing that the time for courage was when he was caring for his mother. There seems to be no escape from sorrow, from the deep wound of grief. The idea of living without his mother is both unsettling and guilt-provoking, as he admits on November 28: "Does being able to live without someone you loved mean you loved her less than you thought . . . ?" (68); the question is so disturbing that he ends it with an ellipsis. On November 29 he records a conversation with "AC" in which, citing Kierkegaard, Barthes observes that "I can't endure seeing my suffering being reduced—being *generalized*; . . . it's as if it were being stolen from me" (71).

Many of Barthes's entries are analytical, but he never retreats into clinical theory or impersonal prose. "Don't say *Mourning*," he writes on November 30. "It's too psychoanalytic. I'm not *Mourning*. I'm suffering" (73). His objection to psychoanalysis is based on his belief that bereavement does not soften in time, that it cannot be regulated or normalized. "My distress is chaotic, erratic, whereby it resists the accepted—and psychoanalytic—notion of a mourning subject to time, becoming dialectical, wearing out, 'adapting'" (71). Given his objection to the word, it's surprising that the editors did not title his book *Suffering Diary.*

Suffering takes many forms for Barthes in the months following his mother's death. Melancholy, numbness, and weariness characterize the early entries. Time slows down, as when he writes on November 9, "I limp along through my mourning" (40). He describes his emotional life as dark, with occasional glimpses of light. Desire is part of his past, not his present life. Sometimes he feels lacerating pain, other times inertia. He loses interest in past pleasures, such as being in Paris and traveling. He experiences not a lack but a "*wound*, something that has harmed love's very heart" (65). One of his biggest shocks is his rapid shift of emotion, the discontinuous nature of mourning. The need to retreat from the world appears in several entries written in the fall and winter of 1977–78. The entries penned during this time convey shock, as if he still can't believe what has happened. On December 7 he writes, "Now from time to time, there unexpectedly rises within me, like a bursting bubble: the realization that *she no longer exists, she no longer exists,* totally and forever" (78). "Everything pains me," he records on January 16, 1978 (87). He notes briefly on February 1 that he has developed bronchitis, his first illness since his mother's death. A month later he rejects the generalization that time soothes mourning. "No, Time makes nothing happen; it merely makes the *emotivity* of mourning pass" (101).

Barthes hoped after his mother's death that he would become a better person, leaving aside "all kinds of nastiness, jealousy, narcissism," but this has not happened, he confesses sadly on February 12, 1978; "I am becoming less and less 'noble,' 'generous'" (92). He returns to this theme in two entries written on April 27, both of which reveal his harshest self-judgment anywhere in *Mourning Diary.* "After *maman*'s death I believed there would be a sort of liberation in kindness, she surviving all the more intensely as a model. . . . But it is, alas, the contrary that occurs" (118).

"My Grief Has Not Been Hysterical"

Barthes displays little interest in writing outside his diary in the late fall of

1977 and winter of 1978. It's probably accurate to say he was always thinking about writing, about his work, as he called it (the same word Susan
Sontag used to describe her writing), for there were few days when he did
not write an entry. But he was ambivalent about writing a book about his
mother, partly because he did not want to exploit her memory. "I don't
want to talk about it," he admits in an October 31, 1977, entry, "for fear
of making literature out of it—or without being sure of not doing so—
although as a matter of fact literature originates within these truths" (23).
That literature originates within these "truths" suggests that writing, perhaps all writing, arises from loss. In a November 21, 1977, entry he makes
an even stronger statement: "Depression comes when, in the depths of
despair, I cannot manage to save myself by my attachment to writing"
(62). He realizes that although language cannot convey adequately the
experience of suffering, language can nevertheless help in bereavement.
"My suffering is inexpressible but all the same utterable, speakable," he
discloses on August 1, 1977. "The very fact that language affords me the
word 'intolerable' immediately achieves a certain tolerance" (175).

Beginning in the late spring of 1978, Barthes begins to recover from his
paralyzing grief, and his entries become more positive. In a noteworthy
entry written on May 18, 1978, he declares that his mother's death is the
only event in his life to which he has responded non-neurotically. "My
grief has not been hysterical, scarcely visible to others (perhaps because
the notion of 'theatralizing' my mother's death would have been intolerable)" (128). The next day he reflects on this further, reaching an epiphany: "When *maman* was living (in other words, in my whole past life) I
was neurotically in fear of losing her. Now (this is what mourning teaches
me) such mourning is so to speak the only thing in me which is not neurotic: as if *maman*, by a last gift, had taken neurosis, the worst part, away
from me" (129). Three days later he speaks more self-assuredly about
grasping the "truth of mourning," which is "quite simple: now that
maman is dead, I am faced with death (nothing any longer separates me
from it except time)" (130). It's not that he believes he will be reunited
with her in death; rather, he seems resigned for the first time to her death,
and he is now able to internalize her, as he suggests in a May 31 entry:
"How *maman* is present in all I have written: in that there is everywhere
a notion of the Sovereign Good" (131). These insights ease his grief.

Gaining Recognition for His Mother

Barthes's breakthrough entry occurs on June 5, 1978, when he explores the question of being *recognized*, by which he means having one's work—and, therefore, one's identity—validated and affirmed. He is no longer interested in the recognition he received before his mother's death; now he seeks to gain recognition for her. "Before resuming *sagely and stoically* the course (quite unforeseen moreover) of the work, it is necessary for me (I feel this strongly) to write this book around *maman*. In a sense, therefore, it is as if I had *to make* maman *recognized*" (133). His goal now is to immortalize her, as he writes on March 29, 1979. "I live without any concern for posterity, no desire to be read later on (except financially, for M. [Barthes's half brother, Michel]), complete acceptance of vanishing utterly, no desire for a 'monument'—but I cannot endure that this should be the case for *maman* (perhaps because she has not written and her memory depends entirely on me)" 234. And with that entry he begins writing *Camera Lucida*.

The idea of creating a posterity self for his mother is a turning point in Barthes's life. Suddenly the world seems brighter. "This morning," he writes on June 9, 1978, "walking through Saint-Sulpice, whose simple architectural vault delights me; to be *in* architecture—I sit down for a moment; a sort of instinctual 'prayer': that I finish the *Photo-Maman* book" (136).

There are still moments of sadness in *Mourning Diary*, even tears, but the remaining entries show a movement toward recovery and engagement with the world. Barthes learns not to ignore or dismiss suffering but to transform it into his writing. On June 21, 1978, he reads for the first time his mourning diary. "Tears each time there was any question of her—of her person—not of me" (151). On June 24 he writes that there are virtually "no signs of an internalized mourning," which he interprets as the "fulfillment of absolute internalization." In the same entry he implies he lives in a society that "denies mourning" (155). On July 7 he observes that he would die immediately if there were a chance of meeting his mother in an afterlife. On July 13 he sees swallows flying through the summer air and laments his lack of religious belief: "I tell myself, thinking painfully of *maman*: how barbarous not to believe in souls—in the immortality of souls! the idiotic truth of materialism!" (159). On July 18, his mother's birthday, he buys two roses and places them on his desk. In another entry on the same day he writes, "Each of us has his own rhythm of suffering" (162).

"I Integrate, by Language"

Barthes's rhythm of suffering is intense and protracted even during his recovery. A July 20, 1978, entry implies that his only confidant is his diary, which makes writing in it even more indispensable to his well-being. "I begin crying when I think of *maman's* words that always lacerate me: my R! my R! (I've never been able to tell this to anyone)" (166). On July 27 he recalls that his mother taught him *"you cannot make someone you love suffer,"* adding, "She never made anyone she loved suffer. That was her definition, her 'innocence'" (169). On July 29 he quotes a letter Proust wrote to Georges de Lauris comforting him on the recent death of his mother in 1907. "Tell yourself this, too, for it is a kind of pleasure to know that you will never love less, that you will never be consoled, that you will constantly remember more and more" (171). Proust's words are paradoxically consoling to Barthes. On July 31 he writes what is probably the single most important sentence in *Mourning Diary*: "I live in my suffering and that makes me happy" (173).

Living in his suffering meant for Barthes the ability to convey his suffering through language. *Mourning Diary* reveals the power of writing not only as a lifeline, a way for the living to remain connected with the dead, but as a way to understand and express reality. To live with suffering may not seem an epiphany to some people, but it was to Barthes, as he notes, again, on August 1, 1978. "Always (painfully) surprised to be able—finally—to live with my suffering, which means that it is literally *endurable.* But—no doubt—this is because I can, more or less (in other words, with the feeling of not managing to do so) utter it, put it into words. My culture, my taste for writing gives me this apotropaic or *integrative* power: I *integrate,* by language" (175). Writing gives Barthes apotropaic power, the ability to ward off evil or bad luck, as he repeats in an October 6, 1978, entry. "Exorcise this Fear by going *where I'm afraid to go* (places easy to determine, thanks to the signal of emotivity)" (204). He realizes that this apotropaic power cannot succeed permanently in warding off evil or bad luck, but he affirms human agency, the belief that people use language to achieve (self-)integration.

Reading is also a lifeline for Barthes, a way to connect him with other writers who have experienced love and loss. He singles out Nietzsche, D. W. Winnicott (quoting his line, "I fear a catastrophe that has already occurred" [*Mourning Diary* 203]), and Proust, particularly his agonized separation from his mother, with which Barthes immediately identifies. "I cannot read without pain," he writes on August 1, 1978, "without choking on truth, everything Proust writes in his letters about sickness, courage, the death of his mother, his suffering" (177).

Curiously, Barthes never reveals in *Mourning Diary* how he felt about being his mother's caregiver. For many years he suffered from tuberculosis, which required long periods of hospitalization. Did his experience with illness sensitize him to the importance of caregiving? Did he feel overwhelmed by the many responsibilities of caregiving? Did the experience change their relationship? Did he feel relief when his mother died because her suffering was over? These questions remain unanswered, along with the cause of her death. Apart from telling us about their reversal of roles, Barthes remains silent about the details of caring for her. He never mentions whether his half brother, Michel Salzedo, who lived with his wife, Rachel, in the same building as Barthes, helped him. Nor does he speculate how his mother might have felt if she knew he would later write about her. We don't even know whether Barthes intended *Mourning Diary* for publication.

Throughout *Mourning Diary* Barthes idealizes his mother. She represents to him the embodiment of everything that is beautiful, innocent, and pure. He lauds her "absolute kindness" and her "intact[ness] against all neurosis, all madness" (216). She inspires him by her example. "I try to continue living day by day according to her values," he observes on August 18, 1978, "to recover something of the nourishment she provided by producing it myself, her household order, that alliance of ethics and aesthetics that was her incomparable fashion of living, of constructing the quotidian" (190). In life she encourages his writing; in death she becomes his muse. Is Barthes aware that his idealization renders his mother into a saint? Richard Howard, the translator of *Mourning Diary*, raises this question in the afterword. "Some of Barthes's friends have observed that no mother could possibly be that perfected a being, a life force and in death a paradigm, a phoenix." Howard had once met Madame Barthes and supports Barthes's view of her: "I wanted to translate *Mourning*

Diary, improbable creation though it is, as evidence—as so many writings of Barthes testify so much more flawlessly—to the contrary" (261).

Ironies nevertheless persist. The more Barthes praises his mother's kindness and goodness, the more he condemns his many "egoisms," berating himself on December 31, 1978: "Oh what a contradiction: by *maman's loss* I become the contrary of what she was. I want to live according to her value and reach only the contrary" (221). Her "perfect" love for him serves only to remind him of his imperfect love for others. Her "profound modesty" may also have reminded him of his own ambitions (201), which after her death he channeled into her memory. He admits that his "work was always concretely kept away from her" (218), suggesting the possibility that she would not be interested in, knowledgeable about, or sympathetic to his writing. Nowhere does he comment on her understanding of him or his work. And still another irony: biographer Louis-Jean Calvet reports that Barthes concealed his homosexuality from his mother, fearing her disapproval. Some of his friends, Calvet reports, believed that Barthes's mother "never had the slightest inkling about it" (178). Barthes's refusal to share with his mother an important part of his life reveals a more complicated mother-son relationship than the one we see in *Mourning Diary.*

Barthes admits in a May 10, 1978, entry that his mother had "no presence" in his writing before her death (123). He refers to her briefly in *Roland Barthes by Roland Barthes.* It is an odd autobiography, or perhaps antiautobiography, for he is always undercutting his authorial authority, referring to "R.B." as an unknowable character. *Roland Barthes by Roland Barthes* is evasive and fragmentary, revealing little about the author's affective life. In a paragraph entitled "The unfashionable," Barthes discloses cryptically that "when he loved his mother (what would it have been if he had really known his father and by some misfortune had loved him too!), he was unfashionable" (125). Does this mean that he loves his mother too much? In an October 25, 1978, entry in *Mourning Diary,* he points out a difference between his mother and himself that now strikes him as disturbing: "O the paradox: I so 'intellectual,' at least accused of being so, I so ridden by an incessant metalanguage (which I defend), she offers me in the highest degree her nonlanguage" (209).

"Diary Disease"

Nowhere is Barthes's fear of being "so intellectual" more evident than in his essay "Deliberation," which first appeared in the journal *Tel Quel* in 1979 and later formed the final selection in *A Barthes Reader*, edited by Susan Sontag. The sixteen-page essay, his last publication before his death, focuses on his intense ambivalence over keeping a journal. "Deliberation" is the major countertext to *Mourning Diary*. Reading "Deliberation," one would never suspect that Barthes wrote *Mourning Diary*—or that he would approve of its publication.

Barthes acknowledges in "Deliberation" that in "recent years" he has made "three attempts" to keep a diary: "the first and most serious one—because it occurred during my mother's last illness—is the longest, perhaps because it corresponded in some degree to the Kafkaesque goal of extirpating anxiety by writing" (*A Barthes Reader* 482). The other two attempts to keep a diary are "more experimental," each focused on only one day. Of the nearly two dozen entries he quotes in "Deliberation," only two are about his mother. One entry, written on July 16, 1977, two months before her death, describes her feeling better and sitting in the garden. The other entry, written two days later, on her birthday, indicates that all he can offer her is a rosebud from the garden. He does not mention her death in the last entry, written on April 25, 1979.

Barthes's opening sentence of "Deliberation" is qualified enough to apply to most writers who have contemplated keeping a diary but who have never done so: "I've never kept a journal—or rather I've never known if I should keep one" (*A Barthes Reader* 479). The rest of the paragraph describes his on-again, off-again efforts to start a diary, an impulse that is "faint, intermittent, without seriousness and of no doctrinal standing whatever." He diagnoses the problem as *"diary disease,"* an "insoluble doubt as to the value of what one writes in it" (479).

The long second paragraph of "Deliberation" conveys Barthes's mistrust of writing a diary. He admits that initially he feels a "certain pleasure" that soon turns into embarrassment or disgust. The "text doesn't hold up," he claims, like delicate food that quickly spoils. He notes "with discouragement" the "artifice of sincerity," which, he implies, sounding like Oscar Wilde, is only a "pose." Rereading the diary several months or years later may be pleasurable, not aesthetically but as a "kind of narcissistic attachment." He asks himself, "Is it *worth the trouble?*" (*A Barthes Reader* 479–80). Kafka kept a diary to "extirpate his anxiety" or to "find salvation," but these motives, Barthes contends, do not apply to himself. Nor is "confession" an adequate motive to keep a diary: "psychoanalysis, the Sartrean critique of bad faith, and the Marxist critique of ideologies have made 'confession' a futility" (481).

Barthes rejects in "Deliberation" personal or psychological reasons to keep a diary and instead lists four literary reasons: (1) "poetic," presenting a text "tinged with an individuality of writing, with a 'style'"; (2) "historical," seeing the "traces of a period"; (3) "utopian," showing the author as an "object of desire"; and (4) "amorous," constituting the diary as a "workshop of sentences" (*A Barthes Reader* 481–82). He includes several of his diary entries in "Deliberation," none of which appear in *Mourning Diary.* These entries demonstrate his conviction that "'I' is harder to write than to read" (487). In one of these entries, about the death of old Prince Bolkonsky in *War and Peace,* he mentions "Marie's feeling of guilt because for a moment she wanted her father to die, anticipating that she would thereby gain her freedom" (488)—a statement intimating Barthes's awareness that caregivers (including, perhaps, himself) may feel guilt for desiring their own freedom. He admits in "Deliberation" that he is not sure whether the fragments of diary entries he quotes are publishable, but "nothing tells me, on the other hand, that they are not" (491). The next question he asks himself—*"Should I keep a journal?"*—is immediately followed by a "nasty answer: '*Who cares?*', or, more psychoanalytically: '*It's your problem*'" (491).

I can't imagine any psychoanalyst responding this cynically to the therapeutic use of personal writing. All introspective writing, diary writing or otherwise, is valuable to therapy. Barthes spends the rest of the essay explaining why he believes diary writing is "stricken," in his view, "as though with an insidious disease" (*A Barthes Reader* 491–92). His first reason is that diaries have no "mission." Diaries are about the diary writer, he opines, not about the world, evidently not troubled by this simplistic binary opposition. He contends that writing a diary "implies a pleasure, a comfort, but not a passion" (492)—a distinction without a difference. Diaries are inauthentic, he asserts, not because they lack "sincerity" (of which he has been dismissive earlier in the essay) but because they are "doomed to simulation" (493). This leads to what Barthes calls a paradox:

"By choosing the most 'direct,' the most 'spontaneous' form of writing, I find myself to be the clumsiest of ham actors" (493). Still another argument against keeping a diary is the "instability" of the writer's judgment—the absence of value realized too late. Quoting Kafka, Barthes writes: "When I say something, this thing immediately and definitively loses its importance" (494).

Surely Barthes protests too much. All of his criticisms are, at best, half-truths. The sheer illogicality of his argument reveals his suspicion of all self-disclosing writing, not simply diary writing. His conclusion, in the last paragraph of "Deliberation," that he can "never get away from himself" in his diaries (*A Barthes Reader* 494), precludes the possibility that personal writing, in whatever genre or form, enhances growth and understanding. Diaries can illuminate both the tragic and comic elements of existence, both self and other, both the "trap" of human nature and the possibility of escape.

After reading Barthes's withering criticisms, we can understand why the publication of *Mourning Diary* was delayed for thirty years. Richard Howard's oblique hint in the afterword alerts us to the difficult decision made by the Barthes estate to publish the book. "I believe that after Roland Barthes's death, his friends and his publisher's advisers determined, after some very powerful impulses to resist, to evade, to ignore these agonized markings altogether, instead chose to publish *Mourning Diary* as evidence of creative intention. I don't suppose Roland would have abounded in their sense, neither do I suppose he would have repudiated the enterprise" (260). The mangled syntax of Howard's first sentence and the curiously ambiguous second sentence, imitating, consciously or not, Barthes's uncertainty over the "publishability" of his fragmentary diaries, hardly do justice to the larger question of authorial intent in *Mourning Diary.*

A Theorist of Love, Loss, and Recovery

How does our understanding of "Deliberation" affect our rereading of *Mourning Diary*? Barthes's disclosures of love, grief, and despair in *Mourning Diary* are far more sincere and heartfelt than his cynicism is in "Deliberation." Expressed differently, he is a better literary writer in *Mourning Diary* than a theorist in "Deliberation." Ironically, Barthes is a superb theorist of love, loss, and recovery in *Mourning Diary*. He is supremely aware that mourning is chaotic and indeterminate. The binary opposition between self and other theorized in "Deliberation" is exposed as false in *Mourning Diary* when he reminds himself: "*Memento illam vixisse:* Remember that she lived" (113). There is nothing narcissistic or solipsistic about his insights into mourning, as when he suddenly realizes on November 19, 1977: "For months, I have been her mother. It is as if I had lost my daughter (a greater grief than that? It had never occurred to me)" (56). Nor is there anything self-centered about his "horror," in an entry written on the same day, "when the memory of those words she spoke to me would no longer make me cry" (57). His understanding of Marie's feeling of freedom after the death of her father in *War and Peace* appears in a similar observation in his March 2, 1978, entry in *Mourning Diary*: "The thing that lets me endure maman's death resembles a certain possession of freedom" (98).

To be sure, some of the entries in *Mourning Diary* betray the same self-dissatisfaction, even self-loathing, that we see in "Deliberation." He reproaches himself for his "hardness of heart" (118), his "irritability, impotence to love" and "[desolating] egoism" (178), his "heartfelt bitterness, the propensity to jealousies, etc.: everything that in my heart keeps me from loving myself" (219). We sympathize with Barthes's vulnerability and self-reproaches because they indicate he is a flawed human being, like everyone else (except, in his view, his mother), and because there is value in seeing these flaws in order to overcome them. He might have quoted, in his own defense, the Roman poet Terence's observation two thousand years ago, "Homo sum; humani nil a me alienum puto": I am human; I count nothing human foreign to me. However painful self-knowledge may be, Barthes would agree that knowing is generally better than not knowing—and what better way to understand the devastating grief arising from maternal loss than in keeping a diary?

Many of the entries in *Mourning Diary* are emotionally raw, spontaneous outpourings of the heart. How could they not be? Barthes was writing about the greatest loss in his life, and he had neither the ability nor interest to craft lapidary sentences while reeling from his mother's death. He was not trying to shock his readers, win an argument, or curry favor; rather, he was trying to make sense of the greatest tragedy in his life. We do not see the dazzling aphoristic brilliance that he forged in *A Lover's*

Discourse or *Roland Barthes by Roland Barthes*. *Mourning Diary* lacks the aesthetic virtuosity of his other writings: it is not clever, sparkling, playful, ironic, theatrical, subtle, erotic, euphoric, elegant, provocative, or subversive. It is merely heartrending and memorable. *Mourning Diary* is about depth, not surface; self-revelation, not self-concealment; rawness, not refinement; engagement, not detachment. In his other books he conceives of writing as leading to happiness and bliss, but in *Mourning Diary* he uses writing to plumb the depths of despair. Elsewhere he believed that literature is entirely about language, but *Mourning Diary* reveals that literature is also about life—and death. Barthes often disdained "mere psychology," but now he shows how grief can affect every moment of one's waking and sleeping life. Barthes's master in *Mourning Diary,* not in terms of influence but of tone, is Oscar Wilde—not Wilde the playwright and agent provocateur but Wilde the author of *De Profundis,* his haunting lament on a life gone awry.

Barthes was not able to suspend entirely his aesthetic sensibility while writing *Mourning Diary.* Some of the entries convey the fear of sentimentality expressed in "Deliberation." On April 3, 1978, he complains about his use of the word *despair,* which is "too theatrical" (111). A January 11, 1979, entry strikes him as melodramatic: "the pain of never again resting my lips on those cool and wrinkled cheeks. (That's banal—Death, Suffering are nothing but: banal)" (222). Few readers will agree with this brutal self-judgment. Barthes is aware he is being judgmental, which is why he immediately qualifies his assertion that "Suffering is a form of egoism" with the words, "I speak only for myself. I am not talking about her" (195). Sometimes Barthes's intellectuality momentarily blinds him to the wisdom and power of emotion. In "Deliberation" he claims that the diary lends itself not to tragic but to comic questions, but this is certainly not true of *Mourning Diary,* which reveals the devastating consequences of loss. If at times Barthes expresses dissatisfaction with some of his entries in *Mourning Diary,* at other times he cannot stop crying while rereading an entry, proof of the depth of his emotion, as he reveals on June 21, 1978: "Reread for the first time this *mourning diary.* Tears each time there was any question of her—of her person—not of me" (151).

In listing in "Deliberation" the many bad reasons for keeping a diary, Barthes never points out the many good reasons for keeping one, including those we have already seen: the need to honor the memory of the deceased, the need to work through paralyzing grief, and the need to remain connected with the living and the dead. How could he forget the words he penned in the August 1, 1978, entry about the apotropaic or integrative power of language? This integrative power inheres in all forms and genres of language: novels, poems, essays, and diaries. In his Inaugural Lecture upon being elected to the Collège de France, Barthes make the dubious claim that language is "neither reactionary nor progressive; it is quite simply fascist; for fascism does not prevent speech, it compels speech" (*A Barthes Reader* 461). His denial of human agency is striking.

Barthes never came out of the closet about his homosexuality; had he done so, D. A. Miller suggests, he would have lent support to younger scholars who admired him. In *Mourning Diary,* published thirty years after his death, he has finally come out of the closet with respect to his grief over maternal loss.

We don't know whether Madame Barthes died in character, but we now know, thanks to the publication of *Mourning Diary,* that her death compelled her son to write *out of* character. *Mourning Diary* is more remarkable because of Barthes's antipathy to autobiographical writing. Calvet notes that this mistrust of biography "explains the reluctance of a handful of those who knew him (and who regard themselves as his intellectual heirs) to talk about him" (xii).

The Work of Mourning and the Work of Writing

Mourning Diary will inevitably change readers' opinions of Barthes. The iconoclastic theorist who boldly proclaimed the death of the author will now be remembered as the son who grieved deeply the death of the mother—not simply the universal figure of the mother but his own mother. *Mourning Diary* reveals more about Barthes's inner life than the evasive, detached autobiographical musings of *Roland Barthes by Roland Barthes.* The man who insisted that literature provide the "pleasure of the text" wrote late in his life a text filled with heartrending anguish. The author of *A Lover's Discourse,* filled with theorizings on amorous love, was far more intimately knowledgeable about *maternal* love. "You have never known a Woman's body!" Barthes admits on October 27, 1977, quickly adding, "I have known the body of my mother, sick and then dying" (4). The writer who praised surface and rejected the idea of depth and interiority fell into an abyss of suffering during his extended bereavement. "We often hear it said that it is the task of art to *express the inexpressible*," Barthes declaims in the preface to *Critical Essays;* "it is the contrary which must be said (with no intention of paradox): the whole task of art is to *unexpress the expressible*" (xvii). He reverses this in *Mourning Diary*, summoning all of his linguistic power to express his inexpressible suffering.

Barthes loved his mother more than he loved anyone else in his life, male or female. She awakened his deepest compassion and devotion—and inspired his most emotionally charged writing. His love for others, as revealed in his writings, was fleeting. The title essay in his posthumously published volume *Incidents* describes his homosexual encounters in Morocco in 1968 and 1969, none of them satisfactory. Another essay in *Incidents,* "Soirées de Paris," recounts his ambivalent pursuit of young men the summer before his death. As Jonathan Culler remarks, the essay, which Barthes referred to as "Pointless Evenings," "tantalizes by the half-concealment (behind initials) of friends, who were subsequently annoyed to find that evenings Barthes had spent with them qualified as 'empty.' Above all it seduces by its admission of aimlessness" (Culler 111). There is nothing tantalizing or aimless about *Mourning Diary.* It is a book that anyone would have been proud of—including his mother.

Barthes resolves in a May 31, 1978, entry to transform the "Work of Mourning" into the "real 'Work'—of writing" (132), and he succeeds brilliantly in *Mourning Diary.* In another entry recorded on the same day, he declares that the "great crises (love, grief) cannot be liquidated hastily: for me, it is *accomplished* only in and by writing" (132). And on December 15, 1978, he exclaims that he will continue to be "unwell, until I write something *having to do with her* (*Photo,* or something else)" (216).

Barthes may not have intended to write an end-of-life memoir, but *Mourning Diary* turns out to be just that, a final meditation on love, loss, and recovery. A dialogue between self and (m)other, *Mourning Diary* presents us with an author who turns instinctively to writing as a way to restore meaning to his life. He describes mourning variously as a wound, absence, lack, silence, sadness, nausea. In no other book or essay does Barthes reveal his vulnerability, confusion, or tenderness. In no other work does he create a more compelling character. Madame Barthes's death was a transformative event in her son's life, profoundly changing his writing. *Mourning Diary* bespeaks the power of writing to honor the memory of a beloved parent, to gain recognition for others, to enable one to continue to live following a devastating loss, to express the tangled feelings of bereavement, and to accept the inevitability of one's own death. As Lori Soderlind remarks in her review of *Mourning Diary* in the *New York Times Book Review,* "Writing itself is a form of grieving, of trying to preserve what will otherwise be lost. Barthes expressed distaste for 'making literature' of his mother's death, and yet, faced with crises most profound, he did what an inveterate writer must do: take notes" (January 23, 2011). *Mourning Diary* could not bring Madame Barthes back to life, but it helped her son come to terms with her death—and with his own. "As for death," he writes on October 8, 1978, "*maman's* death gave me the (previously quite abstract) certainty that all men are mortal—that there would never be any discrimination—and the certainty of having to die *by that logic* soothed me" (206).

CONCLUSION

Alive When They Died

~~~~~~~

$\mathcal{M}$any people believe that we live in a death-denying culture where men and women don't "die" but "pass away,"
where dying and death remain hidden from view, where
the terminally ill withdraw silently from life, and where bereavement lasts
only a few months. Geoffrey Gorer argues that death has become "more
and more 'unmentionable' *as a natural process*" (172). He contends that
if social prudery prevents people from coming to terms with the basic
facts of birth, copulation, and death, then such discussions will be done
surreptitiously. "If we dislike the modern pornography of death, then
we must give back to death—natural death—its parade and publicity,
readmit grief and mourning" (175). Philippe Ariès reaches a similar conclusion, that death went into hiding in the twentieth century. He links
the denial of death to the growth of technological medicalization that has
resulted, in his view, in the loss of the art of dying well.

"A Hot Topic"

People may fear death, but they are also fascinated by it. Peter and Elizabeth Fenwick point out that there are nearly eleven columns of entries on
death and dying in *Bartlett's Familiar Quotations*, as opposed to only six
columns on the soul and a single one on immortality. "Death is often still

referred to as a taboo subject, but the evidence suggests that it is now more of a hot topic than a forbidden one" (233). The success of the hospice movement and the deluge of scholarly and popular books and articles on loss and bereavement provide additional evidence of the burgeoning interest in death. Clive Seale notes the growing importance of death rituals. "The implications of this, sociologically, are quite profound, for it enables us to see that dying people, in late modernity, are being offered the opportunity to preside over their own funerals" (110). Partly as a result of the Internet, obituaries have become a booming business, including those written by relatives and friends of the deceased and those commissioned by newspaper editors, who have found a new source of income in death notices.

The dying and their families are writing not only obituaries in record numbers but also end-of-life memoirs. The memoirists, whether writing of their own dying or that of a loved one, reveal grief, mourning, and sometimes guilt. The dying also exhibit a determination to complete their life stories. In Winnicott's words, these memoirists were alive when they died, writing feverishly to the end, trying to have the last word. Writing an end-of-life memoir has become a new death ritual, a secular example of the long tradition of *ars moriendi*, the art of dying. It is no exaggeration to say that we are living in the golden age of the end-of-life memoir. Sylvia Plath's wry observation in her poem "Lady Lazarus"—"Dying / Is an art, like everything else, / I do it exceptionally well" (245)—applies to the end-of-life memoirists in my study, who seek both to enlighten and entertain us amid the onslaught of death.

Writing a memoir while dying requires extraordinary concentration, devotion, and determination. Siddhartha Mukherjee remarks in *The Emperor of All Maladies* that the "daily life of a patient becomes so intensely preoccupied with his or her illness that the world fades away. Every last morsel of energy is spent tending the disease" (398). Mukherjee quotes Max Lerner's statement about his battle with lymphoma: "How to overcome him became my obsession. If it was to be a combat then I had to engage it with everything I had—knowledge and guile, ways covert as well as overt" (398). To write a book about one's dying involves a double struggle, first, with one's body shutting down, and second, with the process of writing, which even when one is in the best of health may feel like a battle with one's demons.

End-of-life memoirists can take us to death's door, but they cannot write about their own deaths. "One can experience the death of another but, paradoxically, cannot experience the death of oneself," writes Edwin Shneidman. "Thus our 'experience' of death is indirect and, on that account alone, is all the more puzzling and tantalizing" (7). In a December 3, 2003, article in the *New York Times,* Jane Brody suggests that "active dying," total body failure, usually takes between ten to fourteen days. Allan Kellehear's estimate, graphically depicted in *A Social History of Dying,* is much shorter. "Biologically speaking, dying only takes a few precious seconds, or occasionally a few minutes. The physical process of dying usually begins in one failing organ of the body and then simply spreads itself, meticulously switching off the lights as it leaves each room of the body" (2). Of the end-of-life memoirists in this book, Harold Brodkey, Tony Judt, Art Buchwald, Morrie Schwartz, and Jean-Dominique Bauby take us close to their own deaths, but they do not describe active dying. We learn about their dying but not about their actual deaths: they ended their stories before organ shut-down. They show us how they wrote, dictated, or blinked their stories, but we do not see them when they are unable to write, dictate, or blink.

In *Memoir: A History* Ben Yagoda describes the fierce backlash against the genre, observing that there has been "about a scandal a year, and sometimes more than that" involving fraud (246). Apart from my discussion of Philip Roth's selective memory in *Patrimony,* I have not raised the contentious question of the unreliability of memory—contentious not because memory is unreliable—everyone knows that it is—but because of the difficulty of knowing precisely when memory is unreliable, misleading, or blank. Suffice it to say that all of the memoirists who wrote about their dying did indeed die and, as far as I can tell (from published reviews and articles), the memoirists seem to have been telling the truth as they saw it. Other scholars, perhaps future biographers, will explore in more detail the reliability and truthfulness of end-of-life stories.

The Reality of Terminal Life

End-of-life memoirs take us into the dying person's bedroom, at home or in a hospital or hospice, where we learn about terminal care for those who can no longer take care of themselves. Such views of naked vulnerability are often wrenching, especially for squeamish readers. And yet these details, when reported by the dying persons themselves, deepen our understanding of the reality of terminal life. Nancy K. Miller's observation about Annie Ernaux's memoir *Shame* applies to end-of-life memoirs like *Patrimony*, *Letting Go*, *Tuesdays with Morrie*, and *The Diving Bell and the Butterfly*: "In autobiography, the acts—performed and witnessed—that might seem to beg not to be revealed are the very ones that produce writing" ("Memory Stains" 210). Writing is a countershame activity, a way of shaming shame: by transforming private shame into public knowledge, we lessen the power that shame has over us. Shameful secrets become less fearful when shared with others. Few people fail to experience feelings of shame and betrayal when their bodies break down and they lose control of their bladder and bowels; "death with dignity" has less to do with the process of dying, the "indignity of death," than with the quality of care received by the terminally ill.

Miller makes another observation, in *Bequest and Betrayal*, that has particular relevance to Roth's *Patrimony*, Rieff's *Swimming in a Sea of Death*, and *Barthes's Mourning Diary*: "Memoirs about the loss of parents show how enmeshed in the family plot we have been and the price of our complicity in its stories. The death of parents forces us to rethink our lives, to reread ourselves. We read for what we need to find. Sometimes, we also find what we didn't know we needed" (xiii).

Surprises

To learn about the loneliness of dying is certainly not surprising. Pascal's statement, "We live and die alone; no one can help us," seems intuitively and experientially correct, and it is easy to find contemporary thinkers who agree with him. The title of Norbert Elias's book *The Loneliness of the Dying* conveys his agreement with Pascal. But I did find many surprises while writing *Dying in Character*. I was surprised by the number of dying writers who conveyed joy, happiness, and contentment while they were dying. End-of-life memoirs are not always elegiac. Brodkey ends *This Wild Darkness* with a feeling of "genuine amazement" over the journey he is about to take into the unknown. He is not crushed, as one might expect, by his sentence of death. I was surprised that Brodkey was willing to die as long as his writings survive: textual resurrection is more important to him than personal immortality. I was even more surprised that

Art Buchwald and Randy Pausch both use the word *fun* to describe their dying experiences. This partly explains why they both became media stars—and media-ized. Dying was not fun for Morrie Schwartz and Tony Judt, but they reveal courage, satisfaction, and fearlessness during the final stage of their lives, when they are nearly paralyzed by their illnesses. Jean-Dominique Bauby expresses optimism and hope in his story, as does Edward Said in his memoir and in his late writings. It is hard to imagine that these writers could feel so upbeat in their situations, but their memoirs are authentically affirmative. The writers are not simply whistling in the dark. They see death approaching, beginning to envelope them, snuffing out their lives, preventing them from holding a pen or dictating, yet they remain stalwart and focused on their writing. Their optimism arises not from a belief in God and an afterlife—only Kübler-Ross looked forward to death so she could experience rebirth—but from their fulfillment in this life and from their gratitude for being alive.

Other surprises included Kübler-Ross's attempt to enlist a friend to help end her life despite a lifetime of rejecting patients' (and her own mother's) pleas for physician-assisted suicide. I was surprised that Susan Sontag, after decades of insisting on the importance of truth-telling to the terminally ill, refused to allow family and friends to speak candidly about her approaching death. Philip Rieff became an unwilling accomplice to his mother's denial. We are still left to ponder whether the Talmudic obligation to tell people what they can hear and not tell them what they cannot hear is helpful or harmful to the dying person—and to the caregiver. I remember how astonished I was when I discovered that Philip Roth wrote *My Life as a Man* to refute Hans Kleinschmidt's discussion in "The Angry Act"—a refutation that is also, ironically, a confirmation of some of his psychoanalyst's observations about the role of aggression in literary creativity. Roth's *Patrimony* reveals the role of reparation in the family romance without entirely concealing the son's anger toward both his parents. I was stunned by Edward Said's deathbed confession that he had not done enough to help the Palestinians, to whom he had devoted much of his adult life. I was startled to find that Mitch Albom doesn't acknowledge in *Tuesdays with Morrie* Schwartz's own end-of-life memoir, *Letting Go*. And I was amazed to learn that after writing *Mourning Diary*, Barthes did everything he could to subvert the value of writing and reading personal diaries.

Resiliency

One sees courage and strength not only in the authors who write about their own dying but also in the memoirists who write about their parents' deaths. Roth, Rieff, and Barthes all felt as if they had lost an essential part of themselves when their parents died. There were times when these writers felt like they were also dying, but they lived to tell their stories and, when they were finished memorializing their parents, they continued their writing careers. All of the writers in my study, the dying and their caregivers, demonstrate *resiliency*. Susan Sontag did not want to believe that she was dying of blood cancer, but she, too, was resilient, surviving two earlier bouts with cancer and hoping for another recovery.

Continuing Bonds

Whether writing about their own deaths or those of loved ones, the memoirists wrote with testimonial fervor, bearing witness to their own and others' lives. This is especially true of Roth, Rieff, and Barthes. They demonstrate a new view of mourning and loss that can also be seen in philosophy, as William Watkin points out. "Thinkers such as Jacques Derrida, Emmanuel Levinas, Jean-Luc Nancy, and Jean-François Lyotard have begun to insist on the responsibility of mourning to the lost other, turning attention away from those who grieve and towards those who have been lost" (199). Writing about their parents' deaths, Roth, Rieff, and Barthes became literary caregivers, demonstrating an ethics—and aesthetics—of care even when they believed, as Roth did, that they were revealing information that their parents did not wish to be disclosed.

In *The Other Side of Silence*, George A. Bonanno, a psychology professor at Columbia University Teachers College, concludes from a large-scale empirical study that the "clear majority of those surveyed felt that their lost loved one was still in some way with them or 'watching over' them" (135–36). The enduring connection between the deceased and the bereft has led to a new theory of bereavement, the "continuing bonds" phenomenon, which helps to explain why the dying feel compelled to write end-of-life memoirs and why so many people feel compelled to read them. Unlike Freud, who theorized that one of the tasks of mourning is to withdraw emotionally from the deceased, J. William Worden argues, along with many other contemporary grief theorists, that the mourner needs to maintain a relational bond with the deceased. "We need to find ways to memorialize the dead, that is, to remember the dead loved one—keeping them with us but still going on with life" (35). Writing is an ideal way for the living and dying to remain connected with each other, forging a continuing bond that survives death.

Through writing we realize that death may end a life but not a relationship. In *Let's Take the Long Way Home,* Gail Caldwell's memoir about her friendship with Caroline Knapp, who died of lung cancer at the age of forty-two, we see how our understanding of the dead continues to change. "It's taken years for me to understand that dying doesn't end the story; it transforms it. Edits, rewrites, the blur and epiphany of one-way dialogue. Most of us wander in and out of one another's lives until not death, but distance, does us part—time and space and the heart's weariness are the blander executioners of human connection" (123). Our relationship with and understanding of the dead change over time, as we ourselves change, and writing helps us to record these changes, whether dramatic or subtle.

Preserved for Posterity

I have limited my study of dying in character to memoirs, but novelists are no less preoccupied with and haunted by mortality, and sometimes their work appears, completed or not, with or without its creators' permission, decades after the writers' death. Vladimir Nabokov died in 1977 at the age of seventy-eight, and he left behind instructions to his literary heirs to destroy a fragmentary and incomplete novel, written on scores of index cards, on which he had been working for several years. Published in 2009 with an improbable subtitle, *The Original of Laura (Dying Is Fun)* survived the author's infanticidal intentions. Nabokov's wife, Véra, who decades earlier had saved the draft of *Lolita* her husband had impulsively thrown into the fire, could not bear to destroy the new manuscript, and when she died, their son, Dmitri, himself a writer, agonized over the decision. Should he honor his father's instructions, on the one hand, or preserve the story for posterity, on the other? In justifying his decision, Dmitri Nabokov argued that his father would have completed the manuscript if he had had more time. "An author may be seriously, even terminally ill and yet continue his desperate sprint against Fate to the last finish line, losing despite his intent to win" (*The Original of Laura* xii–xiii).

Alternately playful, satirical, and melancholy, *The Original of Laura* contains a Humbert-like narrator named Dr. Philip Wild, a writer and neurologist who casts light on the genesis of Nabokov's greatest novel, *Lolita*, while at the same time offering us cryptic insights into his creator's strange musings on death. *The Original of Laura* remains mystifying and bedeviling, but it suggests that Nabokov was writing in character while resurrecting his most notorious fictional narrator. Like Barthes's *Mourning Diary* and Hemingway's late stories, *The Original of Laura* raises the question of whether an author's literary reputation is helped or harmed by unauthorized posthumous publication. Despite the many differences between the wily novelist and his demented narrator, *The Original of Laura* is vintage Nabokov not only because of his delight in poking fun at himself—he mentions slyly a professor of Russian literature, a "forlorn looking man bored to extinction by his subject" (93)—but also because of his faith in the immortality of art.

Christopher Hitchens: Reading about One's Own Death

End-of-life memoirs come in all shapes and disguises. Christopher Hitchens's memoir, *Hitch-22*, reads like an end-of-life memoir partly because it is a four-hundred-page rumination on dying and death, and partly because while on a tour publicizing the book Hitchens was diagnosed with esophageal cancer. There is another reason *Hitch-22* reads like an end-of-life memoir. Hitchens notes in the beginning of the book that he had recently read a publication that referred to him as *"the late Christopher Hitchens"* (2). "So there it is in cold print," he observes ruefully, "the plain unadorned phrase that will one day become unarguably true. It is not given to everyone to read of his own death, let alone when announced in passing in such a matter-of-fact way" (2). Reading one's obituary must be unsettling, but Hitchens might have taken heart from Leopold Bloom's reflections on death in the Hades chapter of James Joyce's *Ulysses*: "Read your own obituary notice they say you live longer. Gives you second wind. New lease of life" (91).

Still another reason *Hitch-22* reads like an end-of-life memoir is that at the beginning of the book Hitchens recalls receiving a note from the writer Julian Barnes thanking him for the letter of condolence he sent on the sudden death of Barnes's wife, Pat Kavanagh, who died from brain cancer in 2008, the same year in which *Nothing to Be Frightened Of* appeared. Like *Hitch-22*, *Nothing to Be Frightened Of* reads like an end-of-life memoir. For both Barnes and Hitchens, the publication of their meditations on dying and death was followed immediately by a catastrophic personal event. Art often imitates life, but sometimes, in an eerie, unexpected way, art, in the form of a memoir on dying and death—seems to foreshadow life. And when this happens, it is almost inevitable that we return to the art, looking closely to see whether there are clues that foretell the future. Hitchens stated in a March 6, 2011, segment on *60 Minutes* that there is only a 5 percent survival rate for esophageal cancer, but he remained feisty and outspoken during the interview.

Hitchens's feistiness continued to the end of his life. Described as "probably the country's most famous unbeliever," he received the Freethinker of the Year Award in 2011. He told Charles McGrath in a *New York Times* interview that he wanted to write a book about dying: "It could be called 'What to Expect When You're Expecting'" (October 9, 2011). Hitchens didn't have time to write that book, but he did write two articles for *Vanity Fair* about his experience with cancer. In the September 2010 issue he recalls, with characteristic wit and verve, the details of discovering that he had metastatic esophageal cancer, which his father died of when he was seventy-nine. Hitchens was only sixty-one when cancer struck. He did not respond to the diagnosis in a formulaic, sequential way. "The notorious stage theory of Elisabeth Kübler-Ross, whereby one progresses from denial to rage through bargaining to depression and the eventual bliss of 'acceptance,' hasn't so far had much application in my case. In one way, I suppose, I have been 'in denial' for some time, knowingly burning the candle at both ends and finding that it often gives a lovely light. But for precisely that reason, I can't see myself smiting my brow with shock or hear myself whining about how it's all unfair: I have been taunting the Reaper into taking a free scythe in my direction and have now succumbed to something so predictable and banal that it bores even me."

In the January 2012 issue of *Vanity Fair* Hitchens recollects wryly a statement he made in *Hitch-22*. "Before I was diagnosed with esophageal cancer a year and a half ago, I rather jauntily told the readers of my memoirs that when faced with extinction I wanted to be fully conscious and awake, in order to 'do' death in the active and not the passive voice. And I do, still, try to nurture that little flame of curiosity and defiance: willing to play out the string to the end and wishing to be spared nothing that properly belongs to a life span." Using imagery and language that recall Harold Brodkey's *This Wild Darkness,* he describes toward the end of the essay the passing of his life. "I am typing this having just had an injection to try to reduce the pain in my arms, hands, and fingers. The chief side effect of this pain is numbness in the extremities, filling me with the not irrational fear that I shall lose the ability to write. Without that ability, I feel sure in advance, my 'will to live' would be hugely attenuated. I often grandly say that writing is not just my living and my livelihood but my very life, and it's true. Almost like the threatened loss of my voice, which is currently being alleviated by some temporary injections into my vocal folds, I feel my personality and identity dissolving as I contemplate dead hands and the loss of the transmission belts that connect me to writing and thinking." Hitchens died at the M. D. Anderson Cancer Center in Houston, Texas, on December 15, 2011 at the age of sixty-two.

The Fallacy of the "Therapeuto-Autobiographical Fallacy"

Julian Barnes often writes on moribund subjects, and when, at the age of fifty-eight, he finished a collection of short stories dealing with the "less serene aspects of old age," he was asked whether such writing "helped." The question annoyed him, and in *Nothing to Be Frightened Of* he refers irascibly to what he calls the "therapeuto-autobiographical fallacy." He quotes from a 1903 diary entry by Jules Renard and then offers his own caustic commentary. " 'The beauty of literature. I lose a cow. I write about its death, and this brings me in enough to buy another cow.' But does it work in any wider sense?" (97). Not for Barnes. His response to the therapeuto-autobiographical question? One has a painful childhood, is loved by no one, writes about it, cannot publish the book—and remains unloved. Barnes concludes that writing is not therapeutic, nor would writers wish it to be.

By contrast, Roger Rosenblatt concedes that writing about his daughter's death is therapeutic, albeit only temporarily. When his thirty-eight-year-old daughter, Amy, a physician and mother of three young children, died suddenly from an asymptomatic heart condition, Rosenblatt and his wife moved into their son-in-law's house to care for their grandchildren. Rosenblatt writes about the experience in his 2010 memoir *Making Toast*. In 2012 he published a second memoir about his daughter's death, *Kayak Morning*. The book might have also been called *Kayak Mourning*, for in it he reflects on love, loss, and bereavement. *Kayak Morning* is not a self-help book in the tradition of *Tuesdays with Morrie* and *The Last Lecture*, but it abounds in sorrowful wisdom and wit. Nowhere in his many books and essays does Rosenblatt write about "dying in character," but he implies this in *Kayak Morning* when he states that "people in grief become more like themselves" (128). Angry at God, Rosenblatt refuses to be comforted or consoled. All he has to keep him afloat, he admits, is writing. He discloses in *Kayak Morning* that following the publication of *Making Toast*, which originally appeared in the *New Yorker*, he received nearly a thousand letters from people telling him their own stories of love and loss and wishing his family well. His response to this outpouring remains terse and unenthusiastic: "Everybody grieves" (14). One of the most poignant moments in *Kayak Morning* occurs near the end when he reveals a conversation with a therapist-friend, whom he allows to have the last word:

> "Why did you write *Making Toast*?"
>
> "It was therapy. As long as I was writing about Amy, I could keep her alive."
>
> "What about afterwards?"
>
> "When the book was finished, it was as if she had died again."
>
> "The book isn't enough," she said.
>
> "No, it isn't enough."
>
> "So what do you do now? Write another book?"
>
> "There has to be something more lasting than a book."
>
> "And what would that be?" (143)

Admittedly, this is not a ringing endorsement of writing as therapy, but it is the best Rosenblatt can imagine. Expressed differently, writers write — that is what they do—and some of them, like Kübler-Ross, Brodkey, Said, Judt, Buchwald, Schwartz, Pausch, and Bauby all wrote to the end of their lives. *They were literally dying to write.* Nothing could stop them from writing, including near-total paralysis. They would have written even if writing made them feel worse, but, instead, writing brought its own gratification. Most of the end-of-life memoirists in my study, those who wrote while dying and the others who wrote about their parents' deaths, would agree with Barthes's statement that writing conveys apotropaic, integrative power, the ability to live with suffering. These writers exorcized their fears by going to where they were afraid to go. Most memoirists would concur with Maureen Murdoch's observation that the "fundamental premise of memoir writing is a belief in the restorative power of telling one's truth; once told, the writer can begin to move on with her life" (81). The only qualification I would add is that telling one's story allows end-of-life memoirists to move on with their own deaths. "We are addicted to language for its sanity-providing," Joyce Carol Oates states in *A Widow's Story* (115), her memoir about the sudden death of her husband. Oates notes that "in the end it is our work that matters," work that is both a "solace and a lifeline" (116). The clinical psychologist Kay Redfield Jamison discloses at the end of *Nothing Was the Same*, her memoir about the death of her husband, Richard Wyatt, that she found her way back to life through her writing. "To hold on to love, I had to find a way to capture and transform it. The only way I knew to do this was to write a book, this book, about Richard" (202).

Reading, too, no less than writing, is therapeutic, for however upsetting it may be to read about others' suffering or death, we can learn from their experiences and, in the process, feel less alone and scared. As we grow older and become closer to death, we read end-of-life memoirs for the same reason we read obituaries. "Obituaries have a pull," Marilyn Johnson suggests, "a natural gravity for those of us who've observed that life has a way of ending" (9). We need not share Johnson's euphoric conclusion—"It's the best time ever to read obituaries, and I'm here to tell you, it's a great time to die" (12)—to share her belief that reading death notices—and end-of-life memoirs—exposes us to life's deepest emotions and provides us with lasting insights into life and death.

Reading may even be life-saving. In a footnote in his memoir, Hitchens recalls a story about a youth of "appallingly dank demeanor" who served William Styron and him in a diner. The server remarked, after returning Styron's credit card, that it bore a name that was "almost the same" as that of a famous writer. "Bill said nothing. Tonelessly, the youth went on: 'He's called William Styron.' I left this up to Bill, who again held off until the kid matter-of-factly said, 'Anyway, that guy's book saved my life.' At this point Styron invited him to sit down, and he was eventually persuaded that he was at the same table as the author of *Darkness Visible*. It was like a transformation scene: he told us brokenly of how he'd sought and found the needful help. 'Does this happen to you a lot?' I later asked Styron. 'Oh, *all* the time. I even get the police calling up to ask if I'll come on the line and talk to a man who's threatening to jump'" (*Hitch-22* 29). In her memoir Alexandra Styron has confirmed her father's efforts to respond to the overwhelming number of letters he received after the publication of *Darkness Visible*. "My father devoted an enormous amount of time, time that might otherwise have been spent on his own work, reacting to his readers" (10).

The Lessons of Love and Loss

Some end-of-life memoirs are didactic, while others are not. Kübler-Ross is an engaging storyteller who offers her compelling insights into death and dying before instructing us on her controversial "answers to life's big questions." Schwartz's *Letting Go* and Mitch Albom's *Tuesdays with Morrie* abound in clinical and philosophical advice for the dying and their caregivers, and Pausch's *The Last Lecture* reads like—a lecture. Said and Judt write their life stories in a style that is intellectually rigorous without being pedantic. Rieff doesn't offer much advice to readers of *Swimming in a Sea of Death*, perhaps because he has enough difficulty simply staying afloat. The other memoirists explore love and loss without counseling readers how to live or die. Oates speaks for these memoirists when she remarks that she was tempted to offer advice to others but then decided against it. The only advice she offers occurs on the last page of *A Widow's Story* when she declares, speaking about herself in the third person, "Of the widow's countless death-duties there is really just one that matters: on the first anniversary of her husband's death the widow should think *I kept myself alive* (416). Jamison mentions the futility of offering advice on grief and limits herself to one statement: "The lessons that come from grief come from its unexpected moves, from its shifting views of what has gone before and what is yet to come" (170).

Dying in Character

The anthropologist and filmmaker Barbara Myerhoff characterizes our species as *Homo narrans*, humankind as storyteller, but even she would be amazed, as I am, by the number of end-of-life memoirs written, dictated, or blinked under near-impossible conditions. These stories are a lasting tribute to the memoirists' courage, strength, and hope. They wrote for themselves and their readers, for the present, of which they have been part, and for the future in which their words will affect new generations of readers. The writers left a paper trail that we can follow in their movements toward death. "We tell ourselves stories in order to live," Joan Didion has observed famously. She has now written two achingly personal memoirs about loss: *The Year of Magical Thinking*, about the death of her husband, and *Blue Nights*, about the death of her only child. Some writers tell themselves stories in order to die. Writing becomes, for them, an act of self-creation amid the process of self-extinction. Few of these memoirists viewed themselves as death educators, but their insights may be helpful in our own preparations for death. They lived and died in harness, writing to the end. They continue to speak to us from beyond the grave, and they remain living for as long as we reflect on their words. We keep alive their stories, just as future readers will keep alive ours. Whenever, wherever, and however we die, at home or away, decades from now or tomorrow, from cancer, stroke, amyotrophic lateral sclerosis, locked-in syndrome, or a car accident, we remember their end-of-life memoirs. Like Winnicott, they were alive when they died, and they inspire us by their examples.

WORKS CITED

Albom, Mitch. *The Five People You Meet in Heaven.* New York: Hyperion, 2003.

———. *For One More Day.* New York: Hyperion, 2006.

———. *Tuesdays with Morrie: An Old Man, a Young Man, and Life's Greatest Lesson.* New York: Broadway Books, 1997.

Allen, Graham. *Roland Barthes.* London: Routledge, 2003.

Anderson, Linda. "Autobiography and Exile: Edward Said's *Out of Place*." In *Edward Said and the Literary, Social, and Political World,* edited by Ranjan Ghosh, 165–75. New York: Routledge, 2009.

Ariès, Philippe. *The Hour of Our Death.* Translated by Helen Weaver. New York: Knopf, 1981.

Astrow, Alan. "Thoughts on Euthanasia and Physician-Assisted Suicide." In *Facing Death: Where Culture, Religion, and Medicine Meet,* edited by Howard Spiro, Mary McCrea Curnen, and Lee Palmer Wandel, 44–51. New Haven: Yale University Press, 1996.

Avrahami, Einat. "Impacts of Truth(s): The Confessional Mode in Harold Brodkey's Illness Autobiography." *Literature and Medicine* 22 (2003): 164–87.

Bakewell, Sarah. *How to Live: or, A Life of Montaigne in One Question and Twenty Attempts at an Answer.* London: Chatto & Windus, 2010.

Barenboim, Daniel, and Edward W. Said. *Parallels and Paradoxes: Explorations in Music and Society.* Edited and with a preface by Ara Guzelimian. New York: Pantheon, 2002.

Barnes, Julian. *Nothing to Be Frightened Of.* New York: Knopf, 2008.

Barsamian, David, and Edward W. Said. *Culture and Resistance: Conversations with Edward W. Said.* Cambridge, Mass.: South End Press, 2003.

Barthes, Roland. *A Barthes Reader.* Edited and with an introduction by Susan Sontag. New York: Hill & Wang, 1982.

———. *Camera Lucida: Reflections on Photography.* Translated by Richard Howard. New York: Hill & Wang, 1981.

———. *Critical Essays.* Translated by Richard Howard. Evanston, Ill.: Northwestern University Press, 1972.

————. *Incidents.* Translated by Richard Howard. Berkeley: University of California Press, 1992.

————. *A Lover's Discourse: Fragments.* Translated by Richard Howard. London: Jonathan Cape, 1979.

————. *Mourning Diary: October 26, 1977–September 15, 1979.* Translated by Richard Howard. New York: Hill & Wang, 2010.

————. *Roland Barthes by Roland Barthes.* Translated by Richard Howard. New York: Hill & Wang, 1977.

Battin, Margaret Pabst. *The Least Worst Death.* New York: Oxford University Press, 1994.

Bauby, Jean-Dominique. *The Diving Bell and the Butterfly: A Memoir of Life in Death.* Translated by Jeremy Leggatt. New York: Vintage, 1997.

Bayley, John. *Iris and Her Friends: A Memoir of Memory and Desire.* New York: Norton, 2000.

Becker, Ernest. *The Denial of Death.* New York: Free Press, 1973.

Berman, Jeffrey. *Companionship in Grief: Love and Loss in the Memoirs of C. S. Lewis, John Bayley, Donald Hall, Joan Didion, and Calvin Trillin.* Amherst: University of Massachusetts Press, 2010.

————. *Death in the Classroom: Writing about Love and Loss.* Albany: State University of New York Press, 2009.

————. *Dying to Teach: A Memoir of Love, Loss, and Learning.* Albany: State University of New York Press, 2009.

————. "Revisiting Philip Roth's Psychoanalysts." In *The Cambridge Companion to Philip Roth,* edited by Timothy Parrish, 94–110. New York: Cambridge University Press, 2007.

————. *Surviving Literary Suicide.* Amherst: University of Massachusetts Press, 1999.

————. *The Talking Cure: Literary Representations of Psychoanalysis.* New York: New York University Press, 1985.

Birkerts, Sven. *The Art of Time in Memoir: Then, Again.* Saint Paul: Graywolf Press, 2008.

Bloom, Claire. *Leaving a Doll's House.* Boston: Little, Brown, 1996.

Bloom, Harold, editor. *Till I End My Song: A Gathering of Last Poems.* New York: HarperCollins, 2010.

Bonanno, George A. *The Other Side of Sadness: What the New Science of Bereavement Tells Us about Life after Loss.* New York: Basic Books, 2009.

Bowen, Alexander. *The Betrayal of the Body.* New York: Macmillan, 1967.

Bowlby, John. *Attachment and Loss.* 3 vols. New York: Basic Books, 1969–80.

Brodkey, Harold. *First Love and Other Sorrows.* New York: Dial Press, 1957.

————. *My Venice.* New York: Metropolitan Books, 1998.

————. *Profane Friendship.* New York: Farrar, Straus, & Giroux, 1994.

————. *The Runaway Soul.* New York: Farrar, Straus, & Giroux, 1991.

————. *Sea Battles on Dry Land: Essays.* New York: Metropolitan Books, 1999.

————. *Stories in an Almost Classical Mode.* New York: Knopf, 1988.

————. *This Wild Darkness: The Story of My Death.* New York: Metropolitan Books, 1996.

————. *Women and Angels.* Philadelphia: Jewish Publication Society of America, 1985.

———. *The World Is the Home of Love and Death: Stories.* New York: Metropolitan Books, 1997.

Brody, Jane E. "Frank Talk about Care at Life's End." *New York Times,* August 23, 2010.

———. "A Humorist Illuminates the Blessings of Hospice." *New York Times,* January 23, 2007.

Brookes, Tim. *Signs of Life: A Memoir of Dying and Discovery.* New York: Times Books, 1997.

Broyard, Anatole. "Good Books about Being Sick." *New York Times Book Review,* November 11, 1990.

———. *Intoxicated by My Illness and Other Writings on Life and Death.* Compiled and edited by Alexandra Broyard. Foreword by Oliver Sacks. New York: Ballantine, 1992.

Buchwald, Ann. *Seems Like Yesterday.* New York: Putnam, 1980.

Buchwald, Art. *I'll Always Have Paris.* New York: Putnam, 1996.

———. *I Think I Don't Remember.* New York: Putnam, 1987.

———. *Leaving Home: A Memoir.* New York: Putnam, 1993.

———. *Stella in Heaven.* New York: Putnam, 2000.

———. *Too Soon to Say Goodbye.* New York: Random House, 2006.

———. *We'll Laugh Again.* New York: Putnam, 2002.

Buck, Ross. "The Gratitude of Exchange and the Gratitude of Caring: A Developmental-Interactionist Perspective of Moral Emotion." In *The Psychology of Gratitude,* edited by Robert A. Emmons and Michael E. McCullough, 100–122. New York: Oxford University Press, 2004.

Buckley, Christopher. *Losing Mum and Pup.* New York: Twelve, 2009.

Buckman, Robert. "Communication in Palliative Care: A Practical Guide." In *The Oxford Textbook of Palliative Medicine,* 2nd ed., edited by Derek Doyle, Geoffrey W. C. Hanks, and Neil MacDonald, 141–56. Oxford: Oxford University Press, 1998.

Byock, Ira. *Dying Well: Peace and Possibilities at the End of Life.* New York: Riverhead, 1997.

Caldwell, Gail. *Let's Take the Long Way Home: A Memoir of Friendship.* New York: Random House, 2010.

Callanan, Maggie, and Patricia Kelley. *Final Gifts: Understanding the Special Awareness, Needs, and Communications of the Dying.* New York: Bantam, 1997.

Calvet, Louis-Jean. *Roland Barthes: A Biography.* Translated by Sarah Wykes. Bloomington: Indiana University Press, 1995.

Cassell, Eric J. *The Nature of Suffering and the Goals of Medicine.* 2nd ed. Oxford: Oxford University Press, 2004.

Chaban, Michèle Catherine Gantois. *The Life and Work of Dr. Elisabeth Kübler-Ross and Its Impact on the Death Awareness Movement.* Lewiston, N.Y.: Edwin Mellen, 2000.

Ching, Barbara. " 'Not Even a New Yorker': Susan Sontag in America." In Ching and Wagner-Lawlor, *The Scandal of Susan Sontag,* 52–77.

Ching, Barbara, and Jennifer A. Wagner-Lawlor, editors. *The Scandal of Susan Sontag.* New York: Columbia University Press, 2009.

Chochinov, Harvey Max. "Dignity-Conserving Care—A New Model for Palliative Care." *Journal of the American Medical Association* 287 (2002): 2253–60.

Conrad, Joseph. *Nostromo.* Garden City, N.Y.: Doubleday, 1929.

Critchley, Simon. *The Book of Dead Philosophers.* New York: Vintage, 2008.

Csikszentmihalyi, Mihaly. *Creativity: Flow and the Psychology of Discovery and Invention.* New York: HarperCollins, 1996.

Culler, Jonathan. *Barthes: A Very Short Introduction.* New York: Oxford University Press, 2002.

Davies, Douglas J. *A Brief History of Death.* Malden, Mass.: Blackwell, 2005.

De Beauvoir, Simone. *A Very Easy Death.* Translated by Patrick O'Brian. New York: Warner, 1965.

Didion, Joan. *Blue Nights.* New York: Knopf, 2011.

———. *The Year of Magical Thinking.* New York: Knopf, 2005.

Dillard, Annie. *The Writing Life.* New York: HarperPerennial, 1990.

Doka, Kenneth J. "Historical and Contemporary Perspectives on Dying." In *Handbook of Thanatology: The Essential Body of Knowledge for the Study of Death, Dying, and Bereavement,* David Balk, editor in chief, 19–25. New York: Routledge, 2007.

Dolby, Sandra K. *Self-Help Books: Why Americans Keep Reading Them.* Urbana: University of Illinois Press, 2005.

Dumas, Alexandre. *The Count of Monte Cristo.* Translated and with an introduction and notes by Robin Buss. New York: Penguin, 2003.

Ebbern, Hayden, Sean Mulligan, and Barry L. Beyerstein. "Near-Death Experiences Are Not Glimpses of an Afterlife." In *Death and Dying: Opposing Viewpoints,* edited by Paul A. Winters, 163–68. San Diego: Greenhaven Press, 1998.

Edelman, Hope. *Motherless Daughters: The Legacy of Loss.* New York: Delta, 1995.

Egan, Susanna. *Mirror Talk: Genres of Crisis in Contemporary Autobiography.* Chapel Hill: University of North Carolina Press, 1999.

Elias, Norbert. *The Loneliness of the Dying.* Translated by Edmund Jephcott. New York: Continuum, 2001.

Eliot, George. *Middlemarch.* London: Zodiac Press, 1967.

Emerson, Ralph Waldo. *Ralph Waldo Emerson.* Edited by Richard Poirier. Oxford: Oxford University Press, 1990.

Erikson, Eric H. *Identity: Youth and Crisis.* New York: Norton, 1968.

Facing Death: Elisabeth Kübler-Ross. Directed by Stefan Haupt. DVD. 2003.

Fenwick, Peter, and Elizabeth Fenwick. *The Art of Dying: A Journey to Elsewhere.* New York: Continuum, 2008.

Frank, Arthur W. *Letting Stories Breathe: A Socio-Narratology.* Chicago: University of Chicago Press, 2010.

———. *The Wounded Storyteller: Body, Illness, and Ethics.* Chicago: University of Chicago Press, 1995.

Franklin, Benjamin. *The Autobiography of Benjamin Franklin.* Berkeley: University of California Press, 1949.

Freud, Sigmund. *Beyond the Pleasure Principle.* In *Standard Edition of the Complete Psychological Works,* 18:1–64.

———. "Dostoevsky and Parricide." In *Standard Edition of the Complete Psychological Works,* 21:177–94.

———. "Preface to the Second Edition." *The Interpretation of Dreams,* in *Standard Edition of the Complete Psychological Works,* 4:xxv–xxvi.

———. *The Letters of Sigmund Freud.* Edited by Ernest L. Freud. New York: Basic Books, 1960.

———. "Mourning and Melancholia." In *Standard Edition of the Complete Psychological Works,* 14:243–58.

———. *The Standard Edition of the Complete Psychological Works of Sigmund Freud.* Edited and translated by James Strachey. 24 vols. London: Hogarth Press, 1953–1974.

———. "Thoughts for the Times on War and Death." In *Standard Edition of the Complete Psychological Works,* 14:273–300.

———. *Totem and Taboo.* In *Standard Edition of the Complete Psychological Works,* 13:1–161.

Fulton, Robert. "Anticipatory Mourning: A Critique of the Concept." *Mortality* 8 (2003): 342–51.

Gay, Peter. *Freud: A Life for Our Time.* New York: Norton, 1988.

Gilbert, Sandra M. *Death's Door: Modern Dying and the Ways We Grieve.* New York: Norton, 2006.

Gill, Derek. *Quest: The Life of Elisabeth Kübler-Ross.* With an epilogue by Elisabeth Kübler-Ross. New York: Harper & Row, 1980.

Glaser, Barney, and Anselm Strauss. *Awareness of Dying.* Chicago: Aldine, 1965.

Goodman, Lisl Marburg. *Death and the Creative Life: Conversations with Prominent Artists and Scientists.* New York: Springer, 1981.

Gordon, Andrew. "Jewish Fathers and Sons in Spiegelman's *Maus* and Roth's *Patrimony.*" *ImageTexT.* www.english.ufl.edu/imagetext/archives/vi_1/Gordon.

Gorer, Geoffrey. *Death, Grief, and Mourning in Contemporary Britain.* London: Cresset Press, 1965.

Greenberg, Joanne. *I Never Promised You a Rose Garden.* New York: Holt, Rinehart, & Winston, 1964.

Gross, Charles G. *A Hole in the Head: More Tales in the History of Neuroscience.* Cambridge: MIT Press, 2009.

Hall, Donald. *Goatfoot Milktongue Twinbird: Interviews, Essays, and Notes on Poetry, 1970–1976.* Ann Arbor: University of Michigan Press, 1978.

Harrington, Anne. *The Cure Within: A History of Mind-Body Medicine.* New York: Norton, 2008.

Harris, Darcy. "Healing the Narcissistic Injury of Death in the Context of Western Society." In *The Shame of Death, Grief, and Trauma,* edited by Jeffrey Kauffman, 75–86. New York: Routledge, 2010.

Hick, John. *Between Faith and Doubt: Dialogues on Religion and Reason.* New York: Palgrave Macmillan, 2010.

Hitchens, Christopher. *Hitch-22: A Memoir.* New York: Twelve, 2010.

Horowitz, Mardi, Nancy Wilner, Charles Marmor, and Janice Krupnick. "Pathological Grief and the Activation of Latent Self-Images." *American Journal of Psychiatry* 137 (1980): 1157–62.

Jaffe, Lois, and Arthur Jaffe. "Terminal Candor and the Coda Syndrome: A Tandem View of Terminal Illness." In *New Meanings of Death,* edited by Herman Feifel, 196–211. New York: McGraw-Hill, 1977.

Jamison, Kay Redfield. *Nothing Was the Same: A Memoir.* New York: Vintage, 2009.

Janoff-Bulman, Ronnie. *Shattered Assumptions: Towards a New Psychology of Trauma.* New York: Free Press, 1992.

Johnson, Marilyn. *The Dead Beat: Lost Souls, Lucky Stiffs, and the Perverse Pleasures of Obituaries.* New York: Harper Perennial, 2007.

Jones, Ernest. *The Last Phase, 1919–1939.* Vol. 3 in *The Life and Work of Sigmund Freud.* New York: Basic Books, 1957.

Joyce, James. *Ulysses.* Corrected ed. New York: Modern Library, 1961.

Judt, Tony. *The Burden of Responsibility: Blum, Camus, Aron, and the French Intellectuals.* Chicago: University of Chicago Press, 1998.

———. *Ill Fares the Land.* New York: Penguin, 2010.

———. *The Memory Chalet.* New York: Penguin, 2010.

———. *Past Imperfect: French Intellectuals, 1944–1956.* Berkeley: University of California Press, 1992.

———. *Postwar: A History of Europe since 1945.* New York: Penguin, 2005.

———. *Reappraisals: Reflections on the Forgotten Twentieth Century.* New York: Penguin, 2008.

———. *Thinking the Twentieth Century.* With Timothy Snyder. New York: Penguin, 2012.

Kafka, Franz. *Letters to Friends, Family, and Editors.* Translated by Richard Winston and Clara Winston. New York: Schocken, 1977.

Kamenetz, Rodger. *Terra Infirma: A Memoir of My Mother's Life in Mine.* New York: Schocken, 1985.

Kastenbaum, Robert. "Last Words." *Monist* 76 (April 1993): 270–90.

Keats, John. *Selected Poems and Letters.* Cambridge: Riverside Press, 1959.

Kellehear, Allan. *Dying of Cancer: The Final Year of Life.* Chur, Switzerland: Harwood, 1990.

———. *A Social History of Dying.* Cambridge: Cambridge University Press, 2007.

Kennedy, Valerie. *Edward Said: A Critical Introduction.* Cambridge, Mass.: Polity Press, 2000.

Khalidi, Rashid. "Edward Said and Palestine: Balancing the Academic and the Political, the Public and the Private." In *Writing for the Barbarians: A Tribute to Edward W. Said,* edited by Müge Gürsoy Sökmen and Basak Ertür, 44–52. London: Verso, 2008.

Kleinschmidt, Hans J. "The Angry Act: The Role of Aggression in Creativity." *American Imago* 24 (1967): 98–128.

Kohut, Heinz. *How Does Analysis Cure?* Edited by Arnold Goldberg. Chicago: University of Chicago Press, 1984.

———. *The Search for the Self: Selected Writings of Heinz Kohut.* 4 vols. Edited and with an introduction by Paul H. Ornstein. London: Karnac Books, 2011.

Konigsberg, Ruth Davis. *The Truth about Grief: The Myth of Its Five Stages and the New Science of Loss.* New York: Simon & Schuster, 2011.

Koppelman, Kent L. *Wrestling with the Angel: Literary Writings and Reflections on Death, Dying, and Bereavement.* Amityville, N.Y.: Baywood, 2010.

Kübler-Ross, Elisabeth. *AIDS: The Ultimate Challenge.* New York: Macmillan, 1987.

———. *The Cocoon and the Butterfly.* Edited by Göran Grip. Barrytown, N.Y.: Station Hill Openings, 1997.

———. *Death Is of Vital Importance: On Life, Death, and Life after Death.* Compiled and edited by Göran Grip. Barrytown, N.Y.: Station Hill Press, 1995.

———. *Death: The Final Stage of Growth.* Englewood Cliffs, N.J.: Prentice-Hall, 1975.

———. *Healing in Our Time.* Edited by Göran Grip. Barrytown, N.Y.: Station Hill Openings, 1997.

———. *Living with Death and Dying: How to Communicate with the Terminally Ill.* New York: Touchstone, 1984.

———. *The Meaning of Suffering.* Edited by Göran Grip. Barrytown, N.Y.: Station Hill Openings, 1997.

———. *On Children and Death.* New York: Macmillan, 1983.

———. *On Death and Dying.* New York: Macmillan, 1969.

———. *On Life after Death.* 1991. New foreword by Caroline Myss. Berkeley: Celestial Arts, 2008.

———. *Questions and Answers on Death and Dying.* New York: Macmillan, 1974.

———. *To Live Until We Say Good-bye.* Text by Elisabeth Kübler-Ross. Photos by Mal Warshaw. Englewood Cliffs, N.J.: Prentice-Hall, 1978.

———. *Say Yes to It.* Edited by Göran Grip. Barrytown, N.Y.: Station Hill Openings, 1997.

———. *The Tunnel and the Light: Essential Insights on Living and Dying, with a Letter to a Child with Cancer.* Compiled and edited by Göran Grip. Photographs by Ken Ross. New York: Marlowe, 1999.

———. *The Wheel of Life: A Memoir of Living and Dying.* New York: Scribner, 1997.

———. *Working It Through.* Text by Elisabeth Kübler-Ross. Photos by Mal Warshaw. New York: Macmillan, 1981.

Kübler-Ross, Elisabeth, and David Kessler. *Life Lessons: Two Experts on Death and Dying Teach Us about the Mysteries of Life and Living.* New York: Scribner, 2000.

LaCapra, Dominick. "Trauma, Absence, Loss." *Critical Inquiry* 25 (Summer 1999): 696–727.

Larson, Thomas. *The Memoir and the Memoirist: Reading and Writing Personal Narrative.* Athens: Swallow Press/Ohio University Press, 2007.

Lavine, T. Z. *From Socrates to Sartre: The Philosophic Quest.* New York: Bantam, 1984.

Lawrence, D. H. *Studies in Classic American Literature.* New York: Viking, 1969.

Lear, Jonathan. *Radical Hope: Ethics in the Face of Cultural Devastation.* Cambridge: Harvard University Press, 2006.

Leavitt, David. "The Way I Live Now." In *The Story and Its Writer: An Introduction to Short Fiction,* 3rd ed., edited by Ann Charters, 1470–71. Boston: Bedford Books of St. Martin's Press, 1991.

Le Comte, Edward S. *Dictionary of Last Words.* New York: Philosophical Library, 1955.

Leibovitz, Annie. *A Photographer's Life.* New York: Random House, 2005.

Lerner, Max. *Wrestling with the Angel: A Memoir of My Triumph over Illness.* New York: Touchstone, 1991.

Lewis, C. S. *A Grief Observed.* 1961. Reprint, New York: HarperCollins, 2001.

Lindemann, Erich. "Symptomatology and Management of Acute Grief." *American Journal of Psychiatry* 101 (1944): 141–48.

Lutz, Tom. *Crying: The Natural and Cultural History of Tears.* New York: Norton, 1999.

Martin, Terry, and Kenneth J. Doka. *Men Don't Cry . . . Women Do: Transcending Gender Stereotypes of Grief.* Philadelphia: Brunner/Mazel, 2000.

May, Todd. "Happy Ending." *New York Times,* November 2, 2009.

McInerney, Fran. "Cinematic Visions of Dying." In *The Study of Dying: From Autonomy to Transformation,* edited by Allan Kellehear, 211–32. Cambridge: Cambridge University Press, 2009.

McInerney, Jay. *Brightness Falls.* New York: Knopf, 1992.

Mead, George H. *Mind, Self, and Society: From the Standpoint of a Social Behaviorist.* Edited and with an introduction by Charles W. Morris. Chicago: University of Chicago Press, 1934.

Melzack, Ronald, and Patrick Wall. *The Challenge of Pain.* Rev. ed. New York: Penguin, 1988.

Miller, Arthur. *Death of a Salesman.* Edited by Gerald Weales. New York: Viking Critical Library, 1967.

Miller, D. A. *Bringing Out Roland Barthes.* Berkeley: University of California Press, 1992.

Miller, Edwin Haviland. *Salem Is My Dwelling Place: A Life of Nathaniel Hawthorne.* Iowa City: University of Iowa Press, 1991.

Miller, James. *Examined Lives: From Socrates to Nietzsche.* New York: Farrar, Straus, & Giroux, 2011.

Miller, Nancy K. *Bequest and Betrayal: Memoirs of a Parent's Death.* New York: Oxford University Press, 1996.

———. "Facts, Pacts, Acts." *Profession* 92 (1992): 10–14.

———. "Memory Stains: Annie Ernaux's *Shame.* In *Extremities: Trauma, Testimony, and Community,* edited by Nancy K. Miller and Jason Tougaw, 197–213. Urbana: University of Illinois Press, 2002.

———. "Regarding Susan Sontag." *PMLA* 120 (2005): 828–33.

Moller, David Wendell. *Confronting Death: Values, Institutions, and Human Mortality.* New York: Oxford University Press, 1996.

Moody, Raymond A., Jr. *Life after Life: The Investigation of a Phenomenon—Survival of Bodily Death.* Harrisburg, Pa.: Stackpole, 1975.

Morris, Virginia. *Talking about Death Won't Kill You.* New York: Workman, 2001.

Mukherjee, Siddartha. *The Emperor of All Maladies: A Biography of Cancer.* New York: Scribner, 2010.

Murdoch, Maureen. *Unreliable Truth: On Memoir and Memory.* New York: Seal Press, 2003.

Myerhoff, Barbara. *Number Our Days: A Triumph of Continuity and Culture among Jewish Old People in an Urban Ghetto.* New York: Touchstone, 1978.

Nabokov, Vladimir. *The Original of Laura (Dying Is Fun).* Edited by Dmitri Nabokov. New York: Knopf, 2009.

Nadeau, Janice Winchester. *Families Making Sense of Death.* Thousand Oaks, Calif.: Sage Publications, 1998.

Nelson, Judith Kay. *Seeing through Tears: Crying and Attachment.* New York: Routledge, 2005.

Nuland, Sherwin B. *How We Die: Reflections on Life's Final Chapter.* New York: Vintage, 1995.

Nunez, Sigrid. *Sempre Susan: A Memoir of Susan Sontag.* New York: Atlas, 2011.

Nussbaum, Martha. *Upheavals of Thought: The Intelligence of Emotions.* Cambridge: Cambridge University Press, 2001.

Oates, Joyce Carol. *Where I've Been, and Where I'm Going: Essays, Reviews, and Prose.* New York: Plume, 1999.

———. *A Widow's Story: A Memoir.* New York: Ecco/HarperCollins, 2011.

Parkes, Colin Murray. "What Becomes of Redundant World Models? A Contribution to the Study of Adaptation to Change." *British Journal of Medical Psychology* 48 (1975): 131–37.

Pausch, Randy. *The Last Lecture.* With Jeffrey Zaslow. New York: Hyperion, 2008.

Plath, Sylvia. "Lady Lazarus." In *Collected Poems,* edited by Ted Hughes. 1981. New York: HarperPerennial, 1992.

Plimpton, George. *Shadow Box.* New York: Putnam, 1977.

Prosser, Jay. "Metaphors Kill: 'Against Interpretation' and the Illness Books. In Ching and Wagner-Lawlor, *The Scandal of Susan Sontag,* 188–202. New York: Columbia University Press, 2009.

Quill, Timothy, and Margaret Battin, editors. *Physician-Assisted Dying.* Baltimore: Johns Hopkins University Press, 2004.

Rando, Therese A. "A Comprehensive Analysis of Anticipatory Grief: Perspectives, Processes, Promises, and Problems." In *Loss and Anticipatory Grief,* edited by Therese A. Rando. Foreword by Robert Fulton, 3–37. Lexington, Mass.: Lexington Books, 1986.

Ratekin, Tom. *Final Acts: Traversing the Fantasy in the Modern Memoir.* Albany: State University of New York Press, 2009.

Rieff, David. *At the Point of a Gun: Democratic Dreams and Armed Intervention.* New York: Simon & Schuster, 2005.

———. *A Bed for the Night: Humanitarianism in Crisis.* New York: Simon & Schuster, 2002.

———. *The Exile: Cuba in the Heart of Miami.* New York: Simon & Schuster, 1993.

———. *Going to Miami: Exiles, Tourists, and Refugees in the New America.* Boston: Little, Brown, 1987.

———. *Los Angeles: Capital of the Third World.* New York: Simon & Schuster, 1991.

———. *Slaughterhouse: Bosnia and the Failure of the West.* New York: Simon & Schuster, 1995.

———. *Swimming in a Sea of Death: A Son's Memoir.* New York: Simon & Schuster, 2008.

Rieff, Philip. *Freud: The Mind of the Moralist.* Garden City, N.Y.: Anchor Books, 1961.

Roberts, Robert C. "The Blessings of Gratitude: A Conceptual Analysis." In *The Psychology of Gratitude,* edited by Robert A. Emmons and Michael E. McCullough, 58–80. New York: Oxford University Press, 2004.

Robinson, Ray. *Famous Last Words.* New York: Workman Publishing, 2003.

Rollyson, Carl. *Reading Susan Sontag: A Critical Introduction to Her Work.* Chicago: Ivan R. Dee, 2001.

Rollyson, Carl, and Lisa Paddock. *Susan Sontag: The Making of an Icon.* New York: Norton, 2000.

Rose, Jacqueline. "The Question of Zionism: Continuing the Dialogue." In *Edward Said: A Legacy of Emancipation and Representation.* Edited by Adel Iskandar and Hakem Rustom, 314–20. Berkeley: University of California Press, 2010.

Rosen, Jonathan. "Rewriting the End: Elisabeth Kübler-Ross." *New York Times Magazine,* January 22, 1995, 22–25.

Rosenblatt, Roger. *Kayak Morning: Reflections on Love, Grief, and Small Boats.* New York: Ecco, 2012.

———. *Making Toast: A Family Story.* New York: Ecco, 2010.

Roth, Philip. *The Anatomy Lesson.* New York: Farrar, Straus, & Giroux, 1983.

———. *Conversations with Philip Roth.* Edited by George J. Searles. Jackson: University Press of Mississippi, 1992.

———. *The Counterlife.* New York: Farrar, Straus, & Giroux, 1986.

———. *Deception.* New York: Simon & Schuster, 1990.

———. *The Dying Animal.* Boston: Houghton Mifflin, 2001.

———. *Everyman.* Boston: Houghton Mifflin, 2006.

———. *Exit Ghost.* Boston: Houghton Mifflin, 2007.

———. *The Facts: A Novelist's Autobiography.* New York: Farrar, Straus, & Giroux, 1988.

———. *The Ghost Writer.* New York: Farrar, Straus, & Giroux, 1979.

———. *The Human Stain.* Boston: Houghton Mifflin, 2000.

———. *The Humbling.* Boston: Houghton Mifflin, 2009.

———. *I Married a Communist.* Boston: Houghton Mifflin, 1998.

———. *Letting Go.* New York: Random House, 1962.

———. *My Life as a Man.* New York: Holt, Rinehart, & Winston, 1974.

———. *Operation Shylock: A Confession.* New York: Vintage, 1974.

———. *Patrimony: A True Story.* 1991. New York: Vintage, 1996.

———. *The Plot against America.* Boston: Houghton Mifflin, 2004.

————. *Portnoy's Complaint*. 1969. Reprint, New York: Vintage, 1994.

————. *The Professor of Desire*. New York: Farrar, Straus, & Giroux, 1977.

————. *Reading Myself and Others*. New York: Farrar, Straus, & Giroux, 1975.

————. *Sabbath's Theater*. New York: Vintage, 1995.

Said, Edward W. *After the Last Sky: Palestinian Lives*. Photographs by Jean Mohr. New York: Columbia University Press, 1986.

————. *Beginnings: Intention and Method*. New York: Basic Books, 1975.

————. *Culture and Imperialism*. New York: Knopf, 1993.

————. *The Edward Said Reader*. Edited by Moustafa Bayoumi and Andrew Rubin. New York: Vintage, 2000.

————. *Freud and the Non-European*. Introduction by Christopher Bollas, with a response by Jacqueline Rose. London: Verso, 2003.

————. *From Oslo to Iraq and the Road Map: Essays*. Foreword by Tony Judt. Afterword by Wadie E. Said. New York: Pantheon, 2004.

————. *Humanism and Democratic Criticism*. New York: Columbia University Press, 2004.

————. *Interviews with Edward W. Said*. Edited by Amritjit Singh and Bruce G. Johnson. Jackson: University Press of Mississippi, 2004.

————. *Joseph Conrad and the Autobiography of Fiction*. Cambridge: Harvard University Press, 1966.

————. *Music at the Limits*. New York: Columbia University Press, 2007.

————. *Musical Elaborations*. New York: Columbia University Press, 1991.

————. *On Late Style: Music and Literature against the Grain*. Foreword by Mariam C. Said. Introduction by Michael Wood. New York: Pantheon, 2006.

————. *Orientalism*. 1978. Reprint, New York: Vintage, 2003.

————. *Out of Place: A Memoir*. New York: Knopf, 1999.

————. *The Pen and the Sword: Conversations with David Barsamian*. Monroe, Maine: Common Courage Press, 1994.

————. *Power, Politics, and Culture: Interviews with Edward W. Said*. Edited and with an introduction by Gauri Viswanathan. New York: Pantheon Books, 2001.

————. *Reflections on Exile and Other Essays*. Cambridge: Harvard University Press, 2000.

————. *The World, the Text, and the Critic*. Cambridge: Harvard University Press, 1983.

Scarre, Geoffrey. "Dying and Philosophy." In *The Study of Dying: From Autonomy to Transformation*, edited by Allan Kellehear, 147–62. Cambridge: Cambridge University Press, 2009.

Scarry, Elaine. *The Body in Pain: The Making and Unmaking of the World*. New York: Oxford University Press, 1985.

Schur, Max. *Freud: Living and Dying*. New York: International Universities Press, 1972.

Schwamm, Ellen. *Adjacent Lives*. 1978. Reprint, New York: Knopf, 1987.

————. *How He Saved Her*. New York: Knopf, 1983.

Schwartz, Morrie [Morris S.]. *Letting Go: Morrie's Reflections on Living while Dying*. Introduction by Paul Solman. New York: Walker, 1996.

Schwartz, Morris S., and Charlotte Green Schwartz. *Social Approaches to Mental Patient Care*. New York: Columbia University Press, 1964.

Schwartz, Morris S., and Emmy Lanning Shockley. *The Nurse and the Mental Patient: A Study in Interpersonal Relations*. With the assistance of Charlotte Green Schwartz. New York: Wiley & Sons, 1956.

Seale, Clive. *Constructing Death: The Sociology of Dying and Bereavement*. Cambridge: Cambridge University Press, 1998.

Servan-Schreiber, David. *Anticancer: A New Way of Life*. New York: Viking Penguin, 2009.

⸺. *Not the Last Goodbye: On Life, Death, Healing, and Cancer*. With Ursula Gauthier. New York: Viking, 2011.

Shneidman, Edwin. *A Commonsense Book of Death: Reflections at Ninety of a Lifelong Thanatologist*. Lanham, Md.: Rowman & Littlefield, 2008.

Shohat, Ella. "The 'Postcolonial' in Translation: Reading Said in Hebrew." In *Paradoxical Citizenship: Edward Said,* edited by Silvia Nagy-Zekmi, 25–47. Lanham, Md.: Lexington, 2006.

Sontag, Susan. *Against Interpretation*. 1966. Reprint, New York: Delta, 1979.

⸺. *AIDS and Its Metaphors*. New York: Farrar, Straus, & Giroux, 1989.

⸺. *Alice in Bed: A Play in Eight Scenes*. New York: Farrar, Straus, & Giroux, 1993.

⸺. *At the Same Time*. New York: Farrar, Straus, & Giroux, 2007.

⸺. *The Benefactor*. New York: Farrar, Straus, 1963.

⸺. *Brother Carl: A Filmscript*. New York: Farrar, Straus, & Giroux, 1974.

⸺. *Conversations with Susan Sontag*. Edited by Leland Poague. Jackson: University Press of Mississippi, 1995.

⸺. *Death Kit*. New York: Farrar, Straus, & Giroux, 1967.

⸺. *Illness as Metaphor and AIDS and Its Metaphors* (combined edition). New York: Anchor, 1990.

⸺. *In America*. New York: Farrar, Straus, & Giroux, 2000.

⸺. *On Photography*. New York: Farrar, Straus, & Giroux, 1977.

⸺. *Reborn: Journals and Notebooks, 1947–1963*. Edited by David Rieff. New York: Farrar, Straus, & Giroux, 2008.

⸺. *Regarding the Pain of Others*. New York: Farrar, Straus, & Giroux, 2003.

⸺. *Styles of Radical Will*. New York: Farrar, Straus, & Giroux, 1969.

⸺. *Under the Sign of Saturn*. New York: Vintage, 1981.

⸺. *The Volcano Lover*. New York: Farrar, Straus, & Giroux, 1992.

⸺. *Where the Stress Falls*. New York: Farrar, Straus, & Giroux, 2001.

Spanos, William V. *The Legacy of Edward W. Said*. Urbana: University of Illinois Press, 2009.

Spence, Jonathan. *The Memory Palace of Matteo Ricci*. New York: Viking, 1984.

Spiegelman, Art. *Maus: A Survivor's Tale: My Father Bleeds History*. New York: Pantheon, 1986.

⸺. *Maus II: A Survivor's Tale: And Here My Troubles Began*. New York: Pantheon,. 1991.

Spivak, Gayatri. "Thinking about Edward Said: Pages from a Memoir." In *Edward Said: Continuing the Conversation,* edited by Homi Bhaba and W. J. T. Mitchell, 156–62. Chicago; University of Chicago Press, 2005.

Stanton, Alfred H., and Morris S. Schwartz. *The Mental Hospital: A Study of Institutional Participation in Psychiatric Illness and Treatment.* New York: Basic Books, 1954.

Steiner, George. *Lessons of the Masters.* Cambridge: Harvard University Press, 2003.

Stewart, Garrett. *Death Sentences: Styles of Dying in British Fiction.* Cambridge: Harvard University Press, 1984.

Styron, Alexandra. *Reading My Father.* New York: Scribner, 2011.

Styron, William. *Darkness Visible: A Memoir of Madness.* New York: Random House, 1990.

Tolstoy, Leo. *The Death of Ivan Ilych.* In *The Short Novels of Tolstoy,* translated by Aylmer Maud. New York: Dial Press, 1949.

Updike, John. *The Witches of Eastwick.* New York: Knopf, 1984.

Watkin, William. *On Mourning: Theories of Loss in Modern Literature.* Edinburgh: Edinburgh University Press, 2004.

Weisman, Avery D. *On Dying and Denying: A Psychiatric Study of Terminality.* New York: Behavioral Publications, 1972.

Wirth-Nesher, Hana. "Roth's Autobiographical Writings." In *The Cambridge Companion to Philip Roth,* edited by Timothy Parrish, 158–72. New York: Cambridge University Press, 2007.

Worden, J. William. *Grief Counseling and Grief Therapy: A Handbook for the Mental Health Practitioner.* 3rd ed. New York: Springer, 2002.

Yagoda, Ben. *Memoir: A History.* New York: Riverhead, 2009.

Yalom, Irvin. *Existential Psychotherapy.* New York: Basic Books, 1980.

Young, Jeffrey R. "After His Last Lecture, a Computer Scientist Contemplates His Final Months." *Chronicle of Higher Education,* October 12, 2007.

Zinsser, William, editor. *Inventing the Truth: The Art and Craft of Memoir.* Boston: Houghton Mifflin, 1998.

Zipperstein, Steven J. "The Two Tony Judts." *Chronicle of Higher Education,* September 10, 2010.

INDEX

7/13